NASHVILLE 1780–1860

From Frontier to City

 **Anita Shafer Goodstein**

University of Florida Press
Gainesville

The University of Florida Press thanks Mrs. Jack C. Massey for her gift to aid in the publication of this book.

Copyright 1989 by the Board of Regents of the State of Florida

Printed in the U.S.A. on acid-free paper

The University of Florida Press is a member of University Presses of Florida, the scholarly publishing agency of the State University system of Florida. Books are selected for publication by the faculty editorial committees of Florida's nine public universities: Florida A&M University (Tallahassee), Florida Atlantic University (Boca Raton), Florida International University (Miami), Florida State University (Tallahassee), University of Central Florida (Orlando), University of Florida (Gainesville), University of North Florida (Jacksonville), University of South Florida (Tampa), University of West Florida (Pensacola).

Orders for books published by all member presses should be addressed to University Presses of Florida, 15 NW 15th Street, Gainesville, FL 32603.

All illustrations were obtained from the Tennessee State Library and Archives, Nashville.

Library of Congress Cataloging-in-Publication Data

Goodstein, Anita Shafer.
  Nashville, 1780–1860: from frontier to city / Anita Shafer Goodstein.
    p. cm.
    Bibliography: p.
    Includes index.
    ISBN 0–8130–0940–5 (alk. paper)
    1. Nashville (Tenn.)—History. I. Title.
F444.N257G66   1989
976.8'5504—dc20   89-33186
                                      CIP

CONTENTS

Acknowledgments	vii
Introduction	ix
1 Leadership in a Frontier County	1
2 Leadership on the Urban Frontier	19
3 Building Institutions on the Urban Frontier	44
4 Black History on the Nashville Frontiers	71
5 Municipal Politics in the Age of Jackson	93
6 Growing Apart	116
7 Growing Apart: Black Nashville	136
8 Whig City	157
9 Urban Success and National Disaster	179
Appendix	205
Notes	211
Bibliography	253
Index	271

This book is dedicated to the memory of

Sadye and William Shafer

Jessie and Elliot Goodstein

ACKNOWLEDGMENTS

IT is a great pleasure to acknowledge the debts accumulated in the course of this study. Paul Wallace Gates heads my list of benefactors because, as teacher and role model, he introduced me to the joys of working in the sources and convinced me that life without an on-going research project is sadly incomplete. Support and encouragement came always from Robert F. Berkhofer, Bertram Wyatt-Brown, and Mary E. Young. Don H. Doyle offered the kind of constructive criticism that made reworking the manuscript a rewarding experience. My thanks go also to Carl Abbott and David R. Goldfield. Although I have not always followed their suggestions, their criticisms helped to clarify my ideas and have made this a stronger study.

I shall forever sing the praises of the staffs of the Tennessee State Library and Archives and of the Jessie Ball duPont Library and Archives of The University of the South. Nan Thomas, Cathy Young, Jim Jones, Minnie Childers, and all the other tireless and ingenious workers in the Word Processing Center at The University of the South must know that without their cheerfully granted skills I would have given up long before completing my task. Jacqueline Avent patiently and carefully transcribed the 1860 Nashville census for my use.

I am also indebted to Sarah Goodpasture Little for the use of her extensive pamphlet collection and to the late Isabel Howell who was always an enthusiastic supporter of my work and who opened her family papers to me.

Earlier versions of chapters 4 and 7 appeared in the *Tennessee Historical Quarterly* 35 (Summer 1976) and 38 (Winter 1979). I thank the editor for permission to reprint.

Financial support came from a Social Science Research Council faculty research grant in 1967–68, when I was just beginning my work, and from a National Endowment for the Humanities Fellowship in 1979–80, when I was beginning to see the end of this project. In between, two University of the South faculty research grants provided funds for a sabbatical semester in 1973 and for work in the summer of 1974. I am most grateful.

Finally, I want to thank my husband, Marvin, not so much for the specific help he gave with this book but for a more fundamental gift. He is always there when I need him.

INTRODUCTION

NASHVILLE'S antebellum history was shaped by the same momentous forces that conditioned the history of the United States: the development of a market economy, the democratization of political institutions, the implacable reality of slavery, and the debacle of secession. Nashville was a stockade fortified against hostile Indians in 1780, a boomtown after the War of 1812, and a political, shipping, and banking center during the decades preceding 1860. There are many ways to tell the story of a city emerging from the wilderness during these years. This account is shaped by political questions. Who were Nashville's leaders? How did they understand the definitions and the responsibilities of community? What was the social structure that was reflected in Nashville's politics? What was the impact of Jacksonian politics on the city? Why and how did the Whigs maintain their ascendancy in Jackson's own city during the life of the second American party system and, afterward, into the period of sectional crisis? I believe that the history of antebellum Nashville reflects in microcosm the political history of the new American nation as it moved from republican to Jacksonian America and then into the crises of the 1850s.[1]

Some time ago I set out to explore Nashville's urban frontier. Stimulated by the essays of Stanley Elkins and Eric McKitrick,[2] shored up by Richard C. Wade's *Urban Frontier,* and enticed by the resources of the Tennessee Historical Society and the Tennessee State Library and Archives, I began to investigate the Nashville of the first two decades of the nineteenth century. Pressed by questions from readers of my first paper on the subject,[3] I undertook to move backward in time to the city's eighteenth-century beginnings, and, inevitably, I was drawn forward into the history of the mature city.

I say "inevitably" because during the years I have been at work on Nashville, urban history has come into its own. Stephen Thernstrom has described the copious work done in this area during the seventies as applying "social theory to historical data," developing the use of quantitative evidence, and describing the lives of "ordinary anonymous city dwellers."[4] Following Thernstrom's own lead, there were studies of social mobility in the cities[5] as well as important studies of what held cities together, of the nature of community.[6] Urban biographies have been published in sufficient numbers so that one can now recognize how much antebellum cities had in common, whether they were located in the North, in the South, in the Midwest, or on the frontier.[7] More recently, class formation has been a major concern of urban historians,[8] while other studies have been painting a wider picture of the city within a regional context.[9]

I have learned from all of these studies, especially about the use of new research resources and new ways of testing and teasing research material. I have counted—a lot—in census and tax records and in slave lists. And I have attempted collective biographies of more or less anonymous groups in Nashville—early merchants, mechanics, immigrants, black people. But I have also relied heavily on newspapers and on letters and diaries, on the more traditional tools of the historian, in an effort to blend frontier, urban, and political history.

The questions of political history are once more being urged upon us for study, often as an important aid to understanding the data that social historians, urban historians among them, have unearthed.[10] The political questions are both old and new. Political historians have traditionally asked how democratic American society has been in any given time and particularly in the Age of Jackson. I have culled from Sean Wilentz's agenda for political history some current questions that seem apt for this study of Nashville: "How were the ideological tensions between republicanism and the market handled by politicians and their allies . . . ? What *was* the political culture of the frontier . . . ? How did the parties turn popular perceptions to their own uses?"[11]

Three interrelated themes lend themselves to an examination of Nashville's antebellum years. The first is the association of political leadership with successful entrepreneurship. Nashville knew two frontiers, the Indian fighting frontier that began with the first settlements on the Cumberland River in 1780 and a second, overlapping urban frontier that extended by at least two decades the possibilities of heightened economic opportunity, social mobility, and access to positions of authority—possibilities that scholars since Frederick Jackson Turner have associated with the frontier.[12] Only slowly did Nashville become urban. Merchants, bankers, and lawyers began to take over the leadership of the community from the squires of the first frontier. Not surprisingly, during these phases of its history Nashville's leaders were characterized by their involvement in the most lucrative economic activities of the new society—land speculation on the first frontier and the staple trade and banking on the urban frontier.[13] Cash, credit, and connections with powerful land speculators back east were major components of successful economic and political careers.

The egalitarian stripping down of Turner's frontier thesis had only marginal validity during the Indian fighting years between 1780 and 1795. On the other hand, while the town was building, new men who found room at the top came closer to meeting one of the criteria suggested by Elkins and McKitrick as necessary for establishing an urban frontier experience: the absence of a "readymade structure of leadership." Room at the top gave full vent to extraordinary entrepreneurial energy. The "expectant capitalists" of Richard Hofstadter's and Bray Hammond's interpretations of the Age of Jackson took center stage in Nashville long before the town's favorite son entered the White House.[14] However, room at the top did not mean "widespread participation" of the bulk of the population in the political arena.[15] The political culture of these frontiers, Jeffersonian republicanism, cultivated democratic manners, but political leaders, once established, long retained a monopoly on municipal as well as state offices. Nashville's eighteenth-century origins and its slave-based social system undoubtedly worked against the possibility of the Elkins-McKitrick model of participatory democracy on the urban frontier.[16] The rapidly developed social and political hierarchy of the frontier cities examined by Richard Wade seems a closer fit.[17] To it must be added the reality of conflicts of interest among expectant capitalists and between them and other groups of settlers, as suggested by Allan Bogue. Simple response to environmental opportunities is not a sufficient explanation of the political institutions developed on the frontier.[18] The panic of 1819, for example, witnessed savage infighting among Nashville's merchants and bankers and, intriguingly, the development of the democratic rhetoric associated with the Age of Jackson.

Moreover, almost before the frontiers had disappeared, Nashville leaders were forced to share political office with and to develop a political rhetoric that would more fully include the "respectable" classes: master mechanics and workingmen, taxpayers and expectant taxpayers. The democratization of political life, briefly evident in the aftermath of the panic of 1819, was officially restricted on the municipal level in 1829 but grew once more with the enthusiasm that greeted Jackson's presidencies and that climaxed in the post-Jacksonian creation of a second American party system. In the late thirties master mechanics began to appear regularly and in impressive numbers on the board of aldermen, one of the chief results of the Jacksonian revolution in Nashville. In 1840 the tax requirement for voting in municipal elections was removed. However, democratization was far from total: although the pool of candidates had been significantly widened, political office continued to be contingent on property ownership.

My second theme—changing definitions of community, particularly those of the community's leaders—stems naturally from the exploration of municipal politics. Historians have observed the absence, and sometimes the loss, of a sense of community in nineteenth-century cities where boosterism could divide as well as unify the business sector, where the rich and comfortable fled into private societies, and where the poor were outside the definition of community.[19] Early Nashville experienced vivid instances of frontier individualism and chaotic breakdowns of order, but these were mitigated by the strong bonds of family, the relative homogeneity of the frontiersmen, and the rapid emergence of a leadership cadre that deliberately sought to maintain eighteenth-century standards of law and deference. On the urban frontier the leaders were new and usually young men who within a generation had built a network of voluntary and public associations—not the least of which was the municipal corporation itself—to bolster their own positions and to act out the static definition of community that they expected to reproduce. *Hierarchical* and *deferential* may be adjectives too strong to have been voiced in a society where republican manners were moving toward democratic politics, but it was certainly assumed that leadership belonged to the economically successful, again an assumption not really surprising given the work of Edward Pessen in synthesizing the data on political leadership in the Jacksonian period.[20] The role of voluntary associations in providing instruments of social control and self-control and in defining an emerging American middle class continues to be a subject of intense concern to historians.[21] Nashville's case demonstrates that voluntary societies played all these roles and, most importantly, helped to mediate the divisiveness of the growing city, for in the immediate post-Jackson years there was again a significant break in continuity, this time in the idea of community.

Urban historians have supplied us with rich materials on the social experiences of American cities in the years between 1825 and 1860, but municipal politics have often been slighted.[22] Yet the second American party system addressed the realities of a widened electorate within the cities as well as on the state and national levels. The political party became the premier voluntary society and a major means of social as well as political identification.[23] Democrats in Nashville updated the traditional Jeffersonian-Jacksonian stance— the people versus the interests, producers versus speculators. The Whigs introduced a new rhetoric, one more clearly adapted to a commercial society and specifically aimed at including the "respectable" workingman, the "expectant" taxpayer. The Whig party was particularly successful in Nashville in creating support for the image of a Good Village peopled by strivers— sober, hardworking, socially mobile citizens. The notion of the farmer's and mechanic's place in a social hierarchy gave way to the ubiquitous success ladder. It was an idea that won Whig majorities in Nashville, in part because working-class solidarity was hard to come by in a slave society, in part because it echoed new and national hopes for a good society despite phenomenal growth and diversity.[24]

The third theme, then, traces within the city the real divisions that Whig-party dominance could at best paper over. The divisions made by race were the first, the most consistent, and the most pernicious. Black history requires separate chapters because its course was determined very differently from that of whites, whether native or foreign-born. Slaves and free blacks were the most vulnerable people within the city because they were excluded from the public definition of community at the same time that their labor, their very presence, ensured a native, white, middle-class political majority and thereby helped keep the city a Whig city and made it a southern city. Despite all the similarities that Nashville shared with cities of the North and the West, it remained unalterably southern.[25]

Leonard Curry has argued that antebellum southern cities were in many senses more urban than southern; indeed, from their governmental organization to their voluntary societies to their "housekeeping" problems and solutions, southern cities were hardly different from northern cities.[26] In the very diversity of their populations they resembled cities of the North and the Midwest. Foreign immigrants made up a far from negligible percentage of Nashville's white population in the 1840s and 1850s. In Nashville, as in other cities, immigrants, especially Catholic immigrants, were forced to create their own institutions, which were separate from and usually paralleled those of the native community; or, more commonly, they lived in the city as strangers or transients.

One other group lived outside the fellowship of the native community. The poor, a category that included not only widows, orphans, and the incapacitated but also the working poor, had no place within the boundaries of the Good Village; they were not citizens but objects of charity. Their example provided the stick to drive the villagers up the ladder and the nightmare vision, the other side of the American dream. Here, too, Nashville was neither unique nor especially southern.

Nor were the increase in absolute amounts of wealth held by individuals and the steady concentration of wealth in the city peculiar to Nashville. Urban studies have amply documented these phenomena in the antebellum years and afterward. Yet the notion of a mobile middle class, taking in millionaires and mechanics, bankers and hordes of young clerks—strivers all—was being born. Helped along by the democratic suffrage and the general prosperity of the forties and fifties, it sidestepped the potential divisiveness of class.

We must come back, then, to the essential division of white and black in the city. Black history on the frontiers and in the settled community is made distinct from white history by the limits imposed upon blacks, who, though workers, could not become part of a working class and, even in the rare instances when they became property holders, could not expect to transcend caste. Race, more so than foreignness or poverty, was never addressed as a social problem to be overcome but was instead accepted as a social given. Southernness begins here.

Nashville was as bustling, as growth-conscious, as "progressive" as any city of its size in the nation. During the paranoia of the fifties, however, Nashville experienced the extraordinary pressures of sectionalism. There was never any doubt of the city's southern loyalties, but here, until the last minute, a clear majority called for union and the political resolution of sectional problems. The Whig majority survived the dissolution of the national Whig party, regrouped under new names, and maintained its control of the city. The Whig agenda, concerned with economic growth and social improvement, with railroads and public schools, retained its hold on the city's electorate. Here, as in other border areas, there was faith that the political system, still viable, could be trusted to protect the South and slavery.[27] John Bell, the candidate of the Constitutional Union party in 1860 and one of Nashville's earliest Whigs, was the city's favorite son. Even the success of Lincoln at the polls did not destroy faith in the Union for most in the city. Secession did not come until Lincoln's call for troops, and it came then as a stampede rather than as a measured move.

This history of antebellum Nashville proceeds, then, via three themes. The monopoly of political office by economic elites is true even, and especially, of the frontier periods and is ultimately tempered by the democratizing impact of the second American party system. More clearly, democratization did mean the change from a static idea of community based on property ownership and place in the social structure to a dynamic concept of the community as white, Protestant strivers. The rivalry between Whigs and Democrats dramatized and hammered home the rhetoric describing Nashville as a socially mobile, ever more complex, and ever-growing city. These political and ideological processes at the municipal level are perhaps the core of the study. Nevertheless, the third theme is essential to understanding the political and social development of the city. Economic and ethnic divisions were clear, and the latter were insisted upon, but Nashville foundered ultimately on its deepest division, race.

Every American city was once a frontier outpost. Yet, in viewing Nashville's antebellum history as political narrative, one sees an easy continuity between frontier and town. Traumas came with democratization and then again with the crises of slavery and sectionalism. When the war did come, it ended one period of Nashville's history, a period that had embraced both the bleak failures and the profound rewards of the antebellum decades.

Leadership in a Frontier County

CHAPTER 1

THE politics of this frontier community were surprisingly complex. From the initial surveys and the first settlements a leadership group emerged. First-comers, survivors, and men of some capital, they were usually also closely associated with eastern political figures and absentee landholders. But it was the men on the scene who actually shaped a community. The immediate aims were survival and land exploitation. Then, in a rough way reflecting the scarce resources available on the frontier, the community's leaders tried to reproduce the world they had known.

In December 1779, James Robertson's band of land seekers—eight white men and a black slave—reached the Bluffs, sixty to eighty feet above the Cumberland River and not far from the salt springs called French Lick. Others had been there before them—Indians, intrepid fur seekers called "the long hunters," among them an occasional French trader from the Illinois country. These men had accepted the bounty of the land and left, but Robertson's men meant to claim the land itself. They cleared fields for a first crop of corn and began to build

Nashborough, a stockade cradling a land office. Within a few months they were joined by their families and friends and by strangers, many of whom came via the tortuous water route from the Watauga settlements in the party led by John Donelson. Other land hunters from Virginia and both the Carolinas arrived. Too quickly for safety, a number of stations fanned out along the bends of the Cumberland, each station made up of rough cabins strung out from blockhouses.[1]

Two problems faced the pioneers—physical survival and secure title to these lands. They were both geographically and politically isolated. They had come out to the Cumberland under color of the treaty of Sycamore Shoals, a private treaty negotiated in 1775 with some of the Cherokee by Richard Henderson for the Transylvania Company.[2] However, this treaty was not recognized by any political authority, nor was it recognized by most Indians with some claim to the area. The pioneers were on their own: to the north, the new Kentucky settlements could offer little aid; neither could the closest North Carolina settlements, 150 miles to the east; to the south lay potentially hostile Spanish territory. And from almost any direction an Indian threat was real and exacerbated by white duplicity in private and public treaty making and by the obvious danger any white settlement posed to Indian sovereignty.

The first settlers were gambling their lives on the Transylvania Company's dubious claim and also, and more certainly, on their own experience. Most of them came from the westernmost regions of North Carolina and Virginia. Making frontier claims into settlements was their way of life. In May 1780, 256 adult men signed the Cumberland Compact, thereby creating a voluntary association to provide law in the wilderness and, specifically, to protect their land claims.[3] Necessity, experience, and a high order of leadership created and maintained the first institutions of their community—the court of "triers" and the militia. Many of these men were strangers to one another, and among them were wide gradations in status and experience. There were long hunters and surveyors, farmers and speculators, men of distinction and property and unknown men with only a few tools and a rifle. Moreover, Nashville's first settlers did not plan to build a city in the wilderness. The stations were temporary quarters, sufficient unto the day when the itch to get out to the land might be satisfied.

Frontier democracy served as an alternative to legal authority. By electing their court of notables the first settlers established a temporary government. Robertson had already proved his capacity; others may also have done so. Nevertheless, the compact, which provided that each station had the right to recall its elected "triers" should the inhabitants be dissatisfied, indicates an understandable degree of hesitation among men who had little to bind them beyond the drive to acquire land. Between 1780 and 1783 the settlers elected eleven men to serve as their judges.[4] All had demonstrated their stubborn will to remain on the frontier and had participated in the Indian fighting. Heydon Wells lost an eye, Samuel Barton was wounded at least twice, Robertson lost a brother and two sons in Indian raids. But they survived.

A few did have special qualifications. Isaac Lindsey, one of the true long hunters who had visited the Cumberland country as early as 1769, was an obvious choice even in this group of experienced pioneers. Samuel Barton and Thomas Molloy, like Robertson, were surveyors, and surveying was a singularly important skill on this frontier. Barton served on occasion as a surgeon, and Molloy was this frontier's first lawyer; both were probably self-taught. The "triers" chose Andrew Ewing as their clerk. His ability to write legibly and spell phonetically singled him out, but more important was his ability to find financial backers to go security for him in the sensitive clerk's office. All of the original triers were successful pioneers. The surveyors would be especially successful in acquiring lands for speculation. None of these men seems to have arrived on the frontier with much capital. True, they were not poor men or squatters. They owned horses and some of them a few slaves, but their skills would be the source of their success. They were men of phenomenal energy; moreover, their entrepreneurial talents were demonstrated against a background of bloody conflict.

After an initial lull came repeated Indian raids which left a toll in dead, mutilated, and kidnapped. Shortages developed, especially of powder. In addition, there was increasing anxiety about the validity of title to the lands for which the settlers were risking their lives. A good many families were driven out of the Cumberland country altogether. At one point Robertson's strongest argument in maintaining the settlements was that it was more dangerous to go than to stay.

Robertson demonstrated heroic capacities in these years.[5] He was thirty-seven when he led the first party to the Cumberland, and he had behind him years of intensive schooling in the wilderness. Before the outbreak of the Revolution he had explored the area west of the Alleghenies and led the pioneers who established the Watauga community. During the first years of the Revolution, as agent for North Carolina and Virginia, he lived among the Cherokee and learned their language. He could have claimed land anywhere along this first Indian border, land sufficient for a farmer or planter. Obviously, he sought not just this but rather land in quantities large enough to create capital, to speculate with, lands that could be turned into the basis of position for himself and his children. The resourcefulness and the individualism that we attribute to frontiersmen were part of Robertson's makeup, but though he faced the loneliness of the wilderness again and again, he was not a loner. He sought authority, honor, and wealth, and he helped create a society that might accord them to him.

It was Robertson who made the trip through Indian country to Kentucky to find the powder for the threatened colony. It was Robertson again who made the hazardous journey to Kaskaskia to find George Rogers Clark, who was believed to hold a Virginia claim to the Cumberland area. Robertson's courage and woodsman's intelligence were beyond question, as were his diplomatic talents. Robertson brought about a lasting truce between the Chickasaw and the settlers. His negotiations with the Cherokee and the Creeks were less successful, but here too he assumed the responsibility of diplomacy, sending emissaries, letters, and an occasional bribe.

The insistent question remained the settlers' claims. By 1782 it was clear that Henderson's title would be ignored by the new American governments and that North Carolina would take possession of "her" western lands. Shunting aside Henderson's claims, North Carolina nevertheless decided that the Sycamore Shoals treaty had cleared the Indian title. The "empty" lands would provide payment for the state's veterans of the Revolution—and a field day for speculators.[6] In 1783 North Carolina created a military reserve and organized Davidson County as a political unit. The little stations in the wilderness immediately became the focus of the complex world of land speculation. With members of the North Carolina legislature Robertson had already forged alliances that assured his settlers' stake in the land. By an act of 1783 the first settlers who had remained on the frontier and the heirs of those who had been killed in the Indian fighting would earn their preemptions as a kind of blood right—640 acres to each of 152 persons.[7]

However, the recognition of preemptions was an end to just one phase of the pioneers' venture. Pioneering was clearing land of trees and Indians, of wild beasts and other men's claims. Pioneering also encouraged a vast entrepreneurial appetite that looked upon the wilderness as a source of capital and power. James Robertson was once more a key figure in this next phase of frontier development. By 1783 Robertson had become the land agent and partner of William Blount, land speculator extraordinary and a member of the North Carolina legislature. Blount's influence in the legislature gained some favors for the settlements and helped create Blount's own enormous stake in the western land. Even before he had visited the West Blount was elected its representative to the North Carolina legislature through the efforts of the Robertsons and their friends. By 1790 he was appointed the first governor of the Territory Southwest of the Ohio River, and by 1796 Blount owned or held an interest in more than a million acres. His brother, John Gray Blount, owned another million and a half acres. Such gross appetite for land was accompanied by a genuine, almost bubbling enthusiasm for the western country itself. "It is certain that every man who arrives here and determines to become a Citizen appears to feel and I believe does in reality feel an Independence & Consequence to which he was a Strainger in the Atlantic States." Blount was a startling mixture—an aspiring aristocrat, a very occasional democrat, a grandiose dreamer, and an effective politician.[8] The ambitious men of the frontier quickly joined his bandwagon. The impact on the frontier community was direct. Land monopolists not only left a heritage of confused and fraudulent land titles but also perpetuated a political system in which a few men determined major policy issues.[9]

After 1783 there were two significant areas of political leadership that concerned the frontier community—the county court and the state or territorial legislature. The settlements depended upon the handful of elected representatives to the legislature to gain preemptions and guard rights, legal surveys, Indian presents and treaties, militia payments and federal troops, roads, and postal services. In return for such services these men helped make the bonanza of western lands available to eastern legislators, often offering their own services as locaters. Of the eight men who served as representatives to the North Carolina legislature in the eighties, seven were major speculators, and at least four acted directly as Blount locaters. Very different in age, experience, and attainments, these men had in common their link to the special world of the land speculators.[10]

The county court was the immediate source of political authority in the community. It held a monopoly of political power tempered significantly by the chaotic conditions of the frontier—constant flux in population, lack of funds and hands to administer any law with vigor. The justices themselves were new men busy making their own way; their unpaid public services were at best a peripheral concern. Authority probably derived less from their office than from the kind of men they were. After 1783 the justices no longer were elected directly by the frontier's settlers but were appointed by the North Carolina legislature. Between 1783 and 1788, twenty-four men were appointed. An interest in land speculation and a place in the Blount organization were clearly important qualifications of this governing elite. With the exception of young William Polk, they all were also local men. Polk, as surveyor of the middle district, was immediately a power on the Cumberland. Ten of the justices of the eighties had survived the desperate years from 1780 to 1782; five had served on the court of notables. James Robertson, Elijah Robertson, Isaac Bledsoe, and Anthony Bledsoe were experienced frontiersmen and surveyors and were tied to the land speculators in the North Carolina legislature. Anthony Bledsoe had been appointed surveyor of North Carolina's western lands by an act of 1780. As commissioner for Virginia, Daniel Smith had surveyed the boundary line between Virginia and North Carolina; he would become Blount's secretary of state when Davidson County was reorganized as part of the Southwest Territory in 1790.

The fact that so much can be pieced together about their careers and patterns of operation indicates an unusual level of activity among the justices.[11] The skills they brought to the Cumberland were not simply those of the farmer or planter. In addition to nine surveyors, there were a lawyer, a surgeon, a doctor, and two merchants, one of whom claimed more than 100,000 acres in North Carolina grants. The overriding business concern of the justices in the eighties was land speculation. Eighteen of the twenty-four justices acquired title to more than one thousand acres each, eight of them to well over 20,000 acres each. Armed with military warrants for the most part procured east of the mountains, these eight men were in effect in the land business. Most of them ultimately became planters in Middle Tennessee. In the midst of Indian raids they cleared fields, planted orchards, built stills and mills, and in a few cases even raised stone mansions. But for them the plantation played a secondary role, at least during the frontier decades.

There were, in addition, what one might call the middling speculators, men like James Mulherin, one of the first settlers and an Indian fighter, teacher, and surveyor. Mulherin married into the Buchanan family, and his pattern of operations was similar to that of his brother-in-law, Captain John Buchanan. Mulherin accumulated just under 10,000 acres in North Carolina grants and seems to have used speculation as a means to acquire capital to plow back into a prosperous plantation. By 1798 Mulherin's home was one of the fifteen in the entire county valued at more than $1,000. His brother-in-law's establishment was more modest, but John Buchanan owned one of the half-dozen mills and one of the rare barns assessed in the county. Both were major landholders of developed lands by the turn of the century.[12]

Still a third pattern of speculation, a modest one, was evident among the justices of the eighties. For Isaac Lindsey, the old long hunter who had been a signer of the compact and had fought throughout the Indian campaigns, the North Carolina grants he had acquired as a preemptioner and guard to the surveying commissioners provided his stake and his children's inheritance. The tax lists of Sumner County tell part of his story. By 1790 he had accumulated 1,600 acres. In the next year he began to sell land, and during the nineties he sold or gave to his children almost all but his own farm, 320 acres on Lindsey's Bluff. His son Ezekiel farmed an adjoining 320 acres, and there was land left for his son Isaac, "if he returnes from his traveling enjoyments."[13] Jacob Pennington, Robert Ewing, Robert Edmiston, Dr. John Sappington, and William Simpson, whose cow was sold after his death in 1788 to provide schooling and a hat for his daughter, each acquired between 1,000 and 2,000 acres. Only two justices held as little as 350 and 388 acres; just one owned only a single lot in town.[14]

The justices, then, were men of property and of that peculiar property, undeveloped lands, that promised handsome returns but whose value in the eighties and nineties was not readily convertible into huge sums.[15] At the end of his life Robertson was still taking on public jobs for cash. Nevertheless, even if title to land did not ensure wealth, it did provide political status in the new community.

In 1790 the Cumberland settlements became part of the Territory of the United States Southwest of the Ohio River, and William Blount was made governor, with extensive powers of appointment. He listed with pride and a positive joy the offices he now had to fill— "Justices, sheriffs, constables, clerks, registers, etc. and militia officers of every grade below a General." For a man who later insisted, "It is a principle with me never to be departed from if I can avoid it not to stand between a Friend and a Benefit," this was a rich opportunity.[16] It was also, of course, a step further away from frontier democracy. Blount appointed twenty-eight justices to the Davidson County Court between 1790 and 1795. He was clearly well satisfied with the character of the court of the eighties, for he reappointed nine men of the older court, and the characteristics of the new justices continued the pattern earlier established.[17] Of the nineteen new appointees, four were major speculators with land claims upward of 20,000 acres, five claimed between 5,000 and 10,000 acres, and another five claimed between 1,000 and 5,000 acres. Only five held less than 1,000 acres.

The speculator contingent among Blount's appointments was especially reinforced by Robert Weakley and Robert Hays. Weakley was a cousin of Griffith Rutherford, member of the North Carolina legislature, speculator, and shortly to become president of the first Tennessee territorial legislature. Robert Hays had married Jane Donelson in 1786 and in the following year had served as Davidson County's representative to the North Carolina legislature. These two young men were immediately of the inner circle. Both had been officers in the revolutionary army, had come out to the settlements as early as 1785, and had served as strategic links between the eastern capitalists and the land locaters in the field. They were two of that coterie of young, active, ambitious men who created important positions for themselves on the frontier and who became part of a wider group of Blount appointees that included the very new lawyers—Andrew Jackson, John McNairy, and John Overton. Jackson was an untried lawyer, only twenty-two, when in 1788 he was appointed public solicitor for the Western District of North Carolina by his friend Judge John McNairy, himself just appointed judge of the superior court of North Carolina for the Mero district. Both were reappointed by Blount, who was shortly to appoint as collector of the federal revenue Jackson's fellow lodger at Widow Donelson's, John Overton. Working with older agents and partners of Blount, such as the Robertsons, these young men would make up a powerful political circle on the frontier.[18]

From this group were to come not only some of the major political figures of the then western part of Tennessee but also the men who would help to build the varied economic institutions of the new area. Yet, whatever their talents and whatever their prospects, most of these justices had very little cash. Even those who, like the Robertsons, had accumulated land in princely quantities had to scratch for the wherewithal to maintain their holdings. When one examines their pattern of operations, what becomes clear is their almost frantic entrepreneurial drive: the justices kept inns and operated ferries, opened stores and competed for federal contracts to supply forage for troops and trade goods for pacified Indians, sought posts that carried with them fees or salaries, served as lawyers, doctors, carpenters and house builders, slave traders, and moneylenders.

James Robertson has come down to us as a sober man, resourceful, decisive, but above all solid, the rock of the Cumberland. One of the Indian chiefs with whom he treated reported, "He had winning ways and makes no fuss." Yet this sobriety went along with the furious pace of a man on the make. Among the public offices he filled were commandant and major general, treaty commissioner, Indian agent, and representative to the North Carolina legislature. Though the responsibility and honor were undoubtedly of great importance, the salaries ($1,200 as Major General, $400 as Indian agent) were not insignificant. Robertson owned horses and slaves and soon great tracts of land, but the need for hard money was always evident. Neither his public career nor the real threat of hostile Indians prevented him from taking on the surveying for major North Carolina speculators. The thirty-three thousand acres entered in Robertson's name by 1787 represented his fee for locating for absentee speculators. He was busy buying up warrants on the frontier with paper money sent by Blount. By 1787 a beginning had been made on his home plantation at Richland Creek: about thirty acres were under fence, and a blockhouse providing a minimum of safety and comfort had been built. But the plantation could not provide a source of ready profit; it was left to his sons, white hired hands, and black slaves to do the basic jobs there while Robertson surveyed, repaired the public tobacco scales in the town of Nashville (for which he received a remission of taxes), bought and sold town lots, kept an inn, developed an iron furnace that by 1802 was producing about three hundred tons a year, and tried to collect debts from debtors often protected by the very county court he sat on.[19]

Robertson was the most important figure in the settlements, but his career parallels that of most of the justices. Whatever they were to become, in the eighties and nineties they were men with careers and fortunes still before them. They included no men of leisure and no men who lived solely on the proceeds of a profession. Almost all were involved in farm making along with their other pursuits. So few had much formal education that this became the mark of personal eccentricity rather than social differentiation.

When, in 1796, the legislature of the newly created state of Tennessee took over the appointing power, thirteen of the justices of Blount's era were retained, including those stalwarts who had consistently retained their positions since the days of the court of notables—both Robertsons, Samuel Barton, and Thomas Molloy. Moreover, the forty-two new appointments made between 1796 and 1799 maintained the characteristics the court had always demonstrated.[20] They were, by and large, significant landholders and active entrepreneurs. Most eventually became planters.

After twenty years of Indian fighting and land speculating, Davidson County had overcome some of the more obvious conditions of a frontier society. The Indians had been eliminated. The unauthorized massacre of the Chickamauga Cherokee at Nickajack in 1794 was the last Indian "battle" of this frontier. The lands of the county had passed into private hands. But at least a third and perhaps as much as half the lands of the county were still being held for speculation. Given the size of their holdings, about eighty-five of the approximately seven hundred landholders on the 1798 tax list can be classified as speculators, some of whom also farmed.[21]

New residents were swarming into the area. In Davidson County the population almost tripled between 1795 and 1800, and most of that population was still landless in 1800.[22] The range of holdings varied enormously: in 1798 one or two individuals claimed less than an acre; at least a dozen men held more than 5,000 acres each,[23] one of them—as yet an absentee—more than 19,000 acres. More than half the landholders, 362 individuals, claimed between 100 and 1,000 acres; however, the value of the property of 63 percent of the property holders in the county was assessed at less than $1,000, of 38 percent of the property holders at less than $500. Most land was still virgin land; section and half-section grants and purchases were finally being broken up and sold for farms at the turn of the century, twenty years after the first settlements. Only thirteen barns and nine mills were assessed in 1798. Stills were more plentiful: in 1795 John Overton reported five hundred of them in the Mero district.[24] Corn was always the first crop of the frontier, but most of these stills must have been producing for home consumption; only five were assessed in Davidson County in 1798.

By 1800 Davidson County had in its county court justices a leadership cadre. Initially, frontier leaders had been selected by their fellow pioneers, but the radically democratic institutions of the first frontier were temporary. The security of North Carolina land titles was the most pressing concern of the pioneers whose leaders allied early with Blount and company and coopted the ambitious young men who rode into the settlement with their law books or surveying tools. The Blount connection aided immediately in the process of gentrification that turned "daring adventurers seeking fortunes in the public lands" into recognized leaders of the community.[25] It absorbed as well and very quickly the older men who had brought capital with them when they began to move in as the Indian raids were eliminated. Land speculation was an almost universal pursuit of the local justices. However, land speculation, gamble though it might be, was the pursuit of men whose total pattern of operations adds up to a picture not so much of adventurers as of eager, commercially minded, unspecialized entrepreneurs building capital however they might. Land speculation was one of a number of economic opportunities offered by the open frontier to men who were at the outset neither yeomen farmers nor patriarchal planters. The justices did not deal in the millions of acres of the Blounts. Ownership of 75,000, 50,000, 10,000, or even 1,000 acres separated them from the pioneer farmers but did not of itself provide a fortune or assure social status. Perhaps this helps account for the democratic aura that pervaded the Tennessee frontier even after the loss of frontier autonomy.

The Blount machine and an appointed local government coexisted with broadly based institutions that acted to draw together the dispersed population. Even the Blount organization had to be sensitive to public opinion, had to fashion a machine and win votes. Territorial status would, after all, give way to statehood. Blount's lieutenants had to be available in the taverns, on the public square during court sessions and public meetings, and, above all, on the militia grounds. The militia was the premier institution of any frontier; here all adult males, including free blacks and excepting only the superannuated, were enrolled, and, after statehood, militia elections were the most democratic of Tennessee's institutions. All freemen, aged eighteen to fifty, elected their field officers, who in turn elected their generals.[26] The justices of the county court operated, then, within a world where democratic public manners were encouraged. The rhetoric of politics was aggressively republican, antiaristocratic. To be perceived as a Fed or a Quid meant political death; officeholders styled themselves as Jeffersonian republicans by 1800. Even the legendary bellicosity of the frontier was tempered by the local party leadership when it threatened criticism of Jefferson's peace policy in 1807. A public meeting called after the firing on the *Chesapeake* branded the incident an "act of war." But the war hawks of Nashville—Andrew Jackson, John Overton, Jenkin Whiteside—pressured by James Robertson, agreed to amend the resolution of the meeting by adding a statement of support and approval of President Jefferson.[27] There was no hint of divisive interest politics. The young merchants of the village were powerfully attracted to Judge Jackson and his aggressive nationalistic style; they eagerly sought places in the town's militia and followed him into the War of 1812 and the Creek wars.

The basic political reality remained the Blount connection, which was kept viable by his successors. Blount's agents occasionally squabbled for place among themselves, but they were agreed on fundamental issues—easy access to land and low taxes on land. Along with and despite republican rhetoric, they initiated on the frontier the politics of a regrouped and self-proclaimed gentry. Their candidates relied on the caucus in the state legislature and the traditional deference accorded a prominent landholder or lawyer. Hard-fought contests tended to emerge only from personal or factional feuds like that of Jackson and General Sevier, both Blount lieutenants, over the office of major general of militia.[28] When a brash newcomer, Felix Grundy, broke the rules, contested for office against the establishment's candidate, and won, he made do with traditional labels, calling his opponents Federalists; by attacking the nominating caucus, he did indeed introduce a new democratic argument, but in 1811 it was too early to see in that argument the basis of a new politics. Grundy, a winner, was quickly absorbed into the single viable party.[29] A political stance and a political mechanism remained in place until after the panic of 1819.[30]

At the end of twenty years a community had in fact been hacked out of the wilderness. The county court was its chief institution, the only institution charged with overall competence for the community's concerns.[31] The justices shared with the community a fierce commitment to getting lands into private hands, preferably their own, and a profound need for capital. The first concern, then, was to establish a working respect for property. The court began with the need to protect land claims. It continued to function as the register of preemptions, land boundaries, and cattle brands. It guarded the property of the dead, appointing administrators and recording detailed inventories of the smallest estates. The widow Lefever's petticoat and scarlet cloak, even her "bundle of Trumpery," were carefully entered into the court's books.[32] In a world in which cash was very scarce, the court was preoccupied with debt cases. The cows and preemption rights of small holders were perhaps more vulnerable than the notes of hand of land speculators and traders to the court's action. Still, the court did its best, occasionally summoning a blue-ribbon jury of merchants to determine a complicated debt case.[33] The squires did not find it easy to collect from debtors and occasionally were themselves the debtors. Corporal punishment was routinely administered for theft, and the punishment for horse theft was savage—thirty-seven lashes on the bare back. By comparison, conviction for assault and battery brought fines of sometimes no more than a penny.[34]

The court assumed considerable responsibility in the area of economic regulation and physical development. Road building was a prime necessity, and here one sees the court at its most effective. Without financial resources, the court acted as coordinator of the available labor. It appointed overseers to view and then to mark out roads and commandeer the labor of those who lived along them. But it accepted with good grace the reports of overseers that some roads were "useless" and would not be undertaken and fined very lightly the overseers who did not finish their jobs on time.[35]

The first ferry license was issued by the court in 1784, and at the same time a detailed schedule of rates was drawn up and imposed upon ferrymen. The assumption of the right to regulate suggests little of the stereotype of the individualistic pioneer. Not only ferry rates but also tavern rates and millers' fees were fixed by the court. Ordinary keepers were required to give bond and fix securities. Inspectors were appointed for tobacco and after the turn of the century for cotton. However, enforcement of the regulations tended to be lax and punishments of violations lenient.[36] If the patterns of the East were in fact to be imitated, the copy was at best a pale one.

Responsibility for the poor, the unfortunate, and the orphans was accepted as a matter of course. Here again formulas for handling welfare problems were traditional. Orphaned children with property had guardians appointed for them; propertyless orphans were bound out. Most often, the court apprenticed orphans with the stipulation that the children be taught the trade of the master. Wardens of the poor were elected as early as 1788, but it was the court that determined whether or not an individual was incapable of providing for himself and allocated fixed sums for relief.[37]

The court attempted to enforce an orthodox, even puritanical, moral code. Adultery, profane swearing, buying and selling or grinding corn on the Sabbath, and bearing or siring bastard children were all crimes. However, juries rarely brought in harsh punishments. In a case of adultery the guilty couple was fined twenty-five shillings each and the man was held in bond for $500, in case a child should be born, "to indemnify the county for the trouble of a bastard."[38] The rule was pragmatic. Evan Shelby in bed with the tavernkeeper's daughter; Mark Robertson accused of siring a bastard; Elijah Robertson up for assault and battery, and again for swearing in the court's presence, and twice again for drunkenness; Squire Molloy emancipating his slave daughter and making her his heir; Andrew Jackson and Rachel Donelson Robards eloping on the rumor of her divorce[39]—the frontier was not an easy place to maintain standards. One sympathizes with the justices when faced with the widow Lefever. Fined for bearing a child out of wedlock, she turned on her accusers and charged them with not only producing but also murdering their own bastards. She shocked the court into fining her two hundred pounds—an impossible sum. The court's purpose was clear when the next day she was pardoned on condition she apologize.[40] The community was small enough to know intimately its neighbors' sins and determined enough to uphold standards of respectability by bringing those neighbors to court, but the squires were practical enough to punish lightly.

Education and religion remained basically private matters. For the most part, education was left to part-time schoolmasters and to preachers who could be prevailed upon to take a few scholars. In the late nineties an occasional planter supported a tutor and organized a school at his plantation. It is true that the frontier leaders intended to provide a classical education for their sons. As early as 1785 Davidson Academy had been chartered on lands adjoining the village. Eight land speculators and the Reverend Thomas Craighead made up its board of trustees.[41] Craighead was a graduate of Princeton and a "new-light" preacher, an intellectual come-outer whose Spring Hill School was kept at the meetinghouse, eight miles from Nashville. It was this school rather than the academy, which for a long time existed only on paper, that had the most regular history as a teaching institution.[42] The curricula of both institutions reflected the notion that heavy doses of Latin and Greek made the educated man, and, in part for that reason, the number of scholars accommodated was never more than a token of the young people in the community. Education traditionally helped make a gentleman. Upon William Blount's death his brothers remembered that above all else, even if sacrifices were to be made, Blount's sons were to be sent to the best schools.[43] In one way or another, the children of the leadership cadre acquired an education. The education typically sought for sons was nonutilitarian and aristocratic, dictating a life-style that these men on the make pursued.

Religion, too, was essentially a family affair on the frontier. Old Isaac Lindsey, an enthusiastic convert of the first circuit rider on the Cumberland, joyfully split up his set of John Wesley's sermons, leaving one volume to each daughter.[44] But religion was not yet institutionalized. The silver crucifix on the wall of Timothy Demonbreun's home may have been the lone symbol of Catholicism in the settlements.[45] The handful of German settlers were hungry for familiar preaching, but the only German preacher to appear before 1799 turned out to practice not as he preached and was dismissed by the congregation.[46] The multiplicity of sects undoubtedly hindered organization, but more important was the condition cited in Bishop Asbury's shrewd comment: "When I reflect that not one in a hundred came here to get religion; but rather to get plenty of good land, I think it will be well if some or many do not eventually lose their souls."[47]

The traditional sects of the eastern establishment had made no great inroads by the turn of the century. There were scattered Episcopalians, a small number of Scottish Dissenters, and a good number of devout Presbyterians. It may be that Craighead was supported to some extent by the subscriptions of some of the Presbyterians.[48] But it was left to the Methodists to make the first onslaught on the irreligion of the frontier. Benjamin Ogden rode the circuit as early as 1786 or 1787 and left behind him enthusiastic exhorters and classes. In the nineties the Methodists had acquired in Nashville a stone building on the public square that seemed to be open to preaching by all comers. It was still unfinished in 1800, when Bishop Asbury made his first visit to Nashville. He thought that if floored, ceiled, and glazed it "would be a grand house." Instead, it was pulled down, and Methodist preaching in town was held in the jail for a number of years. In the nineties the number of reported conversions fluctuated drastically from year to year but never assumed significant proportions. Although Asbury reported a couple of thousand in his audience in 1800, and although during the year of the Great Revival camp meetings did succeed in attracting hundreds and occasionally thousands, church membership itself remained small. John A. Granade, "the wild man" of the circuit, tackled a group in a tavern on the road to Nashville in 1799 and was told, "If there was such a man as Jesus Christ, and if he had done so much for him, he was much obliged to him, but that he thought Tom Paine a greater man than Jesus Christ."[49]

General Martin Armstrong commented that "in Nashville and in the surrounding region, especially among the upper classes, deism and irreligion ruled beyond all bounds."[50] Still, it was not usually an aggressive deism, and a decent respect was paid a preacher of education. The male leaders of the community, however, expressed little interest in developing churches. An examination of the membership rolls of the Mill Creek Baptist Church, organized in the spring of 1797, indicates that not the justices but their wives and their slaves probably joined this church.[51] The tight discipline of small knots of Baptists and the enthusiasm of tolerant Methodists were the major achievements of organized religion in the last decades of the eighteenth century.

Just as the first settlers brought with them the plan of their stockade, by this time part of the folk experience of American pioneers, they brought with them also a clear if simplistic notion of town planning.[52] In 1784, when Nashville was chartered, only the presumption of the frontiersmen could label it a town. Aside from hastily built cabins, or "huts," there were only the storehouse of Nashville's first merchant, Lardner Clark, and possibly one other sturdy log building. In 1785 a Spanish emissary to Robertson reported "only 40 souls, 20 able to bear arms," in the Cumberland settlement.[53] Pelts and some tobacco were the sole items brought to the store for trade. The incorporation act named five trustees and a treasurer for the town. Two hundred acres were set aside from the lands adjoining the salt lick to make the town. Thomas Molloy drew the first plat of the town—165 one-acre squares drawn in regular lines that paralleled the river. Four acres were left open to form a public square fronting on Water Street. The plat was that of a real-estate salesman, its function almost entirely restricted to the sale of lots. Tree-covered, one-acre lots seemed spacious enough to guarantee privacy to individuals, and the four-acre reservation seemed adequate to community needs, defined as a courthouse and jail.

It was much too early to expect any greater concern for city planning. The community was concentrating on getting out to its lands, not on building a town. Only a few were interested in town lots as a permanent holding. At least fifty-three lots were quickly conveyed by the trustees in 1784 and 1785. But the condition of sale, that each purchaser erect a frame or log building at least sixteen feet square and eight feet in the pitch, was too rigorous a requirement given the instability of the period and the few confirmed townsmen available. The county deeds show a very rapid turnover in lots: in the three years between 1786 and 1789, forty-four lots changed hands at least ninety-three times. Most of the subscribers to lots were obviously buying for speculation, and speculation did not prove too profitable.[54]

Responsibility for the government and development of the town was left up to the county court and to its leading member, James Robertson. As the county's first representative to the North Carolina legislature, Robertson sponsored not only the act establishing Nashville but also the acts that placed the land office in Nashville, made Nashville the inspection point for tobacco, created Davidson Academy on lands adjoining the town's, and ordered a road cut from the Clinch River to Nashville. Proceeds from the sale of town lots were to provide the funds to build a courthouse, a prison, and stocks. The court appointed the necessary officers of the town: a constable and jailer, tobacco inspectors, patrolmen of the bounds to watch out for strayed cattle and strayed slaves, and overseers of the streets, who had the power to command the labor of the inhabitants. It provided funds for plastering and repairing the courthouse and for erecting tobacco scales, a pen for stray cattle, and a jailhouse, divided into a "dungeon" and a "debtor's room." The court provided a bell, presumably to warn of Indians or fire, and, ominously, branding irons for the jailer's use. Like the rest of the county, the village was governed on a minimal basis. Though property in town was evaluated and assessed, taxes were light and seemed to be difficult to collect. A reminder of the fragility of the community leaps out of the formal records of the court for 1792: "N.B. The court did nothing of consequence at the aforesaid term but just met and adjourned the same day ... by reason of the incursion of the Indians in the county at this time."[55]

In its first two decades the village of Nashville grew very slowly, meeting the limited needs of the county. In the eighties store goods were traded for pelts and land warrants. As corn and tobacco became more available, farmers began to barter crops for goods and services. But throughout the period Nashville remained basically the county's seat, coming to life when the courts met. The justices of the court set their stamp upon the county. Like all pioneers, they had come to the frontier seeking economic well-being and enhanced social status. But unlike the bulk of the white settlers, they had been able to make entrepreneurial energy, land speculation, and political associations with North Carolina legislators their means of entry into a leadership cadre. In the interest of secure land titles, the initial democracy of the frontier had given way very quickly to traditional political forms. As appointed rather than elected officials, the justices became part of the Blount machine that ran the territory and later the state without significant opposition. Yet Jeffersonian rhetoric, democratic manners, and an openness to talent and capital, so easily assimilated on the frontier, tempered the hierarchical framework they created for politics. As men on the make, the frontier leaders were trying to fashion neither a "citty on a Hill" nor a new democratic society. They applied traditional, remembered formulas to the challenge of the new environment. They were republicans. Their definition of community remained minimal, defensive; physical protection of persons and legal protection of property sufficed as community goals.

Leadership on the Urban Frontier

CHAPTER 2

IN 1800 Nashville was a village, the county seat. Twenty years later it had become a mercantile town, the focus for the shipping and distributing needs of a wide agricultural hinterland, its growth dependent on the initiative of its merchants and bankers.[1] Merchants, bankers, and lawyers—often the same people—began to assume positions of leadership in Nashville after the turn of the century and more obviously after the War of 1812. These were the men who "persisted," who were drawn to the town by boom times and remained through panics and recessions, developing a trade in tobacco and cotton, utilizing first flatboats and then steamboats, and opening banks and lines of credit to the East. Nashville's first merchants were drawn from among the land-speculating pioneers, but soon these men were joined by more specialized merchant migrants, whose bourgeois ethic seemed to blend quite well with that of the entrepreneurs of the first frontier. Within a generation young men on the make had exploited the opportunities of the urban frontier, the direction of Nashville's commercial development had been plotted, and a merchant elite had established itself, dominating the cotton and tobacco trades and the shipping and banking concerns of Middle Tennessee.

"Expectant capitalists"[2] seemed to have made it when the panic of 1819 dealt them a considerable blow. It proved to be only a temporary setback, but it did shatter for a short while the stance of authoritative leadership that the merchant-banker-lawyer alliance had assumed. The infighting also produced a startling political rhetoric of the people-versus-establishment kind that we usually identify as Jacksonian and that was to play a role in the democratization of the political culture of the town. Meanwhile, however, cotton and tobacco merchants rallied, allied again with professionals and representatives of the county leadership, and took their place at the top of the town's social hierarchy.[3]

The census of 1800 provides a rare snapshot of the village of Nashville: 345 people, almost half of them black and all but three of these slaves. Of the 191 white people, just 12 men were older than forty-five. Only 100 men and 35 women were older than sixteen. Fifty-six youngsters, 41 of them under ten, completed the total.[4] Few were settled residents. During the nineties, however, the village had begun to acquire a physical center, the public square, four acres fronting on Water Street above the boat landing. On and around the square were clustered at least two of the town's taverns as well as artisans' sheds, lawyers' offices, merchants' warehouses, the courthouse, the jail, and the Masonic hall—all frame or log structures. Within what today must represent two or three short city blocks was concentrated an enormous amount of energy. The taverns, one and a half or two stories high, were the most impressive buildings; Talbot's boasted nine rooms and twenty-three windows. Here was heard the talk of land and politics that most intrigued the county, and here also were often begun the assault and battery cases handled by the court.

Government was in the hands of the court. A newcomer to Nashville at the turn of the century would have looked to the county for the town's leaders. Land speculators turned planters were making of Middle Tennessee a distinctively southern world. Slavery was entrenched. County and state governments were dominated by planters, prospective planters, and their lawyer allies. Although most of the squires still lived in log mansion houses, their children were inheriting the fruits of frontier speculation— expensive educations in

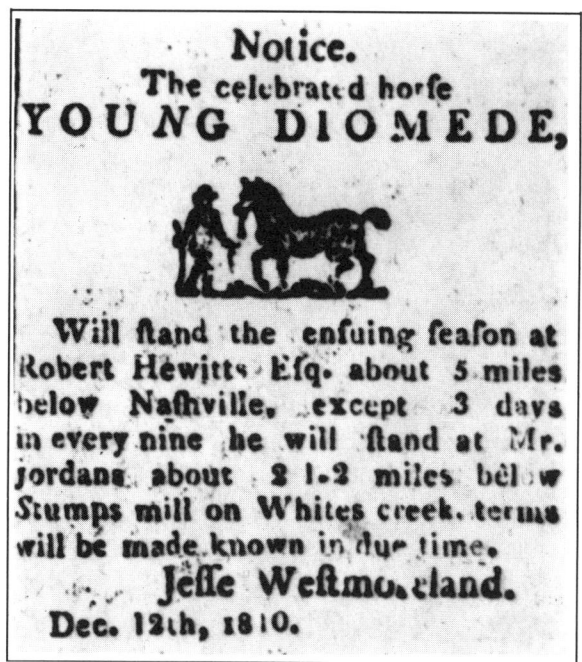

Philadelphia or New Salem or at home with private tutors. They were redecorating with furniture brought by wagon from Philadelphia or Baltimore. In the next two decades brick, stone, and frame houses would replace log structures around the countryside. One generation's priority did not make for a closed establishment, but it did mean that the county provided the first institutional framework for the urban frontier: county court, militia company, public meeting, Masonic order.

In the next decade Nashville's population began to soar, initially without benefit of a transportation revolution. In 1811, 287 men signed the militia roll. The War of 1812 and the aftermath of the Creek wars, clearing Indian titles in Tennessee and Alabama, drew more immigrants to the Nashville basin and into northern Alabama. The major catalyst for growth was the production of tobacco and cotton in sufficient quantities to support a market town. By 1816 the undeveloped lands of Davidson County had disappeared. Farmers and planters rather than speculators had become the favored customers and clients of the town.[5] The first steamboat docked in Nashville in 1818 and signaled a further impetus to the town's growth despite the panic of 1819. The 1820 census recorded 855 adult white males in the town and its "suburbs."⁶ Nashville's white population was now almost eleven times and its black population approximately six times greater than they were in 1800.⁷

In 1820 Nashville's white population was young, predominantly male, still growing dramatically, and still transient. The greatest part of the population was made up of young adults. More than one-third, 39 percent, were young people under sixteen; children under ten, however, made up only 27 percent of the population, less than the national average of 33 percent. Only 66 men and 45 women were older than forty-five. There were less than half as many adult women as men (408 as compared with 855), which may account for the relatively small number of young children and which was perhaps more typical of the urban than of the agricultural frontier.⁸ The 1820 census listed 367 white households; 81 (22 percent) were all male, and 54 of these represented a single male. In addition, almost every mechanic's household and most merchants' households included extra men and boys—apprentices, journeymen, and clerks. Taking in boarders and lodgers was one response to housing a rapidly growing population. Never again would the rate of growth approach that of these first twenty years of the century.

However, the still shots provided by the census figures, if they suggest simply a steady building up of population, tend to falsify the record. Only sixty-eight names on the 1811 militia roll can be found in the 1820 census.⁹ Again, something like 70 percent of the heads of household in Nashville in 1820 had moved on by 1830.¹⁰ A huge in-and-out migration had to be happening to account for absolute population growth. Transiency, the constant movement of large numbers of people out of the city, has been emphasized by urban historians as a major factor in the workings of the nineteenth-century city.¹¹ It helps explain the American ambivalence about urban life that has been the heritage of generations of boosters and decriers of the city. It explains in part how the problem of poverty was handled—by poor people moving on. Its opposite, persistence, or continuous residence in one city, correlates well with property holding and the achievement of status positions in a given community.

In the five decades between 1811 and 1860, Nashville's transiency level ranged between 77 percent and 70 percent. Such figures mean that from 1830 to 1860 Nashville's population seems to have been somewhat less stable (by 8 percent and 14 percent) than the populations of the great metropolises of Philadelphia and Boston.¹² In the decade of the fifties Nashville experienced also a transiency level higher than that of Richmond, an older and larger southern city, and higher than that of Milwaukee, a much newer and dynamically expanding river city of the Midwest.[13] Its level was closest to that of Jacksonville, Illinois, a "frontier community" founded in 1825.[14] Transiency seems to have been typical of cities, and it would be most evident to contemporaries during the frontier stages of development, when total population was small. Such turnover of population provided a premium in status and influence to those who dug in.

A few of the first settlers and their sons chose to live in town, where they often held key government posts: clerk of the courts, postmaster, state treasurer, clerk in the land-registry office. These men made up a crucial leadership element in part because they represented continuity with the first frontier. They owned or came from families that owned thousands of acres; they often maintained farms or country seats as well as homes in town. Many of the doctors and lawyers in town also came from the families of the first land seekers. The professions may have been regarded as more honorable than the trades, but they did not in themselves lend status to their new practitioners. They may well have been attractive because they called for family connections and patrons rather than capital.

Doctors ran the gamut from transients and quacks to dedicated and well-educated men. Nashville's first physician, luckily perhaps, never practiced but was sent to Congress instead. Dr. White "would dress up in buckskin and march through the streets with a gourd of whiskey under his arm, and almost compel every person he met to drink with him." Yet he had been educated at Edinburgh. Dr. William Yandell, who trained many doctors, practiced for years "without his ever having heard a lecture."[15] On the other hand, Felix Robertson was graduated from the University of Pennsylvania's medical school, then the best in the country. Doctors were farmers, politicians, cotton traders, retailers of drugs and house paint. Attempts to organize as doctors were limited to setting minimum price scales—and these were honored only in the breach and resulted in public quarrels.[16] In 1824 four doctors and the preacher and teacher William Hume offered a series of medical lectures, but there were neither medical establishments nor medical standards on the urban frontier.[17] The Creek wars did produce experienced surgeons, and more and more doctors came to town. In 1802 three doctors and in 1823 thirteen doctors advertised in the Nashville papers. Medicine seemed to attract both men on the make and men with more than common education and substantial landholdings to secure them.

Of all the professions the law carried the greatest weight and opened the most doors. Yet here, too, standards remained loose to nonexistent. It was not until 1824 that the Tennessee Supreme Court set a "course of study" for candidates and began to insist on "close examination in open court." Sam Houston took time out at the beginning of his adventurous career to study in Judge Trimble's office and "in a few months was admitted to the bar." The next year he was made district attorney for Davidson County, paralleling the career of his mentor, Andrew Jackson. One young merchant, Thomas Fletcher, bankrupted by the panic of 1819, became a lawyer and indeed one of the most successful and least solemn of the breed. Fletcher may have written "History of a Modern Attorney," a series of letters in the *Whig*, which explained that the law was one way for a "busted" businessman, despite ignorance and inexperience, recoup his fortune. "Get what you can" was the answer to the novice's question about the proper fee. Law, too, was a business. Lawyers discovered that elevation to the bench was less lucrative than practice and, like Felix Grundy, they gave up judges' positions—though not the title. It is a cliché that eloquence and quickness rather than learning and precedents marked the way to success for frontier lawyers. Loudness might have helped, too, if the descriptions of procedures, or lack of them, in the county courts are to be believed.[18]

However, one can overdo the dramatics and the appeal to the emotions by the bar. Jenkin Whiteside, who "towered above all the Bar," was no orator. We are told that he spoke quietly to judge and jurors, that rational discourse was his normal style. There was, in fact, something of a legal establishment in Nashville early on. Some of the young men of Blount's day had survived and made land law and politics their province. John Overton was perhaps the most studious and the most politically potent of the lawyers of the first frontier. "Overton's Reports" became the standard sourcebook for case law in the area, and his judicial opinions on land law were decisive. After 1800 men of considerable formal education or experience joined Nashville's bar and benches.[19]

Nashville had been a legal and political center from the moment of its founding, first of the scattered settlements, then of what James Robertson had named the Mero district, then of a huge Davidson County out of which were carved the counties of Middle Tennessee.

By the time of the War of 1812, Middle Tennessee's population growth had made it the political center of the state. In 1812 the state legislature began to meet in Nashville, and though it returned to Knoxville in 1816, by 1819 the legislature was once more in Middle Tennessee, where it continued to meet either in Nashville or in nearby Murfreesborough.

Most of the prominent lawyers and judges were not town residents. Felix Grundy was one exception; he built and lived in a town house, but he, too, was taxed on 255 acres—as well as on nine lots in town, which made him the single largest holder of town property in 1816. Indeed, lawyers made up a significant number of the town's absentee proprietors.[20] However, one can identify on the 1820 census nineteen lawyers or law clerks who did live in town. In 1823, twenty-six lawyers advertised their services in Nashville newspapers. When the courts or the legislature met their numbers swelled.

Lawyers seemed to serve as a link between town and country, between merchants and planters. Courthouse and riverfront complemented each other. Some of the lawyers dealt directly with the debt cases and collection work of the merchants.[21] Lawyers invested in steam mills and in the Nashville Bridge Company. But perhaps the area in which professionals and merchants worked together most closely was banking. Even the first bank, the Nashville Bank, set up by merchants in 1807, had on its board in the next year a lawyer, John Dickinson, the "austere and silent" Yankee from New Hampshire.[22] Lawyers, doctors, and landholders began to appear regularly on bank boards before 1819, but after the panic they made up half or more of the boards of the Nashville Bank and the short-lived Farmers and Mechanics Bank, whereas merchant representation declined. The branch bank of the Bank of Tennessee had from its inception in 1815 more lawyers and landholders than merchants.[23] Banks linked successful professionals to the busy merchants, the dynamic factor in the town's growth.

Indeed, to an early foreign visitor it had seemed that Nashville's "inhabitants (like all those in the new settled towns) are chiefly concerned in some way of business: a storekeeper is the general denomination for such persons, and under this head you may include everyone who buys and sells." A letter from Nashville in 1801 added, "Our traders are beginning to think of establishing Houses at Natchez and Orleans for the reception of produce of this country."[24] Surveyors and land lawyers began to advertise for bearskins and cotton to be carried to New Orleans. A first generation of frontier merchants went about organizing a staple trade; they met the challenges of transporting crops downriver to New Orleans via barge and keelboat, worked out trade routes upriver and overland to Pittsburgh, Philadelphia, and Baltimore, and assembled the cash and credit to move crops. Anyone and everyone entered the trade—lawyers, doctors, land speculators, planters. This was venture capitalism, unspecialized and speculative.

Frontier entrepreneurs like Anthony Foster took on mercantile operations along with surveying and locating lands, debt collection, and the practice of law. Foster was on this frontier as early as 1788; in 1792 he served as Governor Blount's emissary to the friendly Chickasaw and to the more hostile Choctaw, who tore up the peace belt he offered. He was in Philadelphia in 1798 buying land warrants for himself and John Overton and trying to expedite payment to the veterans of the unauthorized Nickajack campaign. In knee breeches, his hair in a queue, Foster was both a frontiersman and an eighteenth-century gentlemen of affairs. His connections with land speculators and political figures undoubtedly enhanced his reputation among the merchants and moneylenders of Philadelphia and New Orleans, and he could command the credit for store goods that would be used in bartering for staples. Foster was involved in at least two mercantile operations before the end of the century, and after 1800 he actively continued in the trade for a few years. However, by the time of the Creek wars he was once again preoccupied with land and land law.[25]

In the fall of 1802, eight firms were represented at a meeting of merchants who announced that they would accept ginned cotton from those "who had given bond and security." Less than three years later twelve firms got together to announce a price for cotton; only two of the firms of 1802 were listed.[26] In each year some merchants dropped out, but more joined in the expanding trade. By the outbreak of the War of 1812 more than twenty merchants in town were bringing in goods from Philadelphia and England, buying or trading for cotton and tobacco, and readying to take advantage of the war boom, many of them while they served in the war; this was a time of dependence on clerks and junior partners. Government spending for rations and saltpeter, and for the means to pack and transport goods, added to frontier opportunities. Fewer than half a dozen of these merchants had been in Nashville before the turn of the century. However, two men not only made the transition from land speculating to urban frontier but played a crucial role in the continued commercial development of Nashville.

William Tait, a Scotsman, arrived in Nashville immediately from Philadelphia in 1786. Typically, our first notices of his presence in Nashville are his bringing a suit for debt and the grand jury's indicting him for retailing liquor without a license. George M. Deaderick was in Nashville by at least 1790. He was then a man in his thirties, an experienced merchant. Tait and Deaderick clearly brought some capital with them. Though they bought land and warrants, neither tied up all his assets in land. They made contact with Robertson and Blount and shared in the federal patronage. The organization of the southwestern territory brought federal money to the frontier to pay for the militia's forage, Indian presents, and salaries. It also brought federal officials, like Blount himself, who were always short of funds for their private ventures in land. Deaderick and Tait both advanced funds to Blount for his public and private needs.[27] Although the contract for supplying the militia went to one of the heroes of the Indian wars, Captain John Gordon, it was Tait who supplied the goods and received the certificates of government indebtedness.[28] William Stothart, Tait's partner, and Stothart's son held the postmastership of the town from 1797 to 1811. Deaderick received the bulk of the Indian supply from 1792 to 1795. This was lucrative enough to cause some rivalry and offers to underbid. A deposition from another frontier entrepreneur anxious to share in the trade suggested that the going rate was 100 percent over Philadelphia costs.[29]

Before the turn of the century Tait and Deaderick were substantial property holders in town, leaders in its commercial life, and participants in its politics. Deaderick moved out to his Brown's Creek plantation, but Tait remained a confirmed townsman, whose two-story frame house away from the clamor of the square was labeled "Best House in Town." Deaderick organized the first bank in Nashville, indeed in the state, and Tait served on its board. Both helped create a staple market.

Business was conducted by both men via a complex system of partnerships that served to pool capital and to provide managers. The organization of the staple trade required capital to buy up the crop or to extend credit to farmers who turned over their cotton and tobacco on a commission basis, and to pay shipping costs to New Orleans. The man with ready funds was always in demand.[30] Partner-

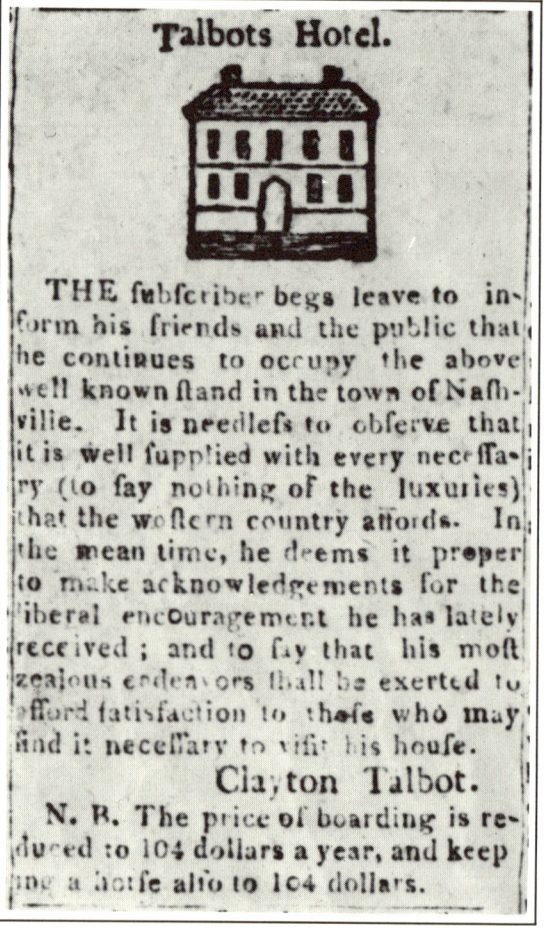

ships helped subsidize and promote younger men. Deaderick drew many of his partners from among the husbands of his nieces, five of whom married into the opportunity-seeking crew of lawyers, speculators, and merchants that made up the bachelor society of Nashville.[31] One niece, Julie Windle, married Stephen Cantrell, the son of a pioneer farmer from Sumner County. During the War of 1812 Cantrell supplied the troops and served as commissary and quartermaster. He was by 1813 a director of the Nashville Bank—Deaderick's bank—and by 1818 president of the bank, secretary of the Nashville Bridge Company, and a power in the merchant community.

Both Tait and Deaderick died in 1816, the year of the "cold plague." They left impressive estates comprising plantations, undeveloped lands, city property, slaves, and bank shares. Tait, taxed on more than 7,000 acres, was the largest landholder in Davidson County, and when Deaderick's executors offered some of his property for sale in 1820, they advertised it as the "most valuable real property in the state." As late as 1832, Cantrell, a Deaderick executor, still owed the estate $39,055.[32]

These first merchants worked out commercial routes when transportation was slow and expensive—overland by wagon and up- and downriver by barge. The eastern markets were one focus of the trade. Goods brought from Baltimore to Nashville from 1790 to 1810 were hauled by six-horse teams at a cost of ten dollars per hundred pounds. In 1811 one shipper offered to take freight to Pittsburgh at four dollars per hundred pounds; cotton was shipped by river to Pittsburgh and Cincinnati and then overland to eastern ports.[33] The produce of the countryside found a cheaper outlet downriver at New Orleans. As early as 1802 cotton worth a million dollars, much of it from the Natchez and Nashville areas, was being exported from New Orleans.[34] However, at that time the difficulties of transporting to market were encouraging migration from the Nashville basin to the Natchez country. The editor of the *Tennessee Gazette* took pains to discourage this emigration, pointing out the uncertainty of land titles around Natchez and insisting that market problems would be solved: "Capt. Caffery proposes carrying any species of produce to New Orleans for the moderate price of one dollar per hundred." A letter published on the front page argued against population dispersion, which would serve only the interests of the land speculator. Home manufactures, it urged, would solve the problems of distance from seaports.[35] However, the self-sufficiency of the Jeffersonian ideal was not most people's goal; the New Orleans trade was crucial. Threats to close the port by Spanish authorities in 1802 triggered agitated public meetings, part of the continuous clamor in Nashville and throughout the West that lay behind the Louisiana Purchase.[36]

The purchase answered one set of problems. Nashville shipped its cotton downriver by keelboat and schooner or carried it in small barges to Eddyville, on the Cumberland below Nashville, where it could be loaded on sloops too heavy to pass over the shoals that sometimes blocked the part of the river closest to Nashville itself. Very little came upriver from New Orleans. The arrival of a barge at Eddyville, eighty-two days out of New Orleans and manned by ten oarsmen poling upstream with a cargo of sugar and liquors, was an event to be memorialized in 1804. Again in 1809 a "barge of 60 tons manned by 35 men reached Nashville. Two skiffs had been prepared which would ... move ahead alternately 50 or 100 yards, fasten the rope to a tree and literally pull the heavy craft upstream."[37] The expense and hardships of transporting crops prompted "a Farmer" to urge a novel experiment in public ownership. He suggested that each county acquire boats and barges to carry produce to New Orleans and upriver. Individuals simply could not handle the problem on their own.[38] Nothing came of his suggestion. However, what individual farmers could not handle, merchants and barge captains began to provide. Between 1810 and 1818, when the first steamboat entered the Nashville trade, a dozen barges and keelboats were making the trip from Nashville to New Orleans in December and back again in May, carrying on the return trip anywhere from fifty to a hundred tons of sugar, cigars, and fancy groceries from the port city to Nashville.[39] Masters of barges and keelboats and their merchant partners or employers were part of the new wave of immigrants to the frontier.

Between 1800 and 1825 more than a hundred individuals and firms entered the cotton and tobacco trade in Nashville. The term merchants may conjure up a picture of solid establishment figures, always portly, somewhat cautious, and at least middle-aged. But these men were also frontiersmen, pioneers in the hazardous keelboat trade, militia colonels, Indian fighters, brawlers, and duelers. Most of them were young when they began their careers in Nashville, some barely out of their teens when they opened their first store. Bachelors or recently married men, they sought opportunities rather than amenities on the frontier. And access to opportunity was wide. Like the first-comers to the agricultural frontier, the merchants needed some capital. How much is problematical. Lewis Atherton, in his pioneer study of the frontier merchant, estimated that five or six thousand dollars would be adequate and observed that this was often advanced by eastern merchants. It was normal for eastern firms to offer credit free of interest for six months and then to carry frontier merchants for as much as a year or two at interest of 6 to 10 percent.[40]

Credit was the lifeblood of trade. The paean to the virtues of credit written by a land speculator in 1796—"my credit rises by my adversity and in my belief, he who is out of debt is out of credit"[41]— was echoed again and again in the activities of frontier merchants. The local court records are full of debt suits, and these do not simply line up creditors against debtors. Creditors were themselves debtors, sued often by merchants in eastern cities who had provided goods for the frontier. Even banker Deaderick, plaintiff in numerous debt suits, was sued in turn by Philadelphia and Baltimore firms.[42] Nor were eastern merchants the only source of credit. The local moneylender soon became a major factor in the business of the square. When lawyer Dickinson died in 1815, he left an estate of more than $70,000, much of it in notes payable by Nashville's leading merchants. Andrew Jackson had cosigned two of these notes for Rachel Jackson's nephew, William Eastin, a merchant who periodically called on his wife's Donelson connections for financial help. Thomas Crutcher, guardian of the Claiborne children, loaned their money to Eastin also. Merchant and shipmaster Lemuel Turner instructed his executors to sell his assets and lend the proceeds out at interest to provide for his family.[43] A sinister portrait of the moneylender was drawn in a letter published in the *Whig* in 1817. "I stroll through the streets to view the trading and laboring part of the community—the honorable and industrious Merchant, the ingenious Manufacturer, the diligent Mechanic, and the Usurer . . . who derives from the unlawful interest of his money its secret and ignominious profit. . . . You will see several of these vultures lounging about the corner of a street, seated upon an old box . . . silently waiting for their prey."[44] The venom in the portrait does not discount the fact that borrowed money was crucial to the fortunes of the young merchants and that the moneylender was not usually a specialized role in the mercantile community. He might be a planter, a lawyer, a retired or a fellow merchant.

Industry, perseverance, and meticulous attention to business were recognized as important in winning credit and success. Young William Nichol made the sixteen-day journey to Baltimore to buy supplies and on his return was immediately dispatched again by his father because William had neglected one item of business.[45] Sons and clerks became partners and then independent businessmen, but they were expected to perform. On the eve of his twenty-first birthday and at the beginning of his career in town as a bank clerk, Ephraim H. Foster received from his father a long letter urging him to study Christ, to "keep at a distance from the gambler and grog drinker," and to "make choice of some worthy female. . . . Be careful that she is of good family, strong mind, sweet temper, good constitution and knowing how to carry the *keys* and make a *pudding* and one that you love most ardently and if she should happen to combine with the above qualifications a little property it will be no material objection."[46] Few fathers and employers on the frontier were more deeply committed to a pious life-style than Robert Coleman Foster, but most would have echoed his advice. Piety, prudence, and sobriety were linked with industry and property in the value system if not always in the workaday world of the urban frontier.

To credit and the bourgeois virtues one has to add the factor of luck. Mercantile enterprise on the frontier could be a gamble. Who of the merchants would not sympathize with young Bedford, who wrote to his brother in New Orleans at the close of the War of 1812, "Peace, a glorious one I hope, has destroyed all my speculations—I intended to purchase cotton, and let it remain, till an arrival from Europe—If peace to sell upon the spot—if not peace to ship it to Pittsburgh—and thence to Philadelphia and New York—as peace has occurred I should have made 8 to 10.000— if I could have gone down in Decr *which ill health alone prevented*—."[47] On the other hand, in 1825 a letter from Nashville reported, "The great rise in cotton is making fortunes for some of our merchants—Yeatman and Woods have now on hand 1800 Bales which cost an average of 15 cents—Sugar has risen in consequence of some Kentucky speculators buying up all they could find—It is now 12 cents. If you had 1 or 200 bbls at 8 cents you could make money on it here—. . . . If cotton keeps up, all property must rise."[48] Merchants used the term *speculations* advisedly. Both the risks and the promises of the trade were great.

While the trade was new and expanding, there were few establishment places to be captured; these had yet to be fashioned. The careers of twenty-eight men whose names appear on both the 1811 militia roll and the 1820 census may serve to illustrate some of the characteristics of merchants and some of the patterns of mercantile operations.[49] They are chosen because they had been in town for at least a decade, but it turns out that their "persistence" in Nashville was even more remarkable: twenty-four remained in town until they died. In fact, the persistence rates of men identifiable either as mechanics or as merchants were significantly higher than those of the overall population. Forty-six percent of mechanics identified on the 1811 militia roll reappear as household heads on the 1820 census schedule, while persistence overall was less than 25 percent. Forty-eight percent of household heads identified as "in commerce" on the 1820 census were again on the census roll in 1830, when overall persistence of household heads was less than one-third. Continuous residence in Nashville, as in other cities, typified town leaders.[50]

Five of these men were clearly entrepreneurs of the first frontier. By 1820 only two of the five might still be called merchants; the others served as bank directors or owned warehouses and town lots. Indeed, the father-in-law of one refused to leave town property to his daughter "for reason that I conceive Mr. Wm. Lytle holds a sufficiency of town property."[51] Another five of these merchants began to advertise for cotton and tobacco between 1801 and 1805. The others came still later; in fact, for half a dozen of these men, their names on the 1811 militia roll are the first notices of their presence in Nashville.

They were a cosmopolitan lot. Five of the seventeen for whom we have pertinent data came originally from Ireland, and one came from Scotland. As might be expected, only one, Stephen Cantrell, had been born in Tennessee; five had been born in Virginia and Kentucky, one in Maryland, one in Vermont, and three in Pennsylvania. Perhaps more to the point is that most of these men, and especially those who came after 1805, came as merchants rather than land speculators or prospective planters. They came from such great mercantile centers as Philadelphia or Baltimore or from such trading towns as Pittsburgh and Lexington. Unlike prospective planters (Andrew Jackson and his partner in commerce and in war, John Coffee, come to mind)[52] who at the turn of the century had engaged in trade for a season or two, serving their neighbors from a country store, most of these men were products of a mercantile network, probing the possibilities of the Nashville area.

They were young; of the twenty-one for whom we have data on age, none was older than thirty-nine, and a third were twenty-five or younger when they first appeared in Nashville. The sources of their capital or credit were varied. At least three began as clerks to other Nashville businessmen. Another five established themselves in Nashville with backing from merchants in other cities. Family connections provided capital for a number of them. Robert Armstrong's mercantile career was initiated after he eloped with Josiah Nichol's daughter. Andrew Jackson interceded for his protégé, one of the heroes of the Creek wars. In his most bristling fashion, Jackson wrote Nichol that the bridegroom, "without a cent of property . . . is worthy of any lady of any grade, of any family of any fortune!"[53] Nichol capitulated, and young General Armstrong was in business in 1815.

Irish-born Josiah Nichol was one of the older men; he was thirty-nine when he came to Nashville in 1808. Three years later he was a director of the Nashville Bank and an alderman. Between 1812 and 1815 he was a government contractor for saltpeter. By the twenties he, his son, his son-in-law, and two of his ex-clerks were commission merchants with substantial investments in steamboats.

A few of the younger merchants, such as the Kirkman-Hannah-Jackson clan of young, Irish brothers-in-law, also brought considerable capital to the frontier.[54] The last of this trio, James Jackson, ultimately gave up a successful mercantile career for a plantation near Florence, Alabama. However, although some of the merchants invested in land and retired to plantations, the opportunities of the expanding trade and of the real-estate and banking concerns associated with expansion clearly absorbed the energies of most. Alexander Porter, another Irishman, opened a general-merchandise store in Nashville in 1806 and built up a commission business which he maintained through the panic of 1819 and into the twenties. When he died in 1833 he left three plantations but also a good deal of city property. His eldest son, James, was left "a piece of ground on the Public Square, 20' front—on which I wish a store house to be built no less than two stories high." Porter obviously felt that economic opportunity was to be found in town. He suggested that one of his sons should become a lawyer, one a doctor, and one a merchant. Being a planter was incidental, not in itself a compelling ambition.[55]

Specialization of economic function was as characteristic of the urban as of the land-speculating frontier. Most of these men started with a store or a "manufactory." Storekeepers and artisans traded for country produce; those with staying power concentrated on the cotton and tobacco crops and rented warehouses and gins. Most continued to put together partnerships on an annual basis. A pioneer textile manufacturer followed the same pattern. George Poyzer's cotton-thread factory was in operation by 1802. Poyzer accepted raw cotton, flax, and hemp in exchange for thread, but, with the creation of an active market for the raw product, his modestly capitalized factory, like others through the twenties, tended to be overshadowed by the trading activities of its owner.[56] The action was on the waterfront.

Moving crops to market meant involvement in shipping and banking. Andrew Hynes's career is illustrative. He opened a store in Nashville in 1809, when he was twenty-four. By 1813 he was manufacturing copper stills; by 1814, with his ex-clerk, Thomas

Fletcher, he had invested in a hemp factory and was involved in the keelboat trade, bringing goods upriver from New Orleans. Indeed, he met one of his own boats coming upriver as he was going down to New Orleans with Jackson's forces during the war. Jackson commandeered blankets for his troops from Hynes's keelboat.[57] In 1817 Hynes and Fletcher were active in founding the Farmers and Mechanics Bank. None of the merchants remained simply retail shopkeepers. Sixteen of the twenty-eight served as bank directors before 1820, and three were officers of the company that built the first bridge over the Cumberland in the midst of the panic. At least two had invested in a steam-powered mill. Entering the twenties, Nashville's leading merchants and ultimately most successful businessmen were those who invested in steamboat transportation and in banking.

Even before the end of the War of 1812 William Carroll had made contact with the agent of steamboat patentees in Pittsburgh, his hometown, and was urging a subscription of thirty thousand dollars to build a boat for the Cumberland. Carroll continued to push the project when he returned from service in the war. The Nashville Steamboat Company was in fact incorporated in 1819 and built the *General Robertson* in 1820. By then Carroll had already entered the field; in partnership with Daniel Whiting, a ship captain, he owned the *Andrew Jackson*, which was in operation by the spring of 1818 and was the first steamer in the Nashville–New Orleans trade.[58]

In the first half-dozen years of steamboat transportation, all of the Nashville investors seem to have been merchants despite the early interest of a few lawyers in town. Perhaps the merchants' keener interest in the trade led them to gamble on the high risks. In 1823 the boat company's *General Robertson* sank after hitting a snag in the river. In the next year the *General Greene*, weighing three hundred tons and the largest of the steamers, also hit a snag and sank. Nevertheless, by 1824 a dozen steamboats traveled between New Orleans and Nashville; at least six were owned by Nashville merchants. Though only three steamers had docked at Nashville in 1819, 33 arrivals were recorded in 1824 and 112 in 1829.[59] Cheap, fast transportation helped produce the merchant elite in the twenties.

Thomas Yeatman and the Woods brothers, Joseph and Robert, were the most spectacularly successful of all Nashville businessmen who began their careers during the frontier years. Engaged in the river trade as very young men, they made the transition from keelboats to steamboats, from merchandising to banking and, uniquely for Nashville men, to large-scale manufacturing. Tradition has it that advance information of a rise in the price of cotton prompted Yeatman and his brother to buy up the crop in Nashville and in Huntsville in 1825, the only year after the panic of 1819 during which the crop brought twenty cents a pound. This coup presumably helped to provide the capital for the banking firm of Yeatman and Woods, organized in 1825 with a specie capital of $100,000. In the same year they invested in an ironworks, located in nearby Stewart County, that by 1833 included two blast furnaces, forges, and a rolling mill, employed two hundred slaves, and was valued at $300,000. In that same year their bank was also credited with a capital of $300,000. At his death, in the cabin of a riverboat where he was struck down by cholera, Thomas Yeatman was reputed to be worth $500,000.[60] Few of the commission merchants fared as well as Yeatman and the Woodses. More typical of the most successful merchants' assets after more than a decade of steamboat traffic were those of Josiah Nichol, who left an estate of more than $150,000, and of Alexander Porter, whose property was valued at more than $75,000, when they died in 1833; like Yeatman, they were victims of the cholera epidemic.[61]

All of these men were associated with Nashville banks. Banking necessarily grew to keep pace with the staple trade. Within ten years of its founding in 1807, the Nashville Bank had a capital of about $1 million and had created branch banks in four Middle Tennessee county seats and one in eastern Tennessee. By 1814 a second bank, a branch of the Bank of Tennessee, which had been organized in Knoxville in 1811, was in operation. Judge Overton was a major subscriber; he and at least five other lawyers and land speculators joined the board of the new institution.[62] Boom conditions motivated the drive for a third bank. Jesse Wharton, a Nashville lawyer and a U.S. senator, wrote Overton in 1815 urging a branch of the Bank of the United States (BUS) for Nashville. Credit creation was his main concern; Wharton specified the need for a bank that would not be confined to specie payments.[63] However, Overton was by this time deeply involved with the Bank of Tennessee, whose president, Hugh Lawson White of Knoxville, was determined to block competition and perhaps to monopolize banking facilities in Tennessee.[64] Despite the resolutions of public meetings and the championship of Felix Grundy, the group of lawyers and businessmen who sought a branch of the BUS were outmaneuvered in the Tennessee legislature, where a prohibitive tax was placed on "foreign" banking corporations. A combination of populist reaction to the BUS, soon to become "the monster," and the old guard of the banking community won. In later years Andrew Jackson was to insist that it was "the aristocratic few in Nashville" who had sought a branch of the BUS, but in fact a significant part of the merchant community and a good many lawyers were enthusiastic, while the principal opponents were the established bankers, "the aristocratic few" indeed.[65]

A group of merchants, many newly involved in steamboat transportation, and their lawyer allies countered the opposition to the BUS by organizing their own Farmers and Mechanics Bank, which went into operation in 1818. The largest single stockholder and the bank's cashier was Moses Norvell, brother-in-law of the Woodses and one of the most bustling of the new entrepreneurs. Norvell's investment amounted to $16,250; a number of the other stockholders invested less than $1,000. In 1820 the Farmers and Mechanics Bank reported $166,900 in paid-in stock. Its stockholders had borrowed $142,919; of the seventy-four stockholders, only one, Robert C. Foster, had not borrowed a penny.[66]

In years when cotton was bringing a good price in New Orleans, Nashville banks loaned generously to the mercantile community. In fact, they earned a reputation, at least among the conservative bankers of eastern Tennessee, for speculative operations. In 1820 a correspondent of Overton, arguing for consolidation of the Nashville Bank with the Bank of Tennessee, insisted that Knoxville be the headquarters of the parent bank because "we all are too well acquainted with the irresistible mania for speculation in the good people of Nashville."[67] When times grow difficult banks ought to contract their operations and maintain a specie basis, wrote a Knoxville banker.[68] Yet to draw in one's belt, to stop buying, was a contradiction in terms to the Nashville business community.

When the economy slowed down and government spending decreased after the boom times during the War of 1812, the banks' response was not to contract but to refuse to redeem in specie. In 1815 both the Nashville Bank and the branch bank suspended specie payment. The editors of the *Whig*, which was owned by the Norvell brothers, were quick to justify the move as one geared to protect local merchants from the drain of specie to the North. A public meeting, chaired by a major stockholder in the Nashville Bank, presented resolutions in favor of the banks' move and urged against penalties for suspension. A committee of bank directors published in the banks' defense a letter explaining their course in chauvinistic terms. It was charged that the bank notes of other states were being brought to Nashville and sold at a discount for the notes of Nashville banks so that specie could be drawn out of the state.[69] Contraction was not to be considered, especially when cotton prices were high. First-class cotton brought twenty-eight cents a pound in New Orleans in 1816 and thirty cents a pound in 1817 and 1818.[70] These prices not only permitted specie resumption but also prompted the demand for greater banking facilities.

Boom times meant that almost all the merchants owned taxable property within a decade of their arrival in town. Nineteen of the twenty-eight were freeholders by 1816, and this is especially significant because so few townsmen actually owned real estate in town.[71] All owned slaves, although only two claimed numbers sufficient to suggest they were building plantations.[72] Only nine of the merchants were taxed on acreage in Davidson County in 1816, and three of these on small properties valuable because they were close to town. At least eight of these men died before 1829, the year for which another tax list exists. One had suffered severe reverses by 1816. Eleven others, however, had more taxable property in 1829 than in 1816, and two had held their own despite the difficult few years that followed the 1819 panic.

The panic spelled disaster for many merchants, but of this group only four or five were wiped out. Thomas Hill's 1820 advertisement, offering his store, dwelling, stock, and trade for notes of the Farmers and Mechanics Bank, suggests that his involvement with that bank was to bring him down.[73] William Carroll was reported to have lost as much as $66,500,[74] but in 1821 he was translated into the governor's office in the teeth of and indeed through use of the panic. The reverses of the panic tended to be temporary; continuous economic growth meant that the credit to start again was available. Though the panic brought confusion to the merchant community, it also demonstrated the strength of the institutions that community had created.

Disaster hit in 1819 when the bottom fell out of the cotton market. Cotton dropped from thirty to nineteen cents per pound and was to fall to a low of twelve cents in 1826. Something like five hundred debt suits were filed in the Davidson County Court in the first six months of 1819.[75] The first reaction of the banks was suspension. Once more the newspapers and public meetings chaired by prominent citizens supported the move. But the depth and duration of this depression made it impossible for the business community to maintain a solid front. The bank directors were cast as the villains of the day. The *Clarion* warned, "Well may the banks fear a call of Legislature. . . . They are the horse leeches of the country." The *Whig* published a satirical poem, "The Bank That Jack Built": "These are the *Rags* all tatter'd and torn, / That were issued as money, noon, evening and morn / By the cunning Directors." The charges became even more sinister. Stockholders were urged to examine the conditions of their banks and to note that everyone was in distress except the directors. The *Clarion* fervently supported Felix Grundy for the legislature; Grundy's relief proposals included a state bank whose paper would be based on state lands and that would lend to indebted farmers. Opposition to this loan bank was bitterly condemned as emanating from a conspiracy of bank directors. One letter described Nashville's commerce as dead, destroyed by banks and shavers, shavers being defined as "those who pounce on merchants. . . . whose credit is shaken and suck them dry." The *Whig* widened the field of villains to take in the judges of the county court who had determined to go through their docket and handle all debt suits even if sessions continued from 7:00 A.M. to 9:00 P.M.[76]

The newspapers, like their rural readership, were insisting upon a scenario that lined up on one side the debtors—farmers and merchants—and on the other "the monied aristocracy"—bank directors, judges, land speculators, and the conservative bankers of eastern Tennessee. The changes in membership of bank boards in these years, when some merchants were bankrupted and others came dangerously close to bankruptcy, undoubtedly created bitterness, but factional politics also accounted for some of the venom.

The *Clarion*, which supported Grundy, went so far as to offer support for stay laws, usually anathema to merchants. It published a letter attacking not just bank directors but specifically the "bog-trotters," the successful Irish merchants who were charged with attempting to control elections and town meetings. Associated with the *Clarion* were some of the "busted" businessmen like William Carroll and John P. Erwin. The *Whig* opposed Grundy and stay laws and was backed by John Overton, who was at once part of the anti-Grundy political faction and a principal stockholder of the Bank of Tennessee, which had earlier blocked Grundy's attempts to bring a branch of the BUS to Nashville.[77] To complicate matters further, one of the *Whig*'s owners was Joseph Norvell, a director of the Farmers

and Mechanics Bank in 1820 and a brother of that bank's cashier. The directors of the Farmers and Mechanics Bank blamed the older banks for their plight. Both newspapers, then, had ties with the merchants and bankers of Nashville, and it was clear that some merchants, too, had turned on the bankers and the "foreigners" in their midst and on the legal establishment. But merchants, though bitter, and some of them frantic, wanted relief, not revolution.

When Patrick Henry Darby bought the *Clarion*'s presses and began to issue the Constitutional Advocate in 1822, his paper maintained the barrage against banks and bankers. Darby, a flamboyant lawyer dealing especially in disputed land titles, had become a member of the Nashville Guards and was busy building a political following.[78] In 1823 Darby charged that Stephen Cantrell, president of the Nashville Bank, had, as pension agent, made personal profits through premiums in exchanging government specie for the bank's paper money. The result was a no-holds-barred indulgence in what we have come to call Jacksonian rhetoric. Published in the *Whig* was a scurrilous anonymous letter calling Darby a Yahoo, a barbarian, a renegade, and finally a "Kentuck Mongrel." It was followed immediately by a letter from Cantrell, who accused Darby of being a hypocrite and a pharisee who would "rise from his knees and go direct to a ballroom"; Cantrell charged that Darby had no right to his middle name, was connected with Burr's treason, had tried to sell free blacks, had stolen horses, had hunted land titles while others died in the war, and, closer to home, had bought defective titles and served his own clients as witness. Darby countered by calling conspiracy, conspiracy of the rich and the established against a man of the people. "For myself I have neither parchments nor diplomas from universities or college. . . . Neither am I connected with Banks, or Bank directors, or corporations or companies." "Being raised a mechanick," he favored lien laws and the concerns of working people. Darby also charged Judge Overton with taking part "in a very corrupt combination to destroy Darby."[79]

All this might have been powerful ammunition for an attack on the establishment. Cantrell was in fact dismissed from his post as pension agent, and even Andrew Jackson, Overton's old friend, was sympathetic to Darby's position. The *Whig*, of course, far from jumping on the antibanker bandwagon, published Cantrell's countercharges against Darby and published no defense of the lawyer when he was inexorably pushed out of town. In the summer of 1823 Darby lost the election to the state legislature by a wide margin. Judge McNairy struck him from the roll of attorneys in 1824. The cause, again peculiarly "Jacksonian," was Darby's appeal to the people, to public opinion, as against the courts. Darby had written a pamphlet defending his position in a suit pending before the circuit court, and this was ruled contempt of court. Then Grundy, the democratic champion, evidently convinced the elders of the Presbyterian church to deny Darby communion.[80] By the fall of 1824 Darby's press had been bought with money supplied in part by Overton; it would be run by a man who would "deport himself accurately."[81] Darby moved to Kentucky.

No matter how shaken it had been by the situation following the panic, Nashville's merchant and lawyer leadership did not succumb to the-people-versus-the-privileged rhetoric. The conflict that developed within the entrepreneurial community after 1819 is perhaps one way to sum up the group experience on this urban frontier. Merchants who counted on continuous economic expansion to give them an assured status in the community were frustrated and challenged. They allied with the debtor farmers of the state to place one of their own, General Carroll, in the governor's office.

Carroll was one of the first spokesmen for what was later labeled Jacksonian democracy. He helped achieve major changes in Tennessee's basic institutions; he sought and ultimately won taxation of land according to value and the stripping of the General Assembly of its wide power of appointment, which had kept county government and the courts in the hands of a planter establishment. At the same time it would be difficult to distinguish Carroll's program from that of his later Whig opponents. In the immediate crisis Carroll's program reflected the needs of Nashville's merchants. Carroll did not favor stay laws, and under his administration the loan bank was cautiously administered. He pushed for the abolition of imprisonment for debt, for penal reform, and for the creation of a public school system. He urged a statewide program of internal improvements.[82] He was initially antibank in no uncertain terms, yet within a few years he was supporting a campaign to bring a branch of the BUS to Nashville.[83] Carroll's program was, in short, concerned with promoting economic expansion and commercial opportunities. One critic summarized Carroll's motives, perhaps better than he knew, when he sneered that one was urged to vote for Carroll "because he *was broke and . . . won't* stay so."[84]

Casting the bank boards as the "monied aristocracy" may have helped relieve the pain but did little to assuage the effects of the panic. In 1826, when forced to resume specie payments, all the chartered banks in Tennessee were liquidated, leaving in Nashville only the moneylenders and the private bank of Yeatman-Woods, and even Yeatman-Woods encountered fierce public opposition. But the panic did not halt economic growth. Steamboats on the river set a new pace. Six thousand bales of cotton were shipped from Tennessee to New Orleans in 1821, and 30,000 bales, worth $1 million, were shipped out of Nashville in 1825.[85]

Throughout the twenties there was development along lines already set out before the panic. Nashville served an ever wider hinterland as collector of country produce and increasingly as distributor of dry goods, groceries, drugs, and manufactured goods. Commission merchants and wholesale merchants gradually began to give up "the store." A major drive for turnpike construction in the thirties was a logical outgrowth of the action on Nashville's waterfront: the turnpikes would confirm Nashville's position as the commercial hub of Middle Tennessee. Banks and bankers retained their "monster" image, but the trade of the city continued to grow, and the need for banks was clear to the merchant community, which wholeheartedly backed Carroll's efforts with Nicholas Biddle of the BUS. In 1827 a branch of the BUS was established in Nashville. By

1833 two new banks were chartered. Merchants and lawyers dominated the lists of directors.[86]

They had not been dubbed the "Nashville Regency" yet, but, as the Darby incident suggests, an economic and political elite was in place. Within a generation a group of merchants, lawyers, and bankers, who were no more representative of the town's population than the justices had been of the county's, had made themselves the establishment within the developing town. A few, especially those whom the panic forced to remember their modest beginnings on the frontier, responded positively, if temporarily, to the popular antibank, antimonopoly rhetoric. More typically, the merchant-lawyer leadership looked upon the new rhetoric as a threat and closed ranks. By the twenties it could call upon effective institutions, religious and social sanctions, and political, legal, and financial power to secure itself.

Building Institutions on the Urban Frontier

CHAPTER 3

THE merchant-lawyer leadership showed itself in more than the economic sector. Inheriting the few sociopolitical institutions of the frontier—militia, public meeting, Masonic order—the entrepreneurs of the urban frontier went on to create debating societies, lyceums, and libraries, private voluntary societies that both entertained them and testified to their pursuit of culture. Their wives sustained the churches, created a Sunday school, and took the initiative in providing for the poor and the helpless. Voluntary societies, including the churches, subtly did their part in confirming a cultural and social elite. A female academy, the college, and membership in the churches began to establish social hierarchies in the community. At the same time, municipal government was dominated by this same elite group of merchants and professionals.

For more than forty years Nashville was a male preserve, a brawling, hard-drinking town, on the surface at least hardly a community. Its transient population gravitated to the riverfront for work and to the taverns for diversion. Young John Dickinson hesitated to move into town in 1800 because "dissipation is carried on in all its branches and there is scarce any opportunity for study." Indeed, Dickinson was forced into a duel with one of the Overtons, and though he swore to be "done with it," he decided to buy pocket pistols.[1] Early Nashville demonstrated the kind of individualism we associate with the come-outer frontier—unusual tolerance of personal eccentricities, of religious persuasions or lack of any, of common-law marriages and divorce, of the visibility of free blacks and slave mistresses. There was at the same time heightened sensitivity to questions of individual honor and reputation. Violent encounters in the streets and in the taverns were commonplace; the line between brawling and dueling was a fine one, and community leaders took part in both kinds of direct action. Not everyone approved. James Robertson tried vainly to restrain Andrew Jackson, insisting, "I cannot find where any honor is attached to dueling." Jacob McGavock registered horror when two of Jackson's protégés, Thomas Hart Benton and William Carroll, faced each other with pistols. Carroll lost a thumb, and when it was feared that Benton might die, McGavock thought not of "honor" but of Benton's "poor old mother who I am told depended on him entirely for his support." However, such sober good sense and prudence did not prevail among aspiring planters, young lawyers, and at least some of the merchants.[2] Here, too, the county set the tone.

Nevertheless, there were factors at work that gave coherence to the village and allowed it to develop an institutional structure of its own. Size was one factor; the activities of the town were concentrated in a few short blocks. The relative homogeneity of the village in terms of ethnic and family background and in terms of the concern for "making it," which was the universal motive of migrants to this frontier, enabled townsmen to understand each other and their county neighbors, themselves frontier entrepreneurs. Family and family alliances provided the strongest social cement. A core of stable residents in a sea of migrants soon accepted responsibility for municipal government and began to put together literary and social groups for their own amusement. The women of the town contributed to church building and founded the first welfare institutions of the community. Churches, voluntary associations, and corporation government began to define a leadership cadre that undertook to speak for the town. A web of complex and enduring relationships based on kinship, friendship, business partnerships, employment, church membership, and participation in voluntary associations cre-

Baptist Church. From the *Nashville Business Directory of 1860*.

ated a community among the large group of achievers and strivers.

Pioneers had moved as families to the first frontier—Robertsons, Donelsons, Shelbys. At seventeen Jacob McGavock was sent by his family to work for his uncle in Nashville's land office. As an old man he wrote his brother that he had not known their father had served as quartermaster during the Revolution. "I was so young when I left his house—that I know very little of his early life."[3] Yet Jacob had inherited from his family a pattern of operations and a specific place on the frontier. For most of his adult life he would serve as clerk of the circuit court, from which vantage point he would collect his fees and supervise the family's land business.

Three Deaderick brothers settled in Nashville; they were joined by their sister and their half brother. The marriages of the Deaderick nieces tied together a surprisingly large number of frontier entrepreneurs in much the same way as the marriages of John Donelson's children tied together land speculators, planters, and merchants. Frontier bachelors gossiped about the marriages of their friends and twitted each other about acquiring "shemale sleepmates."⁴ Complex family alliances provided social and economic support.⁵ Joseph Woods and his brother Robert married the West girls from Lexington. Not only did Robert follow Joseph to Nashville, but so also did the West brothers and at least two other West sisters. Eliza West married Simon Bradford, her sister Hannah married Moses Norvell; both men were involved in the commission business. So was John B. West, who owned a cotton-thread factory; the thread was sold at Joseph Woods's warehouse.⁶ William Carroll married a Bradford, and his brother, Nat, married the daughter of Duncan Robertson, merchant and auctioneer. A third Woods brother, James, a widower, married the sister of Alexander Porter after settling in Nashville, and, when she died, he married a daughter of the Erwin family, who were land speculators and merchants. Thomas Yeatman's second wife was an Erwin. Elihu Hall and Thomas Fletcher each married a daughter of Thomas Talbot, the tavernkeeper. By the twenties there were merchant clans in Nashville. George Deaderick's wife reportedly jeered that each time a niece produced a namesake, her husband was expected to contribute handsomely.⁷

If family was one source of stability, another was the ease with which "foreigners" were assimilated or ignored. There had always been foreigners in Nashville. Indeed, some insist that Timothy Demonbreun, born in Quebec, soldier and trader in the Illinois country, tavernkeeper and storekeeper in Nashville, was the first true inhabitant of the village, his home a cave in the bluff. But aside from the important group of Scottish and Irish merchants, few foreigners took leadership positions in the village. Without sponsors or capital, seeking work, most were men like Jacob Noy, who died in Nashville in 1803 possessed of "one Dutch oven, two pewter dishes, one Basin pewter, one German history and one German catechism."⁸ For those who remained for any length of time, assimilation into the Protestant and English-speaking community was the norm. The first mass performed by a Catholic bishop was celebrated in Demonbreun's home, but at least two of Demonbreun's children were Baptists, one a preacher.⁹ There were never enough Frenchmen or Germans to support a distinct community. In 1820 the census reported only ninety-five aliens in Nashville.

This situation was, of course, not unusual. Massive immigration to the United States had fallen off during the American Revolution, and immigration figures remained low until the 1830s.¹⁰ The French

Revolution and the Napoleonic Wars, the barriers erected to emigration by European governments, the existence of alternative destinations for immigrants, and, finally, American hostility to aliens, all played some part in restricting immigration.[11] Moreover, Nashville was both an inland town, requiring an expensive trip from the seaports, and a southern town, which offered few economic incentives to justify a poor immigrant's traveling so far off the beaten course.

Contemporaries, of course, would take note of accents and cultural differences, yet the only extant evidence of hostility to foreigners emerged after the panic of 1819, when the successful Irish merchants and bank directors were singled out and "bog-trotter" became an epithet. The response was far from defensive; "bog-trotters," it was pointed out, were not debtors. They paid their way.[12] Yankees as well as Irishmen easily and early established themselves in town along with Carolinians and Virginians. Carroll and Tannehill from Pittsburgh quickly became leading citizens. Indeed, Andrew Jackson, writing the secretary of war in 1810, requested that arms be deposited with "Capt. Carrol, Lt. Paxton, and Ensign Tannehill, these officers are gentlemen of Property and standing in society"[13]—high praise indeed when one considers that Tannehill had been in Nashville no more than three years and Carroll had arrived within the year.

Community was founded in the face-to-face relationships made possible by the size of the village. Men were identifiable by their property and occupations, women by their husbands, and slaves by their masters. Two people who knew the village well described it many years later, each using the same technique of recollecting: moving down the streets and alleys and identifying the inhabitants. Colonel Willoughby Williams visited Nashville many times before he settled there in 1818. His brief sketch begins by telling us that in 1809 "none but professional men and merchants lived in town." And, indeed, though he identifies about one hundred people, only nine might be labeled mechanics, and these obviously come within Williams's loose definition of "merchants." Significantly, with one possible exception, all the mechanics were property holders. Williams mentions only four women, one of them because her divorce case was argued by Aaron Burr. Black Bobb's tavern is the only reference to black people.[14]

Jane Thomas's record, a rambling, hodgepodge of genealogical data interspersed with telling details, was put together at the very

Catholic Church. From the *Nasvhille Business Directory of 1860*.

end of the nineteenth century for a series of newspaper stories. Her memories of Nashville began in 1804, when she was brought to the village as a small child. She remembered the "beautiful" women and, that rarity on the frontier, a spinster (like herself). She remembered Granny Nell, the Indian midwife, who got drunk every Christmas and galloped around the square, and Mrs. Estill, the free black woman who kept a bakery. She remembered as well many more of the mechanics. She grew up in the village and seems more grounded in its daily life than Williams, whose orientation was more county than town. But by and large the same people count for both of them. In a village becoming a town, absorbing population at a great rate, open to new waves of strangers each year, a stable center was discovered among those who stayed put, among property holders and their family connections.[15] In remembering, sometimes nostalgically, their community, these memoirists disregarded most others. From the vantage point of the forties, for example, Wilkins Tannehill remembered a Nashville of thirty years before as far more "republican," a Nashville of young lawyers and businessmen, of clerks and junior partners.[16] If there were distinctions between the cultures of rising professionals and merchants in town, they were not obvious, and all townsmen were overshadowed initially by the world of the squires.

In building the first specifically town institutions, townsmen did not start with a clean slate. From the beginning the institutions of the countryside embraced the village. In 1801 Nashville citizens organized their own light infantry company and by 1807 a troop of cavalry. Andrew Jackson described the town's infantry corps in 1810 as made up "of respectable merchants and mechanicks."[17] The Indian fighting frontier was a vital memory in the area, and when the War of 1812 and the Creek wars broke out, merchants and mechanics would become military heroes or at least captains, colonels, and majors. The war experience, the ancient blood tax, gave them the kind of prestige, even legitimacy, previously associated with the first settlers. William Carroll became a major general, Andrew Hynes a colonel; Wilkins Tannehill served as judge advocate, and Stephen Cantrell as commissary and quartermaster.[18] Even a black soldier, Jeffrey Lockelier, acquired special status as a result of his service at Horseshoe Bend and New Orleans.[19]

Like the militia, the public meeting was an institution inherited from the first frontier, calling on all the free men in the community and geared to rallying effective popular support for a specific goal. The public meeting was not an official institution. It was called to petition the legislature for the right to build a market house on the square or for the right to town government itself, to raise subscriptions for a fire company or for a bridge across the Cumberland. After the village had acquired its own government, it was this kind of meeting that provided the stimulus for improvements or voiced the "town's" position on relief legislation during the panic. Active participants in the meetings tended again to be merchants and lawyers. The meetings were open, the community was small, and the ability of any given individual to influence the meeting was at least a possibility, but the initiators of a public meeting were usually seeking consensus. They organized the meeting and stood ready to elect its chairman and secretary. The public meeting did not readily lend itself to the airing of alternative views. On the other hand, like the militia, the meeting did provide a stage for relative newcomers to demonstrate their talents and prove themselves gentlemen of "standing."[20]

The Masonic order was a third inheritance from the first frontier. Freemasonry held an honorable position among the Cumberland's frontiersmen; a lodge had been licensed by the North Carolina order as early as 1796. The generalized and secularized Christianity of the Masons was more universally supported than any given religious sect by the leading men of the community. The log Masonic hall had its place on the square by 1800, and, unlike the first church building, it was not torn down until it could be replaced in stone. By 1812 Cumberland Lodge, based in Nashville, was organized. The speeches and balls that marked the feast of Saint John the Evangelist were sponsored by a mixed crew of merchants, master mechanics, lawyers, a handful of "farmers," and an occasional "gentleman," men who could afford the dues and the lottery tickets to raise money for a splendid new Masonic hall.[21]

Early on there was also a Nashville mechanical society that embraced mechanics from all over the county and took the lead in organizing the annual Fourth of July celebrations.[22] However, this society disappears from the record after 1803. The celebrations on Independence Day, February 22, and, after 1815, January 8 (in honor of Jackson's victory at New Orleans) seem to have been the responsibility of the tavernkeepers and community leaders.[23]

In 1835 the Frenchman Beaumont described the American community leader: "He obtained successively all the honorific titles to which an influential citizen of the U.S. can aspire: he was a member of the Historical Society, the temperance society, the Colonization Society, Inspector of Prisons and Asylums, and he was, besides, an anti-Mason."[24] It was exactly this conglomeration of titles and memberships that taken together described a place in American society that was being created in Nashville in these years.

Wilkins Tannehill's career is a case in point. Tannehill was a compulsive joiner. He arrived in town in 1810, and by 1813 he was serving as judge advocate in the militia and, unlike Beaumont's solid citizen, had joined the Masons; he served seven terms as Grand Mason. He kept the books of a newly organized library company (1814), was appointed trustee of Cumberland College (1814), and was elected town alderman (1813–16), treasurer of the thespian society (1818), recording secretary of the Tennessee Antiquarian Society (1821), trustee of the University of Nashville (1825–26), treasurer of the Nashville Theater Stock Company (1826), and trustee of the Presbyterian church (1826). He was a sponsor of the Sunday-school union (1829), vice-president of the colonization society (1830), and vice-president of a resuscitated and rather vigorous lyceum (1830). All these activities were carried on in addition to his career as merchant, cashier of the Nashville Bank, and editorial writer for the *Whig*. Prodigious energy! and there would be more activity to come.[25]

Aside from the Masonic order, the voluntary associations Tannehill joined were new. Rather than the associations according status, individuals had to create and gain support for the associations. Perhaps that was why Tannehill could later write about the republican simplicity of an earlier Nashville. Initially, at least, social organizations had been founded by young men on the make. In the twenties a not so subtle change began. The earlier do-it-ourselves, self-culture associations gave way to social and cultural uplift societies. Thespian societies became stock companies to build theaters for professional actors. Discussion societies gave way to lyceums designed to raise the sights of clerks and apprentices. Ministers and professionals were heavily represented on the boards of such newer, church-related, and religiously oriented organizations as the colonization society, the Sunday-school union, and the temperance society. These organizations of the twenties reflected the coming of age of the frontier entrepreneurs.

The earliest attempts to develop the cultural life of the village, like the Nashville Discussion society of 1807 and its successor, lyceums, subscription libraries, and reading rooms, came from a limited number of professionals, merchants, and editors.[26] These organizations tended to be short-lived and poorly endowed, but they were reconstituted over and over again. In 1817 there was the Nashville Musical Society, in 1818 the Nashville Thespian Society, one of whose performers was Sam Houston.[27] These societies were concerned with entertainment and self-expression rather than charitable or civic endeavor. They were male societies, although women may have attended the concerts and dramatic performances. Perhaps the societies were an early indication of the community sorting itself out, of a self-proclaimed elite consciously striving for cultural status. As early as 1806 one newspaper correspondent urged Shakespeare rather than the currently available "entertainments" as moral uplift. The *Whig* announced that "a philosophical oration on Conscience; or the Moral Consciousness" would be delivered "to the Thinking part of the Citizens of Nashville."[28] However, these societies were mostly for fun; they provided a stage for amateurs and served the needs of a limited but hardly exclusive constituency.

During the bitter years following the panic of 1819, at the same time it was attacking bank directors, the *Clarion* published a series of letters on Nashville's "literary" scene that was anything but

Presbyterian Church. From the *Nashville Business Directory of 1860*.

booster literature. It called the debating society presumptuous, the newspapers dull, the bar untutored, Cumberland College "a single dilapidated building without professors or scholars." Even the female academy, which the writer had to admit was "flourishing," was in danger because its trustees were not "literary" men. But the most devastating and the most personal abuse was heaped on the antiquarian society, labeled a "mockery of literature"; its members were described as amateurs who assumed they did not need scientific training for the analysis of the Indian relics they were busy collecting.[29] The leading figure in the antiquarian society was Judge John Haywood, Nashville's first published author, leading scholar and historian, and one of the most influential figures of the Tennessee bar. Haywood's opposition to stay laws singled him out as one of the "Aristocratic few," and resentment could be turned to ridicule of Haywood's penchant for mixing scientific inquiry with speculation about the spirit world.[30] This attack on Nashville's literary institutions was based not on the anti-intellectual bias that is usually associated with the frontier but on the grounds that they were amateurish pretensions to culture. Pretensions to cultural *leadership* may have rankled even more at this moment as a result of the mayhem created by the panic, when it would seem that who was whom in Nashville was being sorted out in a devastating and fundamental way.

The antiquarian society, like the college, suggested the possibility of invidious distinctions. By 1820 there were indeed graduates of the college in town. Davidson Academy, founded by the first settlers, had become Cumberland College in 1806. Under the administration of James Priestley, a Presbyterian minister, from 1809 to 1816, it was in fact a superior classical school. Priestley was evidently a dedicated teacher whose interest in geography, chemistry, and physics complemented his school's concentration on the classics; however, one little fellow complained that though he was "very much pleased with Dr. Priestley. . . . it is a very loansome place, and the fare extremely bad."[31]

It was the lawyers who joined county leaders on the board of trustees of Cumberland College, with a few, almost predictable exceptions made for prominent merchants, and it was the sons of lawyers and of planters who earned degrees at the college. Merchants' sons entered the business at fifteen or sixteen. Actually, very few degrees were awarded—only nineteen in the seven years from 1809 to 1816, when the school was "suspended."[32] In 1825 the University of Nashville was organized as a successor to Cumberland College, and under an innovative educator from Princeton, Philip Lindsley, a more sophisticated college was projected. Enrollment increased substantially. By the thirties the sons of Robert Smiley, the tailor, and Samuel Stout, the carriage maker, as well as the sons of important merchant families were enrolled. However, this testified to the economic success of these families, not to the democratic appeal of the college. Although a few more merchants joined the trustees, the university remained an exclusive club; except for three years, annual enrollment through 1850 remained below one hundred students.[33]

There was certainly not a rich intellectual life in Nashville during the frontier decades, but there were books and readers.[34] Merchants and lawyers wrote satirical sketches for the Nashville papers and

Wilkins Tannehill compiled his "History of Literature from the Earliest Period to the Revival of Letters in the Fifteenth Century." When the river fell and commercial activity slowed down, there could be more attention given to concerts and plays, homemade or imported. Balls and assemblies were eagerly attended despite the suspicions of the evangelicals. In 1806 a letter to the editor urged dances as one way of introducing women to the social scene and thereby improving the manners of the town.[35]

The isolation of women in the village must have been almost as great as the isolation of their sisters in the countryside. Their lack of numbers, their absorption in childbearing and childrearing, their work load in maintaining huge households, and their identification by their husbands' occupations meant that the household tended to define the limits of every woman's role. The luxury of sisterhood awaited at least enough women in town to create a critical mass. Some women lived on one-acre lots, supervising children and servants, keeping a garden and a cow to provide for the table; until 1801 there was no market house, and what was not raised at home had to be bargained for with farmers in the countryside. After the market house was built, it was the man of the house who usually did the shopping, a servant walking behind to carry the produce.

Most of the women were young. In 1800 twenty-two of the thirty-five adult women were between sixteen and twenty-six; in 1820 more than half were between sixteen and twenty-six.[36] Some, in moving to the frontier, were separated from mothers and sisters. As role models they might have chosen the wives and widows of the first frontier.[37] These were strong women who had hitched up their skirts and carried the ammunition and the whiskey ration to the men during the Indian raids, who had given birth in the stockades and seen sons and husbands killed, who had managed plantations while their husbands were off surveying or in the legislature. The relative independence of action that the Revolution had necessitated for many American women left to manage farms and plantations was clearly part of the experience of frontier wives.[38] Most had been brought up in a traditional Calvinism that at least made sense of their losses. For years they did without regular churches and depended on itinerant preachers to baptize their children. They were not genteel women; they heard and probably spoke a language that was free of Victorian euphemisms and perhaps indelicate to the ears of their granddaughters. If they were disturbed by General Winchester's common-law marriage, they made no cabals. Divorce, though it created scandal, did not prompt them to ostracize those involved, and it was not uncommon in their generation. They continued to live, after the first hazards and hardships were over, in "the old vulgar style." And they died toothless but straight-backed. The day before her death at ninety-one, Charlotte Robertson, wife of the founder, had been stitching a dress for a slave.[39]

Widows in town were often keepers of boardinghouses or taverns. Ann Hay maintained her husband's tavern after his death. She was not of the great county families, but her message to her son, "walk uprite be faithfull to your offesers trust in the Lord an pray god to direct you in all thing he is able and willing to relieve all that put thare trust in him," would not differ substantially from the messages of the Robertson women or of Margaret Tait, who lived in the "Best House in Town," either in content or in punctuation and spelling. Indeed, Margaret Tait may not have been literate. The great ladies of the first frontier did not change much in the more settled decades to come, except, perhaps, to become more pious.[40]

Women could lend vigorous support to institutional development in only one area outside the household—in religion—and here they were aided by the convictions of their husbands and fathers. Charlotte Robertson, herself the daughter of a minister, would not have had to urge James Robertson to persuade Craighead to come out to the frontier. Encouraging a preacher to join them would have been as natural to the builders of the first settlements as providing so quickly for state support of a classical academy. Spending time in church or money and energy on church buildings was something else again. Some men did. After the evangelical crusade swept down from Kentucky, small chapels and meetinghouses appeared in the countryside. In 1797 there were two Baptist meetings; by 1808 there were at least five. Methodist circuit riders left classes behind them. Presbyterians found reassurance in Craighead's presence, and the tiny group of antiburgher Scottish seceders sent to Edinburgh for William Hume in 1801. But in town it was the women who made up the first regular congregations. Here they could and often did appear without husbands or fathers. Like the slaves, white women found breathing space in church.[41]

There had always been preaching in town by itinerants of every sect. Frontier Nashville was tolerant—perhaps just curious. Father Badin, the Catholic priest who had all of Kentucky and Tennessee as his parish, traveled across "the horrid Cumberland Mountains" in 1810, took tea with the Reverend Mr. Priestley, and preached in

Methodist Episcopal Church. From the *Nashville Business Directory of 1860*.

the courthouse.[42] Indeed, preaching took place more often in the courthouse than in a meetinghouse. When Bishop Asbury made his third trip to Nashville in 1812, he was put up at the jail, whose keeper was a devout Methodist. Asbury was bitter about the pulling down of the old stone church on the square and about a community that put the courthouse in the central location, where the church "ought to be."[43]

Presbyterians held priority in Nashville. The first minister to locate in the settlements was Thomas Craighead, a graduate of the College of New Jersey. Ordained in 1780, he moved to the frontier five years later. Craighead operated in the traditional fashion of Presbyterian ministers: almost the first thing he did was to open a school. Yet there was about him a touch of the unorthodox, which was perhaps what led him to the frontier. He took part in the camp meetings that signaled the Great Revival, was accused of the Pelagian heresy and of giving comfort to Shakers by his liberal views on regeneration; he fought the charges of presbytery, synod, and General Assembly for more than a dozen years. Yet Craighead was not given to "enthusiasm"; he relied on careful, theological argument when he preached in Nashville and was suspicious of "come-outers" who broke with the church establishment.[44] Like Hume and Priestley, who were to come later, Craighead was a schoolmaster in fact and in temperament. All three were respected by the community and the county, but they ministered to small, if influential, groups.

Frontier Nashville was given more to cockfights and horse races, to duels and balls, than to building churches. In 1811 there was no church building in town. The *Clarion* urged a committee to collect subscriptions;[45] the committee was formed and included Presbyterians Felix Grundy and Randal McGavock, George Deaderick, who was raised a Lutheran, and Robert C. Foster, whose piety led him into a number of such unpopular causes as the outlawing of billiard tables and who moved from the Baptist church to the Campbellites. In fact, two churches were begun in the next year— one, on the outskirts of town, by the Methodists and one, more centrally located, by the Presbyterians.

The men organized the finances and had adequate meetinghouses built, but it was the women who were the members. In 1813 the Reverend Gideon Blackburn organized the First Presbyterian Church around seven women and one man, the ruling elder, tailor Smiley. Blackburn organized a female prayer meeting and in 1816 the women acquired a society house. Another twenty-two people joined his church, twenty of them married women. Blackburn's rigidly orthodox brand of Calvinism and his "very distant" manner were not encouraging. He and the congregation ultimately parted company: "Mr. Blackburn did not please the Inhabitants of Nashville. . . . he is illiberal."[46] By the twenties more men were joining the church, perhaps because Blackburn was gone. Felix Grundy, who persuaded the new minister, Allen Campbell, and the ruling elders to exclude Darby during their great controversy, was one. Prominent merchants and bankers like Hynes, Tannehill, and Robert Woods became trustees. It was evidently the Reverend Obadiah Jennings, who came to the church in 1828, who began to persuade the "gentlemen" of town to join the congregation in some numbers.

"Being himself a lawyer for years, he could sympathize with the doubts which perplex educated minds."[47]

Leaving the men to raise the pew rents, the ladies kept the church going. In 1820 at their society house they listened to Blackburn preach—for three and a half hours.[48] With few exceptions these were indeed the "ladies" of the town, women whose husbands and fathers could afford to rent pews and who had the leisure for sermons and charity work. They were better educated and less burdened, and there were now enough of them in town so that their energy could be directed to institution building; not just the church but by 1817 the Female Bible and Charitable Society of Nashville were their contributions. The Bible society was the first welfare organization in town. The women divided Nashville into districts and made rounds to see who was "sick, hungry, suffering" in order to relieve their wants. These women had no problems writing constitutions and electing directresses and lady managers. Mary Hayes, who read law with her father, was secretary of the Nashville society in the panic years, when the society had its work cut out for it. Nashville women, like women all over the nation, were beginning to fashion a dramatically new public role for themselves, one that reinforced the leadership positions of their husbands and fathers. Though they called on their sister society in Philadelphia for donations of Bibles to distribute among the poor, the Nashville women were hardly behind the women of the great metropolitan centers in their concerns. Rather, their society exemplified an urban pattern taking shape, women adapting the voluntary association for charitable purposes in cities and towns.[49]

Vigorous women, like Ann Grundy, launched the first Sunday schools in 1819 despite the objections of most churchgoers, who called them "Sabbath breakers, violators of the law of the land . . . disturbers of peace."[50] Ann Grundy was undaunted. Her seven daughters helped make her home an especially attractive place for the young bachelors of Nashville, whom she conscripted to teach the illiterate white youngsters of the town on Sunday morning. Some support came from the editor of the *Whig*. This was one way to keep boys from congregating on the Sabbath "in ways that vitiate their morals" and annoy the citizens. Once the school was in operation an election of male managers was in order. By 1823 the Nashville Sunday School Union was organized with a membership of twenty-three women, six men, and one boy. These women's organizations cut across sectarian lines. Methodist as well as Presbyterian "divines" addressed the ladies, and indeed the male managers of the Sunday school in 1819 included more Methodists than Presbyterians.[51]

By 1817 the Methodists had decided that the brick church on Broad Street was too far from the "center of population" and built a new church on Spring Street. In the following year Nashville became a separate charge, and by 1820 seventy-two white and thirty-two black members were reported.[52] The Methodist church was the most popular in town, perhaps because of its hesitations about wealth and education in the ministry. John Johnson, the first settled minister, rejected $1,000 a year as too great a salary; he instead accepted $232, $100 for each adult and $16 for each child in his family, and table expenses—and his wife trimmed hats at 75 cents a day.[53] Methodist women, though they were "great workers in the church," were not so visibly the mainstay of the church.[54] Among the Methodists the role of the preacher was less central, and the congregation was more active. Merchant John Price, for example, "zealous in the cause of the church, and a great lover of the peculiarities of Methodism . . . was partial to class meetings, and contended earnestly for the doctrines of justification by faith, regeneration, and the witness of the Spirit. He was very fond of camp meetings, and was always zealous in revivals of religion."[55] Perhaps the greater participation by laymen in doctrinal matters made for a lesser role for women, whose place was to be quiet.

Methodists confronted religious skepticism and what they perceived as upper-class attitudes. Learner Blackman, presiding elder of the Cumberland district from 1808 to his death in 1815, accepted the position of chaplain to Jackson's troops during the War of 1812 after searching his own soul to determine whether the monetary reward, which looked too good to a Methodist preacher, was part of his motive. His diary reveals both concern and timidity about preaching to the officers, whom he saw as profane, skeptical, and better educated than himself: "I felt some embarrised to speak to a few officers of information but not one of them religious—Thank God they have been civil polite and agreeable."[56] In town Methodists did not auction or rent pews, did not observe a distance between laymen and ministers, and in these years usually did not attract the most successful lawyer and merchant families. However, the Methodists did build the largest congregations in town, congregations swelled by black communicants.[57]

A new concern with religion was apparent in Nashville a few years after the war. By 1818 the *Clarion* was proposing a religious column, though that did not materialize. In 1820 the Baptists finally moved into town, organizing a congregation of nineteen members. Ten years later a desperate split with the Campbellites left this first Baptist church with only three women and two men. The new Christian church, led by Philip Fall, claimed even the church building.[58] Meanwhile, the Cumberland Presbyterian church also came to town in 1828. Fifteen years earlier a Cumberland Presbyterian preacher had been blocked from using the courthouse as a pulpit by the regular Presbyterian clergy. Now members of the First Presbyterian Church subscribed to the building fund of the Cumberland Presbyterians.[59] Some townspeople began to suggest the need for an Episcopal church, and in 1831 a church was completed. Its membership was limited, but non-Episcopalians subscribed for pews on the grounds of public spirit or political alliances.[60] Despite ideological differences, splits within Baptist and Presbyterian churches, and controversies over ball going and temperance, furthering religion in all its forms had become more important than parochialism for a large part of the leadership group in town.

In 1821 a Catholic chapel had been built on Cedar Knob Hill largely to accommodate the Irish laborers who had been brought to Nashville to build the bridge. Anthony Foster donated the land, and Father Abell, the congregation's first priest, reported that "many of the first families attended Mass." When he asked for fair play after hearing Catholicism denounced, he was given the courthouse as a forum for his lecture, despite the threats of the Baptist revivalist, Jeremiah Vardiman, to compete at the same time and place. After his lecture Abell was congratulated by "a knot of young men" who evidently wanted him to continue the debate.[61] For some of these young men the discomfiture of Vardiman, who preached against dancing, swearing, drinking, and horse racing, must have been the source of their delight with Abell. Catholicism was preferable to militant Baptist exhorting. The little Catholic chapel was never consecrated, however, and, when the bridge was built and the laborers were dispersed, it was rented to a schoolmaster.

During the twenties decorum and order were becoming increasingly important to community leaders, and, as a corollary, they were suspicious of "enthusiasm." Dr. Priestley's obituary read, "His piety was scriptural, rational and unobtrusive. He was in principle a member of the Presbyterian church, but he was no sectarian." When Eleanor Foster, Anthony Foster's second wife, died, her obituary noted that she was "a member of the Presbyterian church . . . in

> **FEMALE DENTIST.**
>
> **MRS. SUSANNA DULANY,**
> LATE from the city of Baltimore, officiates in the capacity of DENTIST, in all its branches—Draws Teeth with skill, and without much pain—makes artificial ones—cleans teeth—plugs the hollow ones with gold or lead; which method not only puts an end to the pain, but also preserves the tooth a great while. She prepares a powder much to the purpose of cleaning the teeth, and preserves the gums—which cures the scurvy perfectly, in a few days. She makes a Pomatum to destroy freckles, pimples in the face, and dark shades on the skin. Apply at Mr. CONDON'S.
> Nashville, May 5, 1817.—37

which she exercised her devotion with fervour and zeal, but without the superstition of a bigot or the enthusiasm of a zealot."[62] Presbyterian schoolmasters were almost always in charge of Davidson Academy, Cumberland College, and the University of Nashville, but all insisted on the nonsectarian bases of their education. The Sunday school sought to spread "Religion and Education without regard to sect or denomination."[63]

By the late twenties joining a church and subscribing to the Sunday school and to the Bible society were expected of a responsible merchant, master mechanic, citizen. The first boards of directors of the Auxiliary Bible Society of Davidson County included Presbyterians and Methodists and Robert Foster. In 1828 the Bible society proudly reported having distributed 220 Bibles in Nashville alone.[64] Evidently the town was saturated. However, its piety was far from oppressive. When Foster tried to convince the trustees of the university to bind themselves not to go to the theater—the students had already been prohibited from going "unless express permission be given"—only one other board member voted with him.[65] Despite the flurry of religious activity, Nashville was in no danger of becoming a puritanical town.

As we have seen, the merchants seemed content to leave higher education to others; their sons went to the "English" schools in town and, if they yearned for a more elegant style, to a French master or a dancing class. Dancing and balls were very much part of the social life of early Nashville, and challenges to their respectability may have been one sign of resentment against the club that ran the town, just as the deprecating of "enthusiasm" may have reflected some self-consciousness about class differences in religious style. Still, denominational divisions could not have been traumatic. The small daughter of one merchant was invited to a dancing party. She was reminded that she had just recently been baptized a Methodist. She thought a bit and decided she would prefer to be a "Piperterian."[66] The story was remembered and repeated as a funny rather than soul-shaking anecdote.

A clearer sign of social division within the community came with the founding of the Nashville Female Academy in 1816. Merchants were eager subscribers: sixteen of the original twenty-five were merchants, and seven were lawyers.[67] Most of the students were boarders from the countryside, daughters of planters and prosperous farmers, but in every division there were the daughters of merchants. The school was expensive, with tuition, room, and board amounting to $175 per year in 1824. Sending a child to the academy was evidence of economic success. In 1825 the trustees tried to refute the charge that the academy inculcated aristocratic habits of luxury. They assured the public that the girls were dressed in the products of the country, not imports, except for the "necessary woolens." Still, the cotillion for the "rise of the Female Academy" became a social event held at the Masonic hall and attended by gentlemen who had purchased their tickets.[68]

Mary Beth Norton sees the education of women, especially middle- and upper-class women, as one significant legacy of the revolutionary era.[69] Nashville's Female Academy, an early achievement, was a sign that the town was outgrowing frontier status and that its leaders shared in the new attitudes toward women's needs. By 1829 there were at least two other schools for girls in town, and a third was projected. The principals of these schools had to tread a narrow line between the piety for which they had been chosen and the social demands of their patrons. Principal Hume would not allow the academy girls to go to public dancing parties or balls during term, but they were permitted to go to dancing schools in the daytime and on Saturday. Somewhat later, "Uncle Crutcher," perpetual trustee, was overruled by the girls who wanted to dance in the "city."[70]

By the mid-twenties the schools were preparing young women to take a place in a more structured, more socially sophisticated world than their pioneer grandmothers had known. On the eighteenth-century frontier there had been Presbyterian ministers and schoolmasters, evangelical revivalists, deists, skeptics. As the churches came to town, however, opinions began to be institutionalized and to some extent associated with social status. Religion was no longer a private concern. At least for the people within them, churches made for public well-being. They could be used to discipline a Darby or to educate the children of the poor. Total church membership was never more than a fraction of the population. The poor could ignore the new emphasis on piety and decorum. However, for the successful and the striving, the classical schools, the female academy, church membership, and membership in specific churches began to be badges of identification.[71]

There were similarities among the voluntary associations, the churches, and the town's governing body, not least of which were their overlapping memberships and clublike atmospheres. The merchants of the town, more specifically the staple merchants and commission merchants, came to dominate town government. In November 1801 the legislature authorized a board of commissioners to be elected by men who owned town lots or who had lived in town for at least six months. The first commissioners were a mixed lot, reflecting the diverse interests of frontier entrepreneurs: three lawyers, a doctor, the editor of the newspaper, a shoemaker, and a tavern-keeper who was also the village's butcher and jailer. Most were investing in lands in the county. Yet they turned to and formulated some rules for the growing community.

Streets had to be laid out and kept clear of "dead carcasses," stud horses, and "stagnant pools." Slaves were to be prevented from hiring out on their own time, from keeping tippling houses, and from assembling in a "kitchen after dark." One senses the hand of Commissioner Foster in the Sabbatarian legislation, which prohibited merchants from selling their goods and anyone from chopping wood on Sunday. However, it was clear necessity that dictated extraordinarily heavy fines to prevent wooden chimneys in town buildings.[72] The commissioners also arranged for the building of Nashville's first market house. All of this was traditional. Like the justices of the court before them, the commissioners were enacting for Nashville remembered law, a good part of which would not be enforced. Only rarely were they too active. Some Davidson County farmers petitioned the legislature to prevent the Nashville sergeant from disposing of stray cattle because, as they explained, they could not keep their stock from going to town, "there being so many incitements in Town and the French Lick near it!"[73] The village was built of wood; its two short streets were narrow and, of course, unpaved; there was no police force, no fire engine, or even buckets provided by the community; no water supply beyond the natural springs and the river. And people kept arriving.

The Incorporation Act of 1806 was undoubtedly prompted by this population growth. The act provided for the election of a mayor and six aldermen, all of whom had to hold property in the town.[74] Voters were defined as "the citizens of said town, and such as possess real property within the same." There is some question as to whether absentee freeholders or resident nonproperty holders could vote. Early historians of Nashville assumed that the act of 1806 excluded from the suffrage all except property holders. If this were so it would mean a retreat from the more democratic suffrage that had elected the commissioners.[75] In any event, political participation seems to have been minimal, confined at most to the relatively small percentage of the population who were committed to Nashville.

The direct election of the mayor has been singled out as a sign of political sophistication in Nashville, providing for a strong executive who might act as a check against the authority of the aldermen and thereby embody the republican rule of separation of powers.[76] Perhaps. We have no record of the debate that fashioned the terms of incorporation. We do know, however, that within five years the "independent" mayor was repudiated in favor of the more traditional method of election of the mayor by his fellow aldermen.

The act of 1811 clarified the suffrage requirement and may have widened the electorate. Property holders, whether resident or nonresident, could vote. Town residents could vote if they had been residents of the county for at least six months. The right to vote, then, was interpreted liberally in 1811. To have restricted voting to freeholders would have resulted in government by a tiny minority indeed. In 1798 twenty-six lot holders had been assessed; in 1816 only 129 owners of town property were reported—and half of them were nonresidents. Any degree of autonomy for townsmen required the wider suffrage. It may well be, however, that as a direct result of the more democratic suffrage the independent mayor was rejected in favor of one chosen by his fellow aldermen—a check on the voters, then, rather than on the aldermen, for the pool from which aldermen could be chosen remained small. As late as 1829 there were only 171 freeholders, and again half of them were absentees.[77] One doubts that there was extended political debate on the terms of incorporation. The anxiety to achieve a more effective corporation government, one more intimately concerned with the life of the village and less an appendage of the court, was the issue.

Between 1806 and 1826, fifty-four men served as aldermen.[78] At least twenty-eight of the fifty-four were merchants, almost all of them identified at some point with the cotton and tobacco trade. Thirty-five of the aldermen were bank directors. Seven might best be classified as government officials and were closely associated with the county leadership—three clerks of the court, including a Ewing and two McGavocks, two constables, state treasurer Crutcher, and postmaster Curry. Professionals were represented by six lawyers, two doctors, and an editor. Only eleven were mechanics, and those who were elected were substantial property holders who mingled easily with the coming merchants and lawyers of the town. Mechanics, too, were frontier entrepreneurs, who, with luck, could move from the shop to real-estate investments and plantations. For example, Joseph Elliston, a silversmith, was elected to the first board and for thirteen of the first twenty years of town government served either as alderman or as mayor. His interests, first as watchmaker and jeweler, then as investor in the cotton trade, banks, and real estate, grew with those of the village. By 1850 he reported himself a "landholder and farmer" with real estate worth $75,000.[79] But in these early decades it was his activity rather than an established position that made him an obvious choice for town office.

Mayors and aldermen were young men. Of the thrity for whom we have age data, twenty-two were under forty when they first served as municipal officers, and fifteen were between twenty-two and thirty-four. Most had been born in Virginia (sixteen), or Kentucky (seven); two or three were born in North Carolina, Maryland, Tennessee, and Pennsylvania. Foreign birth did not impede election: six aldermen were born in Ireland and two in Scotland. But from the very beginning the corporation's government was made up of men committed to Nashville. Forty-seven of the fifty-four remained in Nashville until they died.

Initially, few active contests were waged for town offices. For many years the Nashville newspapers reported only the names of the candidates elected. Conflicts presumably existed, if only on the grounds of personality and clan affiliations, but given the size of the community all who participated would know without benefit of newspapers what was at issue.[80] In 1817, for the first time, both newspapers presented slates or suggestions for aldermen. All but five of the twenty-one men recommended by both papers had been or would be elected to the board. Almost all were merchants.[81] The electorate seemed to recognize a pool of acceptable candidates, almost all of them leaders in the commercial community, from which it drew each year.[82] Only a handful, notably from among the professionals and government clerks, represented a direct link with the county squires.

Under merchant leadership municipal government amounted to very minimal government indeed. The regulation of slaves, streets, and the market house continued to be the proper business of town officials. As in other urban areas, services that required taxation—police, fire fighting, water supply, streetlights—were provided reluctantly and in niggardly amounts, and not just in the frontier years. Expenditures for public services were reported at $1,116.35 in 1808 and twenty years later at just over $4,000.[83] In 1808 the corporation depended exclusively upon the high constable, who was also clerk of the market house, to police the town. In 1810 the corporation instituted a night watch. A Sunday patrol, largely to supervise the black population, was not added until 1823. Two public wells, always out of order, at least according to the critics, were supplemented in 1823 by a waterworks that brought water from Spring Street to a reservoir close to the public square. It was obviously not so much water for domestic uses as water for fire protection that concerned the aldermen, and it was the square, the center of the business community, that had priority.[84] A piteous request for "Lamps! Lamps!" was published in the *Whig* in 1818, and more than two years later a law was finally passed providing for oil lighting. In 1825, however, the board refused responsibility for maintaining the street lamps, but it provided that any who would could "have the use of them."[85] The corporation's commitment to education was also marginal and erratic. It was not until 1819 that it first appropriated funds for the repair of a schoolhouse, a private Lancasterian school. In 1821 the corporation at last appropriated money for a lot and common schoolbuilding, which, after a couple of years, it rented to private schoolmasters.[86]

Except for unusual expenditures, like the repair of the market house in 1818, the largest item in the budget was always that for the hire and board of the slaves who were employed as street hands.

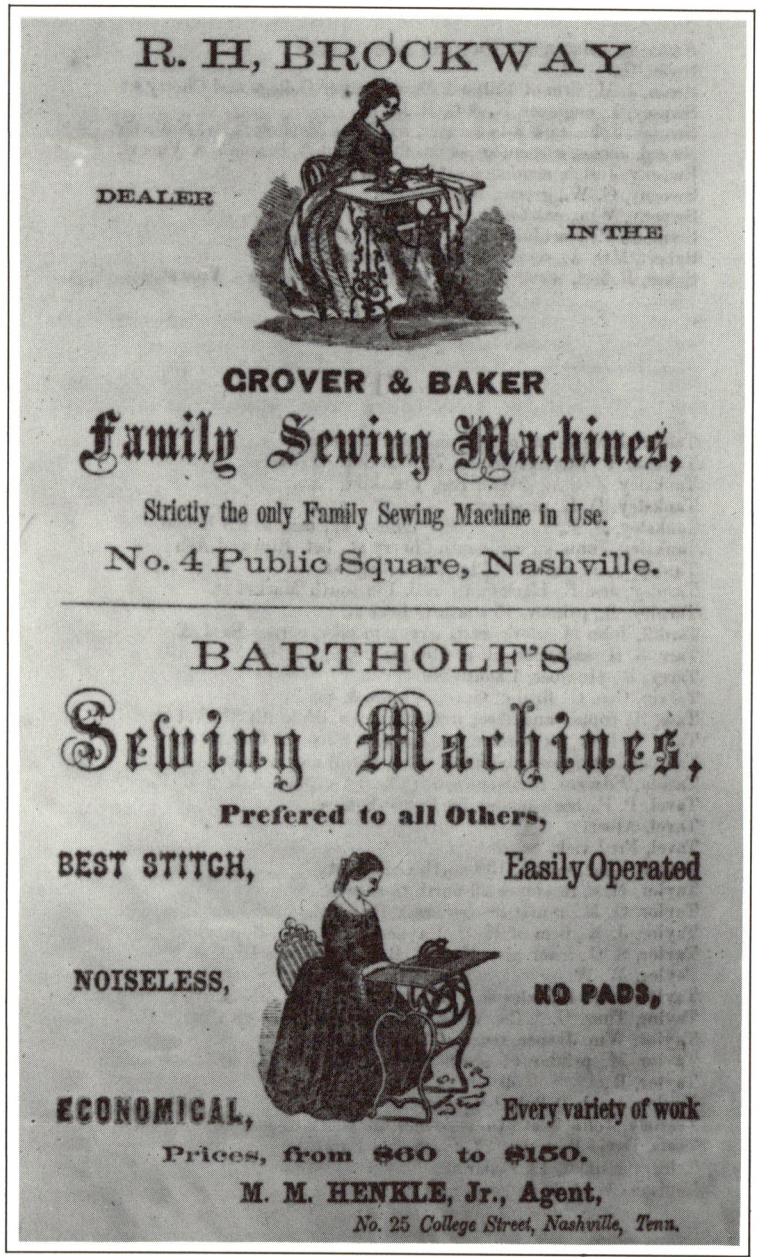

The care of the unfortunate remained for the most part with the county court, which appropriated funds for the support of the temporarily incapacitated, apprenticed orphans, and sent the old, infirm, and lunatic to the county poorhouse. The corporation paid for the coffins and burials of strangers and the destitute within the town limits. Expenses for "the suppression of small pox" amounted to ten dollars in 1825; the next year a steam mill "was turned into a hospital" to house steamboat passengers who were examined on the landing and found infected.[87]

Until the mid-twenties the services demanded and the services provided seem to have achieved a kind of balance, and there was also a rough consensus as to how services were to be funded. Newspaper editors and town meetings initiated demands for improvements. The corporation responded, but the bulk of the bill was paid by private subscriptions. A public meeting, triggered by the burning of a bakery in 1807, established a committee to solicit donations for a fire engine; the corporation provided the engine house. After a disastrous fire in 1814, which destroyed all the buildings on Market Street, Mayor Tait offered a reward of one thousand dollars for the apprehension of the arsonist; the corporation shortly passed laws requiring that each inhabitant own a leather bucket, that all males aged fifteen to fifty-five constitute the town's fire company and that no more than twenty-five pounds of gunpowder be kept in any house. The *Whig*'s editor assumed that it was up to the property owners rather than the corporation to encourage the young men of the town to form a fire company. Their "indifference"—presumably they had not provided the funds for banners, uniforms, complimentary dinners—was the root of the trouble, he contended.[88]

In the boom years after the War of 1812 the movers and doers of the town were concerned with major improvements and investments—bridges and steamboats, for example. They used in this area the same techniques—public meetings to promote and private subscriptions to undertake—as were used in dealing with fire protection for the town. Very little was thought of as a municipal responsibility. At one point, for example, it was decided to provide public funds for the education of poor children. The aldermen were directed to choose two poor boys from each of their wards as beneficiaries.[89] Tax money, suggesting a public commitment, was translated into private benevolence.

Mayor and aldermen met in private to conduct the town's business. Only the laws agreed to and the annual financial statements were published. Municipal government remained a kind of club whose rewards were prestige and whose unpaid responsibilities were hardly onerous. The public meeting tempered the closed quality of corporation government as it had tempered the exclusiveness of the court, but, perhaps more important, the limited scope of corporation activity provided little to challenge in these frontier decades. The creation of the corporation did more to single out town leaders than to provide strong, new institutional apparatuses or guidelines. The membership of town government reflected a traditional pattern of deference that awarded political office to economic and social success.

The young men on the make in the prewar years had become town elders by the late twenties. The town itself, though perhaps less sanitary, was no more genteel and no less violent and disorderly than the frontier village of 1800. It was a river town, and its physical and numerical growth made for anonymity and some fears. A letter to the editor in 1823 complained bitterly of "those miserable wretches of all colors and sexes" who ensured "that in many parts of the town, a lady cannot walk in security from insult."[90] Its politics had become more active; resentment of a now established and prosperous leadership began to be voiced. The editor of the *Banner and Whig* felt compelled to reassure the public that the call for a temperance meeting was not part of a plot to establish a church. The leaders of the meeting were in fact concerned less with new churches than with the new politics; the meeting called for a pledge "not to vote" for intemperate men or those who "treated voters" in political campaigns.[91]

The frontier period was over. A leadership cadre and a social hierarchy were in place. Town leaders were busily fashioning institutions to direct public opinion, to reform the town, to maintain order. Churches and voluntary societies were meant to create consensus, to bring together a disparate community. The raw social climate of the frontier had given way to clearly differentiated and traditional urban social categories. Merchants and professionals in the leadership elite were characterized by their relatively long residence in town, their substantial property holdings, their family connections, their activist wives and daughters, their affiliations with churches and voluntary societies. They topped a hierarchy of shopkeepers and mechanics, respectable workingmen, transient laborers, and slaves. They had made good on the frontier promise of room at the top. Other groups might continue to strive. Only the blacks, at the bottom of the hierarchy, were locked into caste. Even for them, however, the frontier spelled change.

Black History on the Nashville Frontiers

CHAPTER 4

THE black experience was not just a variant of frontier history but an exceptional experience, running counterpoint to the expectations of most frontiersmen. Whether slave or free or, a category unknown to the law, practically free, black people could not participate in the larger community's institutions, much less hope for leadership positions. Neither the rural nor the urban frontier brought liberation to black people. Traditional law and inherited status provided the operative guidelines in race relations even here.[1] However, up to a point, a kind of stripping-down process did work. The masters' early concern with establishing themselves left little energy for reconstituting all the institutional restraints that would have provided a static picture of slavery. Instead, frontier history on the countryside and in the village did mark an episode of black history qualitatively different from settled plantation life and from the more rigorously defined patterns of urban life that would follow. Black people, as individuals, did have more scope, more roles to play, especially within the frontier churches. Paradoxically, however, frontier conditions meant an intensification of the assault on slave families. The maintenance or recreation of a family or a surrogate family had to be a primary concern for most black people. Herbert Gutman traced "a cycle of family destruction, construction, and dispersal" beginning in a newly opened plantation area.[2] A similar cycle clearly was begun on the Nashville frontier. In the short run some of the constraints of slavery were loosened, but the most persistent meaning of the frontier to black people was heightened pressure on black families.

Black people's presence on the Nashville frontiers established and confirmed Nashville's southern character. Black people were ubiquitous, an integral part of the town, a major component of its working class. But slavery made for a peculiar kind of working class. Women and children made up more than half of black workers. Moreover, black workers were legally and historically tied to employers' households in ways that no apprentice, journeyman, or white servant could be. That a leadership elite could remain unchallenged for so long in Nashville may have partly resulted from slavery, which reduced the numbers of and the community's dependence on white workers and made it more difficult for white workers to identify themselves as a working class. The tragic ironies of slavery are exposed here as in every other arena of American life. The very fact that slaves were widely used became one aspect of "community," of homogeneity, and of well-being on the part of the white sector.[3]

The Indian fighting frontier immediately meant an increase in terror. Blacks were at least as vulnerable as whites; they were killed, scalped, kidnapped, held for ransom.[4] In 1796 Governor John Sevier tried to teach Little Turkey, a Cherokee chief, that "it is wrong to swap people for horses, for negroes is not horses tho they are black."[5] The irony rests in the schoolmaster.

Almost all of the black pioneers of Nashville are anonymous. A given name occasionally appears in the record. Abraham, Anthony Bledsoe's servant and a fine marksman, shot and killed Mad Dog, a Cherokee. Sam, James Bosley's "good waggoner and active plantation negro," was taken by the Creeks. Robert, James Robertson's servant, accompanied the first party of settlers in 1779, rode with his master through the Kentucky country in 1780, and lost his life in the Indian attack on Freeland's Station in 1781. Hagar, a black child, fell from her perch behind Mrs. Robertson on a horse as the pioneers fled from Freeland's Station to the bluff. More often we know only the slave's owner.[6]

The legend of Jack Civil suggests another kind of black experience. Jack Civil was a free man of color who probably accompanied the Donelson party and who was wounded and captured by Indians in the raid at Clover Bottom in 1780. Typically, one testimony to Jack Civil's existence is the attempt of the land speculator, Joseph Martin, to make good on Civil's preemption claim. Elijah Robertson gave his oath that he had seen the transfer papers, which had been "lost by the badness of the weather." However, Jack Civil's name does not appear on James Robertson's list of preemptioners. Judge Haywood's history, written in 1823 and the earliest account of the pioneers' story, reports only the wounding and capture by the Indians of Jack Civil and his son. W. A. Putnam's account, published thirty-five years later, reports that Jack Civil went over to the Indians and that after the Indian wars he "denied that he had ever killed or shot at a white person. It was generally believed he lied."[7] The legend evidently grew over time, as did white suspicion of a free black, who was perhaps more easily tolerated on the freewheeling eighteenth-century frontier than by the southern historian writing two years before the Civil War. The sinister connotation, altogether absent from Haywood's work, is clear in Putnam's and tells us somewhat obliquely what would be the free black's experience as the frontier matured.

No white family except the Donelsons initially brought large numbers of slaves to the frontier. Extra mouths to feed were a liability, and, perhaps more to the point, few pioneers had the wealth that coffles of slaves represented.[8] Nevertheless, the number of slaves grew steadily. Most came with their masters from North Carolina or Virginia or Kentucky. Slaves were the property most desired after the land was secured. Indeed, one speculator sweetened his impressive land deals by binding himself to furnish blacks to budding planters; another paid for land with slaves.[9] Recorded sales, gifts, and mortgages of slaves during the first twenty years of the community's history (1784–1803) involve approximately seven hundred black people,[10] sufficient to tell us something of the frontier's impact on slaves.

Above all is the fact of sale itself. Although the number of sales in any one year was not huge, each year the number of those who had experienced sale grew.[11] Sale meant at the least a new master, a new home, possibly a new work routine. It meant also an involuntary break with family and friends. The overwhelming number of sales were of a single slave, man or woman or child. Of the 452 transactions, only 116 involved transfers of more than one slave. Of these

116 transactions, 53 involved women and their children, the matriarchal families created by slavery; only six of the 116 seem to have embraced what we might call a nuclear family—husband, wife, and children; eight may have been transfers of couples, and perhaps 20 others may have included families. Significantly, not until 1802 does one find in a bill of sale the term family to designate the slaves sold, and only once, in 1803, was a sale recorded in which the word *wife* was used.[12]

Sales into a frontier area would carry extra burdens of fear and distance from loved ones. Intensifying the trauma was the fact that these slaves were almost all young people. Of the 98 men over 16 for whom ages were reported, only nine were over thirty; of the 83 women, only eight were over thirty. Almost half of those for whom we have age data were under sixteen. It was not uncommon for children to be sold separately, away from parents or friends. Witness Aron, age six, sold to Andrew Jackson in 1791, and Sylvia, age fourteen, sold for two horse hides.[13] There was also the slave mother whose children had been sold before her master's family came out to the frontier; perhaps her pleas had prevailed, for her master later attempted to find the children his wife had sold.[14]

A master's death, bankruptcy, or suit for debt in any slave area often meant the sale of blacks, and these situations recurred on the frontier, where physical danger was great and men were on the make. The mortgaging of blacks with or without land was a common practice, enabling the master to raise cash or, in one case, to guarantee delivery of a tobacco crop already paid for.[15] Sheriffs' sales of blacks for the payment of their masters' debts were a source of bargain purchases.[16]

Even frontier conditions, however, did not overturn the fact that slaves were a peculiar property whose humanity made claims on their owners. When David Hay's "fellow" Blount was sold for debt on Hay's death, the buyer resold Blount to Hay's son, acknowledging the son's "greater right" and thereby, perhaps, a sense of "family." In some cases blacks were sold with the provision that the seller could substitute others equally valuable within a given period. This is perhaps better evidence of a concern to maintain a given slave/white household. Some transfers were sales within a family; others were gifts to daughters, sons, sons-in-law. When Anthony Foster sold a young woman to Bennett Searcy, he gave to Searcy's daughter a four-year-old girl, probably the child of the slave woman.[17] Despite this evidence of concern for individual slaves, the overwhelming testimony of the bills of sale points to the commercial interpretation of slave property. Impressive evidence of the ability of slaves to overcome sale and dispersion and to recreate the slave family does not minimize the trauma.[18] It does add to our understanding of the special circumstances of frontier blacks who had to and who did begin again the building of a family.

Frontier factors did not act all of a piece. The relatively small numbers of slaves on the frontier initially, the forced intimacy and shared dangers of the journey out and of life in the stockades, undoubtedly intensified the personal ties of blacks and whites in some cases. Some blacks certainly went armed. At the stations blacks helped build the cabins and the walls of the stockade and cooked, fetched water, and nursed. They hunted and dressed the pelts that were the community's first trade goods. Blacks moved with the white pioneers out to the countryside to tackle the job of breaking the land. Relative isolation there must have fostered a special cohesiveness within the larger household, particularly where the white family labored alongside the blacks. Most blacks and most whites were scattered across the countryside. Only a fraction remained in the village of Nashville, but here special conditions obtained.

In 1800, of Nashville's 345 inhabitants, 154 were black. Here all the factors that could affect black people on the frontier were in evidence, and some, especially the commercial needs of a pioneering people, were exaggerated. Land speculators, merchants, and self-made lawyers all dealt in slaves. Indeed, they used slaves almost as currency. One day in January 1789, speculator John Rice assigned a twelve-year-old girl, Jenny, to planter Robert Hays, who sold her the next day for £150 to merchant William Tait, who immediately assigned the bill of sale to another merchant, Anthony Foster. A judgment against speculator Joel Rice was collected in part by the sale of Fran and her two children. Then there is the case of a black woman belonging to banker Deaderick; she was coming home from the spring with water one day in 1807 when she was stopped by a man and told "she was his property, and that she must go home with him." The ensuing lawsuit involved the property rights of Deaderick, not the abduction of a human being.[19] Business failures, debts, and shortage of capital all resulted in the sale of slaves. In addition, the hiring of slaves could mean a new master each week or month or year for the slave.[20]

Yet the other side of this insecurity has to be reckoned with—the wider experience of slaves in town. Many and more diversified lifestyles were exhibited by Scottish merchants and Virginia squires, by pious Baptists and freethinking and free-living bachelors. The village was small enough so that black people could be aware of these different kinds of white people and the different ways they interacted with black people. Who of the black community would not have known that Squire Molloy had fathered a slave daughter whom he cherished, that Senator Jenkin Whiteside kept a slave mistress, or, perhaps more to the point, that Robert Searcy was allowing Black Bobb to work his way out of slavery?

Wherever we have evidence of white men thinking about individual slaves they cared for, that evidence reveals complex and tortured responses to the traditional institutional restraints. Before his death in 1801, Thomas Molloy, Nashville's first lawyer, began the legal proceedings to emancipate and provide for Sophia, his slave and daughter. His will reveals his concern for her future, his evaluation of racial attitudes, and his conviction that Sophia could never make normal life choices. He urged that Sophia never marry; no black man would be worthy of her, and any white man who would marry her must be an "extravagant insensible person regardless of economy or honor, and the opinion of the world, and consequently [he] would destroy the property and reduce the . . . girl to a wretched state of slavery and depression." Molloy's property was left to trustees who were to care for Sophia's "comfort and education" and, should she marry after all, to determine how much she was to be allowed. Sophia did not marry but lived most of her adult life in Nashville with a brother who may also have been one of Molloy's children. Despite Molloy's concern for their emancipation, he and another brother had to earn their purchase money.[21]

Jenkin Whiteside's efforts to please and ultimately to emancipate and be free of his slave, the imperious Fanny, reveal another kind of situation. Because Whiteside was serving his term as U.S. senator in Washington, Fanny's care and emancipation were left to John Overton, the same lawyer who was left in charge of Sophia Molloy's estate. Overton had to deal this time with a woman who would not stay in the country, where Whiteside had provided "she must have her cloathes washed and wood furnished and cut for her." Fanny insisted on coming to town and then complained bitterly about the dirt-floored cabin in which she was placed. Overton finally gave up a room in his office to Fanny. "It was my wish to do anything I could except raising the girl to equality with myself," he wrote in answer to Whiteside's frantic letters. Whiteside understood that his concern

> brush should be used with vigor over the whole surface. Try this method three times a week during the summer months, there is no danger of its sickening you, and there is no calculating its good effects.
>
> We would recommend bathing, when it is convenient, to the whole population of Nashville. To men of sedentary habits it is most desirable. It recruits their exhausted energies, braces up the system and gives a spring and lasticity to the spirits which one can scarcely describe, but which it is delightful to feel.
>
> HOWAR D.
>
> NASHVILLE BATH HOUSE.
>
> On all, both young and old, I call,
> To take a bath prepared by me;
> For bathing's good in spring and fall—
> In summer 'tis a luxury.
>
> It makes the young both fresh and fair,
> Renews the old and sickly too,
> And helps the muscles long to wear;
> The bath for every age will do.
>
> Then come to Frank's old stand, you'll find,
> Attention, comfort, water pure;
> A bath to calm the weary mind,
> That soon effects a lasting cure.
>
> FRANK PARISH.
>
> June 2, 1837.—tf.

for Fanny, his attentions to her comfort, and his anxiety that she trust his promise of emancipation, the most persistent of his concerns, did not follow accepted norms. "If I had reduced my Sentiments to the standard of public opinion I probably would not have taken any notice of her situation but . . . I must always act in such a manner as will satisfy my own conscience." This story has a pleasant resolution: Fanny was freed and reunited with her mother in Virginia.[22] And all the town, black and white, must have been aware of her drama.

There was also another kind of drama to observe. General Coffee was enraged and bewildered when his slave Ben turned on him "more personal abuse than I have ever received during my life." Ben had been an especially trusted slave, the man who carried messages from Coffee on the battlefield to Coffee's family during the War of 1812. Coffee's solution was to send Ben in irons to the Natchez country for sale, but Ben was first to be lodged in the Nashville jail for a few days as an example to other blacks.[23]

Neither Molloy nor Whiteside were southern-born, accustomed from childhood to the institutions of slavery. Molloy was an Englishman; Whiteside had been born in Pennsylvania. As we have seen, a substantial number of Nashville's merchants and lawyers were Europeans or Yankees. This did not prevent them from becoming slaveholders; almost all of them did. But it may have left them more flexible in their response to slaves and slavery. Scottish-born William Tait was the first to emancipate a slave in Davidson County, and by the terms of his will he emancipated four others and looked forward to the freeing of all his slaves on his wife's death.[24] One of Tait's nephews refused to use slaves in his home and employed only free blacks as domestics.[25] Obviously, emancipation was not an act confined to nonsouthern slaveholders. What is suggested here is that the frontier as a place of competing values, where custom had not yet had time to gel, must have played some part in these histories. In one rare case a slave owner freed an industrious slave because he wished her to "enjoy Liberty the birthright of all Mankind."[26] The profound thrust of the Enlightenment was still sufficiently felt on the frontier for opinion on the necessity and duration of slavery not to have yet hardened. In 1803 the *Tennessee Gazette* published, "by the request of a number of subscribers," *The African Complaint*, a fierce denunciation of slavery which insisted upon seeing the slave as a son and lover torn from his home, "forced into a floating dungeon . . . bartered as a slave, exposed to contempt and scorn, unjustly marked with the whip of tyranny—his labor unjustly extorted from him." Both republican and Christian principles were invoked to castigate slavery.[27] Twenty years later this kind of statement could be published nowhere in Nashville.

Emancipation, however, remained an unusual act in Davidson County; only eleven slaves were freed by the county court before 1813.[28] Thus the most important factor for black life in town was simply the substantial presence of black people, the opportunity for blacks to know each other and to share friendship and experience, to build some life outside the purview of employer or master. In the eighties, as the frontier station began to take physical shape, the lean-to kitchens were the living quarters of the slaves, but more general meeting places, like the grounds around the tavern, were established very early. Julius Sanders, a Nashville ordinary keeper, was indicted in 1785 for "allowing a number of Negroes to play at fives on the Sabbath at his battery."[29] One does not know which was the greatest offense: the gambling, the gambling on Sunday, or the assembling of the group of blacks. By 1800 there were perhaps one hundred houses in Nashville; the grand ones had many outbuildings—kitchens, stables, smokehouses, slave cabins. Slaves of rich men generally occupied one-room cabins, perhaps five or six slaves occupying a cabin that ranged in size from 12 feet by 12 feet to 31 feet by 18 feet.[30] Slaves who lived with less affluent masters or employers must have slept in lean-to sheds or kitchens not worth the tax assessor's trouble to enumerate. In these quarters the slaves ate and slept; they worked in the main house or in the master's store or at the wharf. They fetched water from the spring, shopped at the market house, heard a preacher on the public square, visited with each other in kitchens and tippling shops, and found, despite their own tight quarters, a place to talk and to dance.

Slaves knew that black people lived in and around Nashville under all the possible terms of freedom and servitude. The census of 1800 reported only three free persons of color living in Nashville. One must have been Nell, already considered an old woman of fifty-two when she was sold to Edgar and Tait in 1789. In the next six years she managed to earn $100 to buy her freedom. Perhaps she earned her purchase money by washing clothes or cooking for some of Nashville's bachelors. Most of the free black population of the frontier years, however, had acquired their freedom elsewhere. Of the seventy people whose free status was recorded in Davidson County between 1806 and 1818, less than a handful originated in the Nashville area. Most came from Virginia or North Carolina, and a scattering came from other southern states, but one was a Pennsylvanian and one a sailor from Boston. The testimonials to free status give evidence of the variety of experiences of free black people. Anthony Gains was described as a revolutionary war veteran "believed born in freedom." Eighteen people submitted manumission papers or records in their emancipations. Two could offer only evidence of false imprisonment; court acquittal apparently served as evidence of freedom here. Testimony to the free status of one's mother or of one's parents, coupled often with evidence that one had been bound out as an indentured servant until age twenty-one, sufficed in other cases. Two sailors offered certification of their status by a New York notary public. Nine people produced white witnesses who testified that "he was always considered a free person from his birth," that "he was considered free in Baltimore and allowed to make contracts and receive wages," that the witness "knew him in Virginia" or that he knew "no one who claims her as property." Two men had "guardians" who testified that, though they had worked out their purchase money, their masters in New Orleans and in Natchez could not legally emancipate them there. One young woman, Rachel Myers Norris, evidently wanted her freedom papers recorded because she was prepared to accompany her husband, a slave, "to the Western country." Her husband's master had promised "to respect her freedom."[31]

Not all free people sought or obtained registration of their free status. The growth of the free black population after 1800 undoubtedly provided the pressure to get these people identified and registered. Davidson County census returns reported eighteen free persons of color in 1791, six in 1795, fourteen in 1800, and, significantly, 130 in 1810.[32] On the other hand, judging by the skimpiness and sketchy quality of the evidence of free status that was accepted, there was no real effort to control or prevent free black immigration in these years. The free black population was small, largely made up of transients and single men. Only nineteen of the seventy people identified in the free passes were women; the data suggest only two nuclear families and only three families of mothers and children. A couple of the passes noted that the recipients were simply traveling through Nashville. In perhaps a half-dozen cases there is some evidence that the individual was to remain in Nashville or in Davidson County. The most notable was Sherwood Brian (or Sherrod Bryant), who located in the county in 1806, received his free pass in 1811, and had become the richest free Negro in the state by 1850, owning twenty-two slaves and real estate, including a house and lot in Nashville, worth $15,000. He fathered eight sons and six daughters, a number of whom settled in Nashville.[33]

The transient nature of the free black population is of course not surprising in light of the research that has demonstrated that most poor people in nineteenth-century American cities tended to be temporary residents. Steady work was hard to come by, especially for free blacks.[34] As early as 1785 "a certain Mullato fellow called Peter Barnett" had evidently been forced to indenture himself. In 1798 another free black, Jeffrey Scott, felt compelled to indenture himself for six years to W. T. Lewis for forty-five pounds "and to be accommodated as Lewis does his own servants." Within six months Scott sued Lewis on grounds of assault, battery, and false imprisonment. A long and involved court case led first to a mistrial and then to a finding for Lewis. Scott was desperately trying to hold on to his freedom despite the indenture agreement.[35] There were undoubtedly opportunities for casual labor, but without special skills, tools, or capital the free black could be reduced to a form of slavery or, more commonly, could be forced to move on. An 1804 advertisement for an apprentice and journeyman that noted that "a black man would not be rejected" was a rare item.[36]

There were very few success stories like that of Robert Rentfro, who was given permission by the county court in 1794 "to sell Liquor and Victuals on his Good Behavior." Black Bobb's enterprise earned his purchase money, and in 1801 many prominent residents of Nashville petitioned the state legislature for his emancipation. In 1803 the ex-slave bought lot 25 in Nashville from his former master; for more than twenty years he maintained a popular inn and livery stable at the sign of the Cross Keys on the north side of the public square.[37]

County records provide examples of many black lives that fit no rigid slave/free formula. There was Mary, whose mistress wanted to free her but whom the county court judged "too old to be hired out." The court was anxious that legal responsibility for Mary remain with her mistress, but it provided that Mary could "pass and repass in the Town of Nashville"; she presumably had some way of earning her living in town. In another case a master simply recorded in the clerk's office his permission for his "slave Hannah to pass and repass during her good behavior." There were the four Ransom orphans, children of color whom the court bound to Joel Lewis on the same terms, by and large, that it bound out white orphans. Each of the girls was to be provided at age twenty-one with "a feather bed and furniture and a spinning wheel," each of the boys with "two sets of clothes, and a horse, saddle, bridle worth $50."[38] Some masters provided that slaves, though not emancipated, might live independently on their good behavior.[39]

By the 1790s there were in Nashville not only slaves and free blacks but also slaves who were rented from their masters by merchants and craftsmen seeking the labor of slaves without heavy capital investment.[40] Orphans were occasionally supported by the proceeds of their slaves' hire. Some masters who had not yet settled down to planting rented out their slaves. The hiring of slaves was a practice that especially flourished in urban areas, where it was often accompanied by inhibiting regulation. But the brass badges that hired slaves were required to wear in New Orleans or the tickets they were required to carry in Charleston were not adopted in the frontier village of Nashville.[41]

Slave hire quickly became institutionalized. Only seventy-six individuals on the 1820 census roll had been taxed on slave property in 1816, yet four years later 246 households contained slaves. Some of this disparity can be explained by underaged and overaged slaves who were not taxed, but most slaves clearly had to be rented. Duncan Robertson, "the best man that ever lived in Nashville," was also the auctioneer of the services of blacks. Very rarely was a slave family offered or sought: newspapers advertised "3 likely young negro men and a girl" or called for "10 boys of colour between 10 and 15 for work in a Baling Factory" for five years.[42] When produce was low during the depression after 1819, one planter arranged with his wife to send some of their slaves to Nashville to work for others; he allowed to the slaves themselves some choice as to who would go. "If Billy prefers staying at home and Carter is willing to go to town you might send him. . . . I know that Jack will be willing to go [to] town on account of his wife."[43] One gathers that Jack's wife was already working in town. Given the number of households that maintained only one slave and the small size of the community, much of the hiring must have been done between neighbors, without calling on the services of the auctioneer. The size of the town must also have mitigated to some degree the separation of black families. Parents and spouses could maintain some contact even when they lived apart. This was true evidently even when slaves were sent from the countryside into town.

Jack's master was also contemplating sending his slave Bitsy to town, where he thought she could find work for something more than ten dollars a month, "which I know she can earn and find herself."[44] Bitsy was expected to earn enough to send ten dollars a month home and to pay for her own board and lodgings. The casualness of the slave owner's statement suggests an ease and openness about self-hire that would not be true a few decades later. Where would Bitsy find lodging? Most likely in her employer's household— she would have to make herself part of a second black "family" within a white household. There was as yet no substantial free black community to provide an alternative, nor would the planter at any time have seen this as a viable alternative. The black slave family had to be flexible, always open to new adult members as well as children, always prepared for loss.

The practice of hiring blacks was sanctioned by custom and law, but the practice of allowing slaves to hire out their own time, in effect to make their own labor contracts, to find their own food and shelter, and to live independently, also developed. The self-hire of slaves was technically illegal under the North Carolina statutes carried over to Tennessee and under Tennessee statutes, but these were obviously ignored in Nashville. In 1823 state law again prohibited and ordered fines for self-hire, and yet four years later a Nashville ordinance provided for expensive and complicated licensing procedures presumably designed to discourage the practice.[45] Only a few slaves could make these arrangements pay sufficiently to earn their freedom, but some did. Some were in effect set up in business by masters. For others self-hire meant at least a freer existence, if often a marginal one. For all of them self-hire must have provided an extra drive, a goal-oriented existence, and often a deeper despair. Hiring one's own time could be managed for any length of time only with an owner's permission, but the temptation to work even without permission was a strong one. Andrew Jackson, for example, grew furious when his wife's maid washed clothes for people outside the family. He ordered that she be taken to the public whipping post and be given fifty lashes should she try to do it again.[46]

Hiring one's own time could imply either long-term arrangements providing labor and skills or occasional labor provided with or without a master's permission. The town, of course, was the likeliest market for labor, services, and goods. A slave could raise vegetables or provide springwater or bake cakes for sale at revival meetings or in the market square. Slaves who "traded" were in effect hiring their own time. Slaves hiring their own time and slaves trading goods and services became commonplace. Because the first practice was illegal and the second often illegal, there exists no count of black people who lived on this basis. One historian estimates that the number of virtually free blacks living in Nashville ultimately grew to be "perhaps as large as the number who were fully free." Certainly they fooled the census takers.[47]

However, most blacks in Nashville remained slaves in the traditional sense. As the bachelor society of frontier Nashville gave way to families and more settled patterns of living for the white community, the slave quarters undoubtedly received more supervision. At the same time the growth of the village meant more black people, wider communication among them, and a life-style determined in part by contact with fellow slaves and free people of color. Although slave quarters in town were physically closer than those in the country to the white households, the opportunity to lose one's self for shorter or longer periods in the busy streets along the river or off the square was also available. "Houses of entertainment" and "Tipling shops erected on the highway, and in our Towns," establishments run by and catering to blacks, were a source of complaint as early as 1799. Whites viewed them as corrupting agents encouraging slaves to steal so that they might barter for liquor, and whites reacted with anxiety to the spectacle of a "numerous crowd of slaves" drinking whiskey. As the town grew, anonymity became one of its characteristics, and any cluster of blacks became suspect.[48] Nevertheless, the discipline of slaves was left almost entirely to masters and employers despite the fact that municipal regulations governing the activities of black people were among the first to be spelled out by the corporation's government.[49] These regulations allowed considerable leeway for interpretation, and their enforcement was lax. Significantly, the Sunday patrol, instituted in 1823, was an answer to complaints that blacks were taking over the town and especially the market house and public square on Sundays.[50]

During Nashville's early decades, the white community certainly had little to fear from black people. Instances of criminal behavior by slaves were very rarely recorded. In 1791, Cato, Andrew Greer's slave, tried to steal a rifle from Charles Snyder's gun shop; in 1793, Dick, William Nash's slave, was accused of burning a barn; and in 1797, two slaves were accused of breaking into Abner Peak's meat house and stealing a "Quantity of Meat." These seem to be the only recorded instances of serious crime. Worth noting is that the punishment for the attempted theft of the rifle was the same as the punishment for the theft of the meat, thirty-nine lashes. However, we do not know what happened to Dick, who was reported to have told another slave that "he would put his knife" to any man who tried to whip him. Ominously, two pages of the court minutes are missing at this point.[51] The usually unacknowledged fear of slaves does surface repeatedly in one context. Fire was one of the scourges of the village, and after every fire the fear of arson was voiced. When Captain Bosley's barn burned in 1793, "some suspected a negro." When Hynes and Fletcher's hemp factory was burned, the arsonist was supposed to have been a black working in the factory.[52] Fear of slave arsonists would grow throughout the antebellum decades.

Religious revivalism was the only concerted effort of whites to transcend racial distinctions. Early in Nashville's history Methodists and Baptists made a significant impact. Active concern for both black and white souls characterized these denominations. Through the mid-1820s many Methodists, especially those in the ministry, insisted on a vigorous antislavery stance.[53] The Methodist circuit riders and Bishop Asbury himself preached to crowds of hundreds. In these crowds were black people drawn by the excitement and persuaded in some numbers by the message. Services held in the open air, in camp meetings, or on the public square meant there were no fixed galleries for blacks or designated black pews. The Methodists' suspicion of wealth and status, their identification with the poor and uneducated, and their insistence on feeling as opposed to ritual made them natural leaders in the effort to proselytize among blacks. In 1818 Nashville was made a separate charge of the Methodist church, and a year later the Nashville station reported seventy-five white and twenty black members. Within ten years black Methodists made up almost three-quarters of the membership of the Methodist churches of Nashville.[54]

In the countryside, Baptist churches welcomed blacks and whites who came to them "by experience." Baptists, like those who organized in the Mill Creek Church, four miles from Nashville, disciplined their members, demanding of them chastity, sobriety, and church attendance. Very few of the prominent planters, speculators, and merchants were members of the Baptist church, but some of their slaves were. Such masters must have welcomed church discipline for their servants. Mill Creek Church insisted on a rigid Calvinism. On the other hand, the slaves, often freed, if only temporarily, from their masters' supervision, were admitted to new roles. In 1806 Mill Creek Church "resolved that the Black Brethren at the time of the Church's Society Meeting have, and enjoy, the same liberty of exercising public gifts as white members do have or do enjoy." Black members were given the chance "to sing and pray with and exort. . . . fellow servants," to exhort "within the Bounds of the Church," and to judge the worthiness of fellow blacks. If some of these statements indicate an anxiety to restrict black enthusiasm to times and places where white supervision was available, they nevertheless demonstrate that organized religion provided more roles and more potent roles for black people to play within the limits of institutional slavery. One cannot judge too precisely how much scope these new roles actually provided. Still, one is led to wonder by such cases as that of Becky, Anthony Foster's slave, who was tried by the church for "living. . . . in an improper way." Becky was acquitted but was "advised to change her Residence." How much choice could she have had? Anthony Foster was not a member, but his brother, Robert C. Foster, was a deacon and the church's clerk. In

1820 the Baptists moved to town, and here too they eagerly accepted black members, although not quite on equal terms with the white brethren.[55]

Presbyterian proselytizing was much more restrained. A very few blacks were accepted into membership, and the requirements for formal admission remained high. An exceptionally talented black person was occasionally encouraged. John Gloucester, who organized an African Presbyterian church in Philadelphia in 1807, had been converted, purchased, and emancipated by Gideon Blackburn on the Tennessee frontier.[56]

The self-discipline internalized by black church members and the church discipline imposed in part by black brethren cannot be overlooked as major factors in the development of black culture. Here lay some of the roots of the black churches that would continue to develop in the antebellum period. Although many more slaves experienced religion within the quarters rather than in formally organized white churches,[57] black participation in the frontier churches provided both a tradition and the stubborn reality of black members which white rejection of black people in a later period could not erode.

Compared to later years, the frontier decades marked a kind of ease in race relations. Jeffrey Scott did find two white lawyers to argue his case against W. T. Lewis, innkeeper, land speculator, and a powerful political figure. Though Anderson Lavender, schoolmaster, was fined only one cent for beating the free Negro Bob so that "his life was Greatly despaired of," this often was the punishment for assault and battery cases that involved only whites. What is notable is the guilty finding against a white man. Thirty-seven years later a Nashville jury would acquit a white man who, before witnesses, murdered a newly freed black man.[58] Emancipation of slaves, though rare, met with no official obstacles in the frontier period. The petition for Robert Rentfro's emancipation was marked "reasonable and ought to be granted," but after 1831 Tennessee law mandated that emancipation must be accompanied by departure from the state, and exceptions to that rule were hard to win. Free blacks were technically able to vote until 1835, and at least four black citizens were enrolled in Davidson County's militia in 1811.

By 1820 black people in Nashville made up just over a third of the total population.[59] Widely distributed throughout the community, slaves provided above all else a source of domestic labor. They were cooks, laundresses, nurses, seamstresses, gardeners, and coach-

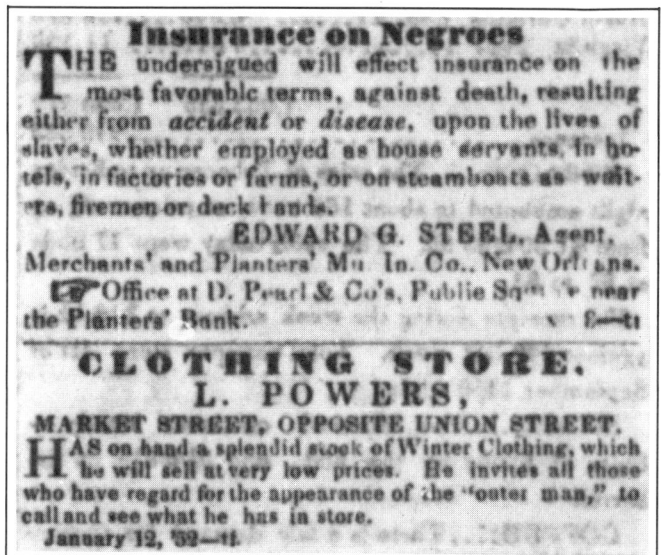

men. The numbers of male and female slaves were relatively balanced at this point and throughout the antebellum years. Black women took up the slack in Nashville's households, where for many years white females were scarce.

Forty-nine percent of Nashville's black population was female in 1820, and 42 percent was younger than fourteen. Women and children, then, described one consistent labor pool. Men were also employed as domestic laborers, but the widespread distribution of adult male slaves among mechanics and shopkeepers suggests that male slaves were used regularly in manufacturing and commercial enterprises. Among the twenty holders of more than three adult male slaves, at least half a dozen were craftsmen: carpenters, a saddler, a tanner. Nicholas Pryor, carpenter and builder, housed three free black adult males in addition to seven adult male slaves. Hoteliers and the steward of the female academy also held many adult male slaves. Still, ten of the twenty large holders of adult male slaves employed them more traditionally in gardening or farming. Most of these large holders were lawyers or successful merchants.

Almost two-thirds of all Nashville households contained slaves in 1820. Slaveholdings ranged from one to thirty-five in 1820, but only fifteen households reported more than ten slaves. Sixty households (24 percent of all slaveholding households) contained only one slave, and another thirty (12 percent), two slaves. Most slaveholdings included children; only 9 percent of slaveholding households reported no slave children, and indeed half or more of the largest holdings were made up of youngsters under fourteen.

Questions about the structure of the slave family are as difficult to deal with in Nashville as anywhere else. In 1820 the census taker reported the number, sexes, and ages of slaves living within a household. Only by assuming that slaves of a given owner or employer constituted a slave family can we venture some guesses. This is, of course, a large assumption, especially for households in town, where it was physically easier for slaves to contract marriages across owners' property lines. In town slaves often worked for and lived in one household but were owned by another. Nevertheless, trying to construct patterns in terms of where slaves lived may be justified. At the very least the slave grouping within a white household provided something of a surrogate family.

In these tentative terms, then, what was the shape of the black family within white households? In the sixty households that employed or owned a single slave, slaves lived without the immediate support of family. On the other hand, 95 percent of all slaves lived in households that employed at least two slaves. The census snapshots make immediately clear the 23 percent of all slave households that were made up of women or of women and children, the "matriarchal" families of slavery. Another 11 percent of slaveholding households included only male slaves or men and children. In only 42 percent of slaveholding households is there a probability of a nuclear family of slaves living under one roof; in most of these cases the data reveal an "extended family," a group that included, along with extra adults, a mother, father, and children. By contrast, and despite the relative scarcity in 1820 of white women, 34 percent of white households represented nuclear families, and 64 percent made up either nuclear or extended families. Most dramatic evidence of the divergence of black and white family patterns was the less than 1 percent of white households that were headed by females. That it was slavery, and perhaps urban slavery, rather than frontier conditions that created these patterns is demonstrated by their perpetuation into the 1850s.

While we can accept as generally valid the census data that indicate the strength of the white family despite frontier conditions, slavery means that the reconstruction of black families from the same kind of data is bound to overstate both the existence and the stability of black families. When Daniel McBean, master carpenter, died in 1816, his property was disposed of at public sale. Sandwiched between the sales of "a lot of scantling" and "one barrel" was the report of the hiring of McBean's Negro man, woman, and two "small" boys. Nelson must have been very small for he brought only ten dollars, while forty dollars was offered for his brother, Hardy. Each member of the family was hired to a different master. Again, when Richard Cross, the tavernkeeper and land speculator, died in 1802, an important part of the support he left for his children was his slave property, whose labor was auctioned off to the highest bidder *annually* for at least fifteen years. In 1817 only two of seven Cross slaves were rented to the same master. One woman was hired by her husband, a free man of color, who purchased her services for the year for thirty-five dollars.[60] If the census were taken annually, these slaves would appear in different households and as members of different black "family" groupings.

The 1820 census recorded seventy free blacks, or 6 percent of the black population and 2 percent of the total population. Eleven lived in white households. One of the two women who did so was Nancy Chavois, "a poor girl of colour who has fits" and who was awarded by the court to whomever bid lowest for her upkeep. Three were children, orphans bound out by the court, like Henry, age seven, bound to lawyer Thomas Washington to be made into "a complete Body servant including shaving," to be taught to read, write, and cipher to the rule of three.[61] Of the adult males three lived with carpenter Pryor and one with a bootmaker.

There were too few free blacks to call any one representative of the group. Jeffrey Lockelier, for example, was born in 1788 to a free woman in North Carolina. At twenty-one, shortly after he had completed his indentures, he came to Nashville. He was caught up in the excitement of the War of 1812, enlisted, and fought through the Creek campaigns, served at both Horseshoe Bend and New Orleans, and went on to fight in the Seminole War. When Lockelier returned to Nashville the town gave him the complimentary title of Major Jeffrey; he made his living as janitor of the courthouse. His was probably the only obituary of a black person published in the Nashville papers in the antebellum years. His war record and the visits made by President Jackson and General Coffee to his deathbed in the house of Colonel Armstrong were the distinguished aspects of his life mentioned in the newspaper account—these and the fact that he died "a Christian."[62]

Some free blacks, like Lockelier, seem not to have married. The burdens on the free black family are sufficient explanation. Nevertheless, of nineteen free black households, only two were matriarchal, and only two were made up exclusively of males. From this small sample but also from the evidence of later years, it seems clear that family organization was typical of the free black households that managed to settle for any length of time. The struggle to put together and keep together families was heroic. Philip Thomas was in Nashville by at least 1803; in 1820 he was described as "a free man of property [who] . . . has a family of children by a former wife who are free and on whose education much care and expense have been bestowed." Thomas, a barber, secured the freedom of his second wife, Aggy, whom he bought from lawyer Hayes for "a stipulated price." The court agreed not only that it would be a good thing to free Aggy Thomas but also that any children she and Philip might have ought to be free. But here again the question arises: what was the family? In 1820 Thomas's household consisted of himself and Aggy, three children, and six slaves, four of them grown men and two of them children under fourteen. Were the youngsters Thomas's children? Aggy's? bought or rented? destined to be emancipated?[63]

Free black households often included slaves who were actually family members and whose purchase money was accumulated laboriously over the years. One free black household head, Samuel Hart, provided in his will in 1832 that his property be sold and the proceeds given to his children, Jack and Hannah, slaves in Mississippi, so that they might buy their freedom. In 1817 Hart had accomplished the emancipation of his daughter, Eleanor, and in 1825 he was granted the freedom of his son Henry, whom he had bought from innkeeper Talbot four years earlier. In his will Hart urged his executor to be kind to his "old Negro woman Rhoda."[64]

At least two free black households resulted from the provision in William Tait's will that his seventeen slaves be freed on the death of his wife. Three of Tait's adult male slaves disappear from the Nashville records immediately after they were freed. The first true test of emancipation for these men may have been the sweet freedom to move. However, Harry and Mary Tate set up house in Nashville; in 1820 their household included two young men, probably their sons. Easter Tate, who was thirty-seven when she was freed, had living with her in 1820 her four youngest children, although all seven of her children were technically bound until age twenty-one to Tait's heirs, merchants of Nashville. Significantly, by 1817 the formula for binding out young black people was no longer always the same as that applied to white apprentices. The Tait guardians were obligated to "teach and instruct . . . the said apprentice [young Franky Tate] all things which the law requires them to do to people of her colour." On the other hand, Billy and Armistead Tate, who were seventeen and eighteen years old, were apprenticed to Nicholas Pryor to learn the house joiner's business.[65]

These free black households represented no threat to the white community; their members had grown up in Nashville; arrangements for the room and board, the livelihood, and the training of the young people were made with little difficulty. Each of the adults who remained in town had a skill or a job. At least three of the free colored household heads were barbers whose clients were the gentlemen of the town. Andrew Jackson himself attended the wedding of barber Reuben Graham, and Dr. Boyd McNairy "danced the reel with the bride," whose father was Philip Thomas.[66] All five free black slaveholders also owned real property in Nashville. Moreover, of the nineteen free black households, six remained in Nashville for ten years or more.

Most free blacks had a white patron, in fact a group of patrons, occasionally ex-masters but more often clients or employers, who could be called upon to arrange the purchase of a wife or a child— and to see the arrangement fairly made. Despite the murmurs against blacks operating tippling houses both Judge Trimble and Felix Grundy went security for Trim Meyers when he received a license to keep an ordinary in 1817.[67] These patrons were part of the leadership cadre in town. Whether from a notion of noblesse oblige or from genuine affection for individuals, they acted to promote the interests of individual blacks. Some blacks achieved free status by living as free persons as the result of the negligence of masters.[68] When, after years of freedom, masters pressed claims, patrons might be found through whom a sale could be negotiated. Patrons would be increasingly necessary as the numbers of free blacks grew and free blacks became the most vulnerable target of racial hostility.

Thousands of black people were brought or had come to the Nashville frontier. Their share of the violence and pain of frontier life was multiplied, for their coming was involuntary and often meant the trauma of separation from immediate family. While they helped to build farms and towns they had also to recreate basic family structures, to rebuild shattered personal worlds. The pressure was intense on the black family, and not on just the slave family. Free blacks had often earned their own purchase money, then were forced to buy spouses and children. It was in family, blood kin and manufactured, that rewards and satisfactions had to come, for there were no churches and no schools and few places in town or countryside that were their own. A parcel or two of town land, a farm or two, a handful of "businesses" were owned by black people. On Sundays, despite protest, black people claimed the market square. Only fragments of the pitifully small numbers of "success" stories remain. For the overwhelming mass, slavery endured.

And yet there was a frontier phase of black history that made a difference in the quality of black life. Obviously, such conditions as the relative ease of emancipation in these years made a substantial difference to the few individuals who gained their freedom, but more important to most black people, slave and free, was the institutional atmosphere, the lack of agencies and energy directed toward the enforcement of racial codes. Allowing black people to hire out their own time began in these early years, and, although the practice did not always or even often lead to legal emancipation, it did make for a different kind of slavery. The presence of practically free people became a constant that all the agitation and legislation of the postfrontier decades could not eliminate. In the same way, the presence of black members in the early churches laid the basis for black church leadership and black congregations. Free people, practically free people, and slaves began to share something of a communal life of their own. As Richard Wade has demonstrated, some of the most crucial conditions of life for the slaves were startlingly changed in urban environments.[69] Nashville's urban frontier saw the beginning of this process.

Municipal Politics in the Age of Jackson

CHAPTER 5

EXCITEMENT and divisiveness characterized Nashville's municipal politics in the 1820s and 1830s. The physical and institutional needs of a growing city created competing demands just as the city's favorite son was making his bids for the presidency. Andrew Jackson's popularity paralleled a new intensity in antiprivilege, equal-access rhetoric and also encouraged larger numbers of men to come to the polls to achieve their own ends as well as to support the Old Hero. A good part of the business community, where it was not overtly hostile, was ambivalent toward Jackson, and it was clearly shaken by the new democracy at the polling places. It succeeded in holding its line by means of suffrage restrictions and then moved into Whig ranks as the second American party system emerged in Tennessee. The battle for voters was heated and stormy in the new wards of the city and was won decisively by the Whigs even though the state Democratic organization forced open the municipal suffrage. Ironically, by 1840 Jackson's own city had become a Whig stronghold, and the Whig party had become the basis of a new consensus.

The consensus politics of the first quarter of the nineteenth century became harder to maintain as the corporation faced the challenges of growth, of economic boom and panic, and, above all, of the emergence of the new national party system. The panic of 1819 had accelerated a process of change that was not peculiar to Nashville. Throughout the nation in the 1820s a political culture based on deference to social superiors was giving way to one based on white male suffrage and an insistence on social equality as the test of true republicanism.[1] Andrew Jackson's extraordinary popularity was not solely a function of his military triumphs; his campaigns stressed an end to privilege and its corruption of the body politic.[2] Even in Nashville the political rhetoric was intense and sometimes bitter. Probably one result of the fear of disorder created by the new politics was Nashville's most publicized lynching. In the long run, however, it was the commercial concerns of an urban community that came to the fore, providing a first glimpse of the issues that would divide the parties of the second American party system. Market houses, wharves, sewers, and schools were some of the needs of a growing town. The functions of municipal government were expanded, and the stakes, therefore, became higher. Master mechanics, men of property, and employers of labor were added to the pool of candidates for corporation offices, and they identified themselves as Whigs.

As one might expect of a successful frontier town, Nashville's population soared spectacularly at least in percentage terms—by more than 200 percent in the first decade of the century, somewhat less in the second. The increase was still a healthy 80 percent in the twenties.[3] Only during the thirties was population growth radically reduced, in part because of a stabilized economy that had yet to feel the impact of turnpike construction, in part because of the panic of 1837. In 1840 Nashville claimed just under 7,000 people. In absolute numbers and in comparison to other growing cities of the West, Nashville's growth was only moderate yet it was the premier city of Tennessee. As population moved into Middle Tennessee and more gradually into western Tennessee, Nashville's central location in the state and its access to the rivers of the West assured its position. By 1830 Middle Tennessee claimed half the population of the entire state and provided the state's political leadership.[4] Knoxville's early importance as an economic and political center had faded, and Memphis, a trading post before 1820, claimed less than a thousand people in 1830.[5]

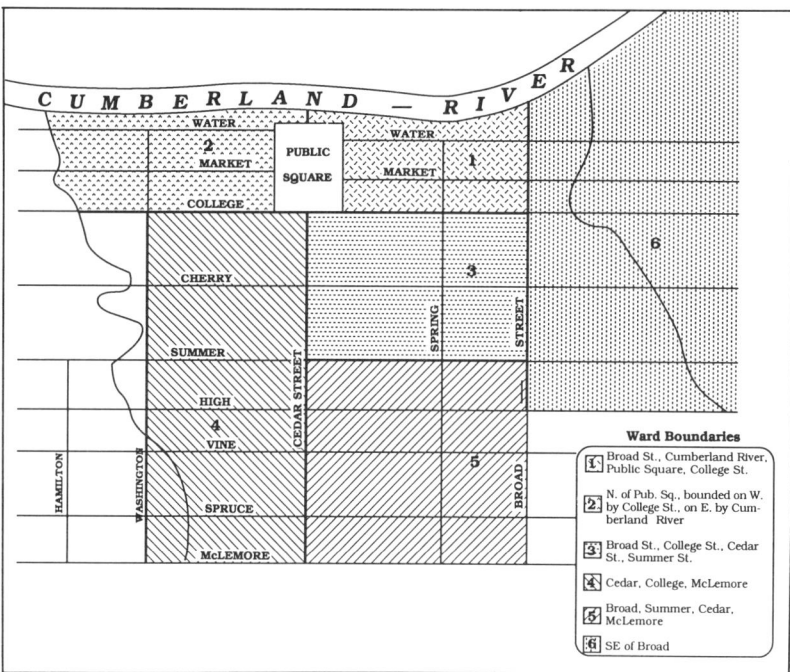

City of Nashville ward boundaries. Source: map of Nashville, 1832, Tennessee State Library and Archives. Drawn by Minnie Childers, The University of the South.

Physical expansion accompanied population growth. As early as 1813 the village's inhabitants had become jealous of encroachments on the valuable waterfront. The original plat of the village, peculiarly, had not taken in the land bordering the river. Judge McNairy, who had purchased the remainder of the 640-acre reservation out of which Nashville had been carved, claimed the waterfront. Almost every man in town signed a petition to the legislature to uphold the town against McNairy. Even Robert Rentfro, the free black tavernkeeper, signed with his mark. A compromise was ultimately achieved, and the town acquired the riverfront immediately along its official border.[6] In 1824 the corporation extended its boundaries by incorporating the 240 acres of Davidson Academy's lands. In 1830 the town extended the boundaries of its second, fourth, and fifth wards, and in 1837 it added to its second ward part of the original McNairy purchase.

The old core of the town, extending from the waterfront to the square and along Market, College, and Cherry streets, became the first and second wards and continued, like the early village, to house close together all classes and conditions.[7] Here merchants, mechanics, and bankers lived next door to or shared quarters with their business establishments. Many of the professionals maintained only an office in these busy streets or in the alleys that branched off them; they settled their families on Cherry Street from Cedar to Broad streets in what would be the third ward. Some of the lawyers moved still farther out to the area south of Broad Street, the corporation's original southern boundary adjoining the academy's lands. But it was Nashville's mechanics who were principally responsible for filling up the streets and alleys of the first and second wards and for pushing beyond them as they sought living and working space. Probably as early as the turn of the century most men in town called themselves mechanics. Craftsmen initially served the needs of planters and farmers, but by 1810 the town itself was generating work, particularly in the building trades. The postwar boom meant that carpenters, bricklayers, and stonemasons could not work fast enough to build shops and homes.[8]

The 1820 census lists 412 individuals "in manufactures," a broad category that took in the three or four owners of cotton-thread factories, their employees, and all the mechanics, from bootmakers and silversmiths to carpenters and house joiners. No more than a quarter of the men listed would have been master mechanics.[9] Most were journeymen or apprentices, men or boys, sons or strangers. In 1820 mechanics' households were typically large, and most of the white members of these households were male adults: six men aged sixteen or older in coachmaker Stout's household, eight men in tailor Smiley's, and seven men in tinner Snow's. Superficially, these bulging households seemed to carry over a medieval tradition of master mechanics gathering about them their apprentices and journeymen, but there was in fact much less stability on the frontier or in expanding cities than that image would suggest. The contemptuous "6 and one half cents reward" offered for a runaway apprentice indicates a more casual commitment on both sides of the contract. The seasonal nature of many of the trades meant that apprentices and journeymen were taken on only "as the weather breaks," and the periodic shortages of skilled workmen also worked against a traditional model. Early in the century, when tailors vied for journeymen, masters advertised that the journeymen would be "paid off on every Saturday night."[10]

As the demand for their services increased, more craftsmen moved into Nashville and began to set up as independent householders even though they might still be journeymen and employees. One can trace in the census data of the next two decades a trend toward reduction in the number and the proportion of households that included three or more adult white males.[11] Even more clear is that the disparity between the numbers of white men and women grew steadily smaller.[12] It was, then, the pressure of workingmen's households that filled in the first and fourth wards and the areas of even cheaper housing along the riverfront and in the low-lying area south of Broad Street in the new sixth ward. By the late twenties a new landing and warehouses at the foot of Broad Street opened up a second commercial district and precipitated a demand for another market house on Broad. The possibility of ward politics emerged.

Public complaints about the corporation's handling of community needs were very rare until around 1819, when dissension within the ranks of the business community, triggered by the panic, began to spill over into the municipal government. In 1818 the *Whig* could suggest, with a bit of humor, "Lamps! Lamps! wanted in the streets. burnt my har to'ther night carrying candle! left in the dark, run over pile rubbish, wish would move it." But by the spring of 1819 the editor had mounted a campaign calling attention to fire equipment, the market house, and the night watch. For the first time the *Whig* advertised the corporation election and urged that "every man who feels a solicitude for the welfare and proper regulation of this town, should attend."[13]

In fact, between 1817 and 1820 an unusual number of changes on the board took place: in 1818 five of the seven aldermen were men who had not served before; in 1819 two new men and a third man who had not served for twelve years were elected; and in 1820 four new men were elected.[14] At least three of the aldermen who were not reelected were victims of the panic, but business failure was perhaps the least significant reason for changes on the board. Public hostility to bank directors and a rejection of the old leadership as a result of the panic were clearly reflected in corporation elections. So also were a new concern for city services and a new source of candidates from among the master mechanics.

As credit was curtailed and property went on the block, bank directors were special targets. In 1818 five of the seven municipal officers had been bank directors. In 1820 only two, in 1821 only one, and in 1822 only two were directors of the old banks.[15] Also in 1820, James Condon, tailor and boardinghouse proprietor, was elected mayor by his fellow aldermen. Condon simply does not fit the pattern of Nashville mayors. Although he had once served as town constable, he had never before been elected to the board, nor would he be elected again. A modest property holder, he took no part in the commission business or the controversial banking business.[16] Nor was he elected as a result of apathy; there were candidates in plenty.[17] Condon evidently conducted a vigorous campaign on a law-and-morality platform that reflected the new concern with order that was sweeping the community. In the midst of the panic the corporation was forced to respond to demands for an increased police force, a corporation school, street lighting, and a waterworks. In 1823 a "clean sweep" was reported in corporation elections as four new men came on the board, including master mechanics Samuel Stout and Thomas Welch.[18]

Minimal as the commitment to new services was, increased expenditures, especially in the postpanic years, tended to be divisive. Fears of monopoly privilege were voiced with regard to the waterworks; favoritism in maintenance of the streets was charged; an auctioneers' tax levied in 1821 pitted auctioneers against other merchants. Services were sought; taxation was decried. Some sought expansion of the corporation's powers through the creation of a mayor's court. Others, alarmed by rising costs, suggested surrender of the charter. The closed meetings of the board were attacked. In 1823 mayor and aldermen were called upon to "unveil; put off the mantle of obscurity which has heretofore concealed all your doings, and exhibit all to the view of the public," and indeed a week later the proceedings of the board appeared in the newspapers. The newly elected board was obviously trying to meet the specific criticisms raised in the *Whig*. It ordered a list of all eligible citizens prepared in order to organize them into fire companies. It organized itself into committees with specific charges and created standing committees to superintend the corporation school, the public springs, street improvement, the fire companies, and the waterworks contract.[19]

Much of the clamor for improvements raised by the *Whig* had to do simply with the exigencies of city living, but it is true that Andrew Jackson's presidential campaigns coincided with and provided fuel and a new vocabulary for urban politics. The editor of the *Whig*, John P. Erwin, was deeply involved in the politics of the twenties. Inheriting a family feud against Andrew Jackson, related by marriage to Henry Clay, Erwin defiantly rejected Tennessee's favorite son and supported Henry Clay in 1824.[20] The *Whig*'s concern with municipal improvements echoed the activist, growth-oriented positions of the future leader of the Whig party. At the same time, the *Whig* published diatribes against electioneering, which it labeled as subversive of republican principles: "No man should sacrifice his honor and independence on the shrine of popularity."[21] However, in 1824 Erwin's decrying the new politics sounded a bit hollow. When Andrew Jackson lost to John Quincy Adams, many in Nashville and throughout the nation saw a "corrupt bargain" between Adams and his new secretary of state, Henry Clay. Old Hickory's popularity would grow in the state, in the South, and throughout the nation in the next four years.

Nashville itself, however, was never solidly in Jackson's camp. A good part of the influential commercial community held back. Jackson's supporters insisted that it was a contingent of Yankees, Irishmen, and Erwins who opposed his election, but most merchants and bankers were favorably impressed by the ambitious governmental programs of Adams and Clay,[22] and no one was sure where Jackson stood on issues like the tariff and internal improvements. At a reception in Jackson's honor in the spring of 1825, Andrew Hynes offered as a toast "the Friends of Internal Improvement—they are the benefactors of their country."[23] John Overton, Jackson's close friend and the principal initiator of Jackson's candidacy, actually preferred Henry Clay. Sponsoring Jackson was evidently a maneuver to maintain his faction's control of state politics.[24] After Adams's victory, businessmen like Thomas Yeatman, neither a Yankee nor an Irishman but, it is true, married to an Erwin, were quickly making recommendations for patronage posts that might be filled by anti-Jackson men. Dr. Boyd McNairy, one of Jackson's most bitter enemies, interpreted his own proadministration, anti-Jackson stand as "opposition to the Aristocracy of our State."[25] Some businessmen saw themselves in opposition not to Jackson but to Jackson's backers, men who, like Overton, were associated with the branch bank, and to the traditional county leadership. The hesitations of the merchant-banker contingent presaged the deep party splits that would develop when Jacksonians increasingly identified themselves as champions of rural rather than commercial interests and, more especially, as opponents of government aid to economic development. But these programmatic differences were hardly apparent in the twenties, when Nashvillians, at the center of the state's politics, were treated to dramatic clashes of personalities and of what were still factions. When, for example, John Erwin was appointed postmaster by the Adams administration, Sam Houston, Jackson's protégé and a candidate for governor, made clear his indignation, and a duel with Erwin was only narrowly avoided.[26]

The new style of campaigning and the new democratic rhetoric crept only slowly into corporation politics. It was Nashville's own William Carroll who was the first to stump the state in the gubernatorial election of 1821, proclaiming his simple origins and his lack of Latin and Greek, which distinguished him from his opponent, a wealthy planter.[27] In 1820 five justices, all Nashville men, protested the attempt of the county court to appoint rather than elect a sheriff.[28] Only then, in the early twenties, do we hear of a "clean sweep" applied to corporation elections.

Still, the new political awareness did not mean mass politics on the municipal level. Though the population grew, the effective electorate remained level. In 1826, in the last town election before reorganization, 325 people, perhaps one-third of the electorate, voted.[29] The clublike atmosphere of corporation government seems to have carried over to the electorate itself. On the one hand, the system of electing from the town as a whole rather than from the wards undoubtedly helped maintain the character of the board. On the other hand, the massive increases in the numbers of voters in national and state elections would not begin until the thirties, so the percentage of Nashville's voters in this city election paralleled the national and, more especially, the southern norms.[30]

In the summer of 1826 the *Banner and Whig* began to voice what must have been a widespread concern to revamp the city government. The city needed to be divided into wards, the number of aldermen increased, the mayor made a justice of the peace within the corporation, and the police and regulatory powers of the corporation increased.[31] Strengthening the corporation vis-a-vis the county court, making it more independent and more effective, was one objective community leaders could agree on. On the other hand, by 1826 the idea of a popularly elected mayor might have been especially attractive to Jackson supporters who saw the merchant leadership holding back from the Jackson bandwagon. Indeed, one suspects that the ease with which Nashville's incorporation act was amended may be explained by the influence within the state legislature of Jacksonians anxious to make Nashville safe for Jackson by widening participation in town politics. A popularly elected mayor and voting for aldermen by ward rather than by the town at large

From the Nashville Business Directory of 1860.

would have looked promising. Just as these changes were being promoted, the county court raised the issue of the town's autonomy when it ordered the market house removed from the square. The noise and the smells of the market, it was reported, offended the lawyers at work in the courthouse. A new courthouse was projected, and the county challenged the town's right to the public square. A public meeting aired the questions of market house and municipal government, and the state legislature responded quickly to a petition that came out of the meeting.

Nashville's government was modernized and democratized. The

city was divided into six wards; each ward was to elect not a single alderman, as the petitioners requested, but two aldermen. Mayor and constable were to be directly elected by the voters.[32] In the election that followed, Dr. Felix Robertson, son of the founder and, like his father before him, a key figure in county politics, was chosen mayor. Robertson was a devoted supporter of Jackson and won again in 1828, when a record vote was registered in an election that pitted Robertson against ex-mayor Tannehill, a vocal Adams and Clay man. Robertson won by an impressive margin—531 votes to 219—and the total number of votes, more than twice the turnout of 1826, was startling.[33]

Even more shocking to the traditional town leadership was the makeup of the new board of aldermen. Nine of the twelve men who served on the newly expanded board had never served before. The following year eight new aldermen were elected, and in 1829, three. Key wards were the first and the sixth—the first, the old commercial heart of Nashville, and the sixth, the recently annexed south side. In the three elections between 1827 and 1829, the first ward chose a tinner, a grocer, and a saddler. The sixth elected four men, among them Jacob Brasher and Josiah Shaw. "Captain" Brasher became, for a brief time, the spokesman of the "suffering" people of the south side; Josiah Shaw was so little known that the newspaper report of the successful candidates carried only his last name. Of the seven men elected from both wards, only two were reported as freeholders on the 1829 tax list.[34] Perhaps more significant, after the restriction of the vote to taxpayers in 1829, none of these men served again.

Community leaders had been evidently counting on master mechanics and workingmen to follow their lead when they sought a more forceful municipal government. They certainly had anticipated no challenge from the working population of the town. For all the heightening of democratic rhetoric, the "real people" in contemporaries' perceptions fell naturally into higher and lower ranks: merchants and professionals, mechanics and journeymen. Day laborers were simply dismissed, not considered part of the community. The Irishmen who were imported to build the bridge in 1819 moved on when that job was done. No significant number of aliens or Catholics existed to fuel ethnic or religious differences. Moreover, "mechanics" included all men who worked with their hands. The dividing line between skilled laborers and master mechanics was not sharply drawn, perhaps as much because few master mechanics approached the wealth and status of the commission merchants as because skilled workers had, potentially at least, the chance to move up to the status of independent shopkeeper. On the other hand, although few mechanics owned real estate, a great many commanded slave labor: 64 percent of all households and two-thirds of the 127 households listed as "in manufactures" on the 1820 census included slaves.[35] Slave labor gave all masters and employers a stake in the social order, while the slave-labor pool, the peculiar working class of southern cities, of course had no part in the political process.

Nashville's leadership was right in one sense. Corporation politics reflected not class interests within the community but rather the popularity of Andrew Jackson. It was national politics that first charged municipal elections with a new energy. Candidates for the mayor's office were clearly identified as pro- or anti-Jackson. And when urban politics did become more than a reflection of national politics, class interests were muted. Local and specific issues institutionalized ward politics rather quickly. The market-house issue was stalemated for a few years while the court refused to rescind its order to tear down the old market house. The corporation ultimately won its major point by agreeing to build a new and more elaborate house on the square.[36] However, the construction of the new market house did not satisfy the property holders and residents of the developing south side, who sponsored a second market house on Broad Street. Broad Street was the border of the fifth and sixth wards, until recently considered the suburbs of the town. A much less elaborate and less expensive structure was built, and the "old" merchants with interests on the square and Market Street and the "new" merchants who were promoting Broad Street began to battle almost immediately. The Broad Street improvements, which included a sewer and a hay scale as well as the market house and proposals for a new wharf and a second bridge, threatened the established interests in the old core of the city. As early as the summer of 1828 objections were voiced against the corporation's investing in a new wharf, and just before the election of 1829 a taxpayers' revolt was threatened. There were also objections against the corporation's providing funds to complete the Broad Street market house when private subscriptions proved insufficient. Candidates for mayor were quizzed on their positions on the issue. Mayor and aldermen proposed alternating market days between the two market houses. Partisans of the square were outraged.[37]

Out of this local battle, waged with increasing heat in the newspapers—itself a new phenomenon—came the effort by potential candidates for office to make political capital and also an intensification of democratic rhetoric. Equal access to economic opportunity, one key to our understanding of the meaning of Jacksonian democracy, was played out in the microcosm of Nashville's urban politics. A public meeting—held at the city hall in the new market house on the square—adopted resolutions that looked like compromises but favored the interests of the square. On the one hand, they rejected the corporation's regulation of market days as a "violation of the rights of a free people" and urged that both markets remain open for business all week. On the other hand, they rejected a proposal that public land be sold for improvements and demanded that the corporation suspend all further improvements until the debts of the corporation were paid, thus promising the eventual building of a Broad Street wharf but effectively tying the corporation's hands so that one could not be built in the near future.[38]

A letter signed "Broad Street" introduced a heightened invective, pointed up the property-versus-people issue, and suggested a new measure of elite status—the clothing of Nashville's merchants' wives. "Broad Street" reminded the public "of the domineering policy and pretensions so long and so arrogantly set up by those *bugs* around the Square, whose females wear such infinitely more fine, valuable and beautiful *shawls* than ours do." "Broad Street" appealed directly to the widened electorate, urging them to consider that the development of Broad Street would mean more work and better housing for mechanics. Significantly, it was in these same weeks that the temperance society stepped up its activities, its spokesmen urging that intemperate candidates and those who provided liquor to prospective voters be boycotted.[39] A populist, democratic theme had been added to the equal-access, antiprivilege appeal, and both were provoking political excitement and anxiety.[40]

Two men were proposed for mayor in 1829. Major Thomas Claiborne was put forward at a public meeting held in Colonel Anthony Johnson's new warehouse on Broad Street. Claiborne, one "of the old Virginia School of Politicians," had earned his military title while on Jackson's staff during the Creek wars and had served both as a state legislator and as a member of Congress. He viewed with regret the "hostility and violence" exhibited by the square toward Broad Street. However, it may be that his very availability as a member of the establishment told against him. Two years later, when he ran for the state legislature (and won), he had to defend himself against charges that he mixed only "with the men of wealth in the town of Nashville," that he sought to take the suffrage from all but freeholders, and, on an interesting new note, that he was opposed to common schools.[41]

The winner in 1829 was a young man, William Armstrong, who was proposed at a public meeting a week after Claiborne was nominated. Armstrong was clearly a Jackson man, one of the political coterie that managed Democratic politics in Nashville from this time on. Only a few months before, his brother, Robert, had been appointed by the victorious Jackson administration as postmaster, replacing John Erwin, and during Robert's long tenure the post office became the Democrats' clubhouse. It was a political plus that the Armstrongs were clearly allied with the mercantile interests of the square; Robert was Josiah Nichol's son-in-law, and both Armstrongs had been commission merchants. The meeting that nominated Armstrong also proposed a full slate of twelve candidates for the board—only five of whom were accepted at the polls. The political scene was still volatile. Only one factor was clearly spelled out: open opposition to Jackson was politically unrewarding. Wilkins Tannehill moved to Louisville for a few years; the prospects for the publisher of a Clay paper seemed dim in Nashville. Erwin, who had refused to run against Robertson in 1828, refused the nomination for mayor once again in 1829.[42]

While Jackson seemed unbeatable in the national arena and more people came out to vote in local elections, the makeup of corporation government would not be allowed to change radically. Two weeks before election day a new twist was introduced into the political debate. "R. S." wrote to the editor of the *Banner and Whig*, "Does not the act of incorporation say that none but freeholders can serve as aldermen!" He went on to suggest, "Would it not be better to have a law passed by the Legislature prohibiting 'all but freeholders' from voting at corporation elections?" The response was prompt and angry. Jacob Brasher demanded the name of this subversive. "Custis" charged that a small but wealthy and therefore influential party was trying to dictate "the terms upon which the legitimate citizens of our town shall enjoy existence—and who would, if they dared, trample upon those rights, which neither they nor their forefathers helped to obtain—rights which at *home*, they could never hope to enjoy."[43] The nativist finger was pointing to the Irish and Scottish businessmen of Nashville, whom some Jacksonians distrusted. Ironically, the same Jackson meeting that had nominated Armstrong had also proposed two foreign-born merchants and bankers; neither was elected. So convenient for the development of populist rhetoric was the charge of a conspiracy to restrict the electorate and so accepted was the notion that once the electorate is widened there can be no retreat, that one would have been tempted to see the letters of "R. S." as the work of Brasher himself. However, on October 26, a few weeks after the election, the corporation passed a law requiring voters to show evidence of the payment of corporation taxes.[44] Property holders were obviously frightened by the new interest at the polls, and most of the new men in office were frightened enough to restrict the electorate.

It may be that the continuing demand for a more active and more expensive city government added to the fears of taxpayers. In late 1829 the corporation sought authority from the legislature to borrow $50,000 to complete a waterworks; this represented the first major debt of the corporation. And still there was agitation for more paved streets, for an extended boat landing, for a "pleasant and healthful promenade."[45] Moreover, the tug-of-war between Broad Street and Market Street continued. A new question was the board of aldermen's support for a second bridge across the Cumberland, which would give Broad Street the same kind of access to the countryside enjoyed by the square. The supporters of the new bridge included many mechanics and retailers but only a few of the commission merchants and bankers, most of whom were stockholders of the old Nashville Bridge Company.[46] The board split eight to four, with eight members advocating petitioning the legislature not to incorporate the second bridge company. Both representatives of the sixth ward voted for a second bridge.[47]

Jacob Brasher became the self-proclaimed champion of the "south end" and campaigned hard for the mayor's office in 1830. Brasher denounced the limitation of suffrage, "enacted no doubt for the purpose of prohibiting the mechanics or laboring men from voting." He attacked the incumbents as afflicted with "internal improvements plague and fever" but reminded the voters that the board "has been opposed to improvements in Nashville, for which reason the mechanics have suffered greatly."[48] He was not being inconsistent. The new $50,000 debt was to be used to buy slave laborers to complete the waterworks. Brasher presumably sought improvements, like the bridge, that would provide jobs in the sixth ward for white workers and raise property values in the ward. Others picked up the sixth ward's grievances. "Nullification" contended that the south

From the Nashville Business Directory of 1860.

end persistently lost in contests with the public square interests and suggested secession.[49]

Brasher lost humiliatingly on election day. Only 36 of a total of 309 votes cast for mayor went to him.[50] The total vote is even more revealing: it was less than half of the votes cast in 1828. The electorate was reduced to about the same number that had voted before the reorganization of town government. Armstrong, the only mayor to serve four consecutive terms, was popular, was obviously Jackson's man, but his popularity alone cannot explain why people did not come out to vote for aldermen or why only forty-four men in the sixth ward voted for mayor.[51] The ordinance restricting the electorate to taxpayers had in fact made a significant difference. Twenty aldermen were elected to office for the first time between 1827 and 1829; only five would serve again after 1829, and none of the men who had represented the first and sixth wards in these years would serve again after 1829.

The politics of the first ward demonstrate the impact of restriction of the electorate. Samuel V. D. Stout (sometimes remembered as Samuel Vexation Damnation Stout), who was first elected alderman in 1823 and who served until 1826, was one of the first of the master mechanics to take part in town politics.[52] His marriage to Wilkins Tannehill's sister in 1813 had not initially made him a part of the inner crew that managed corporation government but did suggest his affiliation with the anti-Jackson camp. Stout was not reelected after the reorganization of the corporation's government. Only after the electorate was reduced was he returned to office, and then he was retained as alderman or mayor (in 1841) for all but four terms from 1830 to 1848. He was joined as representative of the first ward by a commission merchant, Joseph Vaulx,[53] and then by a merchant and banker, John M. Hill.

Maintaining the first ward as the preserve of a prosperous and well-connected mechanic and of leading merchants evidently took some effort. A group of first-ward residents petitioned the legislature in 1831 to prevent nonresident property owners from voting for the first ward's aldermen. They claimed that this practice had already resulted in the nonresidents controlling the first ward's election. Among the petitioners were mechanics, innkeepers, shopkeepers, and a saddler, Henry Cartmell, who had served as alderman in 1828 and 1829. A counterpetition was signed by a considerable number of the capitalists and landowners in the town. These men pointed out that the function of the vote was the protection of property.[54] Voting procedures were not changed. The ward system had opened the city to the possibility of interest politics fought out in the context of a democratic electorate, but men of property, despite cleavages in their own ranks, quickly joined together to limit the range of political participation.

Nevertheless, the Age of Jackson did make some differences in the makeup of corporation government. The most obvious was the increased role of the mechanics on the board. To be sure, almost all of these mechanics were master mechanics, typical not of the workingmen of the city but of their employers. Of the fifty-eight aldermen who served between 1830 and 1840, twenty-one can be classified as mechanics, sixteen as merchants; one was a banker. Mechanics served a total of fifty-nine terms, the merchants and banker, thirty-five. Moreover, of the ten aldermen who served more than three terms, seven were mechanics. Only in the residential third and fifth wards were more of the aldermen merchants than mechanics. Professionals, such as lawyers, doctors, newspaper editors, who were closely identified with the emerging political parties, also began to take a larger part in corporation government.⁵⁵

It is of course not surprising, given the unchanged legal requirement for officeholding, that the aldermen were property holders. Forty-nine of the fifty-eight aldermen were taxed on property in 1839. Their holdings were representative of those of the bulk of the property holders on the tax list and only slightly weighted toward those of the wealthiest taxpayers.⁵⁶ Of the nine aldermen who were also bank directors in these years, only five served more than a single term in the 1830s, and only two served after 1833. Direct connection with the banks and the commission business was not a drawback in corporation politics, but it was no longer a prime consideration in a candidate for alderman. Once the hoi polloi had been eliminated from the polls and uncertainty about the impact of the new corporation government had been quieted, ward politics were by and large reassuring to all property holders despite the change in occupation and status of the aldermen.

At the same time, the politics that would create a second American party system began to take center stage in Nashville. While Jackson was in the White House, open declarations of opposition were not forthcoming even though many whom he had antagonized began to draw together. In addition, Jackson's veto of the charter for the Bank of the United States and the Democratic assault on banks, bankers, paper money, and speculation won few friends in Nashville's commercial circles. Public meetings led by commission merchants, newspaper editors, and bankers, including John P. Erwin, sponsored the preparation of a pamphlet defending the "Credit of the West" and the Nashville branch bank against charges that "seven out of every ten of the exchange operations of the Western Branches of the U.S. Bank, consist of what are termed Race Horse Bills."⁵⁷

Among the state's political figures what may have begun as a rivalry between two ambitious Jacksonians became by 1835 a political revolution. One faction was led by Congressman John Bell, who had married Thomas Yeatman's widow and had a personal stake in the banking and mercantile circles of Nashville. James K. Polk, whose favored position with Andrew Jackson was one source of Bell's antagonism, led the regular Jacksonians. The first major test came in 1835, when Hugh Lawson White of eastern Tennessee, a respected political leader of the old school, was persuaded to challenge Martin Van Buren, Jackson's handpicked successor for the presidency in 1836. The bolt to White signaled the beginnings of the Whig party in Tennessee.[58] Both Nashville newspapers rallied behind White in 1835, and Jackson regulars were forced to subsidize a third paper, the *Union*, to muster support for Van Buren's candidacy. Long lists of supporters of each of the candidates were printed in the papers as each party tried to commit potential voters. Newspaper partisanship was virulent and often scurrilous. So bitter did politics become that by 1838 an ex-editor of the *Union* found it impossible to be ordained within the Episcopal church because of the opposition of Whig members belonging to the church's committee of clergy and laity.[59] By the late thirties the Whig party seemed to sweep the state, but in 1839 Polk's successful campaign for the governorship revitalized the Jacksonians and made the Democratic party an effective competitor again on the state level. A politically balanced two-party system would remain in place until the fifties.[60]

Within Nashville's wards the years between 1835 and 1840 saw intense partisan battles. The first and second wards became and remained Whig strongholds. These wards saw the fewest changes in personnel. Stout was a perpetual figure in the first ward; Joseph Knowles, also an old resident, successful master mechanic, and early on a committed Whig, was a similar figure in the second. Only one alderman from these wards was assessed at less than $1,000 in 1839; he was the lone Democrat elected to the board that year.

The third ward had become a mixed neighborhood of shops, offices, and taverns as well as the impressive business establishments leading off College Street and the substantial homes along Cedar, Cherry, and Summer streets. John Austin, a carpenter, and Dr. Waters, Felix Robertson's brother-in-law, kept one alderman's slot in the Democratic column through most of the thirties. Until 1839 merchants of considerable means occupied a Whig slot, and in 1839 and 1840 the Whigs took both aldermen's posts, electing two mechanics. In the fourth ward, the fastest growing in population, the division between the parties was close. In 1837 and 1838 the Democrats won both seats, and in 1839 and 1840 the Whigs took both.

The fifth ward was the most fashionable and the wealthiest residential section of the city; it returned only two mechanics in this decade. Most of its aldermen were prominent merchants, bankers, or professionals. The publishers of a Whig and the Democratic newspapers both served, once in the same year (1837). Here again the contests between Whigs and Democrats were sharp in the late thirties and early forties.

By the late thirties the sixth ward, despite a cluster of elegant homes close to the university, was already identifiable as the poorest section of Nashville. The eleven men who were elected aldermen between 1830 and 1840 all together were assessed on only $11,750 in real estate in 1839, far less than the $144,440 assessed on the thirteen aldermen of the fifth ward.[61] The sixth's aldermen were usually mechanics. A tobacconist was the only merchant to serve, and one young lawyer from a wealthy family served a single term in 1832. In 1835 tinsmith Powhatan Maxey was elected; a Whig, he would be returned continuously from 1835 to 1842 except in one year. As national politics entered the arena of corporation politics, Maxey's hold on the "Democratic" sixth ward was a measure of Whig strength in the city as a whole.

For a few years after Armstrong's four-year tenure in the mayor's office, the contests for mayor continued to be more like the consensus politics of earlier years. Mayors, irrespective of party label, were merchants and bankers. In 1833, with the bank veto heating the political arena, Nashville came up with an effective expedient. John M. Bass was not only one of Nashville's leading bankers but also, as Grundy's son-in-law, an undoubted Jacksonian. He was elected with a substantial lead over two other contenders, but he was the last Democrat to be mayor until 1837. In the next year John Erwin, now cashier of the Yeatman-Woods bank, was elected over James McCombs, a cabinetmaker. Both men would be committed Whigs. Status rather than party affiliation seemed to be the relevant issue in these campaigns. William Nichol, merchant, banker, and Whig, won over the *Whig*'s publisher in 1835 and was reelected with no opposition in 1836.

The excitement of political organizing and the strain on old loyalties made Nashville particularly fearful of disorder and susceptible to wild rumors. Volunteer guard companies, young men organized along partisan political lines, undoubtedly contributed to tensions within the community. In late June and early July of 1835, reports of a slave insurrection planned by the notorious Murrell gang had created havoc in Mississippi despite the fact that John Murrell, bandit and slave stealer, was secured in the penitentiary at Nashville.[62] Notices of this so-called slave conspiracy and of a violent confrontation between gamblers and vigilantes in Vicksburg began to appear in the Nashville papers. It was put about that the evicted gamblers would take up residence in Nashville. A public meeting, chaired by

State Capitol, Nashville. From the *Nashville Business Directory of 1860*.

Mayor Erwin, appointed a vigilance committee for Nashville. The committee was supposed to enforce the meeting's resolutions that all gamblers be removed from town within forty-eight hours and that sales of liquor be prohibited on Sundays, after 10:00 P.M., and to slaves.[63]

It was in this tense atmosphere that young Amos Dresser, a Lane seminarian and crusader for emancipation, drove into town. He carelessly sent his carriage, containing his abolitionist and anti-Catholic tracts, to Stout's shop for repairs, and there the workmen discovered the pamphlets. Now there was work for the committee. As a mob gathered, the committee took over and supervised the extralegal trial and the lashing of Dresser, who was then hurried out of town.[64]

Samuel Laughlin, the editor of the *Union*, tried to make political capital of the vigilante actions. He kept up a constant attack on abolitionists, featured reports of incendiaries and riots, and tried to paint the Whig leadership as soft on abolitionism. At the same time, he challenged the town's official and nonofficial leadership by publicizing a handbill then circulating in the town that protested mob rule and vigilante bands claiming authority from the mayor to patrol the streets "and inflict summary punishment upon all suspected persons." Laughlin insisted on a connection between the Dresser lashing and an earlier visit of Benjamin Lundy under the auspices of the

Tennessee Colonization Society, whose Nashville branch included as active members and officers John P. Erwin, R. H. McEwen, Wilkins Tannehill, and William G. Hunt, all of whom were anti-Jackson partisans.[65]

The makeup of the vigilance committee provides further evidence that the town's social and financial leadership was indeed moving into the Whig ranks. Twenty-nine of the sixty-one men on the committee can be identified as Whigs or supporters of White; fifteen can be identified as Democrats. At least thirty-one were merchants and bankers, ten were professionals, and only fourteen can be identified as mechanics; at least twenty-three served as bank directors in the years between 1830 and 1840. These vigilantes were "gentlemen of standing and property." Thirty-two of them signed petitions in defense of the continued restrictions on the electorate in 1837; only three petitioned for repeal of the restrictions.[66] The electorate had been growing larger.[67] Either more men were paying the poll tax or the comparative lack of attention to corporation politics resulted in less stringent application of the ordinances. Just before the corporation election in the fall of 1836, the *Banner and Whig* pointedly published the list of restrictions on the suffrage.[68]

When they went to the polls to vote in the 1836 national elections, Nashville voters chose White over Van Buren by 669 to 514, and Tennessee voters gave White an unprecedented 58 percent of their vote. The Whigs were in place.[69] However, party lines had not hardened altogether. Though Newton Cannon, the Whig candidate for governor in 1837, defeated Robert Armstrong by a resounding 17,000 votes, many of Nashville's most prominent Whig leaders had supported their old friend Armstrong.[70]

Within the corporation, the panic of 1837 undoubtedly played some role in the surprising victory of the Democratic candidate, Henry Hollingsworth, over the Whig incumbent, William Nichol. Hollingsworth, a young, self-made lawyer just back from the Seminole War, evidently used Jacksonian rhetoric, identifying himself as the candidate of the "poor" as opposed to the "favored class."[71] He won decisively, running especially well in the first and sixth wards. In addition, the first ward's voters replaced both Stout and John M. Hill, and the fourth ward elected two Democratic aldermen. But 1838 brought a narrower victory for Hollingsworth, who defeated the Whig candidate by just four votes.[72] It was in this context that the attempt to remove restrictions on the suffrage was reintroduced.

Calling on "Republican liberty" and appealing to the liberal suffrage provided by the newly ratified constitution of Tennessee, almost five hundred individuals signed a petition to the legislature requesting repeal of the 1829 suffrage restriction. Former governor Carroll, leader of the Tennessee Democracy since 1821, headed the list.[73] Hollingsworth fought hard within the corporation's government to gain support for the repeal, but only two aldermen voted with him.[74] Another five hundred names of "citizens of Nashville or property holders therein" were hastily assembled to counter the first petition. Here were the names of most of the influential men in the community: bankers, merchants, landholders, clergymen, lawyers, some of the master mechanics, and even some leading Democrats— Felix Robertson and Robert Armstrong among them—who feared that repeal would place "the property, and the very large revenues of the Corporation . . . under the management of unskillful officers, without their consent, and against their will, by those who had no interest in their judicious selection."[75] The 1829 ordinance was maintained for the moment. The line between Democrat and Whig was clearly less firm than that between substantial citizens and the hoi polloi.

Yet party battles were in high gear. Newspaper invective, log cabins and cider, and political maneuvering at every level characterized the last years of the decade. In 1839 Hollingsworth lost to the Whig candidate; he carried only the sixth ward.[76] At the state level, though, the Democrats were able to reverse the Whig tide. They captured the governor's chair for Polk and both branches of the legislature. Davidson County's representatives and Nashville's government remained Whig, but so close were the margins between parties and so desperate the parties for political majorities that Nashville's electorate was in fact increased despite the objections of its mayor and aldermen. The representative from Weakley County, a Democrat, introduced an amendment to a bill to abolish the mayor's court in Nashville, which removed the taxpaying requirement and was sustained by the Democratic legislature.[77] To no avail. Though 145 more voters came to the polls in 1840 than in 1839, the Whigs won once again. The Democratic candidate carried only the sixth ward, and that by only seven votes.[78] Nashville had become a Whig city. Crushed, the editor of the Democratic paper was ready to dismiss Nashville: "Jefferson said 'these cities are sores on the body politic.'"[79]

Very early in the history of the second American party system, Nashville, Davidson County, and indeed a significant part of the

Cumberland Basin began to vote Whig. The panic of 1819 had exacerbated rifts within the traditional political establishments of the counties and the state, and Andrew Jackson's presidential candidacies introduced a new excitement to the political process. Jacksonian antimonopoly, equal-access rhetoric was applied to battles like that between Market Street and Broad Street advocates. The argument of the people versus the privileged was heard at the hustings. However, Nashville's merchant-lawyer leadership shored up its control of corporation politics, initially by bluntly, if legally, limiting the electorate, often by maintaining its own solidarity across the new party lines, and ultimately by recruiting new ward leaders from among the successful master mechanics who shared their views of the community's future. Politics would provide a surprisingly effective glue to hold together a good part of the increasingly diverse urban population.

Growing Apart

CHAPTER 6

IF democratization was achieved almost as a by-product of party rivalry, party programs now had to court a steadily growing and more varied electorate. In the years between 1840 and 1860, economic growth maintained and developed Nashville's urban status with all that that term implies, including the obvious social and economic divisions within the white population of the city. The lifestyles of merchants and bankers, who represented the top of the social hierarchy, paralleled those of professionals but were clearly different from those of master mechanics, who worked alongside "respectable" workingmen but who were decidedly anxious to distinguish themselves from day laborers, especially immigrant laborers. Social divisions within the city were aggravated by the arrival of foreigners sufficient in number to make ethnic minicommunities viable and visible, and the political enthusiasm and anxiety accompanying the organization of the second American party system stimulated a nativism that became more virulent when the Whigs made it part of their program. Democrats and Whigs addressed themselves to the voters. The party of Jefferson and Jackson maintained its suspicion of the bankers and the "interests," appealed to the whole people, and added immigrant voters to its traditional supporters. The Whigs, insisting on a success ladder in an economically developing city, began to build a coalition of merchants, mechanics, and native workingmen. The party system itself functioned to give coherence to a city that was growing apart.

The thirties had seen only a small increase in population; the forties brought a stronger influx of white population, some of it foreign-born and apparently compensating for a dramatic halt in the increase of the black population. By 1850 Nashville had 10,000 people. In the fifties both black and white populations increased so substantially that Nashville, with almost 17,000 people, ranked fifty-fourth among the 103 cities with populations of 10,000 or more in the United States in 1860.[1] Eleven southern cities had larger populations, including Washington, D.C., and the metropolises of Baltimore and New Orleans. Within Tennessee, Memphis, whose splendid position on the Mississippi and in the center of the cotton belt had promoted rapid growth since the forties, eclipsed Nashville in population by 1860.[2] Nevertheless, Nashville maintained its primacy as the financial and political center of the state.

Commerce and finance rather than industry continued to be the pacesetters in the city's economy. Nashville was dependent upon the agricultural hinterland it served as shipping point for staples and market for manufactured goods, largely imported from the North. Like other southern cities, it did not and indeed could not compete with or reduce the lead the North commanded in industrial output. Nashville and her sister cities "grew, but they did not develop."[3] Turnpikes and railroads extended Nashville's reach to and beyond the river system and maintained rather than revolutionized the character of the city.

The steamboat era created its own special excitement. As the boats grew ever more numerous, larger, and more elaborate, the wharves were center stage. Wagons and carts loaded with tobacco and cotton and increasingly with grain and cattle filled the streets leading to the river. One typical account reports a line of drays half a mile long, each dray with a hogshead of tobacco, proceeding to the *Ellen Kirkman*.[4] Each steamer had as agents or owners one of the firms of commission merchants in town. Celebrity captains, collisions in fog, deliberate and dangerous races, and disastrous fires made steamboating the most glamorous aspect of the staple trade.[5] But just up from the landing, lining the bluffs, the rows of warehouses began, and a few blocks beyond were the impressive new bank buildings of the thirties.[6]

For almost six years, from 1827 to 1832, Nashville had managed with only Yeatman-Woods and the branch bank of the BUS. Jackson's threatened veto of the BUS forced the business community to move quickly. Within a few months it had obtained not only the charter of the Union Bank but also a subscription for one-sixth of its stock from the state of Tennessee. In the same year the Planters' Bank of Tennessee was chartered.[7] On the boards of both banks sat Nashville's capitalists: commission merchants and wholesale dealers, commercial lawyers, a large number of retired merchants, and, very rarely, a master mechanic.[8]

The new bank boards had their work cut out for them as they dealt with the panic of 1837, which became a depression that lasted well into 1842. This time, however, the banks were able to maintain themselves, once again making use of the suspension of specie payments.[9] Through the bankruptcies of commission houses and the forced sales of steamboats, the banks held. In fact, they may have been less than happy to welcome the Bank of the State of Tennessee, which was chartered by the legislature in 1838 as one response to the crisis. This bank was wholly state owned and tied by its charter to the creation of a fund for internal improvements and public education. Its greatest support came from eastern and western Tennessee. Middle Tennessee had its own program of internal improvements under way; moreover, Nashville banks undoubtedly resented the competition. The board of the new bank must have quieted fears, however, for it was in many ways a duplicate of the boards of the older banks, and the new bank led the others in high rates for the discounting of commercial paper during the hard times.[10] Davidson County's representative had voted against the state bank's incorporation.[11] Nevertheless, the principal bank of the state system was established in Nashville, an acknowledgment of the city's financial and commercial primacy within the state.

The banking business traditionally had to do with the financing and shipment of cotton and tobacco, but by the late thirties Nashville was importing hardware, dry goods, and groceries in quantities that also required substantial bank financing. John Bass, president of the Union Bank, tried anxiously to arrange loans in 1837 so as to prevent commission merchants and planters dealing in the southern market from monopolizing the Union Bank's drafts to the disadvan-

tage of dry-goods merchants dealing in the northern markets. Complaints that the banks were playing favorites were especially loud in the panic years.[12] The panic may have intensified the development of specialization among Nashville's merchants. For example, one firm, eager to attract hostile farmers, advertised during the depression that "we have no interest in Steamboats, [nor are we] connected with the owners of steamboats, nor do we deal in produce on our own account."[13]

If the steamers enabled Nashville to import goods cheaply, a complete system of turnpikes leading out of Nashville enabled distribution deeper into the countryside. Railroads had been dismissed as "speculations," and in 1834 there was just one macadamized road, leading from Nashville to Franklin, and even that had not been macadamized straight through to Broad Street, so entry to and exit from it was "almost impossible for wagons and carriages during the winter season."[14] But in the next few years turnpike construction absorbed energy and capital. The liberal aid offered by the state after 1836 undoubtedly provided added stimulus. In 1836 the state was authorized to subscribe for one-third and in 1838 for half of the stock of incorporated turnpike companies, and in some cases funds for not only internal improvement but also the common schools of Middle Tennessee counties were used to subsidize the roads. Building right through the depression, entrepreneurs had completed five roads by 1841, and by 1846 about 410 miles of road, with Nashville as their hub, had been completed.[15]

The same merchants who invested in banks and turnpikes sat on the boards of insurance companies. By the mid-fifties at least five companies were offering insurance coverage of all kinds, including insurance on slaves.[16] Investments in turnpikes and banks and insurance companies were supplements rather than alternatives to investments in commercial ventures. Although often profitable in themselves, they also added to the resources available for the staple and wholesale markets. Indeed, when railroads finally did come to Nashville, their immediate impact was to enhance Nashville's mercantile position.

Nashville, like most cities, grew in fits and starts. Only after the economic doldrums of the early forties had passed did the city begin to develop its monuments. When Nashville was chosen as the permanent state capital, a committee of prominent businessmen worked with the Philadelphia architect William Strickland to turn Cedar Knob Hill into Capitol Hill, with its grand marble wedding cake of a state hall. Strickland also designed an impresive new Presbyterian church building.[17] Elaborate private mansions and neat workingmen's cottages were also going up, but there were whole areas of the city that Miss Jane Thomas would not have recognized, for

Nashville's population, which more than doubled between 1840 and 1860, filled in the alleys of the Bottom and of Smokey Row.

Wilkins Tannehill was undoubtedly indulging in a bit of nostalgia when in 1845 he drew this picture of an earlier Nashville: "The manners of the people were then somewhat different; being more upon an equality in point of wealth, families mixed more freely together; there was then no 'fashionable clique', that looked down upon those of humble fortune. When ladies visited each other, it was in proper person, not by a servant leaving a card. . . . Talbot's ball rooms, about 20 by 40 feet, were large enough to accommodate all who delighted to 'trip it on the light fantastic toe.' "[18] But Tannehill's nostalgia aside, real changes had taken place in Nashville; if public and private had once seemed identical, now some achieved privacy by deliberate withdrawal from the public. As if to underscore Tannehill's point, a report on "the People's Ball," held in the sixth ward a few years later, noted that "there were none of the aristocracy or upper tendon [sic] there, nor any of that soulless, double refined, hearth chilling etiquette. . . . but enough of good manners."[19]

Nashville had never been an egalitarian society. Throughout the antebellum period only a minority of Nashvillians owned either slaves or real estate, the two most common items on the tax collector's schedule. From 1820 to 1850, 69 to 78 percent of household heads claimed no taxable property.[20] The "fat fifties" combined with the more complete reporting of the census taken in 1860 produced a different showing; an extraordinary 55 percent of household heads reporting property ownership demonstrated the reality of a prosperous decade.[21] If indeed some Nashvillians in this last decade before the war insisted upon the viability of a success ladder, these figures support their case. Access to the ladder had been widened.

Nevertheless, the concentration of wealth at the top of the ladder was substantial and resembled the situation in most cities, new and old, northern and western, in antebellum America.[22] Fourteen percent of taxpayers controlled 50 percent of real-estate holdings in Nashville in 1839, 14 percent controlled 58 percent of all taxable property in 1847.[23] The 1850 census confirms this picture; 11 percent of the household heads reporting real estate controlled 46 percent of the total value of real estate reported. Nine percent of household heads reporting real or personal property in 1860 controlled 70 percent of the total value of the assets reported. In the same year 33 percent of property-holding household heads claimed less than 1 percent of the total wealth reported.[24] In addition, the range of wealth had changed markedly by the fifties. If in 1839 and 1847 the top 14 percent had included those with property valued at $10,000 or more, by 1860 those at the top claimed property worth $50,000 or more. Although more people held some property in 1860, by that date the top of the success ladder seemed farther away as one looked up from the bottom.

An upper-class life-style had long been building in Nashville; wealth brought with it education, private clubs, formal manners, and leisure. Young gentlemen, accompanied by free black servants, took grand tours of Europe and of northern cities. Whole families habitually deserted the town for "watering places and summer resorts." Gentlemen took tea on a regular schedule at the homes of the great ladies of Nashville society. They lobbied the city fathers to gain improvements for the University of Nashville, one center of their social activities. They were concerned to build a proper theater, one suitable for Jenny Lind or Ole Bull.[25] As the city center grew more crowded, they began to build along the turnpikes elaborate homes that no longer aped town houses but were suited to more spacious lots.[26] In the fifties they moved to the fifth ward, "now decidedly the most beautiful and agreeable part of the city for private residences." The children of merchants, bankers, and lawyers crossed easily from one to another of the back gardens three or four blocks away from the public square. Their homes always occupied the high ground of the plateau, the center of the city, raised above the gullies, gulches, and bottoms.[27] As every foot of real estate in the city became more and more valuable, prosperous merchants and professionals and their wives organized a horticultural society to make a garden "for the use of the members." The public park and promenade sometimes advocated in the newspapers did not materialize.[28] Nashville's men and women of means carved out a living space that seemed farther and farther apart from the rest of the city.

Nevertheless, as businessmen Nashville's capitalists were all too familiar with the teeming waterfront and with the line of storehouses leading from the landing to the public square which by the mid-fifties were being supplemented by newer establishments along College and Market streets.[29] Of the sixty-four household heads who claimed $100,000 or more in assets in 1860, only three might be labeled "industrialists": Vernon K. Stevenson of the Nashville and Chattanooga Railroad, John W. Walker, who had turned from commerce to iron manufacturing in the past decade, and W. S. Whiteman, who owned a paper mill. There were nineteen merchants, four bankers, and at least seven retired merchants or bankers in this group. Retired merchants now often listed themselves as planters or farmers, suggesting more traditional priorities in their investments as well as in their perceptions of themselves.[30]

Continuity was maintained also in terms of the individuals and families whose names appear and reappear as among the wealthiest Nashvillians in the antebellum decades.[31] Frontier land speculation and early success in the mercantile sector laid the basis for the continued success of Nichols, Woodses, Kirkmans, Fosters, Basses, McGavocks, Ellistons, Erwins, Hills. Even the unprecedented prosperity of the fifties did not swamp that core of wealthy families who made up by now a traditional establishment. More than half of these richest Nashvillians came from or married into the old merchant-banker-lawyer elite. It had always been a flexible elite, open to capital and talent. Adam G. Adams, a young Irish immigrant who came to Nashville in 1839, is a clear example. Adams arrived with a well-stocked trunk—nineteen new shirts, fourteen pairs of socks, four silk handkerchiefs, a pair of gloves, and two Bibles—and perhaps with a bit of capital. Six years later he married Susan Porterfield of an old mercantile and banking family; in 1850 Adams was a partner of the Eakin wholesale dry-goods firm that had taken him on as a clerk; he was one of the founders of the Second Presbyterian Church; by 1860 he was an independent merchant worth $105,000 and lived in the fifth ward.[32]

In a sense, even the old rich were nouveaux riches in the fifties, when the boom in property was unprecedented and economic opportunity seemed unlimited. In 1839 the richest man in town claimed $63,000 in real estate; by 1860 Nashville had at least one millionaire and many runners-up.[33] By and large these richest Nashvillians were in their prime years; only eleven were over sixty. New or old in Nashville, they were almost all southern-born; only five had been European immigrants.

A second group of Nashville's wealthy, sixty-eight household heads claiming from $50,000 to $100,000, were slightly younger on average, contained a few more who were born in the North, and tended to confirm the occupational patterns of the rich: merchants, bankers, professionals. Most of these men met in the board rooms of banks, insurance companies, and, increasingly, railroad companies. A complex web of marriage and kinship ties supplemented their social and business relationships and connected them as well with the planter families of the surrounding counties. They were, of course, also connected with families of lesser fortunes within the city. The sons of less prosperous lawyers, doctors, ministers, and merchants looked to them when they sought places in stores, in warehouses, in telegraph offices, and on steamboats, the routes to business success.[34]

Dividing the population into categories based on assets reported to the census taker is, of course, arbitrary and misleading in terms of contemporaries' perceptions of social status. James Thomas, a black barber, reminds us in his memoirs that consciousness of status was usually reinforced by the older, more stable criteria of "birth and education." The "old Virginia set" could not fall too far or the brick maker climb too high.[35] A tippling-house keeper and three slave dealers were among the richest men in the city, but their occupations undoubtedly were too disreputable to admit them to Nashville's "upper tendon." Nor would the eleven master mechanics in Nashville's second group of wealthiest citizens be found in Nashville's inner circle, though three of them now lived in the fifth ward.

Mechanics controlled little capital, and much of what they did have was tied up in tools and materials. As late as 1829 only fifteen mechanics in the town were freeholders. Ironically, the steamboats that had made Nashville prosperous and had attracted craftsmen also brought stiff competition to many like the local hatters and cabinetmakers. But mechanics did provide the weight of numbers and something of their own life-style. Mechanics, from masters to apprentices, worked with their hands. Like the early merchants, master mechanics lived above or next door to their shops, but, unlike the successful merchants, successful mechanics tended to remain close to their workshops. Samuel Stout, mayor of Nashville, made his home on Water Street. His wife, Catherine Stout, sister of Wilkins Tannehill, oversaw the board and lodging of Stout's apprentices and journeymen. Although two of their sons became physicians, a third took over the coachmaking business. Mechanics tended to choose marriage partners from among their own ranks, but there were enough exceptions, especially in the frontier decades, to help validate the notion of republican equality. Oliver Johnson's family provides a case in point. His five daughters married each in her turn a tinner, a tailor, a cooper, a farmer, and a Methodist minister. But Anthony Johnson, one of his sons, who began his career in the tinner's shop of his brother-in-law, moved into a successful mercantile career after his marriage to a young woman of some property.[36]

Few of the mechanics participated in corporation politics until the late twenties. Only the tailor Smiley took a leading role in church affairs, though young Isaac Paul and Henry Ament, barely out of their apprenticeships as carpenter and smith, were to help with the Sunday schools of the twenties. Few mechanics were among the directors of the insurance companies or the banks, among the sponsors of turnpikes, or among the vice-presidents of Whig or Democratic conventions. However, the limited economic development of the thirties tended to confirm the position of the few mechanics who had managed to accumulate property. They were sought out as ward leaders and aldermen. Stout, Austin, and Cartmell appeared on the vigilance committee of 1835; master mechanics might well be capable of directing the mob.

But better times were coming for the mechanics. Of the 372 Nashvillians recorded as household heads in both the 1850 and 1860 censuses, 37 percent who had claimed no property in 1850 did report some by 1860, and another 32 percent reported a gain in assets by 1860. Moreover, of the 123 mechanics within this group, only 17 percent claimed no property in 1860, while 44 percent claimed between $50 and $4,999—more than half $1,000 or more—and 38 percent claimed property worth between $5,000 and $300,000.[37]

Two mechanics claimed more than $100,000, and both were immigrants. Michael Burns, born in County Sligo, Ireland, in 1813, came to Nashville as a saddler in 1836, married the daughter of another Irish immigrant, queensware merchant William Gilliam, and in the fifties became a director of the Nashville and Northwestern Railroad, of the Bank of Tennessee, and the Union Bank.[38] William Stockell had come from England as a young boy. His father superintended the construction of buildings at the University of Nashville in the early forties. William became a "master plasterer" in time to work on the new state capitol, the Masonic hall, the Maxwell House, and the Tennessee Hospital for the Insane. The building boom and his own talent, especially with interior stucco work, made him one of Nashville's richest men in 1860. Stockell was also the driving force of Nashville's fire department, one of the bases from which he built a career in city government, cut short by the Whigs' swing into the Know-Nothing camp.[39]

Many other self-made men were among the mechanics. From 1850 to 1860, plasterer Hurt's real estate holdings went from $12,000 to more than $70,000, printer Bang's from $8,000 to

$45,500, carpenter Spain's from $10,000 to $40,000, and coachmaker Monohan's from $6,400 to $16,300 in addition to the $52,500 he claimed in personal estate. Saddler Morrow claimed no property in 1850 but almost $20,000 in real estate and $40,000 in personal estate in 1860. Tinner B. S. Weller, who had been one of the very few mechanics to subscribe immediately to the horticultural society—his wife was an ardent gardener—saw his real-estate holdings appreciate less grandly, from $20,000 to $25,000 over the decade. In 1850 he also had $25,000 invested in his tinworks which employed seventeen hands. His had been a slow climb to the status of substantial property holder. He had not appeared on the list of lot holders of 1829, but in the next year, at age thirty-one, he was listed as a householder; four apprentices and journeymen lived in his home. In 1839 he was taxed on a single lot; by 1847 he had acquired a second lot and a slave. In 1850 his household included not only his eight children but five young tinners, a clerk, and a seventh boarder. It is a wonder that Syntha Weller had time for gardening, although the five slaves the family now owned undoubtedly helped. The life-style of the master mechanics tied them closely to the working world. They literally lived among their workers, and their wives continued to take in boarders. Their newfound prosperity, however, made them likely candidates for corporation officeholders, spokesmen for political parties, or recruits for the temperance society, positions that were proof of the viability of the success ladder.

The coming of the railroad in the fifties stimulated industrial activity, and a few master mechanics became factory owners. Mason Vannoy and W. J. Turbeville, carpenters and house joiners in the forties, had become proprietors of the Nashville Car Manufactory by 1860, when they employed thirty hands in their factory close by the Nashville and Chattanooga Railroad yards. By 1860 the machine shop of Noble Ellis had become a boiler yard employing sixty workers, and four shops producing machinery and steam engines together employed 442 workers, twice as many as any other manufacturing enterprise reported by the census. Most factories, however, still remained close to the old model of the craftsman's shop—relatively small and dependent on skilled workers.[40]

The bulk of the mechanics did not make it into the ranks of substantial property holders but blended into the body of "respectable workingmen." Some new workers were in demand by the fifties: pipe fitters who found employment at the new gasworks, plumbers serving the extended waterworks, machinists and founders employed by the railroads. The overwhelming concern of these men was steady work. John M. Seabury, for example, had been in Nashville at least as early as 1830. He worked for twenty years as a metalsmith and plumber, raised a family, rented a shop and an apartment above it, took in boarders. In 1849 he served as corporation alderman. Two years later, when a block of buildings owned by Major Allison burned to the ground, Seabury's family lost its " 'little all,' " perhaps three thousand dollars in tools, furniture, and clothes.[41] He recouped his losses as superintendent of the city's waterworks and by 1855 had moved his family across the river to Edgefield. Respectable working people tried to move out to the suburbs. Attractive rentals within the corporation were described as too expensive for most workers and the rest so shabby that the "respectable" would not have them.[42]

The village of South Nashville, incorporated into the city as the seventh and eighth wards in 1854, became one magnet for Nashville's stable working class. By 1860 these wards claimed the highest percentages of household heads with property, although, by and large, these were relatively small amounts of property. Sixty-five percent of household heads in the seventh and 74 percent in the eighth wards claimed property. Of the 170 who claimed some property in the seventh ward, 46 percent claimed less than $1,000, and 28 percent less than $200; in the eighth ward 331 of 451 household heads claimed property, 40 percent less than $1,000 and 28 percent less than $200. Here, then, were clustered the hopeful, a rung up on the success ladder and eager for the climb. Before its annexation to the city, South Nashville had pioneered a public school that reformers held up as a model for Nashville to follow.

It is, of course, not surprising that Nashville workers did not form unions. The printers, the aristocrats among craftsmen, and the tailors alone had a tradition of organization. As early as 1832 there was a typographical society in Nashville, acting largely as a benevolent association to help the indigent of the trade, to mourn the death of members, and to celebrate Benjamin Franklin's birthday. The society tended to fade away and then be "resuscitated." In 1847 it claimed twelve members. Twice the printers did call strikes, in both cases over the firing of journeymen. In 1849 the society called for a walkout of employees, and strikers attacked a scab with brickbats. We have no record of the settlement of either strike, but the society maintained itself and in 1855 affiliated with the National Typographical Union, becoming Typographical Union No. 20.[43] Journeymen tailors, too, had some tradition of association and could occasionally affect the price of their work. In 1833 a group of journeymen opened shop on their own account because their masters had reduced their wages but not prices, and in 1840 the "Society of Journeymen Tailors" voluntarily reduced their own wages so that prices could be lowered during this depression year. Their sacrifice was applauded by the editor of the *Republican Banner,* who urged all Nashvillians to "buy at home."[44]

At least once a strike was called in the South Nashville Furniture Manufacturing Company, one of the new steam-driven plants of the fifties, because of the "behavior of the foreman" and the "irregularity of the prices," but this was quickly met by a counternotice of workingmen organized in support of the foreman and the company, and indeed the "president" of the strike organization was still at work for the firm six years later.[45] Whatever their grievances, workers in any given shop were few, and their bosses were close at hand; foremen were important figures whose names appeared in the city directory. The anonymity that may have been essential for later industrial strikes was clearly lacking.[46] Only the highly skilled workers could earn as much as two dollars a day, but even at less than that the workers in these new establishments were men who had a trade and steady work and could afford the rents of the tenements being built in the fifties close to the railroad yards and the machine shops. Workers who were family men helped keep the fourth ward the most heavily populated in the city. Young single men competed with steamboat engineers and the ubiquitous clerks for living space in the stores and offices off the alleys of the first three wards.

The possibility of work drew newcomers without the skills of "respectable workingmen," laborers hired by the day or the job. Working along with or in lieu of slave labor at the boat landings or on construction sites, the laboring poor were a group that Nashville took little cognizance of until late in the antebellum years. In 1837 a petition, trying to make a political point, it is true, insisted that Nashville was peculiarly free of the pressures of transients, and as late as 1848 another report had it that Nashville was "free from poor immigrants its situation being out of the usual track of emigration. There are but very few poor. . . . The lower class are principally mechanics." When Nashvillians were not pointing with pride to growth figures, they were, paradoxically, praising the isolated position of the city as an "inland town" with "a settled population."[47]

However, transiency figures for Nashville do not vary greatly from those for other cities; throughout the antebellum decades 70 to 75 percent of household heads disappear from the census records within a ten-year span.[48] An increasingly large number of these "transients" would have been white day laborers. In the thirties gangs of laborers were imported to work on the river and on the turnpikes.[49] Building construction in the late forties and the railroads of the fifties meant a fairly constant demand for labor. Contemporaries recognized a pattern of in-migration in the spring and summer, when construction was at a peak, and out-migration in winter, when work was scarce and the price of coal and wood soared.

Despite this pattern of moving on, so common among the poor all over the country, laboring-class districts grew larger. In 1845 the sixth ward was the second most heavily populated in the city.[50] Here, in the Broad Street Bottom, regularly flooded by the streams that ran into the Cumberland and Nashville's most undesirable location, population grew more dense. Though its residents might have to "camp out" in the bitter months of winter and early spring, the sixth ward was still second only to the fourth ward in population in 1860. This ward, which had the smallest number of substantial property holders and the highest concentration of Irish immigrants and which was the most overcrowded in terms of available housing, was home to the bulk of Nashville's suffering poor on whose behalf soirees and entertainments were held uptown—often to little result— and whose largely unsuccessful Democratic politics set them as much apart as their poverty or their foreign accents.

The presence of immigrants, and most especially of poor immigrants, marked a clear social division in the town. Early in Nashville's history, foreign-born settlers had easily made their way into the leadership of the community. If a nativist voice had been raised, it had turned its abuse against Irish bank directors and had been quickly stilled. By the thirties both a Saint Andrew's Society and a Hibernian Society held annual celebrations that toasted the memory of the Scottish and Irish founding fathers of Nashville and that were well attended by native community leaders. These were high-status associations, as the list of the toastmakers and the elaborate entertainment provided demonstrate. Indeed, throughout the antebellum period Nashville's cultural elite could and did welcome into their society foreign-born professionals, academics, and successful or promising businessmen, and they could with impunity take an interest in the growing Catholic institutions of Nashville.

However, the political crisis of the thirties stimulated a new, negative image of the immigrant. An article in the *Republican* referring to the "parrish sweepings" of England and Ireland elicited a conciliatory response from the editor of the *Banner and Whig* and a vituperative one from the editor of the Democratic *Union*. In the *Union* "Erinensis" charged that the underlying issue was Irish support for Jackson and Van Buren rather than for Judge White.[51] Long before Nashville's immigrant population was statistically significant, a nativist attitude was building directly out of partisan politics. The Whig party saw immigrants as Democratic recruits. In 1841 the editor of the *Banner* reported from Washington on the "locofoco" policies of Senator Thomas Benton, a Democrat, which were encouraging the "canaille" of Europe to emigrate and take up cheap American land. The editor of the *Whig* linked the "abuses" of the naturalization laws, foreign votes, and the defeat of Clay in 1844. The *Union* was accused of sympathy for popish domination. Tannehill's *Orthopolitan* favored more stringent naturalization laws and favorably associated the Native American program with the elimination of "the pauper element."[52]

Nashville's religious press, which was by the mid-forties a considerable establishment, became almost rabid on the subject of Catholic subversion. Protestantism alone was equated with true Christianity. The arrival of the Sisters of Charity, a Catholic Order, in Nashville especially triggered the wrath of the Methodist paper. Although the *Whig*'s editor protested that he would not enter the controversy with regard to Roman Catholic tolerance or intolerance, he reprinted articles tracing the Catholic church's intolerance all the way back to the fourth century—with the disclaimer that "we cheerfully admit that it does not apply to the Catholics of the present day, and particularly to those of our own country."[53]

Compared to the frenzied rhetoric of the fifties, however, the zenophobia of the forties was subdued. The increase in the numbers of immigrants and the demise of the national Whig party, which left the local party groping for a new formulation, operated to hammer home ugly stereotypes. Know-Nothings denounced "'drunken, red mouthed Irishmen, louzy Germans'" and gathered in front of Saint Mary's on Christmas Eve in 1855, forcing Bishop Miles to cancel services.[54] Nashville was no Cincinnati; its foreign-born population never remotely threatened to dominate the institutions of the city. Yet immigrants were more and more visible and an easy target, for on them could be projected some of the phenomena made visible by urban growth: poverty, drunkenness, crime, and diversity itself.

In 1850 the total foreign-born population amounted to 810 men, women, and children: Frenchmen, Italians, Poles, a lone Swede, but mostly Germans and Irishmen, in all 10 percent of the city's free population. Ten years later the foreign-born population had tripled and accounted for 20 percent of the free population.[55]

In 1850 the foreign-born population was typically young and male; men from twenty-one to forty-five made up more than half of all male immigrants and more than the female immigrants of all ages. These were young men looking for work and not always finding it. The persistence rate from 1850 to 1860 among the foreign-born was 16 percent—substantially below that of the population as a whole. Very few claimed real estate in 1850, and the handful who claimed substantial amounts tended to be products of the "old" immigration.[56] Thus their alien character was compounded.

Nevertheless, families were settling in and providing the impetus for the ethnic and religious institution building that startled, confused, and occasionally appalled traditional Nashville. By 1860 the male-female ratio among immigrants was closer to the norm for the entire population.[57] The "five families and eight young men" who made up Nashville's Jewish population in 1850 had grown by 1860 to 105 households containing perhaps 325 people in all.[58] Immigrants from all over Europe (a high proportion of them single men), Nashville's Jewish newcomers exemplified the melting pot working within the salad bowl. The English-born Powers brothers all married in America; two took New York brides and one a Kentucky-born wife. The eldest married in New York, settled for a time in Ohio, where his four eldest children were born, and then moved on to Tennessee. Alexander Iser, Russian-born, and referred to by a police court reporter as "a Hebrew slayer of cattle," married a German woman who bore him a child in Tennessee. Sinai Nathan's German-speaking household included boarders from Prussia, Hesse, Baden, and Poland. Mayer Lasky, who kept a kosher boardinghouse, was Polish, but his boarders came from Prussia and Hesse.[59] Most Jews were shopkeepers, retail merchants, and peddlers; only three called themselves laborers. By 1860 about half of Jewish household heads had acquired some property, although only three claimed more than ten thousand dollars in assets, and these three, clothing and dry-goods merchants, lived in the center city wards in homes adjoining or above their shops.[60] In Nashville Jews from these different backgrounds began to constitute a community; they supported a rabbi, a kosher butcher, and a kosher boardinghouse.

The burial association, typically one of the first organizations of immigrants, was in operation in 1851; the first Jewish congregation began to meet in a rented room on Market Street two years later. At the end of the decade the Young Men's Benevolent Society was established. Half of the Jewish household heads had emigrated from the German states, and some of them would have been members also of the turnverein, the Yaegers, and the German Relief Society, organized as early as 1846. Each religious and ethnic group turned to voluntary associations to protect its members and to preserve its identity. Congregations, benevolent societies, privately sponsored orphanages, and fraternities were typically American institutions, yet they also worked to maintain cultural uniqueness.

Nashville newspapers began noting the closing of Jewish stores for the Jewish new year observances, and the police court reporter varied his accounts of brawling Irishmen with vignettes of quarreling "Hebrews" whose concern about the validity of oaths taken with uncovered heads seemed bizarre.[61] The native population of the city began to build its stereotypes.

The Germans who came to Nashville brought with them more capital and skills than the Irish who were fleeing the famines of the forties. Skilled workers and craftsmen opened shops in and around the square. By 1860 Germans were widely distributed in neighborhoods throughout the city.[62] By 1854 a German Methodist Episcopal church had been organized in the center of the city, and in 1859 a Lutheran church was established. However, like other respectable workingmen, the Germans, too, were looking to the suburbs. Many began to buy or rent in the eighth ward and in North Nashville, outside the city limits, even when their businesses were conducted off the square.

In North Nashville they built a community closely paralleling the Good Village of Whig rhetoric but one that was specifically German. By the mid-fifties a second Catholic church, the Church of the Assumption, was being constructed in North Nashville to accommodate a German congregation. Shepherded by a Flemish priest, Ivo Schacht, and supported by successful businessmen like the grocer, J. H. Buddekke, and the confectioner, G. H. Wessel, the German Catholic community insisted on its ethnic church. The actual building was undertaken by workingmen who gave their time and were superintended by a German master mason, Jacob Geiger. The bulk of the shopkeepers and master mechanics as well as most of the doctors and clergymen among the entire immigrant group were Germans. In what would later be called Germantown, they lived and worked in solid brick or neat frame homes, organized benevolent associations and the turnverein, and supported a German-language newspaper.[63] But the nativist stereotype operated here too. Efforts to incorporate North Nashville as the ninth ward of the city were unsuccessful until after the Civil War.[64]

As a group the foreign-born were heavily weighted to the bottom of the economic and occupational scale. Immigrants made up 51 percent of unskilled free workmen and 33 percent of skilled free workmen in Nashville in 1860; ethnic and religious differences as well as skill levels kept them from cohering as a working class, while mutual antipathy with blacks and hostility from native workers ensured the fragmentation of any notion of working-class solidarity.[65] In addition foreign-born women were unusual among Nashville women in listing occupations—of the 225 women who listed occupations, 138 were servants. The 461 foreign-born individuals who reported some assets (ranging from $50 to $342,000) constituted approximately one-sixth of all immigrants.[66]

Immigrants were poor, the Irish were the poorest among them, and more than half of the immigrant population was Irish: 437 of 480 immigrant laborers were Irish; 124 of 138 female servants were Irish women. In addition, the Irish were overwhelmingly Catholic. All the elements of the nativist stereotype were focused here. The police reporter of the *Republican Banner* emphasized the Irish nationality of offenders charged with drunkenness and disorderly conduct. By 1860 Irish mechanics and craftsmen, merchants, bookkeepers, and clerks were at work in Nashville. Many had accumulated a bit of property.[67] But just as proper Nashvillians tended to equate free blacks and Smokey Row, they confounded Irishmen and the sixth ward, where more than 30 percent of all the Irish were housed and where the per-capita holdings of Irishmen were dramatically below those of Irishmen in other wards of the city.[68] Here, where the newest and poorest immigrants were crowded together and doubling up in backyard shanties, the alien "other" was identified.

Even their church was not located among these poorest Irishmen, although it was close to another slum at the base of Capitol Hill. In 1837 Nashville had been made a diocese of the Catholic church, and in the following year the Right Reverend Richard Pius Miles had been consecrated as bishop of Nashville. Miles carried through the building of the Church of the Seven Dolors, Saint Mary's Cathedral, in 1847. But Saint Mary's, for all its handsome architecture, and Bishop Miles, for all his urbanity, were suspect. The building of the cathedral was delayed by the hostility of Nashvillians who objected to a Catholic church so close to the state capitol, who evidently were able to frustrate Bishop Miles's expectations of bringing a Jesuit school to Nashville, and who saw in another Catholic institution, the Sisters of Charity, an underhanded Catholic plot.[69]

Once built, the cathedral remained for the Protestant religious press a symbol of the enemy within the gates, and for many Catholic Nashvillians it was perhaps too imposing, too cosmopolitan. Although and perhaps because the Christmas Eve mass became the occasion for the gathering of music lovers of all denominations and the cathedral became the venue for lectures on Christianity and Catholic doctrine often aimed at more than Catholic audiences, German communicants, as we have seen, sought their own church and German-speaking priests. Much of the cost of Saint Mary's was borne by subscriptions in Philadelphia. The Sisters of Charity organized a school, a hospital, an orphanage; the Catholic Ladies' Benevolent Association supported their efforts. Institutions were being built, but the huge gap between those on their way up the ladder, the respectable workingmen, and the newest and poorest immigrants remained.

One does not want to exaggerate the ethnic and religious diversity of Nashville's population or the significance of its social and economic divisions. The divisions were no greater than in most American cities, and the diversity was considerably less than in most northern cities.[70] But these did contribute to Nashville's urban character and to the need to achieve some semblance of political consensus out of the urban mix. Democrats insisted on the dangers of aristocratic and banker control of government, inherited and began to champion the "new" Americans, and by the late forties began to emphasize southern nationalism and the dangers to slavery posed by northern aggression. Whigs beat the drum for social mobility and economic development, self-improvement and social morality, native rectitude and foreigners' degeneracy, and they put together a solid coalition of Nashville voters. The urge to organize the city, to hold it together under its traditional leadership, was one of the spurs to the development of the party system within the city. Nashville was no mere county seat. On the other hand, Nashville did share with its rural neighbors the decisive division between black and white.

Growing Apart: Black Nashville

CHAPTER 7

SLAVERY was a momentous issue in antebellum America. It shaped the social structure of the South in the cities as well as in the countryside. It was ultimately the crucial issue in the dissolution of the political system and the Union. But in the years before 1860, black people in the South remained without any power to effect political outcomes. Their options were rigidly limited. One was to build their own institutions within the bounds of slavery and racism, yet the growth of such institutions did not ease but often seemed to exacerbate the fears of the white community. Not even the bottom rung of the success ladder was accessible to black people. Neither white nor black people participated in an open, public debate on slavery, but black people were excluded totally from the political system, which in effect carried on the covert debate.

Black people were everywhere, in homes, streets, shops, and factories, in the theater, in the churches, at the cockfights, and at political rallies, but they were nevertheless a people apart. Blacks, whether slave or free, had to expend enormous energy simply in building and preserving families and surrogate families. However, from the thirties on they were also able to create increasingly autonomous churches and Sunday schools and even a few precariously maintained secular schools. The black church was a major achievement of antebellum urban history, was, in historian Leonard Curry's phrase, "both the cement and the symbol of the black community."[1] Nashville's black community could not support the literary and fraternal orders that flourished openly in northern cities and among free blacks in southern cities like New Orleans and Charleston.[2] But free blacks, semifree blacks, and slaves did fashion legally or, more often, sub rosa the support groups that characterized urban life. Black churches were the most visible and the least vulnerable institution of the black community in Nashville.

Separate churches did not mean total independence in religion or in other spheres of life. Blacks remained dependent on whites for livelihood and physical security; they made up a working class with a large component of women and children workers and without independent leverage. Used and abused, they were sometimes coddled as individuals but always subject to the scapegoat's role. The presence of black people periodically became the focus of the fears of the white population not because real threats were initiated by slaves or free blacks but rather because of the great strains on white political institutions.

Between 1820 and 1840 black people made up over a third of total population, but in the forties the rates of increases for white and black sectors diverged significantly. The influx of European immigrants paralleled a dramatic decline in the proportion of black people in the city's population. The white population grew by 85 percent; the black population remained virtually static, and indeed the number of slaves reported in 1850 was smaller than in 1840. As a result, black people made up only 25 percent of the population of the city in 1850 and only 23 percent by 1860, although black population had increased by 55 percent over this decade. Nashville nevertheless contained the largest number of black people in any Tennessee city. Memphis, which closely rivaled Nashville in numbers of blacks, had seen a much more precipitous decline in the percentage of blacks in the city, from 28 percent to 17 percent in the last decade before the Civil War.[3]

In 1860 there were 3,226 slaves and 719 free blacks living in Nashville; free blacks made up 18 percent of the total black population, and a great many of the slaves were hired rather than owned by their employers. In the first through the fourth wards, the com-

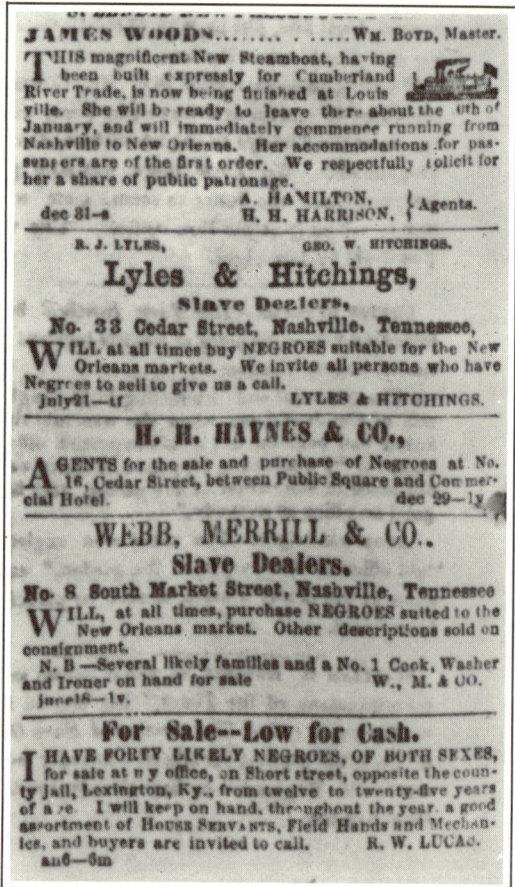

mercial center of the city, almost 500 slaves, 28 percent of the slaves there, were reported as hired. Black people were not as securely attached to specific white households. Moreover, the distribution of slaves among masters and employers was significantly changed. Fifty-nine percent of all households in 1840 had contained slaves. In 1860 at most only 37 percent contained slaves, and there was a wide divergence in slaveholding patterns among the wards: in the silk-stocking fifth ward, 78 percent of households claimed slaves; in the first through the fourth wards, 45 percent; in the sixth, seventh, and eighth wards, 24, 26, and 14 percent, respectively.[4] The distribution of slaves is one indication of the disparity in wealth among white Nashvillians, but it suggests as well a greater isolation of blacks from a large part of the white community, one condition of the pervasive hostility directed toward blacks and especially the vulnerable free blacks in this period and also one condition of greater community among blacks.

The black community that was emerging within the larger Nashville society was never entirely separate from white patrons and persecutors, employers and masters; it embraced slaves, free people of color, and the quasi free; it was characterized by its peculiar institutions, memories, and personalities. The New Year's Day hiring ground was, unhappily, one such institution, which was described by James P. Thomas, a free black barber: "Any number of people with their worldly goods in a bundle in hand for sale or hire. A woman sometimes with her children sometimes without.... It sometimes occurred that the man and wife would be near enough to see each other nightly, a little further would make it weekly, increase the distance the man may feel satisfied with monthly, six months; it was not uncommon if it were made indefinite, possibly never."[5]

The market house on New Year's Day represented the precariousness of even the most intimate of relationships, the family itself. We will probably never be able to provide a satisfactory statistical account of the numbers of black families that were able to maintain continuity under slavery.[6] The obstacles to family life, especially in the city, were formidable. In 1860, two-thirds of slaveholdings—that is, the slave property claimed by individual owners and employers—were made up exclusively of women, or of women and children, or of men, or of children. Most slaveholders, then, did not maintain nuclear families but instead bought or rented slaves according to the services they required—cooks, laundresses, coachmen, gardeners, brick makers, teamsters, laborers, and errand boys. There may have been an exception: some masters were willing to buy or to maintain the children of their female slaves. In 1850 and again in 1860 children made up more than a third of the slave population (37 and 36 percent, respectively). Slave children could prove a profitable investment. Thomas reported that "some men with small means would from a small beginning in the course of twenty years have several likely boys to hire out."[7] Profit and sentiment combined to ensure that one major type of slave family centered around the mother, grandmother, or "auntie."

Although black women outnumbered black men in every census tally from 1830 to 1860, the imbalance was not great, and it was physically easier in the city to contract marriages across slave owners' property lines.[8] The drive toward family life in the black community was strong even where husbands and wives could share housing only sporadically. Thus the market house on New Year's Day along with the whipping place behind the jail and the slave traders' pens were the sites of some of the bleakest experiences of black people and perhaps made even more intense their involvement with the African church.

Crucial to the maintenance of any kind of black community in the city were the legally free and the quasi free, who could pass on the memories of better times when blacks were pilots as well as stewards on the riverboats and when free blacks could vote in the days of the "old constitution."[9] In the thirties, however, fears about slavery and abolition were transferred onto free blacks, the most available target. The otherwise democratic state constitution of 1835 deliberately disfranchised free blacks. The following year the state legislature prohibited free blacks from keeping groceries or any other establishments that sold liquor. Nashville's ordinances followed suit, and the constable was ordered in 1837 to enforce the vagrancy laws against free persons of color and mulattoes and in the following year to check on all free persons of color to determine whether they were in compliance with the state laws of 1831, which made it a condition of emancipation that free people be removed from the state and which prohibited free persons of color from entering the state.[10]

Hostility toward free blacks and toward slaves who hired out their own time antedated the abolition movement, but as the movement gained strength in the North, the rage of southerners turned upon abolitionists and upon free blacks. Abolition itself became a forbidden subject. The editor of the *Banner*, who insisted that he himself would never hold slaves, refused to publish any letters on the subject of emancipation, and merchants, local as well as northern, publicly denied any suggestions of sympathy for abolition in their advertisements.[11] Amos Dresser, the Lane seminarian who was lashed in the public square for his alleged attempts to spread abolition propaganda, reported of one of his accusers that "he was under the influence of very highly excited feelings—his whole frame indicating agitation, even to trembling."[12] The murder of Guinea John, "an inoffensive negro . . . who had by the most unremitting industry just purchased his freedom by the payment of one thousand dollars," angered some law-abiding citizens, including the editor of the *Union*. But when the case was brought to court, the judge found first that there was no prosecutor, then that the jury did not appear, and then that the jurors, to avoid serving, made it clear that they had "formed an opinion after they were summoned, and before the cause and evidence was submitted to them." A jury was finally impaneled, but not before the exasperated judge had fined the first set of jurors and the sheriff, who "had failed to keep order in the court." The jury acquitted the murderer.[13] The only organization in Nashville that might have addressed slavery as a problem was the colonization society, but the Nashville Colonization Society, like its sister organizations throughout the country, seemed dedicated exclusively to removing free blacks from the United States.[14]

Still, city life permitted free blacks to create at least a measure of living and breathing space for themselves and for all black people. In part this meant physical space. Nashville more closely resembled northern rather than other southern cities in the degree of segregation of free black housing.[15] Almost three-fourths (72 percent) of free blacks lived in the second or fourth wards of the city, at most six or eight blocks from either the waterfront or the public square.

The second ward bordered the river; here lived 124 of the 719 free blacks, some of them on Smokey Row, the most notorious of the red-light districts. Of the ten white households that also housed free blacks, three were maintained by white prostitutes, one was a tippling house, and one was a family grocery, an establishment usually synonymous with a tavern. Prostitutes, drunkards, and brawlers—black and white—gave Smokey Row its unsavory reputation. Here as well as at the Bottom, back of the race track, could be found the "genuine sports." It may have been along Smokey Row that a free black barber, Solomon Porter, strutted in a blue coat that had "five dollar gold pieces instead of brass buttons" and in boots whose heels were silverplated.[16] But perhaps even more disturbing to the white community were the evidences of racial mores violated. Delphi Grainger, a black cook, rented space to three black workingmen and to three white railroad men. Ned Dunson, a black steamboat hand, and his family rented a room to a white keeper of a tippling house, a man of considerable property. Richard Fenn, a mulatto, lived with and was perhaps married to a white woman, Letha Fenn. Richard may have been the son of Robert Fenn, a white man who kept a tippling house and a widower whose household included two mulatto women.[17] The police court reporter made great sport of a black woman and a white woman fighting over a lover's picture and lock of hair. One of the most frequent "crimes" charged against free blacks, on the other hand, was that of entertaining slaves in their homes, and they were frequently accused of hiding and aiding runaway slaves.[18] Although individual white people respected individual free blacks, white society feared and distrusted the free black community. It was easiest simply to equate free blacks and Smokey Row and to insist on the exclusion of both from the respectable community.

Yet most free blacks were in fact working people, anxious to maintain families and accumulate a bit of property, eager to build churches and schools. More than half of the free black people in Nashville made their homes in the fourth ward, where large numbers of immigrants also found housing. Sixty-three percent of the free black adults there listed an occupation with the census taker. Perhaps the single greatest difference between black and non-Irish white households recorded by the census was that black women worked to earn their living. Indeed, if there were seven prostitutes and a madam in the fourth ward, there were also fifty-four laundresses, eight chambermaids, and six seamstresses among the free black women. Only twelve men called themselves simply "laborers." Most indicated a specific skill or trade; there were, for example, hackmen, stewards, barbers, cooks, shoemakers, blacksmiths, and stonemasons. Free blacks worked alongside slaves and white men on construction sites and in the brickyards and shoemakers' shops. Rewards for work were minimal: only sixty individuals among all free blacks in Nashville, at most 35 percent of black households as compared with 55 percent of all households, reported either real or personal property to the census taker in 1860, and the range in assets was narrow, from $200 to $1,500. The total wealth claimed by the black population, $162,850, was by far the lowest figure for any segment of the population. Only in the sixth ward did the holdings of free blacks surpass those reported by either German-born or Irish-born immigrants.[19]

These figures reveal neither decadence nor decay in the free black economic position but rather that black people were a peculiar working class; their economic record, no matter how positive, could not have won them respectability in the eyes of the white community. And yet free black people tended to remain in Nashville at a rate that resembled more closely the persistence record of the population as a whole rather than that of the new immigrants.[20] They made certain trades, especially service trades, peculiarly their own. Hacking and barbering were apparently the most lucrative and stable occupations among free black men, and hackmen and barbers occasionally employed white men. Of course, carriages, wagons, horses, and bathhouses could not be hidden easily from the tax collector; hackmen and barbers therefore tend to show up in the records as the more substantial property owners.[21] And hackmen like Peter Lowery and William Napier and barbers like Alonso Summer, who took the lead in the difficult struggle to create and maintain churches and schools, are evidence of a nucleus of black families pursuing the typical goals of the larger society, despite untypical obstacles.

Above all, free blacks maintained strong, supportive families. Despite the desirability of having white patrons, relatively few free blacks chose to live in white households: only five families, four of them headed by females, and fifteen individuals did so in 1850; seven families and forty-five individuals in 1860. Roughly a quarter of independent black households were made up of women and children. Black households were most often complex; earning the rent money meant doubling and tripling up. In 1850 only twenty-eight and in 1860 only twenty-four black households could be described as nuclear families where parents and children lived by themselves. Yet the family unit persisted despite the enormous pressures upon it. Fifty-five percent in 1850 and 45 percent in 1860 of free black households were extended families, including husbands and wives, parents and children, and adult siblings.[22] Like many white households, almost all black ones embraced "extra" boarders or dependents. In 1860 at least fourteen free blacks owned slaves, in most cases members of their families.

Sally Thomas was a slave who managed to maintain her family of three sons independent of a feckless master. One son acquired a new master and patron who took him to Alabama and ultimately freed him. A second escaped north to freedom. Sally's third son, James, named Judge John Catron as his father, but the liaison profited Sally little. She worked as a laundress and squirreled away her earnings in a tin hidden in the loft of her rented house. When her master made ominous noises she arranged through a lawyer, E. H. Foster, to purchase not herself but her son. Some neighbors thought her quixotic, but her first concern was her children. In time she bought her own freedom, but she made sure that James received what schooling was available despite the dollar-a-month charges. James was apprenticed to another quasi-free man, barber Frank Parrish, and in 1846 opened his own shop in his mother's house across the street from the post office. Here Sally Thomas's grandchildren were sent from Alabama so that they, too, might go to school.[23]

Peter Lowery had managed to save enough money by the time he was twenty-seven to buy his own freedom, a hack, and horses. The petition of merchant Samuel Seay to emancipate Lowery was accompanied by a long list of character witnesses that included Governor Carroll. Although this petition was granted, two years later, in 1839, Lowery was denied immunity from the law requiring that freed slaves leave the state, so Seay was vested with "the right to him." Nevertheless, Lowery behaved like a free man; his name appeared on the tax list in 1839, and he continued to accumulate real estate, carriages, horses, and slaves, including probably his mother, three brothers and two sisters. In 1860 he claimed an estate worth $18,000. He lived with his wife and five slaves and rented part of his house to a white machinist and his family. Lowery had by this time become a prominent figure in the Christian church, acknowledged as the "Colored Divine" in charge of the Disciples of Christ's black congregation. Samuel Lowery, his son by his first wife, a Cherokee, was legally free and at sixteen had found employment at nearby Franklin College, a Christian institution. There he received some instruction from Tolbert Fanning, head of the school. Samuel, too, served as a preacher for the Disciples from 1849 to 1857, when, like a number of other free blacks who may have done too well to please the white community, he found it prudent to move north for a few years.[24]

The Napier family started off with some educational and financial backing from William C. Napier's white father whose will provided both the injunction and the funds for them to leave Tennessee for a free state. But after some years Napier returned to Nashville to open a livery stable. William Napier and his wife raised three sons and a daughter in Nashville. He helped maintain one of the "illegal" schools of the fifties, brought a schoolmaster from Cincinnati, and, when this school was closed, sent his sons to Wilberforce University and to Oberlin College in Ohio.[25]

The Thomases, the Lowerys, and the Napiers all produced children who would play effective roles in the black community after the Civil War. More important for our context here, they exemplified the strong family ties and the concern for property accumulation, church affiliation, and school attendance that prevailed in one sector of the antebellum black community.

Numbers, continuity, and family made possible the black institutions developed in the city. Except for the family, black churches were the most complete and enduring of all social institutions fashioned during slavery. In this area the contradictions of slavery were clear and prevented a concerted attack against a limited but real black autonomy. Black churches paralleled the appearance of white churches and in part at least were offshoots of the growing religious commitment among whites.

It was the Methodists' "Nashville Station" that claimed the greatest number of black members. Throughout the twenties black members accounted for roughly half of the Methodist congregation, and in some years in the thirties black membership was reported as greater than white membership, while total membership was outgrowing the "preaching places." For example, there were 780 white and 810 black Methodists in 1832 and 1,108 white and 986 black Methodists in 1860 when 87 probationers increased black numbers.[26] Patterns of segregation seem to have a close relationship to increased numbers, but as early as 1829 blacks and evidently some young whites began to remain after the services were technically over—to sing, perhaps to exhort, certainly to enjoy religious fellowship among themselves. Anxiety was voiced in the white community. "Shrieks and yells" that kept the town awake were only one factor. The suspicion that slaves were using church services to get out from under their work loads was advanced as an argument against "Negro Meetings." Charges of "plots and conspiracies" could also be expected when blacks congregated without supervision.[27]

The white community was faced with a dilemma. On the one hand, a separate black church in an "isolated" part of town or in "their" part of town seemed desirable. On the other hand, separation and isolation suggested a threat. It was a dilemma met by the reality of the black congregation's existence and persistence; these overrode all objections, especially in the face of the white community's growing sensitivity to organized religion. A correspondent to the local paper indignantly objected to the editor's description of the goings-on at the Methodist church and demanded that the editor address himself instead to the nightly goings-on at the theater.[28]

By the summer of 1829 a separate African church had been organized at Sulphur Spring to accommodate black Methodists, and by 1834 the African mission claimed 616 members despite the fact that the year before blacks outside the city had been removed from the Nashville charge.[29] These numbers undoubtedly reflect the intense concern of the Reverend James Gwinn, whose commitment to the African charge is graphically conveyed in his 1833 report to the

Methodist Conference: "'The work of the Lord was greatly increased in this mission among the colored people.... Our camp meeting for this state closed last Thursday, about one thousand colored people attending.... I have never seen so great a display of divine goodness. During the meeting thirty professed to find peace with God, 59 joined the church on trial; the work spreading all through the city. At our 3 o'clock meeting in the brick church last Sabbath about 100 fell round the altar, apparently deeply sensible, of their lost state.' "[30] By the thirties the Methodists had put aside their early rejection of slavery and had substituted a new image of the converted slave as "the noblest prize of the gospel."[31] Once slavery was interpreted by white Methodist ministers as a blessing to the slave, the ministers seemed to have been spurred on to the business of conversion.

They met an enthusiastic congregation. Black people entered the church eagerly, emotionally, and intellectually. Shouting, jerking, handshaking, singing, falling exhausted and unconscious formed one kind of release. Arguing the fine points of doctrine, Methodists disputing with Ironside Baptists and Campbellites and with each other, provided another outlet.[32] But the church itself, the African church, the black church, was the great magnet. On Sunday afternoon and evening "a great crowd would stand outside to display their own shape at the same time to witness the passing into and from the church." If the white minister did not appear, "there were any number among the members who would make an effort to officiate. In case they did not have an opportunity to preach they would seize the first chance to deliver an exhortation.... When a woman felt she was well dressed she walked far up the church with a rustling sound which would cause a craning of necks."[33] Even more for black people than for white, the church was the social center of their lives, the place where black people could define themselves to each other—whether by their prayers or by their clothes.

The "old African church" was sold in the late forties, and a new building, Capers Chapel, was planned. A grand "fair and supper" was held for white patrons whose contributions would go toward the church fund. Such patrons were assured in a local paper that they "will in no wise be incommoded by the presence of colored persons," though the food would be prepared by Sarah Estill, a free woman of color whose cooking skills were well known by the paper's subscribers.[34] In 1853 a second Methodist church, Andrew Charge, "a frame building for colored members," was built on Cherry Street.

By the forties and fifties it was clear that segregated if not officially separated churches for black people would be the rule in the churches that embraced a significant number of black members. Accompanying physical segregation were a harder tone in the white press and at least a promise of closer supervision by civil authority. The corporation restricted the number of meetings each week and the hour of the meetings and sent "one of the watch . . . to keep order there on Sabbath nights immediately after dark." Restrictions were most in evidence in the years when rumor of slave unrest was circulating, but most of the time it was a matter of course to grant permission for black churches to meet in order to regulate their Sunday schools and organize the business of their congregations as well as to hold their services.[35]

The Baptists moved into town at approximately the same time as the Methodists. In 1820 nineteen members were housed in a brick building on Church Street, but in the twenties a factional struggle saw the bulk of the congregation following the Campbellites; by 1830 only a handful of the old congregation was left. The thirties were dedicated to rebuilding, especially after the coming of R. B. C. Howell in 1834. Howell's ministry marked a real departure from frontier tradition within the Baptist congregation. He was as much teacher as preacher and introduced both theology and a respect for learning into the services and practices of the congregation. His insistence upon decorum and literacy carried over into his ministry to the black members of the church and helped dictate a policy of separation, then segregation.[36]

In Howell's first year at Nashville his church claimed 105 members, at least 46 of whom were black. Between 1831 and 1848 it admitted 175 black members.[37] Not surprisingly, the greatest number of these were slaves and women; however, among the free black members were two licentiates and their wives and the "Reverend" Nelson Merry. Persistence in church membership was impressive. Black membership peaked in the revival year, 1833, when twenty-eight new members were admitted. That year's new membership also accounts for half of all the black members dropped by the church from 1831 to 1848, which may be a commentary on the nature of revivalism. Not until 1842 was such a large number admitted again in a single year. The 1842 increase undoubtedly reflected the presence of the black apprentice preachers, to whom Howell was transferring considerable responsibility, and the gradual development of some autonomy for blacks within the congregation.[38]

White membership as well as black was growing, and once more segregation followed a long-term policy of at least partial separation. Howell arranged to meet with black parishioners at least twice a week; at these sessions he presented scriptural readings and then catechized his audience "in the manner of examining classes in a school." He helped train David Anderson and George Brentz, the free black licentiates, and Nelson G. Merry, who was accepted into the First Baptist Church in 1845, when he was just twenty-two years old. Three years later Merry and sixty-five other black members transferred to the Baptist Colored Mission. Although Howell prefaced his explanation of the separation of his black and white parishioners by reference to the problem of numbers, he dwelled more heavily on the special needs of the blacks. His characterization of them reflects not only the realities of their social condition— "Their temptations and trials are peculiar"—and the all-pervasive prejudice of the white community—"They are generally dull of apprehension"—but, significantly, the special aspects common to all traditional Baptists whom Howell was most anxious to discipline— "They are naturally inclined to fanaticism; as church members they are litigious and difficult to govern." These stubborn black Baptists were first separated out for teaching and preaching and were then organized in their own church, "authorized to hold conferences, receive, baptise, dismiss, and expel members."[39] The new colored mission initially held meetings in the corporation's schoolhouse; a white minister "wholly devoted to their interest" was provided. Success was clear. Within a year there were 102 black members and more than that number attending.[40] In 1853 Nelson Merry took over as pastor and built one of the most successful of Nashville's black churches, leading it throughout the Civil War and the Reconstruction period and until his death in 1884, when his congregation numbered more than 2,000.[41]

In 1827, when the bulk of the First Baptist Church broke away from the Concord Baptist Association to form the First Christian Church (Campbellites or Disciples of Christ) in Nashville, slightly more than half of the congregation was black.[42] The new Christian Church maintained integrated worship as befit rebels in the name of primitive, egalitarian church practice. David Lipscomb, a young man then, reported that in 1832 "if not all, most of the brethren were teachers, exhorters, and men capable of conducting the worship of God—male and female, white and black, bond and free."[43] Nevertheless, a black witness reported that blacks took their places in the gallery, although they took communion at the same time as the white communicants, downstairs and to one side of the church.[44] By 1835 the Christian church claimed 600 members and 546 by 1849; in that year half of the congregation was black. In 1849 the Christian church was also sponsoring two "colored Sunday Schools, with 125 pupils, that were under the control of the negro members."[45] Even here, then, where religious commitment was defined most radically when it touched on questions of hierarchy and status, separation continued to be the trend. In 1859 one of the Sunday schools, with 200 "pupils," was officially organized as "the first and only negro congregation of the Christian church in the South." In fact, this Sunday school had been operating as a church for some time. The 1853–54 Nashville city directory listed a Second Christian Church (colored) at North Vine Street, and in 1857 Peter Lowery's petition for night meetings of "his church" was submitted to the board of alderman and rejected.[46]

The Episcopal church may serve as a control when one tries to characterize black religious life and the building of black institutions in Nashville in the antebellum decades. Christ Church was not organized until 1820; it was more insistent on formal church ritual than were the Methodist or Baptist congregations; it provided somewhat more independence to priest and bishop vis-à-vis the lay congregation; and there is evidence that the rectors of Christ Church were sincerely concerned to develop a ministry to the blacks.[47] Yet the number of black Episcopalians was always minute. In all of Tennessee there were perhaps 25 actual communicants in 1850, and 60 in 1860, when an estimated 350 blacks were under Episcopal ministration.[48] The failure of the Episcopal church to attract blacks in any number has been explained in terms of its demands for participation in the formal and traditional service, yet a rector of Christ Church was enthusiastic about the "devotional ardor" of black parishioners and their enjoyment of the "responsive parts" of the service. Lack of numbers cannot be accounted for in terms of black people's inability to appreciate and take part in the service. Nor can it be explained solely in terms of the hesitations of priests to bring blacks into the church. The rector reported, "I have not thought it best to bring them forward immediately, *as I could readily do,* to confirmation and the Communion. I have chosen to give them a long training."[49] Such hesitations were common to all the white ministers of the community. Rather, what is clear is the absence of opportunity for the advancement of blacks in this church. None were priests, none were deacons, and "only rarely" anywhere in the South were blacks employed as Sunday-school teachers or catechists. Moreover, as the church of many of the large slaveholders, the Episcopal community offered less of an escape from immediate supervision. It could not supply that crucial bit of living and breathing room. If the chance to act out a leadership role in any church was limited to a very few, the absence of black leaders even as exhorters or teachers affected the ability of most to experience the sense of fellowship that was central to the church's own mission.[50]

Thus, the thrust of black religious life was toward the congregations that provided a modicum of personal growth, of freedom. Neither the Episcopal nor the Presbyterian church attracted many blacks. Peter Lowery, despite the sympathetic support of his patron, Samuel Seay, chose not Seay's Presbyterian church but the Christian church. Countless other blacks chose deliberately the fellowship of other blacks, the freedom from a master's eye. The pressure of blacks in large numbers, the fears of white congregations, their anxiety to maintain decorum and respectability, and their inability to deny religious identity to the blacks were all factors in the equation that led to the formation of black churches in Nashville. But most important was the delight that black people took in *their* churches. By 1860 these churches were an impressive part of Nashville's black culture. Perhaps a third of the total number of black churchgoers were enrolled as Methodists; at least 200 more were Christians; another 200 were Baptists; to these we might add a scattering of Episcopalians and Presbyterians and even a few Catholics, although most found "no sense in counting dem beads."[51] By 1860 more than half of all black people over the age of ten claimed a religious affiliation.[52]

Schools for blacks were a considerable achievement of the antebellum decades, especially when their existence and dogged maintenance are contrasted with the skimpy provision made for poor white children. Their appearance coincides with the development of black congregations; indeed, black congregations were in some instances first organized as Sunday schools. However, the opposition to black schools was much more intense than the opposition to separate black churches.

The best record that we have of black schools was compiled after the Civil War by Daniel Wadkins, the only black teacher ever listed as such by the census.[53] Wadkins's brief narrative suggests some of the basic characteristics of these schools. They were run at high risk to the teachers. No one school had a long history; continuity was provided only by individual teachers. Broken up time and again by white hostility, the schools' persistence is testimony to the stubborn determination of parents and teachers. There is no evidence of financial or political support ever offered by the white community.

Wadkins reports that the first school was organized in 1833 by a black barber, Alonso Summer, in a church building. There was "an understanding" that the school would serve free children only, but we can only surmise who were partners to the understanding. Municipal authorities were not to consider the possibility of a school for blacks until 1837, and then a resolution to permit such a school, introduced by the mayor, was laid on the table and finally withdrawn.[54] Nevertheless and despite the "understanding," individual slave owners like "Mr. H. R. W. Hill, a high toned Christian gentleman, and a few others permitted their slaves to attend." When the school's teacher was attacked, however, these patrons did not intervene. Summer "was accused of writing and sending two letters containing important information to two fugitives, then living at Detroit, Michigan. . . . These letters were discovered . . . and in consequence . . . Summer was nearly whipped to death, and compelled to leave the State."[55] The story is fascinating as much for what it does not tell as for what it does. We do not know who the accusers were, who intercepted the letters, who carried out the whipping and banishment. Another source tells us of a band of "slinks" led by the son of a prominent jurist.[56] There is no record of official intervention. Wadkins, who tells the story, was then Summer's assistant and his substitute when Summer was in the barbershop.

In January 1838, that is, after the petition for a free black school was withdrawn, a school was once more organized, taught this time by a white man, John Yandle of Wilson County. For about a year Yandle taught reading, writing, arithmetic, and geography to about thirty scholars; then he found work "that paid better." In the forties a number of black teachers appeared once more. Wadkins himself began a school in 1842 "in a house on Front Street near the jail." Wadkins taught continuously through 1856 though his schoolroom was moved at least six times in that period, in 1854 to the Second (colored) Baptist Church. In some years he employed assistants and ran his school at night as well as in the daytime. His students were both free and slaves. By 1855, sixty scholars were attending. All through the forties and early fifties a number of black women kept schools for longer or shorter periods.[57] The manuscript census of 1850 counted thirty-three black children in school.[58] A good many whites must have been aware of the schools' existence, but black schools had to operate as far from public view as possible. In 1850 the editor of the *Union* commented, "Until yesterday, we were not aware that there were several schools for free negroes in the city, and all of them in a flourishing condition."[59] Such genial notice of the schools was not to be counted upon, however.

Wadkins's school was closed in 1856 by "citizens" who called upon him and ordered him "not to teach another day." His response that he was doing "nothing against the law" was answered by the threat that he "watch out for the consequences." Wadkins reopened his school in 1857, but this time the captain of police ordered the school closed. The Negro insurrection scare in December 1856 added an extra pressure against black schools; an emergency resolution of the city council forbade schools for free blacks or slaves whether taught by whites or blacks. A fifty-dollar fine was ordered for any white found teaching blacks. Nevertheless, black parents persisted; in 1859 William Napier brought Rufus Conrad back to Nashville from Cincinnati to teach. His school operated for a few months but was closed down "by a man authorized by the powers that be in Nashville."[60]

These private schools could have reached at best only a small fraction of Nashville's black children. Another potential source of education was the Sunday schools. Here children and adults probably acquired some of the skills of literacy despite the lack of regularity, the problem of numbers, and the competing demands on these schools. Tolbert Fanning, Christian evangelist and educator, and his wife, Charlotte Fall Fanning, the sister of a Christian preacher, taught a number of blacks at their schools outside of Nashville. Samuel Lowery, Rufus Conrad, and perhaps also Daniel Wadkins were pupils of Fanning at Franklin College. All three were to preach, and all three taught school.[61] Sally Porter was a free woman who married a slave with some education acquired through "the very excellent family of white people" he belonged to; she taught and also kept a bakeshop. Mrs. A. L. Tate had been born in slavery in Mississippi; freed by her owner with "some" of her children, she began the long trek to Ohio but settled for a time in a German community in Tennessee, where she was "sent to school with whites." Mrs. Tate eventually went to Nashville, where she married and "taught other colored people."[62] One way or another, black people acquired skills and transmitted them. Perhaps 60 percent of adult free blacks in the city could read and write in 1850.[63] And yet a year later, when Colonel

40 DOLLARS REWARD—RUNAWAY on Sunday laſt from a boat at Harpeth Shaols, a Mulatto man named DICK and calls himſelf RICHARD INGRAM, he is about 5 feet 6 or 8 inches high, has a complexion lighter than ordinary mulattoes, face freckled, forehead low and a ſmall ſcar thereon; as he has much impudence and difpoſed to be witty, can write legibly, it is probable he will forge a paſs—he has been much uſed to trading, and will perhaps attempt his late occupation of baking cakes, felling butter, &c.—If any perſon will deliver him to me in Naſhville, I will pay the above reward, or if he be ſecured ſo as to enable me to recover poſſeſſion, I will pay thirty dollars with all reaſonable charges.

JOHN B. CRAIGHEAD

Foster arranged for James Thomas's right to live in Nashville as a free man, Thomas's signing his own name to the legal document was considered astonishing.[64] What may have been uncommon was that a black man would reveal his skills to a group of whites. Most black institutions thrived on the lack of notice by whites.

City life for black people was not just or mainly churches and schools. Individuals eagerly went to see Shakespeare performed and bargained for standing room in the wings when Jenny Lind came to Nashville. Many more filled the black galleries when John Diamond and the Sable Harmonists danced, sang, and burlesqued black speech. Black people attended the outdoor political meetings, despite the attempts of the police to keep them away. They followed national politics and the politics of the corporation with apprehension and occasionally with hope. James Thomas reported that most blacks supported Jackson enthusiastically because of the bank veto. They blamed the Bank of the United States for supplying credit to slave traders. Thomas himself had been called "Andrew Jackson" on the advice of his mother's patron, E. H. Foster, until Foster became a Whig.[65] Blacks celebrated Van Buren's victory in 1836 with special enthusiasm, for Vice-President Johnson's mistress had been black and Van Buren opponents had earlier burned an effigy of "Mrs." Dinah Johnson's petticoat.[66] On the local level, blacks serenaded a newly elected mayor whom they sensed was sympathetic; they knew which aldermen were approachable. The need for patrons was real in bad times and in easier ones. During the 1856 insurrection scare all of the black community was threatened. Indeed, the scare itself may have been precipitated in part by the wild hopes of blacks, incautiously expressed, that a victory for John C. Fremont and the new Republican party would mean freedom.[67] As election day drew near, the papers reported rumors of a slave insurrection planned for election day in Memphis and then, when election day had come and gone, for Christmas Eve in Clarksville.

On December 4 the Nashville aldermen adopted Godfrey Fogg's resolution closing all schools for blacks, banning all black preachers and all churchgoing for blacks after sundown, prohibiting free blacks from moving into the city from other counties, and providing for the arrest of free resident blacks "under suspicious circumstances." These draconian prohibitions were to be enforced by additional policemen and a raise in pay for the night watch. On Christmas Day it was reported that Fogg had introduced a further resolution authorizing the mayor to call upon a guard company. During these few weeks nine slaves were hung at the Cumberland Ironworks in Stuart County, four by a court and five by a mob. In the Nashville area eighteen or twenty slaves were arrested on charges based on confessions extorted by torture. It was clear to many prominent men in the community, as one of them said, that "we are doing our best to produce a negro insurrection without the slightest help from the negroes themselves. . . . Our better citizens are at work and I hope will succeed in preventing an outbreak—among the whites."[68]

It may be that Fogg's resolutions and especially the curfew kept the hysteria within the city from doing greater damage. One report had it that the worst attacks upon blacks occurred in the "suburbs of the city and the country places where little or no protection could be offered slaves by their masters." Still, the blacks in the city were "thoroughly panic stricken," and so were the whites, some of whom sought to prohibit the passes and free papers that enabled some blacks to move about legally after dark.[69] The pressure on free and semifree blacks continued long after the first panic was over. On a single day in January, forty to fifty blacks were brought into court, charged with living illegally without white supervision.[70] Laws on the books began to be enforced, and many free blacks left for Ohio.

One result was that free blacks, indeed all blacks, needed to call on their white friends. At all times survival meant finding work; clients or employers had to be analyzed closely, dealt with, accommodated. Almost always a specific role had to be adopted. The petition for the emancipation of Peter Lowery stressed that "he has always demeaned himself submissively and humbly towards white persons."[71] One dimension of black life in the city was defined by the patron: employer, master, go-between. And patronage helped condition the attitudes of black people toward class. From the vantage point of his barbershop in the center of Nashville, James Thomas remembered a city in which class lines were clearly drawn.[72] His aristocrats claimed "a heritage from the mother country transplanted in Virginia.... If one of the old Virginia set had run down and grown poor he was entitled to consideration being a 'gentleman by birth and education.'" But "if a fellow had come up from a teamster ... and grown independent he remained Sam or whatever his name might be.... He could never become a gentleman.... The children of the two classes never mixed." If aristocrats did not live up to their responsibilities, they were dismissed as exceptions. Thus, as Thomas commented on a leading citizen whose son led the mob attacking Alonso Summer, "A good father had a bad son." According to his own account, Thomas's father, Virginia-born Judge Catron, gave him a quarter, once. Nor did Thomas quite know how to categorize one of those who had come up in the world but who demonstrated civic consciousness and democratic manners—Sam Watkins, the brick maker, who drank his coffee out of a teacup as his own bondsmen did. The new egalitarian rhetoric was not available to black people, and, particularly for those who could claim kinship or a close relationship with white "aristocrats," class consciousness provided emotional rewards. Identification with aristocrats also provided some license to hate openly at least one group of whites—poor whites, "useless to anybody or any community," and especially the Irish immigrants, "flannel mouths and bog trotters," who by the fifties had begun to compete for jobs as domestics and laborers, as hackmen and barbers.[73]

Blacks were vulnerable to the violence and the gratuitous meanness of poor whites and of the city's watchmen. Indeed, on one occasion a police reporter gleefully announced that one of the day police had "outwitted" a lawyer trying to defend a slave who had come to the assistance of his master during a fight on Broad Street.[74] As a counterweight, perhaps some blacks had to believe in the goodwill of Nashville's masters and employers, although they could never expect these men to become their public champions. In 1856 no patrician leader publicly denounced the insurrection as a delusion.[75] Affection and respect between blacks and whites did exist. "Twenty-eight carriages and upwards of a hundred on horseback" attended a slave's funeral in 1847.[76] Nevertheless, slaves continued to be sent to the jail by their masters for whippings, and slaves continued to escape from Nashville and sometimes to Nashville on their way to freedom. And the petition of a free black barber to erect a lamppost in front of his shop on Market Street, the petition of free blacks to form a band "for the benefit of the city and their own amusement," and the petition of the free black barbers to form a mutual benefit association were all rejected by the board of aldermen.[77] By 1860 the notion that free blacks should be reenslaved could be put forward seriously.[78]

At least a part of the black community defined itself by voluntary associations that shadowed those of the white community, from churches to semiclandestine schools to legally unrecognized mutual-aid societies and musical bands. However, in terms of providing protection or leverage in Nashville, these were a poor substitute for inclusion within the multiplying associations that were attempting to organize greater or smaller segments of the white population. Indeed, whites and blacks were pulling away from each other in the churches, the only community organizations that accepted black members. Blacks were certainly excluded from politics, and it was the Whig party, more than any other of the associations, that reached, sporadically engaged, and provided a measure of consensus for a good part of the city.

Whig City

CHAPTER 8

NASHVILLE'S WHIGS overwhelmed their Democratic opponents in municipal elections. Traditional Democratic objections to government-sponsored economic development and moral improvement crusades did ultimately give way in the city, but the Whigs had claimed as their own an activist agenda that stood squarely behind the city's commercial interests, insisted on self-improvement via education and temperance, and proposed the moral, political, and material elevation of mechanics and workingmen. The Democrats, left to champion the "people," often found their people reduced to immigrants, Catholics, and the poor. Nashville's Democrats felt increasingly compelled to attack their Whig opponents with the sectional issues that national party debates were churning out.

Whig electoral successes at the municipal level were overwhelming. For fifteen years, from 1839 through 1853, the mayor of Nashville was a Whig. Even when the Democratic party won at the state and national levels, Nashville remained the self-proclaimed "Gibraltar of the Whigs." In 1839 only one Democratic alderman was elected, and in 1840, none. Never again would the division be so dramatically weighted toward the Whigs, but a Whig majority remained conclusive.[1] In some years—1842, 1845, 1846, 1848—the Democrats fielded no candidates for mayor. The disclaimer was repeatedly heard that corporation elections were nonpartisan. Indeed, Whigs often could afford the luxury of running against each other, and Democrats could not afford to admit their weakness at the polls.

Nashville's Whig commitment needs to be explained if only because it was the capital of a state that developed an extraordinarily balanced two-party system; margins of victory remained extremely narrow in Tennessee. As the site of the most exciting rallies and conventions and of some of the most influential newspapers in the state, Nashville was bombarded with the campaign rhetoric of both parties. Moreover, the candidates for state offices of both parties during the forties came from Middle Tennessee. Indeed, Middle Tennessee as a whole tended to maintain its allegiance to Jackson's party, while the less populated eastern and western thirds of the state voted Whig. Nevertheless, Nashville and the counties within its political district in Middle Tennessee remained within Whig ranks from 1836 on.[2]

Whig organization and a Whig orientation dominated Nashville as they did other Tennessee cities and many other southern commercial centers.[3] The Whig party's positive stance toward economic development and toward government sponsorship of economic development gave it a decisive edge in an urban or urbanizing community. Whig political activism also extended to areas like the public education and temperance movements, which promised both personal and social rewards, the means toward social mobility. In Nashville many mechanics and skilled workers also were drawn to the Whigs, who made room for them in the local party mechanism itself and thereby helped to demonstrate the theme of social mobility as the reward of labor. The watchword of the Whigs was respectability; reform movements, voluntary associations, even charitable organizations reiterated the Whig message. The Democratic party, so long identified as the party of little government and of rural interests arrayed against banks and corporations, slowly but surely would change its posture as the transportation revolution made inroads on all of American society.[4] Meanwhile, in Nashville in the forties the Democrats were placed on the defensive, often left to bring up the rear with a "me-too" campaign or to champion the poor against the privileged in an urban context where striving workingmen fought against being associated with "the poor."

Much has been made of the hoopla, the intense but issueless campaigning, that accompanied the birth of the second-party system. Perhaps not enough can be made of the equally intense organizational efforts that not only brought extraordinary numbers of voters to the polls but also bound them to a party identity.[5] The victory of James K. Polk, "Young Hickory," in the gubernatorial race of 1839 was narrow, hard fought, and attributed by the crestfallen Whigs to his directive to "organize."[6] The Whigs of Nashville in their turn began to organize with vigor. To the traditional stumping and barbecues were added party conventions that brought thousands into the city. Cannon, drums, campaign canoes on the river, "illuminations" in the town, and lighted candles in the windows of party supporters provided hoopla indeed. Devices that would maintain party affiliation were hit upon. Young men casting their first votes were marched to the polls in groups. Private guard companies, uniformed by Whig subscriptions and presented with flags stitched and embroidered by Whig ladies, gave glamour and status to young men in the town. In 1844 there were five companies of Whig guards in Nashville. Among the elected officers were the sons of the old social elites and a few of the master mechanics. The ranks were filled with mechanics who erected liberty poles and sent well-publicized gifts to Henry Clay, among them a set of horseshoes manufactured by William Driver, Henry Ament, and William Stewart, all master metalworkers. A deliberate appeal was made to the mechanics of the town. It was to "the Whig Mechanics of Nashville" that electoral victory in Davidson County was attributed in 1839. One guard company, using Henry Clay's nickname, called itself the Mill Boys of the Slashes, and its flags were presented by the Spinning Girls, a dozen young ladies headed by Aduella Norvell, the daughter of the *Whig*'s editor.[7]

Perhaps the single most important organizational device was the ward club. Young men's Clay clubs and vigilance committees in the wards chose delegates to the county convention, where the delegates in turn selected official nominees for office on the corporation as well as the county level. "Resolved that Nashville is Whig, thoroughly Whig," was the first order of business when all the Clay clubs of the city met at the courthouse in 1844. Whig candidates withdrew from competition with each other in order to ensure party unity. In the short run the clubs helped organize electoral victories; in the long run they involved more and more people in the apparatus of party. Men who perhaps would not be heard in a citywide meeting would be recognized at the first ward's club room next door to Colman's shoe store or in the "frame schoolhouse" where second-ward Clay club members met. And ward leaders within the city took leadership roles in the county meetings.[8]

Party affiliation made a social statement. The Whig party insisted upon its identification with sobriety and piety; it invited women to and banned liquor from its conventions. Brawling and dueling between political partisans were never eliminated; newspaper editors were peculiarly responsible for and peculiarly vulnerable to the violence of the campaigns.[9] However, early on there was a concerted effort to make political meetings attractive to the respectable. At the Whig conventions there was a ladies' table, and women marched in a body to the great Whig meeting of 1844. Many of these women became fierce partisans. When Henry Clay spoke in Nashville in 1840, women swooned in excitement. Some years later, Hettie McEwen, whose husband, a merchant and banker, was a leading figure in Whig politics in Nashville, was reported as holding "her head about two inches higher" after a party victory.[10] And among the marshals of the Whig conventions was Isaac Paul, one of the leading temperance crusaders of Nashville. Indeed, the editor of the Democratic *Union* tried to turn the respectability theme against the Whigs by insisting that the cannon and drums of the Whig convention profaned the Sabbath. He accused the Whigs of mocking religious meetings by singing camp-meeting hymns and drumming up enthusiasm by a tactic that resembled the calling up of mourners at a revival meeting.[11]

After the 1844 campaign the extraordinary excitement and frantic organizational activity wound down, not to be resumed again until the mid-fifties. In Nashville the Whigs had won. Political commitment, once made, tended to be permanent.[12] Military companies, ladies' tables, flag ceremonies, and vigilance committees had all played a part. The urban middle classes, from bankers to respectable workingmen, had lined up decisively in the Whig ranks.

Although the notion that antebellum political parties divided along class lines has been refuted, it remains a truism that "rich men were evidently pro-Whig."[13] Nashville proved no exception.[14] In 1839, of the twelve richest men in the city, six were Whigs and three were Democrats; in 1847, of Nashville's sixteen richest men, eleven

Nashville Suspension Bridge. From the *Nashville Business Directory of 1860*.

were Whigs and four were Democrats.[15] Merchants and bankers tended to be the rich men in town, and bankers especially swung into the Whig ranks.[16] In addition, of twenty-seven lawyers listed in an 1845 business directory, twelve are easily identified as Whigs, but only two of the rest can be assigned definitely to the Democrats.[17] One of these Democrats was William F. Cooper, who reported that he differed from the majority of his friends in Nashville and, therefore, had been relatively quiet on political issues. "The weight of the intelligent youth of this county is still on the side of the Whigs."[18] Obviously, there were Democrats among the economic and social elites of Nashville. The Grundy-Bass-McGavock family circle was one center that would absorb also the railroad promoter, Vernon K. Stevenson. The Ewing brothers, who practiced law together, provided an activist for each of the political parties. Nevertheless, Whig preponderance among Nashville's business and professional leaders is clear.

Perhaps more surprising is that Whig victories on the corporation level provided city governments dominated by mechanics. From 1840 to 1857, when city government was reorganized, about half of the aldermen in any given year were mechanics. The resounding victory of the Whigs in 1844 brought eight mechanics onto the twelve-man board. Commission merchants, wholesalers, and bankers seem to have given up this political arena. Few ran for office. Some may have refused to take part in what they saw as a demeaning quest for votes, but others may have withdrawn from the ward contests because they were conscious both of their own limited contacts among workingmen and of the need to enlist a large electorate.[19] Professionals, on the other hand, continued to serve regularly, and they were joined by steamboat captains and livery and stable keepers, men who had a wide acquaintance among the workingmen of the city.[20] Seventy to 75 percent of the aldermen during the forties and early fifties claimed property ranging from $500 to just under $10,000, placing them in the middling ranks of propertied Nashvillians. No more than a handful from the wealthiest category of taxpayers was elected.[21] Still, it must be stressed that the mechanics on the board were clearly a propertied and relatively privileged few.

At the height of party excitement in the first years of the forties, a few master mechanics gained the mayor's office as well; coachmaker Stout, butcher Coleman, and tinner Maxey succeeded each other in office (1841–43). W. H. Horn, a painter, served in 1853, and foundry owner Anderson served in 1856. But these five men, experienced in ward politics, were the only "mechanics" to serve as mayor. Three mayors came from the merchant community. Irish-born Alexander Allison was on his way to becoming one of the richest men in Nashville when he was elected mayor in 1847 and reelected in 1848, just a few years before his fellow Whigs locked themselves into the Know-Nothing zenophobia. Merchants S. N. Hollingsworth and Richard Cheatham were elected in 1859 and 1860 as Opposition candidates.

The mayor's office remained sufficiently prestigious to attract politically ambitious young lawyers, some of whom were identified with the county squirearchy. Among the mayors was John A. Goodlett, the son of a vigorous Whig partisan who early introduced him to the new campaign style; the younger Goodlett was just twenty-three when he served as mayor in 1846. John Hugh Smith, who had been elected the year before, served again from 1850 to 1852, and he continued to be hungry for political office even when his candidacies brought him into conflict with his fellow Whigs.[22] Smith may indeed represent Nashville's first professional city politician. John M. Lea, wealthy in his own right, married John Overton's daughter.[23] Robert Castleman, clerk of the county court in the forties, married the daughter of merchant James Woods. John McEwen's parents' home was one of the centers of Whig politics. Randal McGavock, Nashville's lone Democratic mayor after 1837, was not only a scion of the McGavocks but also a grandson of Felix Grundy. Only Goodlett and Smith had served as aldermen. The other mayors came forward from the top of the social and financial hierarchies of town and county.

The board of mayor and aldermen was broadly representative of propertied Nashvillians. The weight of the substantial commercial interests, of bank directors and merchants, had been with the Whigs from the moment the break with Jackson had become politically viable. What remains startling is that mechanics and workingmen should follow their lead in such satisfying numbers. Two factors seem to be operating here: the effective Whig organization that opened itself to active participation by middling property holders, and the creation and extension of what has been called a Whig political culture, a dedication not only to economic development but also to self-improvement and social mobility.[24]

Clay's "American system" translated into a vote of approval for the transportation and commercial revolutions which dramatically changed the nature of the old republic. The Whig party never achieved all the specific planks of the American system, and in time the Democratic party came to accept the opportunities and achievements of a road-building, banking, and industrializing society, but in the early forties especially the Whigs championed urban and commercial values.

In Tennessee, the demise of the Bank of the United States led to a system of mixed private and state banking which took up the slack most successfully. Though the Democratic press objected to the board of directors of the Bank of Tennessee as overwhelmingly Whig and the Whigs insisted some years later that the Bank of Tennessee was "shamefully mismanaged by Democratic bank directors," a radical antibank position was not possible in commercially oriented Nashville, nor did an ideological commitment to limiting the power of bankers surface except in times of panic.[25]

Nor did a specific program of internal improvements at federal expense provide grounds for effective party division. If Democrats were opposed on principle, leading Whigs in Nashville were against such a program because they already had under state aegis all the improvements they sought. State subscriptions to the turnpikes that radiated from Nashville had played a major part in financing the roads, and further agitation for internal improvements, it was feared, would only enhance the position of rival cities to Nashville's disadvantage. On the other hand, federal grants for the improvement of the Cumberland River won eager support from leaders of both parties.[26] The Whig press in Nashville dutifully supported the idea of tariff protection for American manufactures; however, it was not foreign manufactures but competition with the production of other American cities that preoccupied Nashville's mechanics.

Boosterism was the stock-in-trade of both Democratic and Whig organs. Articles in praise of almost any kind of business enterprise were regular features of the local news. The *Orthopolitan*, edited by Wilkins Tannehill, not only pointed with pride to the Lebanon textile factory of Allison and Morgan, Nashville merchants, but also used that example to insist that slaves could be used in manufacturing with profit and without danger to southern institutions.[27] Though Whigs supported and Democrats opposed a more lenient bankruptcy law in 1842, Democratic merchants were as eager as Whigs to take advantage of the law.[28] Whigs pointed with pride in 1842 to the reform achieved by their party: abolition of the last vestiges of imprisonment for debt. However, by 1850 the Democrats claimed the reform stance for blocking reintroduction of imprisonment for debt.[29] Nevertheless, the Whigs stood foursquare for a program of economic development. Banks, credit, and turnpikes were the lifeblood of the city, and Democratic hesitations about the uses of government to promote the market economy lost the votes not only of bankers and merchants but also of mechanics and workingmen.

Moreover, identifying with the Whig party in the city meant identifying with a set of attitudes that reinforced a drive for respectability and status of many shopkeepers, mechanics, and workingmen. From the onset of the new party politics the Whigs were conscious of the need to reach out for working-class support. Polk's victory in 1839 prompted John Bell, Nashville's leading Whig politician, to protest, "I am *done done* as a public man, unless we have some better understanding with each other, and all will agree to give the working men more assistance than we have heretofore done." Indeed, one of the Whig parades of 1840 featured a banner with the slogan "One Presidential Term and Fair Wages for Labor."[30] Beyond slogans and banners, what could the Whigs offer? Piety, sobriety, education, and self-improvement as the essential glue of community became one peculiarly Whig answer.

Nashville was reflecting an urban and national pattern in the complex connections that became evident among organized religion, benevolent and reform societies, and Whiggery.[31] Long before the division of parties in Nashville was clear, one can detect the Whiggish temperament among the old merchant leadership, the organizing and disciplining temperament, which had moved from the churches to the voluntary societies, to institutionalize morality, charity, and culture. Church membership, in both evangelical and nonevangelical churches, characterized Nashville's leadership circles, which were also overwhelmingly Whig. For example, the religious identification of forty-four of the sixty-one men on the vigilance committee of 1835 can be determined. At least fourteen were members of the Presbyterian church, among them the elders Amos Dresser looked to in vain for understanding of his mission. Another eleven paid pew rent to the First Presbyterian Church, perhaps only to accommodate their wives.[32] Eleven were Episcopalians. The rest were Methodists, Baptists, and Christians. These men and their wives were the social activists.

Calls for lyceums and orphanages, libraries and schools were old themes now more persistently advocated, especially in the *Orthopolitan*. Tannehill claimed to be publishing a paper independent of partisan politics, but his Whig credentials were never more credible than in the forties, when he defended tariffs and industrial development and took on the job of scolding a "southern" lack of enterprise vis-à-vis New Englanders whose support of libraries and lectures put Nashville to shame. As early as 1831 Tannehill had advocated better educational facilities in Nashville and especially for the "middle class," which could not afford to send its children off to school. In the mid-forties he objected to the newly formed mechanics' society as too "exclusive"; a more broadly based young men's society, he urged, would be able to maintain a stronger library and, more important, would draw all classes together, would be "more Republican."[33] Education was seen as a prime means of holding the community together.

Temperance was another major panacea offered to forward social peace. Nashville had never been known for its sobriety; even the corporation's slaves received a regular liquor ration at least until 1829. They may have been the first to feel the impact of the temperance enthusiasts. Tannehill's *Orthopolitan* as well as the regular party organs gave ample coverage to the issue, and a temperance society was organized by 1829. Yet a movement was slow in developing.

Throughout the country the temperance cause began to involve more and more people in the thirties and forties, in part as a development of revivalism, in part as an acting out of the self-improvement rhetoric, in part as a rejection of Irish and German immigrants.[34] In Nashville the successful attempt to get a "quart law" prohibiting the sale of liquor by the drink through the state legislature in 1838 was only one maneuver in a long and inconclusive battle. Tippling-house owners were more vulnerable than the wholesale grocers who dealt in whiskey and wine, and tippling houses were coupled with "fancy houses." This link with prostitution may have made temperance even more appealing to women. The wives of Democrats and of Whigs and even unmarried ladies signed petitions against repeal of the law.[35] Politics entered here, too, however. The *Union* published a letter charging that the editor of the *Republican Banner* ran a distillery on the side. The *Whig* made stronger political capital when it insisted that ex-mayor Hollingsworth, a Democrat, now the "locofoco" candidate for the state senate, was in favor of repeal of the anti-tippling-house act.[36] Temperance societies took over the town's Fourth of July celebrations. One procession involved all the Protestant churches, a thousand Sunday-school children, government officials, university students, military companies, and even a visiting group of Hungarian singers.[37]

However, the temperance movement seems to have done relatively little to affect liquor consumption among the unconverted. After the passage of the antitippling act a sarcastic letter to the *Banner* reported, "There are as yet a few houses in Deaderick St. that might be obtained for carrying on the liquor business in a *small way.* The *eight* establishments of this kind already in successful operation should not be considered an obstacle."[38] Unlike the industrial towns in the North where employers of large labor forces, themselves imbued with the cause, could enforce the cold-water pledge on their employees and their colleagues, Nashville had a leadership structure that was never so monolithically committed to temperance, nor was its control over white or black labor exercised in this area.[39] At the height of the campaign the editor of the *Whig* could make fun of the pretentious and inept metaphors he discovered in the *Cold Water Song.*[40] Enforcement of temperance legislation was obviously weak to nonexistent. In 1846 the anti-tippling-house act was repealed, licensing and regulation were once more substituted, and in 1857 there was a return to the quart law.[41]

Perhaps more important in terms of the Whig consensus was the organization of temperance societies. In 1846 the Sons of Temperance boasted twelve hundred members in the state and three hundred in Nashville. The United Sisters of Temperance combined with its advocacy of temperance the functions of a mutual benefit society, proposing a sick fund and a burial fund for members and their husbands. This organization was obviously intended for the wives of workingmen. Initiation fees were set at $2.50 to $3.00 and weekly dues at ten cents.[42] Workingmen and their wives might join to provide themselves a bit of health and life insurance and at the same time to reaffirm their sobriety and self-discipline.

The Whig appeal to respectable workingmen and aspiring mechanics was crafted along lines that led from the respectability of labor to social mobility as the reward of labor.[43] Yet the idea of social mobility was still unsettling, not yet fully accepted as the fundamental promise of American institutions. Early in the century, public manners had stressed the equality of citizens while recognizing the reality of social class. A petition to the state legislature in 1827 opposed the appropriation of public funds for a monument to the memory of General Robertson, contending that such an act smacked of "royalty": "Not long since the Legislature expended a considerable sum of money in making a sumptuous entertainment for Lafayette; now a monument over General Robertson, next a Pyramid in honor of Governor Carroll."[44] Republican simplicity was offended. But the petition was ignored; the petitioners seemed to be speaking an old-fashioned idiom.

The question of class sometimes was addressed jokingly, yet the definitions reprinted by the *Banner and Whig* obviously contained the home truths its readers acknowledged in the Jacksonian years: "Lady. A female who cannot cook her husband's dinner, but is expert in reading novels, playing on the piano, etc. . . . Lower-class. Those who support themselves and their neighbors by labor . . . Upper-Class. Monopolists, Capitalists, Lawyers, Doctors, all who live without work on the labor of others. . . . University. An establishment where the rich obtain education at the expense of the poor, and learn to live without labor."[45] Jacksonian definitions were given to upper-class and lower-class labels. The idea of a middle-class America was in the process of becoming.[46] Meanwhile, the old categories were not easily discarded. "A friend to Mechanics" could lecture them on the "vice of false pride." The "too easy attainment of wealth" meant the breaking of old social ties; the children of successful mechanics became "arrogant."[47] Nevertheless, climbing ladders, and discarding notions of a fixed place in society had become a good deal easier, especially in urban America, while dropping down the ladder continued to be the national nightmare. One virtually bankrupt merchant, demanding aid of a partner, protested that, come what might, he would not ruin his children "and cause them to be in lower ranks of life if my debts go unpaid for years."[48] The consciousness of rank was deep-rooted. Gentlemen, professionals, merchants, mechanics, respectable workingmen, day laborers—these were fundamental categories providing immediate identification in the anonymous city. But the new political realities required a change in the way these orders were addressed. A two-pronged, not always consistent argument was increasingly heard; it stressed the dignity of work and at the same time that the discipline of hard work, thrift, and sobriety would provide the way out of a life of manual labor.[49]

In the early forties, with bankruptcy notices filling the newspapers, with laborers leaving a city where work was no longer available, the social mobility argument could seem a bit hollow. Tolbert Fanning, a self-educated, idealistic farm boy who early joined the Campbellites and became an educator dedicated to the manual-labor system and an editor of *The Agriculturist*—himself a prime example of social mobility—grew tired of hearing about hard times and prepared an article insisting that "any industrious mechanic can get from 75 cents to $2 per day for services, and with such prices anyone should get rich." Fanning argued that in Nashville "we know not a man, who is industrious that does not have a sufficiency of the comforts of life." As he saw it, indolence and drunkenness alone accounted for poverty, and the problems of the economy were the result of mechanics who leave their calling for "a higher profession. . . . 'take a high fall' and generally become robbers." An indignant "Mechanic" replied, "A mechanic, with a family to support, get rich on 75 cents a day! . . . Is he *demented,* or naturally deficient in common sense? . . . Do *they* expect to get rich on 75 cents a day?" Here we receive not only a more realistic appraisal of living conditions but also in the sarcastic "they" a hint of the hard line of class. "They" preached and patronized the others who lived on seventy-five cents a day. Fanning responded that he had done more than most for the "working class" in promoting their "respectability," in spreading the gospel of the dignity of manual labor.[50]

In these years of intense political campaigning, the theme of the respectability of mechanics' callings began to gain attention, and the mechanics themselves began to insist upon it. For decades there had been no official mechanics' associations in Nashville. In 1831 an abortive effort at organization to deal with the competition of eastern cities demonstrated the weaknesses of the mechanics' position in terms of both leadership and program. Among the officers elected by the mechanics' meeting were ex-mayor Erwin, Wilkins Tannehill, and banker John Bass. A committee appointed to prepare a report urged the need for a "protective system," some kind of "tariff" based on the sentiment of the community to buy goods made in Nashville. Henry Clay and boosterism provided one answer, if not too satisfactory a one. Closer to a realistic program, the committee urged a reduction of prices to meet outside competition and an association to regulate the conduct of journeymen. Journeymen's conduct would need regulation if price reductions were agreed on because their wages would be the first to feel the pressure. "A Mechanic," most probably the *Whig*'s editor, also urged a library designed specifically for apprentices and held up the example of Benjamin Franklin to employers who objected that apprentices had no time for reading. The uplift program, promoted from above, fell on deaf ears, and the association itself faded from view.[51]

Notices of mechanics' meetings did not begin to appear in the newspapers again until 1837, when the mechanics took the lead in organizing a Washington's birthday celebration. A parade was scheduled, with most mechanics marching under the general banner depicting a beehive with the motto "In Union Is Our Strength." Only the typographical society, the coachmakers, and the tailors provided special banners, the tailors appropriately featuring Adam and Eve with the message "And they sewed fig leaves together." This time, committees were made up almost entirely of master craftsmen.[52]

The newly established penitentiary raised a sensitive issue. Responding to the reform impulse that had created it, the penitentiary was in the process of rehabilitating prisoners by teaching them a trade; the mechanics objected to the competition and even more intensely to the association of mechanics' trades with convicts. They petitioned the legislature and even gave the legislators a dinner, hoping to persuade them to halt the new program. They were not successful; in 1853 the mechanics were still objecting to a program that they felt reflected poorly on their reputation just as they were bettering their public image.[53]

The Mechanics Library Association of Nashville was formally organized in August of 1841. Only those who were "mechanics by profession" could be active members.[54] The library association had a continuous career if an uncertain impact. It is, however, evidence of the increasing assertiveness of the master craftsmen and of their new eagerness to promote education and be identified with it. A winter's course of lectures was soon organized by the association. The lecturers included six Protestant ministers, two professors at the University of Nashville, a doctor, two lawyers, a schoolmaster, and Wilkins Tannehill—Nashville's literati and leading examples of high culture. Single tickets were sold for 12-1/2 cents and a family ticket for a dollar. The first lecture was entitled "Aborigines of America," the second was a defense of the study of Latin and Greek! More to the point, the library was maintained, and apprentices could read free of charge. A room in the market house was open every Saturday night for lending books; by 1848 the library reported two thousand volumes on its shelves, and by 1860, five thousand.[55]

Participation in what resembled the old lyceum program meant for the ambitious master mechanics an association on a new basis with men like John Berrien Lindsley, son of the distinguished president of the University of Nashville and himself an esteemed educator and an organizer of the medical school at the university; Alexander Hume, son of William Hume, the Presbyterian minister, and one of Nashville's foremost classical schoolteachers; Professor Nathaniel Cross of the university, leading spirit of temperance, Bible, and colonization societies; and lawyer Return J. Meigs, a leading advocate, with Hume and the Fogg brothers, of public education for Nashville. These men began to bring round the master mechanics on the subject of public education. What had been dismissed as a tax burden came to be seen as a springboard to the higher rungs of the success ladder.

The Mechanics' Institute was also a product of this new concern. John Lindsley was elected to its executive board, and among its chief promoters was Samuel B. Ament, one of the young men Ann Grundy had recruited years ago to start her Sunday school. Ament had made his way in Nashville as a carpenter, farmer, and dry-goods merchant. By 1848 he was a founder and machinist and another example of the efficacy of the ladder. It was Ament who asked that the *Union* publish a letter from an anonymous "son of a mechanic" who, "though not of you," encouraged mechanics to create an institute. Lecturers, reading room, and library would enable mechanics to go about "ameliorating the condition and elevating the character and standing of the class with which you are connected, to that position in society to which their works and their merits so justly entitle them."[56] Class was not to be denied; the writer made clear that he was no longer "of you." But the goal held out was "elevation." The

Morgan & Co. Dry Goods. From the *Nashville Business Directory of 1860*.

committee to prepare a constitution for the institute was made up largely of successful artisans, men who in the booming decade of the fifties were securing their economic positions. The next step was status.

The course of lectures delivered under the auspices of the institute in the fall of 1854 spoke more directly to the issue of status than had the older lyceum programs. Certain themes were repeated over and over again. For example, when John McEwen addressed the public on "reform of social ranks," he took as his thesis what was fast becoming the great American promise: "In this country all the avenues to [wealth] are open, free and ample. . . . The man who is a stranger to it today, may walk hand-in-hand with it tomorrow." But McEwen also warned against demagogues who set poor against rich: "I would demonstrate the mutual dependence of all classes, and point out the natural and graceful steps from one to the other."[57] The picture of individuals climbing ladders had to be reconciled with the idea of a harmonious community. Henry Fauntleroy followed McEwen with "The Claims of Mechanical Labor to Equality with Other Pursuits." A final eloquent lecture in the series was the address of Jesse B. Ferguson, "The Duty and Dignity of Work." Ferguson was the controversial young pastor of the Christian church whose "experimental" religion led to charges of spiritualism and universalism and to a split in his congregation. He was a compelling, popular speaker, and there were calls for a repeat performance of his speech for the institute. The *Union* printed the entire lecture. Ferguson began with the dignity of labor: "He who earns his own living, is the only independent man." He went on to stress the prime place of the mechanic in modern democratic society: "The producing causes of all free governments have been the mechanic arts." The course of history since Rome had embodied the transfer of "the sceptre from landed capital to mercantile wealth," a transfer accomplished by the "arts of labor." And "King commerce—the only legitimate monarch now upon a throne . . . is the sun of the mechanic arts." Mechanic and merchant were allies in the creation of the Good Village which had replaced the feudal state; merchants were in fact dependent upon mechanics. Indeed, "the representative of labor who pays his poll tax, neutralizes the vote of the man of thousands." Ferguson's address was a full apologia for Nashville society—urban, commercial, potentially industrial. The old squirearchy had been dismissed by history; they were irrelevant. There were, it was true, problems in the new village and city-state. There were poverty— "but very little"—and "too gross labor," but these would be eliminated shortly by machinery and factories. Even slavery was accommodated: "The well fed and well clad negroes, reclaimed from the worst forms of barbarism, and contented under the direction of intelligent, merciful and independent masters are seen advancing in industrial and civil habits."[58]

This was the message that rising entrepreneurs wanted to hear and that professional and political establishments were prepared to deliver: social unity via technological progress, the vote, and material comfort—all sanctioned by a member of the clergy.[59] The blurring of older social divisions based on occupation, the insistence on economic growth as the painless route to the good society, and the reality of economic growth all combined to provide a Whig consensus in Nashville. But that consensus was subject to strain.

By the mid-fifties the breakup of the national Whig party, the increasing pressure against slavery, the influx of immigrants, and the division of the city into working-class and silk-stocking wards made Ferguson's portrait of the Good Village both attractive and elusive. Ferguson was not overtly a spokesman for the Whigs or their successor parties. It was, after all, the Democratic party's organ, the *Union*, that reprinted his speech. But his speech summed up the stance of the old Whig majority. A few years earlier the village of South Nashville, incorporated in 1850, was held up as especially praiseworthy for its achievement of a public school. Letters published in the *Banner* pointed out that in South Nashville there were no idle vagabonds and no aristocrats, only honest workers. "The working man here does not hang his head in shame. . . . We are all poor, and hence upon pretty much of an equality." Poor but striving! South Nashville "has no school for 'poor folks.' She is determined that her free schools shall be not only *her* best, but *the* best schools in the country."[60] When South Nashville became the seventh and eighth wards of Nashville, it claimed the city's highest percentage of household heads with property, albeit small properties. Here lived the respectable workingmen, whose aldermen almost always fell into the Whig, American, or Opposition, that is, anti-Democratic, columns, whose leading citizens, like Isaac Paul, were staunch Sunday-school and temperance advocates. Few free blacks or slaves or foreign-born lived in these wards, which had become a model of the Good Village.

The majority cast its net widely in the antebellum decades, but certain groups were excluded. As we have seen, free blacks and immigrants were excluded by definition, and "the poor," too, were dismissed from the consensus of the respectable. Public resources for poor people were few. The county court continued to bind out orphans and to provide funds for a few of the incapacitated or the indigent aged to be boarded and housed. There was no tradition but that of charity to deal with poverty. Nevertheless, by the mid-thirties the dimensions of the problem had grown so large that the men of the city had to lend a hand to the women.

The poor themselves handled part of the problem by moving on.

Especially during bad winters, when construction ceased and the price of fuel rose, day laborers and their families took to the road.[61] But though the transiency rate remained high, greater numbers of laborers, vulnerable to seasonal and cyclical business layoffs, lived in the city. A letter in the *Orthopolitan,* pleading for a hospital, pointed out what seemed increasingly apparent: "The poor will always be in greater numbers than the healthy, prosperous and happy" and "always compelled to occupy those localities which are known to be unhealthy and the rents of which, therefore, they can defray."[62] All sources agreed that poor whites and blacks were most vulnerable to the epidemic diseases, and once the danger of contagion was brought home, the city authorities did provide for free vaccination of the poor and for pesthouses to isolate the sick. But the city spent little; when absolutely forced to, it paid for the coffins of paupers. There was some anxiety to keep the news of epidemics from injuring the reputation and commercial prospects of the city. In 1835 Mayor Nichol insisted that tales of the smallpox were much exaggerated. Most cases had appeared among the "indigent, neglected class of our citizens, and Blacks." He did recommend that slaves and poor whites be sent to the hospital—read "pesthouse"—rather than to the "outhouses to which they are generally removed." Almost ten years later coachmaker Stout wrote to his son about sixty deaths by smallpox: "Tho that is all kept dark. The Mayor . . . say[s] Nothing about it. There is no Danger to those who are vaccinated."[63]

Lawyer William Cooper analyzed the incidence of the cholera in the same way; he noted that mortality was greatest among blacks, next among laborers, next among women and children—"strong, healthy males, of the better classes, being rarely attacked." Very specifically, he and Lindsley both reported in June of 1849 that the worst of the cholera was confined to the low-lying ground in the sixth ward. In 1850 Cooper reported, "Not more than 5 or 6 respectable citizenry, in easy circumstances, fell under the scourge."[64] The use of "respectable" as opposed to "poor" is a clue to the thinking of these men.[65] They were not writing off poor people. The speakers were among the most charitable. But they were insisting that poor people were qualitatively different from themselves. In this connection one notes that neither pesthouses nor the later workhouse observed either a sex or a color line. Men and women, black and white, beyond a certain line defined as "respectability," were lumped together and slept together.

The poor were not invited into the Good Village, but once there, some of them became "objects" of charity. In 1837 a house of industry was organized in Nashville by upper-class and middle-class women concerned about the condition of those indigent females they considered "deserving." Auctions and soirees raised funds for the house of industry, which in fact became a school teaching young girls to make hats and capes, to cook and launder. In 1846 it was incorporated as the Nashville Protestant School of Industry for the Support and Education of Destitute Girls. An early and more ambitious program of providing work for poor women seems to have faded quickly.[66] In 1837 a Female Orphan School of Nashville was projected and by the next year was educating thirty-five indigent children. In 1845 the Protestant Orphan Asylum was formally organized in the basement of the First Presbyterian Church. By 1850 women from every Protestant church were on the board of directresses. Meanwhile, the wives and daughters of German and Irish immigrants organized a Ladies' Catholic Orphan Society, which augmented the work of the Sisters of Charity.[67] For those who were neither widows nor orphans, there were annual charity drives. Once more the women of the Society for the Relief of the Poor organized themselves according to Protestant church affiliation, but each winter they reported inadequate funds as they "commenced their search, and already find objects worthy of comisseration of a generous public."[68]

Two fraternities took up some of the slack: the Ancient Order of Mystic Chevaliers (AOMC) and the Robertson Association. Their members were young, many of them lawyers and aspiring politicians; most came from wealthy families in the city and the county. With the exception of the architects and builders, William Stockell and Adolphus Heiman, no master mechanics were enrolled. The Robertson Association took a leaf from the women's work. Before each meeting a member dressed "in his robe of office" would go through his assigned ward to solicit contributions and seek "objects of charity." The association's choice of a silk uniform for its officers "similar to that worn by the Campagnia della Misercordia in Florence" suggests its aristocratic tone; some of the members had made their grand tour.[69] There may also have been some political rewards for members. Involvement with charity as well as with public "amusements," parades and illuminations, gave individuals exposure in the wards where they would be campaigning. Mayor Randal McGavock worked through the Robertson Association to inspect and report on the conditions of jail and workhouse.[70]

That the organization of charity remained an elite preoccupation adds to the evidence that the poor remained outsiders in the Good Village. When Charles Tomes, rector of Christ Church, voiced concern for the plight of Nashville's "great numbers" of destitute, his congregation proved willing to support a mission in the heart of the sixth ward's slum. However, when he tried to open up Christ Church by abolishing pew rents, his congregation mutinied, and Tomes felt compelled to resign and to organize the Church of the Advent, which would insist on free seating.[71]

The electoral successes of the Whigs in Nashville made the Democrats, almost by default, the champions of the poor as well as of the ethnic minorities, of the Catholics, and occasionally even of the blacks in Nashville. The rhetoric of the Democratic party since Jackson had pitted the common man against the privileged interests, against monopoly, and against the use of government to serve the purposes of pietistic reforms.[72] In Nashville, too, the Democratic mayor Hollingsworth had appealed to the "poor" as against the "rich" and the "favored class." Hollingsworth's efforts to eliminate the poll-tax requirement for voting were unsuccessful, however, and his resolution to allow free people of color a school was ultimately withdrawn.[73] It was, predictably, a Democratic alderman who tried to get repeal of the city's Sabbatarian legislation. He stood alone in his support for repeal; not even his two fellow Democrats on the board supported him.[74]

Winning, not alienating, the majority was the paramount concern. Like their Whig counterparts, Democratic spokesmen supported the success ladder and the means to climb it—public education, hospitals, and even workhouses. The Democratic candidate for mayor was cheered on Broad Street when he urged support for a public school system and a marine hospital, but "when he said workhouse, someone in the crowd, who had been saying 'good' to school and Hospital, interrupted him with 'That won't do—I'm done with you old fellow.' "[75] Nashville's Democratic leadership had to observe some fine distinctions. When Democrats championed the poor, they were hardly suggesting class war or, for that matter, class interests. The common man was supposed to make up the vast majority. But the Whigs denied the validity of the Democrats' political vocabulary and at the same time claimed a definition of the electorate that embraced all but the lowest rungs on the success ladder.

The state Democratic leadership despaired of making a dent in the Whig majority in the corporation. Indeed, by 1843 Democratic state leaders were willing to trade off the choice of Nashville as state capital for key votes in the legislature, a move that confirmed the perfidy of Democrats to Nashville's Whigs and weakened the position of the party in the city still further.[76] Nevertheless, throughout the forties the Democrats managed to elect aldermen, usually from the first, fourth, and sixth wards, working-class wards.[77]

The Democrats elected to the board in the forties did not represent as wide a spectrum of Nashville society as that of their Whig colleagues. Of ten aldermen positively identified as Democrats, none were professionals or merchants. Only one, a retired merchant, lived in the old gentry mode, and he was elected in 1842 and 1843 from the silk-stocking fifth ward.[78] Seven of the ten were mechanics, one a livery keeper, and one a baker and confectioner.[79] The stalwarts of the city's Democratic organization were Berryman H. Brown, a carpenter, elected nine times from the fourth ward, and John Coltart, who was elected for the first time when he was only twenty-four. Coltart began his career in Nashville running a bakery that grew into a popular restaurant; International Order of Odd Fellows Lodge No. 1 was organized there in the forties, and undoubtedly the restaurant provided a good political base.[80] Coltart was elected seven times from 1843 to 1854 from the first ward. But when he ran for the mayor's office in 1847, he won only 416 votes, half the total of the winning candidate, and when he ran again two years later he won only 266 votes. The gloomy prospects for the Democrats seemed to lighten a bit in the early fifties, when the national Whig party began to fall apart. Democrats rallied under Thomas J. Haile, a shoemaker, whose Democratic loyalties were so staunch he had named his sons Martin Van Buren, Lewis Cass, and Andrew Johnson.[81] Haile amassed 523 votes when he ran for mayor in 1850 as against the winning Whig's 625 votes. With this kind of encouragement William P. Downs, a man of some wealth, came forward as the Democratic candidate in 1851.[82] The Whigs won with a margin of but twenty-five votes this time. However, this was the high point; even given the dramatic demise of the Whigs, the Democrats could not seem to push beyond the roughly 500 to 700 votes that represented their maximum voter strength in the elections for mayor.

The structure of Nashville's municipal politics was solidly based on the alliance of merchants, bankers, master mechanics, and aspiring workingmen—the taxpayers and expectant taxpayers of Whig rhetoric. For more than fifteen years, from the birth of the second-party system, Nashville rejected the party of Andrew Jackson and

Martin Van Buren. The Whigs successfully captured the urban electorate with their appeal to social harmony via economic growth, with their promotion of master mechanics to aldermen's seats, and with their substitution of "elevation" for traditional place in the social hierarchy. The Whig program extended beyond economic development to embrace a self-help ethic that emphasized temperance and education, the dignity of labor, and the promise of social mobility. A great divide was established, at least in the rhetoric of the Whigs, between the respectable classes, the strivers, and the poor, the immobilized. With the breakup of the national Whig party, most voters, because they accepted the promises of the Good Village, would be drawn not to the Democrats but into the diversionary tactics of the Know-Nothings and their successors.

Urban Success
and National Disaster

CHAPTER 9

BY CHANGING their name, the Whigs maintained their hold on office in Nashville in the 1850s. However, the Whig program of development was made frighteningly irrelevant by the threat of secession. Democratic party rhetoric cut across local issues, and here, as throughout the South, began to prophesy mortal danger to southern slavery and white southerners' liberty. Even in the Lower South, where an agricultural economy, an agrarian ideology, and the Democratic party prevailed, commercial development in the fat fifties accompanied by Whiggish arguments created anxieties that, in turn, provided sympathetic audiences for fire-eaters.[1] By contrast, in the border states the two-party system remained viable, and in Nashville itself Whigs, renamed, continued to win. But the Democratic *Union*, which backed the fire-eaters at the Nashville convention in 1850, attacked even Democratic moderates and made slavery the key party issue. The opposition press countered with the "disunion tendencies of the modern Democracy of Tennessee," tried to stop the agitation over slavery, and, true to the old Whig agenda, continued to vilify Andrew Johnson, ironically the antisecessionist leader among the state's Democrats, as a "demagogue," a "leveller," and an "agrarian."[2] Winning in the city may have left Nashville's old leaders unprepared for the emotional and political strength of the thrust toward secession; winning meant for them a chance to continue pressing for a political settlement that would reassure the South. Winning, for an increasing number of southern Democrats, had to mean the South triumphant.

Municipal politics, then, were acted out against the backdrop of the national Whig party's dissolution. The series of crises that began with the Mexican War and ended in the Civil War destroyed, along with much else, the second American party system. In Nashville and in Tennessee, however, the Whigs fought a sturdy delaying action. They regrouped in the fifties as the American party, then as the Opposition party, and at last as the Constitutional Union party, whose candidate for president in 1860 was Nashville's own John Bell. The strength of the Whigs on the local and state level was impressive testimony to the viability of the two-party system here as in other states of the Upper South. The possibility of winning at the state and local levels made surrender to or assimilation by the Democrats unthinkable and indeed put off the decision for secession until after Lincoln's call for troops.[3]

In the course of these confrontational politics the Whigs lost their name but not their party's cohesion. The prosperity of the decade made easier the development of sophisticated public institutions in the city from the waterworks to a school system, products of Whig activism. In addition, the railroad came to Nashville, a product of bipartisan boosterism which contributed substantially to the well-being of the town. This in turn helped keep the city's political leadership unshaken. By 1860 Nashville ranked second in Tennessee in population size; only Memphis, so well situated on the great river, was now somewhat larger. Nashville was comparable in population—and also in the areas of municipal government and public responsibility—with such medium-sized, pre-factory cities of the North as Lynn and Springfield in Massachusetts or Kingston in New York and with such cities as Petersburg and Norfolk in the South. Half the size of Richmond, one-quarter the size of Louisville, Nashville was one of the middling cities in a list of the one hundred largest in the country.[4]

If the early government of Nashville had resembled a club, by the forties the analogy the city fathers themselves favored was that of a business, cautiously and conservatively administered. Though they accepted new public responsibilities reluctantly, they did so steadily and by the late fifties almost dramatically. The Good Village was, after all, a city, and it had to be made to work. The first major debt of the city—$50,000—was undertaken in 1830 to provide an effective waterworks. Though tempted, the corporation withdrew at the last moment, and despite considerable pressure, from investment in the turnpikes of the thirties.[5] The board did reimburse William Nichol, who, at its request, had purchased the site of Capitol Hill as an inducement to the state legislature to locate the capital in Nashville.[6] But not until the late forties was the corporation ready to take on a half-million-dollar debt for investment in railroads. The fifties mark a kind of watershed in city activity as the corporation also became involved in a public school system and, to a greater or lesser extent, in a fire department, a hospital, and a gasworks.

The creation of a public school system in the 1850s was perhaps the most substantial achievement of a national reform ideology in Nashville. Since 1820 there had been sporadic efforts to do something about educating the children of the poor. John Bell, an alumnus of Cumberland College who worked hard to ensure land grants for his alma mater, also urged his fellow alumni to link a program of common schools in support of academies and colleges because education would unify and discipline the public even though the "universal dissemination equally of knowledge is absurd." The prevailing attitudes toward education linked it with privilege, with taxation, and with higher land prices so that land grants might support academies and classical schools for the upper classes. Thomas Claiborne, the Democratic stalwart running for the state legislature in 1831, did insist that he was not opposed to common schools but that he had to believe it was "perfectly ridiculous to be talking about establishing a system of Common Schools without money.... It will not do to tax the people." Two years earlier the editor of the *Banner and Whig* had commented, "The notion of *equalizing knowledge* is to us a novel one ... visionary and theoretical"—and smacking of the philosophy of Fanny Wright, heroine of New York City's radical circles.[7]

State legislation made possible the first regularly supported "Free School." In 1838 a common school law created school districts that could elect commissioners and share in appropriations made for education. Nashville was ready and by 1839 had organized to provide free instruction to students, although they were expected to furnish their own books and stationery and pay a part of the cost of fuel.

For more than a decade the free school operated on the limited sums provided by the legislature.[8] One male teacher, occasionally supplemented by a female assistant, taught from forty to one hundred children, the bulk of them "ABC Scholars." The son of the minister of the First Baptist Church reminisced, "No one attended except the children of the very poorest people. It was regarded as a disgrace to be a free school boy.... I never was acquainted with a boy who went there, nor did I ever know how many pupils there were. Even the negroes spoke of it with contempt."[9]

It was an elite group, however, that sought to go beyond the pauper school. Schoolmasters and university professors, ministers and prominent Presbyterian and Episcopal laymen were the first advocates of public schools. J. H. Ingraham, an Episcopal clergyman and bookseller, corresponded with Horace Mann and published a plan for public education in Nashville in 1848.[10] Meanwhile, a propaganda barrage had been launched in the newspapers, especially in the *Whig*, aimed at creating a public school system common to all the children of the town and coinciding with the new politics of the forties. The public school's reputation for "vulgarity" was countered by the charge that private schools were "aristocratic"; only a common school could inculcate "republican" virtues. Pointed directly at the middling ranks of taxpayers, the argument insisted that tax money for the schools would amount to less than the tuition at the classical schools and that an added dividend would be the education of all children. The plight of the poor, the strength of republican government, the divisive impact of class, all would be addressed positively by an effective system of public education. Education would ensure that demagogues would not be able to pit poor against rich; the community, knit together by public education, would transcend class. Ironically, a significant bias against the "higher" schools emerged at the same time. High schools were reported to be "alike unfriendly to real improvement and republican principles."[11] Here were arguments aimed at the bulk of Nashville's voters, mechanics and workingmen. Common schools would prevent poverty, enable individuals to climb economic ladders, eliminate fear of those on the bottom rungs—and allow expressions of contempt for elitist schooling.

The *Whig* hammered away, reporting the numbers of illiterates in Tennessee, in Nashville. One almost Dickensian description of the target for education was provided by an anonymous contributor: "At the corner of College and Union Streets, there stood, a few Sundays since, with the air and attitude of a Beau Brummell, a lad not more than twelve years old, and not more than four feet high. His hat was rakishly set on one side of his head; his pants tightly strapped down; his Pilot coat closely buttoned . . . and the manikin puffed a cigar as long as his foot . . . I . . . recognized my neighbor's apprentice . . . who does not know his abc's . . . looking with manifest scorn upon the Sunday school children that were passing."[12]

By the end of the forties the greater part of the community had come round. Pauper schools were perhaps appropriate where a static notion of class prevailed, but as the Whig mechanics were coming into their own, the common-school ideology began to make more sense to them. In September of 1848 the mayor and aldermen called for a vote on the schools and the additional taxation that would be required. The response was a resounding "Yes"—668 voted for the schools and only 137 against.[13] It took another six years to implement the people's will, however. It may be that the board, having agreed to invest half a million dollars in railroad stock, was a bit frightened and hung back from any further investments of corporation funds.

Alfred Hume was sent by the city to inspect eastern public schools. Two thousand copies of his report were printed, and the aldermen at long last approved a system that would encompass primary, grammar, and high schools. One primary and one intermediate school were proposed for each of four school districts, serving children ages four to sixteen. In 1853, ground was broken for the first building in the system—the high school. Nashville supporters of public education obviously did not agree on priorities. When the high school was near completion it was clear that no funds were left to build the primary schools. Some manipulating was undoubtedly going on, but in the end Nashville acquired both elementary and secondary public education.

The aldermen promptly voted to convert the high school to a primary school. Both the newly appointed board of education, composed of men who had been strong advocates of a public school system,[14] and the school committee of the aldermen rejected this idea. The high-school building, on the northeast corner of Spruce Avenue (now Eighth Street) just off Broad, would not be easily available to all the children of Nashville, nor could it contain more than half of the school population. They demanded action on the building of primary schools in every district. Alderman Glenn, head of the school committee, gained passage of a bill to prevent money collected for the schools being used for any other purpose. Skirmishing continued throughout the fall. The University of Nashville offered its services as a high school at two-thirds of tuition costs for all graduates of the corporation's schools, and the board agreed to "amalgamate" the high school with the resuscitated university. Finally, in December 1854, the school fund was placed at the disposal of the board of education. More than one thousand students were accepted for the schools, which began operation in 1855 in all kinds of quarters. The high-school building was too small, as the board of education had predicted. Dr. Edgar's private school was rented for one class of girls, and the ancient corporation school made do for two classes of boys who could not be squeezed into the high-school building. In the next few years schoolhouses were built, bought, and rented to accommodate the flood of students.[15]

Registration figures were gratifying to the promoters and more than a little frightening to the cost-conscious aldermen: the poll tax, which had been imposed in aid of the schools in 1850, was neither popular nor lucrative. Alderman Chilton, a carpenter long active in Whig politics, introduced a bill to compel persons to pay their poll taxes before sending their children to the free schools, but this move was rejected. The program of social uplift through education had clearly won popular support. Property taxes for the school fund began to be collected in 1852.[16]

The aldermen tried to introduce two sessions to reduce costs, but the very professional superintendent, J. F. Pearl, fought this move. Not only would it be difficult to keep the schools clean under these conditions, he argued, but, more important, double sessions would make it difficult to keep track of the children. Their parents would fear "promiscuous mixing," and the school would acquire the reputation of a "rag" school.[17] Pearl tried hard to keep the common school from becoming a pauper school, and in order to do so he had to insist on neighborhood schools, a typical urban modification of the common-school philosophy. By the fall of 1858 there were six schoolhouses, including the South Nashville school. One school was held in the Hard Side Baptist Church. Two were one-teacher schools. But the Hume School, the original high-school building, boasted twelve teachers, and the Hynes School, nine. Of the twenty-nine teachers in 1858, eleven were Yankees and sixteen were women. Although Pearl had to defend his employing northerners, the board did not object to women. Only one woman earned more than six hundred dollars; only three men earned six hundred dollars or less. Somewhat less than half of the school fund went for the salaries of the superintendent and the teaching staff. With a minimum of fifty students to a teacher, they earned their keep. By 1859 there were 1,511 students, and by 1860, over 1,800.[18]

Most other city services developed less vigorously. Water, lighting, wharves, and streets continued to be provided—first to serve the business districts. Priorities remained the same. The city beautiful, the city clean, indeed the city sober and safe were often called for but rarely funded. As in most other antebellum cities, the number of policemen was small, their pay low, and their quality dubious. By 1837 there was a night watchman for each ward and a captain of the watch. Not until the end of the fifties were "day police" a regular item in the city's budget. The deputy marshals wore "day crescents" to distinguish them from the night forces, who wore silver stars.[19] The poorly paid job attracted men whose reliability and sobriety were almost continuously in question. The reluctance of the aldermen to fire policemen and the ease with which suspended policemen were returned to the force suggest that the job was part of the political patronage system. Proposals to have policemen elected from the wards were rejected out of hand.[20]

Most of the work of the watch was confined to hauling the drunk and disorderly to the recorder's office. Often at some risk to themselves, they were called upon to put down a "broil."[21] In sporadic clean-up campaigns the mayor and aldermen led the constables in an assault on faro dens or bawdy houses. In 1830 the corporation cooperated with the Alumni Society of the University of Nashville to force the owners of property close to the university to agree not to rent to prostitutes, but prostitution remained a flourishing institution in Nashville, where in 1860 the census taker listed 207 prostitutes and 69 houses of prostitution.[22] The watch also checked on black churches and more or less regularly oversaw and harassed the black population.

When it suited them the watchmen could enforce ordinances, including those that prevented kite flying or bathing in the river in sight of the city.[23] It was, however, very difficult for the police to deal with murder, arson, or theft when they were not confined to Water Street or to the known taverns and brothels. Throughout the period the mayor joined private citizens in offering rewards for the apprehension of criminals; bounty hunters and vigilantes had to supplement the work of the watch. The situation might have been eased had the mayor had immediate criminal jurisdiction, but the mayor's court, which was established in 1836, lasted only four years. It had not been given broad or independent authority and had only a limited ability to exact fines. As a result, costs quickly outweighed benefits in the opinion of the aldermen, and no real attempt to reinstitute the court occurred when the legislature dissolved it in 1840.[24] Policemen continued to bring their prisoners before the justices of the peace; in the fifties one of the city's justices was named recorder and judge of the police court. And as late as 1859 Mayor McGavock complained bitterly, "The dictum of the policeman is equal to that of the Mayor, and he performs his duty or not at his own pleasure. We have no rules for the government of our police."[25]

Once captured, criminals were also hard to hold and, in at least one case, hard to isolate. In the staid minutes of the board of aldermen appears the report that "one John Clark had on Saturday night by some private means . . . [got hold of the jailer's key and] obtained ingress to the calaboose in which was confined one Mary Brown."[26] Poor as both county and city jail facilities were—cramped, promiscuous, unventilated[27]—they cost money that was only reluctantly provided.

Part of this problem was solved when prisoners were made to work out fines and costs if they had no funds. By 1855 there was a city workhouse, and in 1857 the city treasurer proudly reported that the workhouse account showed a profit: 62,550 bushels of rocks had been beaten and prepared for the streets at three cents per bushel. However, no more was said about profits when "a new and elegant Work House" was completed in 1858. Mayor McGavock lauded the new building in which the sexes could be separated and at which divine service was to be held every Sunday afternoon. At this point the workhouse had become part of a complex system of city enterprises. The keeper of the workhouse had charge of the city's steamboat and of the city's gravel boats. Workhouse inmates—men and women—were carried to an island in the river to break rock. The steamboat towed boats up- and downriver, brought wood from the island to the poor in winter, and towed coal boats to supply the city waterworks. The corporation's "stock" were housed in stables adjoining the workhouse.[28]

Despite the constant threat of fire, regular appropriations for a fire department did not begin until 1846, when the city evidently supplied funds to uniform one of the volunteer companies on which it continued to rely until 1860. Fire fighting remained something of an amateur sport. Bankers and commission merchants joined prominent mechanics as directors of engine and hose companies. Younger and less established men tended to be the "hose directors," the older men the officers of the companies. Fire Company No. 1 announced to the world, from which it was eager to solicit funds, "The present company is composed of the very *elite* of our young men." Parades and annual suppers paid for by the newly formed insurance companies made membership in a company a social asset. The young women of the town were eager witnesses of these "most splendid" parades and of the gorgeous uniforms.[29] As they grew larger the companies became not only rowdier and less "elite" but also one of the networks through which political candidates gained support. At the Broad Street Company's supper in 1847, it was announced that harmony prevailed though rival companies joined the festivities; no liquor or wine was served.[30] The fire companies made up one more of the voluntary societies that characterized Nashville in the forties, and their leaders, William Stockell and John Dashiell, for example, were part of the Whig leadership in the town.

Appropriations by the city to buy engines, hoses, and engine houses were regular but modest. In 1856 a fire on the square severely damaged the courthouse, the Nashville Inn, and the warehouses of several merchants and threatened the town itself. Perhaps this and the threat of firemen's strikes prodded the city to somewhat larger expenditures and finally in 1860 to undertaking a professional fire company under the "paid system." Technology must have played an even larger role. By 1860, as a result of the application of steam power to fire fighting, two companies consisting of sixteen men replaced the six companies and nine hundred men who had made up the volunteer companies.[31]

Since 1830 the city had taken the responsibility for providing water for its residents. Like so many other cities, including the metropolis of New York, Nashville discovered that leaving the city's water supply to private enterprise proved ineffective. Made anxious by the dangers of fire and epidemic, the city borrowed $50,000, invested a good part of it in slaves who would dig the trenches and lay the pipes from the Cumberland River to reservoirs and hydrants in town, hired a noted engineer, Albert Stein, and within three years had a waterworks in operation. The initial cost was underestimated by only $5,000, itself a phenomenon, and that was made up, the city fathers gloated, by the rise in value of the slaves the corporation had purchased.[32] A users' tax was imposed that through the mid-fifties was roughly equivalent to the cost of the growing system of hydrants and reservoirs. But the superintendent of the waterworks was urging still further expansion in the early fifties, and in the last four years of the decade the city spent just under $185,000 on the works, almost twice as much as it received in users' taxes.[33]

In February of 1851 gaslights were turned on in parts of Nashville for the first time. One editor exulted that Nashville was now truly entitled to be called a city. The Nashville Gaslight Company was chartered in 1849; its directors were Nashville capitalists, many of them lawyers. The 285 subscribers in 1851 were private individuals who paid for "the necessary apparatus" to light businesses and homes. The company also provided lighting for the city, which spent larger sums for public lighting than for the fire department in most years; by 1859 it was paying for 195 gaslights on the streets.[34]

Although the antebellum decades are distinguished by the birth of the asylum as a means of ameliorating the condition of the unfortunate and of society itself,[35] public institutions experienced a hard labor in Nashville; the support for public agencies remained very precarious. The definition of "hospital," for example, would have had to be dramatically changed if it were to gain public support. For generations hospital meant "pesthouse," a place to isolate those sick who were also strangers, black, or poverty stricken. Although there obviously was some altruistic concern, the overriding worry was contagion. It was the regular appearance of smallpox and, after 1832, of cholera that induced the corporation to pay for smallpox inoculations for the poor or to rent houses to isolate the stricken. In 1846 the city's hospital, a rented house, charged four dollars a week for board for all patients, white or black, bond or free. Though the mayor and a committee of aldermen investigated the possibility of actually buying a hospital, when the worst of that year's smallpox epidemic was over, they found it "inexpedient at this time"; the total bill to the city amounted to $778.[36]

For two years, from 1848 to 1850, the Sisters of Charity operated a hospital, but by 1850 it was reported that they needed all their resources for their orphans' care. Newspaper horror stories were now part of a drive to acquire a hospital. One reported on a smallpox victim removed from a house flooded by the river's rise and left under a canvas tent in winter; another report argued that the curing of two women by the sisters had forestalled the need for the corporation to care for twelve orphans. The disastrous return of the cholera in 1849 and 1850 added urgency.[37]

Dorothea Dix's celebrated visit to Nashville in 1847 had in fact furthered a successful effort to obtain a modern state hospital for the insane, and in 1852 the old lunatic asylum was turned over to Nashville for a hospital building on condition that care for paupers be provided. The corporation, in cooperation with the medical faculty of the University of Nashville, quickly drew up rules for the management of the new institution. There was a concerted effort here, as in more cosmopolitan cities, to make the hospital "respectable," that is, to eliminate the pauper stigma and indeed to eliminate paupers altogether where possible. No patients with venereal diseases and no patients with incurable diseases would be accepted as charity patients. Those patients with venereal disease who could pay were charged almost twice the going rate. No unmarried women would be admitted to the lying-in ward.[38] The rule prohibiting religious exercises in the hospital may have been suggested by John B. Lindsley, who was convinced that religious wrangling had added to the troubles of the University of Nashville, which had closed its doors temporarily in 1850, a victim of both competition and the cholera. Lindsley had helped organize a medical school and had kept this university department open. Participation in the city hospital program would clearly support the medical school, but, more than that, it was people like Lindsley, exposed to and concerned with the reform currents of the larger American society, who were self-consciously trying to implement the building of institutions of social betterment.[39]

However, the city fathers were obviously reluctant to take on the burden. Within two years the board was discussing turning the hospital back to the state. With only one negative vote, it resolved to do so, perhaps as a maneuver to force the legislature to come through with an appropriation. Two years later the board leased the hospital to the medical faculty of the University of Nashville, agreeing to pay three dollars per week for each "corporation" patient.[40] One was back once more to the definition of the hospital as a pauper institution. A year earlier the doctor in charge of the hospital had reported the place of birth of each patient; almost half were foreign-born, and this fact would have added a nativist sting to the pauper stigma.[41] The corporation continued to pay for inoculation of children in the free school; it arranged to pay for the medicine of paupers, prescribed after "rigorous examination." The druggist chosen as the city dispenser had agreed to fill all charity prescriptions at fifteen cents each. The corporation also allowed the poor to draw "hydrant water" during cholera epidemics. Nevertheless, its disbursements for the hospital department remained small—$464 in 1859, just under $3,000 in 1860.[42]

The growth in the activity of city government was reflected in its record of disbursements. In 1830 total expenditures were just under $9,000, in 1840 they had risen to $28,000, in 1850 to more than $67,000, and in the next year to over $112,500. Throughout the fifties expenditures swelled until by 1860 they amounted to $382,155.[43] In the forties they were accounted for very largely by the cost of the waterworks, the watch, and the maintenance and building of streets. The cost of these standard items grew in the fifties, and new expenditures were added. The salary account also began to figure as the corporation gradually acquired a staff of paid civil servants, including an engineer and overseers of the city's new enterprises. More than $40,000 a year went to the interest account by 1853, and in 1860 the funded debt of the city amounted to $618,500, the bulk of which had financed investment in the Nashville and Chattanooga Railroad.[44]

In the forties, public meetings, a great railroad convention in Memphis, and the booster press had kept before the public the need of the city for a railroad connection. "Old Chattanooga," Dr. James Overton; Vernon K. Stevenson, who gave up his career as a successful merchant to become president, organizer, chief stockholder, and promoter of the Nashville and Chattanooga Railroad; large contingents of the banking and mercantile establishments; lawyers and men of capital from the county—all opened subscription books for the Nashville and Chattanooga Railroad in their offices.[45] John Hugh Smith, then mayor, was elected secretary of the company in 1845. Agitation began to get the city to subscribe $500,000 to the capital stock of the railroad. City boosters, Democrats and Whigs, insisted on the value of this investment. Both Overton and Stevenson were Democrats, an indication of how far toward the program of economic development the party of agrarian interests had moved, at least within the city. For all that it was touted as the way to make Nashville a great iron and coal center, the railroad was part of the traditional mercantile strategy to tie a wider and wider hinterland to the Nashville market.

In 1847 Nashville subscribed for a half million of stock in the Nashville and Chattanooga. Additional subscriptions were made to the Nashville and Southern, to the Winchester and Alabama, and to the Nashville and Northwestern railroads. By 1859 Mayor

Hollingsworth reported that city subscriptions to railroad stock totaled $872,000 and attributed Nashville's growth to the railroads. There was not total unanimity on railroad investment, but by and large the community supported it.[46] The lecture delivered by *De Bow's Review*—chief propagandist for southern industrialization in the antebellum decades—to cautious Nashville businessmen, chastising them for being "too prone to spend their energies and capital on 'note shaving,'"[47] was hardly deserved by the city fathers. For a city government that was typically conservative about public expenditures, that endured for at least a decade the annual flooding of some of its most heavily populated areas before it succumbed to the demand to raise the streets above flood level, and that then raised a part of the cost by private subscriptions, these railroad investments represented a singular change in pace.[48]

The city fathers had to be mindful of the source of their revenues. The bulk of the city's money came from taxes on real estate, slaves, white polls, and carriages. Every inaugural address or valedictory report by a mayor spoke first to the question of finances. Every candidate for office promised strict economy. While the newspapers waxed enthusiastic over every new manufacturing enterprise opened in the area, the aldermen, in fact, could on occasion report it "inexpedient" to provide water for Samuel Morgan's new works. As soon as the debt for one waterworks project was paid, another was incurred to service the growing population. At one point Alderman Glenn proposed that the second ward secede if it received no more attention to its demand for water and gaslights. Each report of the superintendent of the waterworks ended with a plea for funds for more reservoirs, more pipe.[49] The need for service met the plea for caution, the reminder that taxes were already too high. Nevertheless, services were expanded. In 1842 Mayor Coleman described the city government as the "guardians" of property worth $3 million. Fifteen years later taxable property in the city was assessed at more than $11 million.[50]

Yet the guardians of this property had not changed measurably the structure of corporation government. The business of the city was run as if it were an old-fashioned, loose partnership rather than a hierarchical corporation. The original board had been a small crew of seven men who handled the village's business as the unpaid responsibility of an acknowledged leadership cadre. After 1827 the board became more representative of the larger community of taxpayers. Although election campaigns increasingly centered on the mayor, his powers were circumscribed. The standing committees of the board did the business of the corporation; committee chairmen were delegated the right to let corporation contracts, and the aldermen elected corporation employees, including the police. The aldermen were jealous of their prerogatives; they refused to recommend the election of the night watch by popular vote, and until the plans for the new school system were well under way they kept the election of the board of education in their own hands rather than allow the election by the wards, which had originally been required by the ordinances. Although they earned no salary until late in the fifties, they enjoyed their perquisites, including the oyster supper given them by the corporations' employees.[51]

In 1858 a reorganization of city government took place with the creation of a city council consisting of one alderman and two councilmen from each ward. Councilmen and aldermen sat separately, elected their own presidents, and could override a veto from the mayor's office by a two-thirds' vote of each chamber.[52] Yet there was no division of authority between the two chambers. More people were involved in the city's business, but the old committee system prevailed. Although the mayor chose the standing committees, Mayor McGavock's comprehensive report on leaving office in September 1859 pointed out that neither the executive departments of the government nor the corporation's employees were responsible to the mayor. He urged a longer term, higher pay, and more direct authority for the mayor.[53]

There was a good deal of opposition to the notion that elected city officials be paid. In this, Nashville's government harked back to tradition and more or less consciously rejected the implications of what its size and the extent of its operations might require. It added more employees, more buildings, more slaves, more functions, and a refurbished city hall in 1857, but it continued to operate on the basis of annual elections, annual appropriations, and more committees. A sinking fund for the city's debt had been recommended in 1842; it was finally budgeted in 1860. Nashville lagged behind the practice of larger cities that by 1825 had accepted free markets as opposed to city-licensed and rented stalls.[54] The market house, which carried with it the traditional notion of city control and inspection of its food supply, was made less central only in 1859 with the repeal of laws against hucksters. The city was not yet ready to acknowledge responsibility for indigent strangers. Mayor McGavock suggested a penalty for steamboats or railroads that brought to the city those who would be dependent on charity. He reported that many who sought tickets of admission to the hospital were "proper subjects for the Poor House," that is, the county agency, or did not "belong to the City."⁵⁵ To the very end of the antebellum decades, the definition of city government as an association of taxpayers and expectant taxpayers continued to do battle with the newer expectation that the city promote not only economic growth but also social reform.

Urban structures developed cautiously in Nashville in part because municipal leadership remained almost unchanged despite the upheavals in national politics during the fifties. Continuity in leadership tempered both boosterism and the social reform concerns that promoted change. On the other hand, the local political scene obviously felt some effects of the drama of the debate on slavery. It was the annexation of Texas, opposed by the national Whig party, that gave the Democrats the governor's chair in Tennessee in 1845, and four years later the Democrats won both the governorship and the state senate while southern Whigs had to explain away President Tyler's willingness to admit California as a free state and to sign the Wilmot Proviso.⁵⁶ Indeed, after 1844 Middle Tennessee was counted in the Democratic ranks.⁵⁷ Davidson County dissented and was more and more isolated; in Nashville itself in the early fifties Democrats were once more competing avidly with the Whigs in the wards.

When southern radicals determined to vent their grievances in 1850, their convention was held in Nashville. Whigs disassociated themselves from the Nashville convention, and those Democrats who did take part were evidently fully aware of the hostility of Nashville and of Tennessee to any talk of disunion. The state legislature refused to send delegates. The fire-eaters among the unofficial Tennessee delegation were a small minority.⁵⁸ William Cooper, close to the Democratic leadership in the state, reported that Nashville was "as little ultra as any south of Mason and Dixon's line." But, he added, the "cup is full—one more drop and it will overflow."⁵⁹ The Compromise of 1850, though it seemed to be an answer to the Nashville convention, did not provide sectional peace. The crises escalated: the Kansas-Nebraska Act, the organization of the Republican party, the Dred Scott decision, Seward's "irrepressible conflict" speech, John Brown's raid. Each episode helped create a confrontational politics that moved from the national to the local level. Franklin Pierce, a Democrat, won a landslide victory in 1852, carrying every southern state except Tennessee; shortly afterward, the Kansas-Nebraska Act split the Whig party decisively, and even the Tennessee Whigs had to regroup.[60]

In 1853 the Democrats won five places on Nashville's board of aldermen. But the Whigs of Nashville, though they changed their name, intended to maintain their party. In the municipal elections in 1854 they brought off the kind of coup associated with Know-Nothing stratagems elsewhere. A month before the corporation elections only the Democrat, Haile, and Moses Singleton were in the race. Singleton, Old Tip, was a livery stable owner and a perpetual candidate for the mayor's office, a Whig whom his party colleagues never took very seriously. His populist line was usually reported as a joke. As it turned out, the Whigs ran no serious candidate. Rather, on the morning of the election, the name of W. B. Shapard was announced.[61] Shapard, a banker, had until this point been considered a Democrat; however, he evidently had been converted to the American party, which all over the country was drawing off supporters from both of the traditional parties, who were finding it more and more difficult to find politic answers to the slavery question. The Know-Nothings, or Americans, made zenophobia and anti-Catholicism their special political issues but also sponsored the sort of moralism that had made up familiar Whig planks.[62]

Shapard defeated Haile, 1,188 to 255. The editor of the *Union* was overwhelmed. He protested that one could not be both a Democrat and a Know-Nothing. Throughout the fall and winter the *Union* kept insisting that the nativist issue had been a trick of the Whigs.[63] But thirteen of the aldermen elected, including John Coltart, one of the leaders of the city's Democratic party, would identify within the year as members of the American party; only two were Democrats. Actually, despite Shapard and Coltart, there were comparatively few converts to the Americans, for by and large the American party simply supplied a new name for the Whigs in Nashville and throughout the South.[64]

The committee that invited the American party's standard-bearer, Millard Fillmore, to the city was chaired by Colonel McEwen, always a key figure in Nashville's Whig politics. Democrats like William Cooper argued that the "law, and order and decency party.... has fallen from its high state" by taking on the nativist stance. Nevertheless, the Whig newspapers without exception became Know-Nothing organs.[65] The *Union*'s claim that the only religious issue at stake was the sacking of Joel Smith, Democrat and Methodist, from his long-held post as city treasurer in favor of Samuel Seay, Whig and Presbyterian, held a germ of truth. The Whig leaders were still in the saddle. But it is true that even the Whig editors were initially a bit uncertain about how to attribute this victory at the polls. The editor of the *Republican Banner* rejected the charge of a Whig trick and insisted that Shapard was a Democrat and that Democrats who voted for him were not duped. Nevertheless, about three weeks later Mayor Shapard resigned, explaining that he could not attend to the office properly and continue his own business. The board immediately elected R. B. Castleman, who would be popularly elected the following year as the American candidate.[66]

The American party's ploy worked. In 1855 only one Democratic alderman was elected. The Democratic organization seemed demoralized, and, despite the addition of the seventh and eighth wards, the overall vote fell once more. Dr. C. K. Winston, the Democratic mayoral candidate, polled only a bit more than a third of the vote. The *Union* had proposed a "City Reform and Anti-Know Nothing Ticket" and a platform urging tax reduction. The response was the assertion that to reduce taxes would mean to give up the public school program and thereby to leave in operation only the Catholic schools. The Democrats may be calculating upon the Roman Catholic vote, warned "Third Ward" in the *Banner*.[67]

Although the Know-Nothings in their turn split on a North-South axis and could not maintain their hold in the South generally, the alliance between Whigs and Know-Nothings maintained its hold on the Tennessee legislature in 1855.[68] The height of American party excitement came in the presidential elections of 1856—rallies, mass meetings, women meeting at the ice-cream parlor to prepare banners. The party's vice-presidential candidate was Andrew Jackson Donelson, President Jackson's adopted son and an ex-Democrat. Both candidates for mayor that year ran on the American ticket. Castleman, a lawyer from an old county family, was decisively defeated by Andrew Anderson, a now-wealthy foundry owner whose career was identified with that of the city.[69]

The American party won in Nashville, but it confronted an ever more intense and, in some cases, hysterical barrage of abuse from Democratic candidates and press, abuse that ignored local issues, agendas, and programs. Millard Fillmore was attacked by Governor Andrew Johnson as "an Abolitionist, theoretically and practically."[70] The former governor Aaron V. Brown insisted that Fillmore would not protect the South and that Know-Nothings in fact perpetuated the Whig tradition of ignoring the slavery issue in order to maintain their alliance with "thoroughly abolitionized" northern Whigs.[71] By 1856 "Black Republicanism" as well as "abolitionism" had become key words in the campaign of fear waged by the Democratic party in Tennessee. As it had since 1850, the Opposition cried secession, treason, betrayal of Andrew Jackson. But James Buchanan and the Democrats carried the state in 1856. The fear of Republican control, the slaveholders' long-standing fear of losing access to the territories, and white men's fear of the loss of freedom to define and hold their property, were now the loudest planks in the Democratic platform.

Democratic victories on the state and national level again encouraged Nashville's Democrats in 1857. General B. F. Cheatham offered as mayor. Cheatham not only would benefit by the Democrats' increased popularity all over the South but also, as a Democrat, would carry the votes of foreigners and Catholics, especially the Irish; he was also clearly identified with the gentry. Whig leaders responded with the unusual tactic of persuading two weaker candidates to withdraw in favor of young John McEwen. One of Nashville's literati and most devoted political campaigners, he might be expected to carry not only the mechanics but also the silk-stocking ward. McEwen was "judicious, high toned, dignified and eloquent." Democratic successes on the state level, the *Banner*'s editor insisted, had made the Democrats determined to take Nashville, "the very capital of the enemy," but McEwen would "carry a large number of Democrat votes." Indeed, the contest was hard fought. Five hundred more voters were enticed to the polls, and the American candidate won by a margin of only seventy-five votes. The vote in every ward except the fifth was close; the fifth supported McEwen overwhelmingly. The old-line Whig leadership of merchants, bankers, and successful mechanics beat the bushes and maintained their Gibraltar, though at least four Democratic aldermen were elected.[72]

The Democrats took a leaf from the Whig-American book the next year when they nominated Randal McGavock and deserted Haile. McGavock was clearly a patrician, one of Nashville's native aristocrats. His friends could hardly deny him, and he also accepted the offer of "One Hundred Americans" to be "the People's Candidate." Though Haile insisted on running, he came in a poor fourth in a field of four. The opposition split, but there was no effort this year to agree on a single candidate. The fiercely partisan *Republican Banner* made no direct attack on McGavock but in a more subdued fashion urged, "Let every voter imagine himself the proprietor of the whole city.... Only businessmen are suitable.... Even those who are not taxpayers expect to be sometime, or if not, they should feel sufficient pride in the city which is their home to see its government in the hands of the best qualified to secure its prosperity." The old Whig imagery was invoked, but the split in the Whig-American ranks ensured McGavock's victory. Thus, albeit somewhat equivocally, the Democrats won the mayor's office for the first time in twenty years.[73]

Randal McGavock embodied the notion of noblesse oblige; not at all an ideological democrat, skeptical of the masses, and fearful of "agrarianism," he nevertheless campaigned hard among the ethnic enclaves, at Irish boardinghouses and German balls. On September 24 he reported in his diary, "This morning the revolution in my favor commenced among the masses."[74] But there was no revolution in this election. The combined Whig-American vote was in fact larger than the vote for the two Democratic candidates and larger than McGavock's vote in all but the fifth and third wards. On the south side—the sixth, seventh, and eighth wards—just one of the Whig-American candidates ran ahead of him.[75] The old Whig consensus was intact within the city despite the resurgence of Democratic party organization.

The failure of the American party to present a viable alternative as a national party meant that by late 1858 the Whig-American coalition in Nashville was calling itself simply the Opposition. On the local level at least little else changed. Opposition candidates won consistently at the polls. In 1859 it was charged that John Hugh Smith, Nashville's mayor in 1845 and again from 1850 to 1852, had made a deal with the Democrats, but he lost nevertheless to the regular Opposition candidate. Opposition candidates won at least five of the eight aldermen's places in 1860.[76] Whig, Know-Nothing, American, Opposition—only the labels changed. When old Robert McEwen wrote his daughter about the renewed excitement of politics in the last few years of the fifties—"it carries one back to 40 and to 44 excitement"—he continued to refer to his party as the Whigs.[77]

Partisan excitement was maintained, partisan allegiance was sustained. Nashville was a Whig city; in the worst of times, it was at least an anti-Democrat city. But it was also a southern city. On the local level slavery was clearly not a debatable issue; nevertheless, slavery had been a major issue of national politics since the Van Buren campaign.[78] Southern nationalism grew intense in the fifties, and it was not confined to Democrats. John Bass and Francis Fogg, Democrat and Whig, respectively, and both devoted Episcopalians, helped organize the University of the South to free cultivated southerners from dependence on northern educational resources.[79] Economic dependence may have been even more galling, and the threat of northern domination of federal economic policies might very well have been appreciated by Nashvillians intent on their own region's economic development. However, Nashville's dependence on the northern money markets to maintain its Good Village undoubtedly reinforced its negative view of fire-eaters and secessionists.[80] At the same time, the persistence of the Whig consensus gave rise to the expectation that electoral successes could be achieved, that the party system was still at work, and that secession was a needlessly reckless option.[81]

Committed southerners, in no way "soft" on the slavery issue, Whigs could only dismiss the Democrats' charges as partisan and irresponsible. The Whig agenda had worked, after all; even Democrats had accepted a great part of it, including, most recently, public education, railroads, and workhouses. Yet there seemed to be no fruitful way for the parties to address the slavery issue. Instead, fear and frustration occasionally turned the Whigs' Good Village into a mob, all the while the real prosperity of the fifties kept the vote in the same columns. In 1855 rioters prevented a midnight mass at the Catholic cathedral in Nashville. In 1856 every ward in the city gave a majority of its votes to Fillmore, the Know-Nothing candidate.[82] The only other candidate was the Democrat, Buchanan. John C. Fremont, who headed the new Republican party ticket, was not on the ballot, but he was very much in the nightmares of southerners. Once more, in 1856, blacks became the scapegoats for the tension created by the dissolution of a political system. Patrician leaders who knew there was no slave conspiracy could not say so in public. Democrats and Whigs, they preferred to join in the great public celebration on the completion of the Louisville and Nashville Railroad connection which gave Nashville a north-south road—in 1859.[83]

In the face of the failure of the national political system, the Opposition, the old Whigs, and the new Unionists tried valiantly to find a solution that would maintain the politics they had known. The national Whig party was gone. The Republican party was exclusively northern. To join with the Democrats was unthinkable. In February 1860, in a gamble to build a bridge across the sections, the Constitutional Union party was organized in Nashville, with John Bell, a founder of the Whig party in Tennessee, as its presidential candidate and Edward Everett of Massachusetts as its vice-presidential candidate. Throughout the country the new party sought members and allies, looked for common political ground (sometimes with Douglas Democrats in a fusion ticket), and hoped to have the election forced from the electoral college to the House of Representatives—all desperate maneuvers aimed at preventing the success of both Republicans and Democrats.[84] The new party limited itself to a single platform statement, preservation of the Union, whose strength and weakness were illustrated by the jeers of the Democratic *Union*:

> The Constitutional Union Ticket—
> John Bell
>   Nobody's Man!
>   Stands on Nobody's Platform!!
>   Fights Nobody!!
>   Loves Nobody!!!!
>   E Pluribus Unum!!!!![85]

It was appropriate that the new party be born in Nashville, the Gibraltar of the Whigs in a sea of Democrats, border city and southern city. Here it made sense that, somehow, slavery would be accommodated within the Union; conferences, delegations, compromises—the political process would work. Within the city the new party's partisans pulled out all the stratagems and tactics of traditional party battles. There were floats and processions, liberty poles and guard companies; there were "Bell Pipes" and "Bell Segars." The ladies were once more called upon to impress upon their husbands and sons the urgency of voting the Union ticket.[86] That this activity was met by Democratic parades, barbecues, and guard companies lent an air of normality to the crisis.

But the secessionist orators had been raising the ante. William Yancey, the Alabama fire-eater, roared from the capitol in Nashville to a crowd of thousands that the federal government was obligated to protect slave property in the territories.[87] The Constitutional Union party refused to be baited into discussing the slavery issue but pressed its claim to represent the nation. It maintained the loyalty of the Opposition newspapers in Nashville. Its frantic activity seemed to be rewarded by the split in the Democratic party at its national convention in Baltimore. Bell's supporters were optimistic, convinced that the fire-eaters were fomenting division in order to elect Lincoln and precipitate secession, and with this evidence the Unionists would carry the day.[88] Nashville, almost half of Tennessee, and a good part of the South chose Bell and Union; Nashville gave 59 percent, Tennessee 48 percent, and the South 40 percent of the vote to Bell.[89] The Unionists insisted that the political process was still working. But, ominously, in Tennessee Bell's lead over John Breckinridge, the radical Democratic candidate, was less than 5,000 votes. Some Democrats, like V. K. Stevenson, president of the Nashville and Chattanooga Railroad, did opt for Stephen Douglas, the Unionist candidate, when their party split.[90] Most stayed with Breckinridge, however, and clung to the traditional Democratic suspicion of government by the monied interests and the profound fear of change that underlay and kept fully charged the fear of an attack upon slavery.[91]

After Lincoln's election and throughout the winter of 1861, the Union party and the Nashville majority clung to their national loyalties, despite the secession of South Carolina in December and the rest of the Lower South in January and February. In February, when a divided Tennessee legislature called for a popular referendum on convening to consider secession, John Bell and other Unionists campaigned strenuously against the convention and won, but by a small margin. The strength of the Unionists was eroding.

Nevertheless, the stampede to secession began in the Upper South only after Fort Sumter; April brought Lincoln's call for troops. John Lindsley reported in his diary "waves of revolution tempestuous" hitting the city in the last days of April.[92] Bell, without hope of compromise once southerners were called to fight southerners, declared for the South on April 28.[93] In May the Tennessee legislature voted for secession, and in June a popular referendum ratified that decision.[94] Bell and his supporters had always assumed what finally they could not secure. Their "conditional Unionism" dissolved when guarantees of neither slavery's safety nor the Union's integrity proved possible.[95] The secessionists took over; Union diehards left the city or held their tongues. Ex-mayor McGavock raised a troop of infantry, the "Bloody Tenth," from among his Irish constituents.[96] Ultimately, even in Nashville, the appeal of southern nationalism, aggravated by a decade of confrontational politics, triumphed, and the young men put on uniforms.[97]

Perhaps it is evidence of how late and by what a narrow margin the choice for secession was made in Nashville that in the excitement of the "revolution" few plans seem to have been made to fortify the city. Nashville was the first major city to fall to Union troops. It was taken without a battle and remained an occupied city from February 1862 until the end of the war. Indeed, Nashville became a crucial federal arsenal. Despite the hostility of much of its population to federal occupation and despite the acts of individuals committed to the Confederacy, there was no organized attempt at rebellion or at guerrilla warfare from within the city. Rather, Unionists, both old Nashvillians and newcomers to the city, worked with the northern war effort to advance their own and, as they saw it, the city's benefit in these turbulent years.[98]

Nashville was a mature urban society by 1860. Its continuously voiced concern for progress, property, and morality as well as its municipal and voluntary institutions sometimes made it seem more like other cities, northern as well as southern, than like the southern rural culture around it.[99] But it remained closely tied to, surrounded by, and dependent upon its agricultural hinterland. And it remained a slave-owning society. In the end, southern fears of northern aggression prevailed, the Whig consensus and the political process failed, and Nashville reluctantly went to war.

Nashville's first eighty years saw the transformation of a western frontier into a southern city. The first West of the new American republic was captured in the process that slowly converted a stockade and land office into a county seat. A leadership cadre of land speculators and Jeffersonian republicans, of pragmatic entrepreneurs and aspiring gentlemen, made good use of frontier opportunities to re-create a society in the wilderness, a traditional society tempered by democratic manners and considerable room at the top.

As farms and plantations began to produce for market, Nashville experienced a second frontier, an urban frontier dominated by merchants as eager for success as the pioneers on the land. This second frontier quickly produced the barges, keelboats, and steamboats, the credit and the banks, to build a market town. Based on the cotton and tobacco of the countryside, Nashville's economy knew boom and bust and boom again. Much of its population was transient, but successful staple merchants and their lawyer allies created a stable core of leaders within the town. They dominated town government and began to create the institutions— lyceums, churches, Bible societies, female academies, and charitable organizations—that convinced them of their own position at the top of the town's social hierarchy.

The second frontier inherited much from the first, most significantly its continued dependence on the products of the countryside and its continued reliance on slavery, both of which marked Nashville as a southern community. On the frontiers slavery exhibited its inherent contradictions grossly. Here the value of black people as assets that could be traded in lieu of cash made them even more vulnerable to the vagaries and necessities of unsettled masters, while, at the same time, slaves here worked and lived more closely than ever with their masters. The urban frontier also made it easier for slaves to know other black people outside the master's household. Black people once more put together families and, over time, were able to build their own social networks within the growing city.

Nashville's growth made it impossible for frontier definitions of society and politics to remain static. Republican squires and staple merchants may have rejected hereditary rank, but they retained the notions of "place" and of their own place at the top. However, just as they were creating the wealth and the organizations to confirm their political and social leadership, the town was developing around them, not only physically and demographically but also politically. In the long run, the panic of 1819 may have meant greater political than economic disruption. By the mid-twenties Nashville's economy was on the upswing again and following the patterns laid out in the prepanic years, but politics were changing. A new democratic rhetoric flourished in the twenties, first heard in the antibank, anti-bank-director, and antiprivilege campaigns at the state level, then slowly incorporated into the city's politics. Andrew Jackson's second presidential campaign initiated heated contests at the corporation level; local issues intensified political consciousness; and, as faction began the slide toward party, Nashville's leadership elites had to come to terms with the new democratic themes. The distinction Andrew Jackson drew between producers on the one hand and speculators and bankers on the other was not acceptable to Nashville's merchants and bankers. At least for a time, they were able to insist that the relevant distinction was that between taxpayers and nontaxpayers, between property holders and nonproperty holders. Ultimately forced to widen the electorate to include all adult white males, Nashville's leaders participated in and helped create a Whig party that served as the glue of the good society as they defined it.

Whig rhetoric glossed over, indeed, rejected, the idea of divisions within the city, though they were evident in the disparities and concentration of wealth, in the fixed, hard reality of slavery, and in a growing ethnic presence. Economic prosperity in the late forties and the fifties undoubtedly did ease the rub of financial and social distinctions. Slavery helped make it impossible for working-class solidarity to emerge as an effective counter to Whig politics or Whig rhetoric. Nativism, which associated immigrants with alien Catholicism and the taint of poverty, again reinforced the voting alliance of merchants, bankers, master mechanics, and a sufficient number of respectable workingmen. The strength of the Whig ethos was positive as well as negative, however, and was underlined, ironically perhaps, by the economic success of some immigrants and by the eagerness of some immigrants to duplicate the institutional structures of the Whig majority. By and large, however, immigrants as well as black people and "the poor" were barred from participation in the Good Village. Black people, slave and free, struggled mightily to sustain their churches and schools, which were viable, though threatened, urban institutions by 1860. The Whig, white, native majority defined itself by contrast with the poor; those who had arrived at the top rungs and those who were climbing the success ladder made up the Good Village.

Nashville's Whig consensus lasted for a quarter of a century. It survived the Whig party because it promised much and delivered a good deal. It changed the terms of political discourse and the ways in which society was interpreted. The insistence on economic and technological development as the answer to social problems and the promise of social mobility as the reward for hard work and self-discipline were urban and national rather than rural and sectional themes. Nashville's history in the forties and spectacularly in the fifties complemented the Whig promises: successful mechanics became movers and doers in both city and party government; city services, from the waterworks to the fire department, were expanded; a public school system was implemented; the city invested heavily in railroads to maintain and extend its reach into the countryside. Urban success fueled the intensity of the Unionist campaign, the almost startling strength of the antisecessionist movement, which gave way only with the call to arms.

Just here Nashville's urban history demonstrated its essential southern character. The city, like its hinterland, fully accepted slavery, and ultimately the city moved as a southern city. Most of its leaders tried desperately to find solutions short of secession. Though the party system remained viable to the bitter end, the end did come. The war years brought Nashville its quota of disaster and political turmoil. Much would never be the same. The Whig party would never be resurrected; nor would an effective two-party system emerge from the period of occupation and Reconstruction. Still, some patterns would hold. In 1880 Nashville's leading entrepreneurs continued to be wholesale merchants, building upon the strategic position given the city by the Louisville and Nashville Railroad, and the city's leading men insisted that they had climbed the success ladder rung by rung.[100] The self-made men of the New South could easily build upon the essential themes of Nashville's antebellum Whigs.

APPENDIX

Table 1. Population of Nashville

Year	Total	% increase	White	Black	Slave	Free black	Black population as % of total pop.	Black population % increase
1800	345	—	191	154	151	3	45	—
1810	1,100	219	—	—	—	—	—	—
1820	3,076	180	2,054	1,022	964	58	33	564[a]
1830	5,566	80	3,554	2,012	1,808	204	36	97
1840	6,929	24	4,406	2,523	2,114	409	36	25
1850	10,165	47	7,626	2,539	2,028	511	25	1
1860	16,988	67	13,043	3,945	3,226	719	23	55

SOURCE: U.S. Census.
a. Percentage increase: 1800–1820.

Table 2. Household Heads Claiming Property

Year	Number	Percentage	Number claiming real estate only	Percentage claiming real estate only	Source
1820	87	27	—	—	1820 Census 1816 Tax List
1830	162	22	92	12	1830 Census 1829 Tax List
1840	282	31	232	25	1840 Census 1839 Tax List
1850			369	27	1850 Census
1860	1,359	55	831	34	1860 Census

Table 3. Population by Sex and Race

Year	White Male	White Female	Female percentage of white population	Black Male	Black Female	Female percentage of black population
1800	131	60	31	—	—	—
1810	—	—	—	—	—	—
1820	1,260	794	39	521	501	49
1830	2,006	1,548	44	958	1,054	52
1840	2,337	2,069	47	1,097	1,426	57
1850	4,016	3,610	47	1,233	1,306	52
1860	6,968	6,075	47	1,743	2,202	56

SOURCE: U.S. Census.

Table 4. Persistence: Household Heads

Years	Total persistence (percentage)	No. households	Year
1811[a]–20	23	382	1820
1821–30	30	742	1830
1831–40	25	911	1840
1841–50	28	1,385	1850
1851–60	26	2,472	1860

a. Because the U.S. Census of 1810 did not include data for Nashville, the 1811 militia list for the town of Nashville, TSLA, was used in this instance. All other figures were compiled from the U.S. Census.

Table 5. Mayoral Elections

Year	Total vote	Winner	Winner's vote	Party of mayor
1828	750	F. Robertson	531	—
1830	309	W. Armstrong	273	—
1831	—	W. Armstrong	—	—
1832	—	W. Armstrong	—	—
1833	590	J. Bass	387	—
1834	571	J. P. Erwin	410	—
1835	—	W. Nichol	—	—
1836	—	W. Nichol	uncontested	—
1837	779	H. Hollingsworth	430	D
1838	818	H. Hollingsworth	411	D
1839	855	C. Trabue	517	W
1840	1,000	C. Trabue	599	W
1841	908	S. Stout	333	W
1842	981	T. Coleman	608	W
1843	1,050	P. Maxey	596	W
1844	1,218	P. Maxey	709	W
1845	1,179	J. H. Smith	444	W
1846	1,267	J. Goodlett	463	W
1847	1,438	A. Allison	834	W
1848	849	A. Allison	uncontested	W
1849	1,268	J. Lea	528	W
1850	1,247	J. H. Smith	625	W
1851	1,422	J. H. Smith	719	W
1852	1,553	J. H. Smith	752	W
1853	1,663	W. Horn	567	W
1854	1,443	W. Shapard	1,188	A
1855	1,333	R. Castleman	855	A
1856	1,734	A. Anderson	1,058	A
1857	2,239	J. McEwen	1,167	A
1858	2,438	R. McGavock	948	D
1859	2,394	S. Hollingsworth	1,198	O
1860	2,623	R. Cheatham	966	O

A = American
D = Democrat
O = Opposition
W = Whig

Table 6. Political Affiliation of Aldermen by Wards

Year	\multicolumn{8}{c}{Ward number}	Total
	1	2	3	4	5	6	7	8	
1835	WW	WW	DD	W	DD	WD			6W, 5D, 1?
1836	WW	WW	WD	WD	DW	WD			8W, 4D
1837	W	WW	WD	DD	DW	WD			6W, 5D, 1?
1838	WW	WW	WD	DD	DW	D			6W, 5D, 1?
1839	WD	WW	WW	WW	WW	WW			11W, 1D
1840	WW	WW	WW	WW	WW	WW			12W
1841	W	W	WD	WD	W	WW			7W, 2D, 3?
1842	WW		WW	WD	WD	W			7W, 2D, 3?
1843	WD	D	WW	WD	WD	W			6W, 3D, 2?
1844	WW	WW	WW	WW	WW	DD			10W, 2D
1845	WD	W	WW	WW	WW	D			8W, 2D, 2?
1846	WD	W	WW	DD	WW				6W, 3D, 3?
1847	WD	WW	WW	DD	WW	W			8W, 3D, 1?
1848	WD	W	WW	D	WW	D			6W, 3D, 3?
1849	WD	WW	WW	WD	WW	D			8W, 3D, 1?
1850	DD	D	WW	WW	WW	WW			8W, 3D, 1?
1851	D	W	WW	WW	WW	WW			9W, 1D, 2?
1852	DW	DW	WW	WW	WW	WD			9W, 3D
1853	DD	DW	W	D	WW	WD			5W, 5D, 2?
1854	AD/A	A	AA	AA	AA	DA	DA	AA	12A, 2D, 1?
1855	AA	AD	AA	AA	AA	AA	AA	AA	15A, 1D
1856	A	AD	A	A	AA	AA	D	AA	10A, 2D, 4?
1857	A	DD	A	A	AA	A	AD	AA	9A, 3D, 4?
1858[a]		O		O	O			O	4O, 4?
1859[a]	O	O	O	O	O	O	D	O	7O, 1D
1860[a]	O	O	O		O		D	O	5O, 1D, 2?

a. Reorganization of city government had reduced the number of aldermen to eight.

A = American
D = Democrat
O = Opposition
W = Whig

Table 7.

**Nashville: Municipal Disbursements in Selected Years:
Totals and Selected Items (in Dollars and Percentage of Total)**

Year	Total ($)	Watch ($)	%	Streets and street hands ($)	%	Water-works ($)	%	Fire ($)	%	Hospital ($)	%
1828	4,061	897	22	1,324	33	540	13			60[a]	2
1830	8,975	1,152	13	4,475	50						
1840	28,072	3,382	12	3,206	11	3,997	14				
1845	38,804	2,971	8	3,520	9	3,597	9			131[a]	<1
1851	112,503	6,861	6	16,518	15	12,032	11	2,790	2		
1855	171,198	9,423	6	11,039	6	10,952	6	2,901	2	2,960	2
1858	239,268	14,391	6	7,850	3	39,756	17	4,266	2	1,431	1
1859	225,399	15,503	7	22,386	10	39,878	18	7,452	3	464	<1
1860	382,155	15,551	4	50,233	13	56,833	15	17,690	5	2,888	1

Year	Work-house ($)	%	Charity ($)	%	Interest ($)	%	Salaries ($)	%	Bills payable[b] ($)	%
1828										
1830										
1840							1,200	4		
1845					6,060	16	1,150	3		
1851					20,301	18	5,498	5	32,975	29
1855			386	<1	41,636	24	8,488	5		
1858	5,848	2	1,009	<1	51,268	21	9,593	4	30,240	13
1859	21,847	10	965	<1	49,061	22	10,036	4	4,443	2
1860	12,130	3	1,302	<1	54,003	14	9,545	2	33,061	9

SOURCE: Annual reports of the Board of Aldermen.

a. Expenditures for medical purposes.
b. New and undifferentiated accounts, such as "Bills Payable," were added in the fifties and make it difficult to determine exactly where all tax monies were going.

NOTES

Abbreviations Used

DC	Davidson County, Tennessee
MBA	Minutes of the Board of Aldermen, Office of the Metropolitan Clerk, Metro Courthouse, Nashville, Tennessee
PMLT	Petitions and Memorials to the Legislature of Tennessee,
THS	Tennessee Historical Society
TSLA	Tennessee State Library and Archives

Introduction

1. I use the terms *Jacksonian America* and *Age of Jackson* to cover the period from the mid-1820s through the 1840s. Although Lee Benson has provided important insights into Jacksonian politics, his suggestion that the period might be called the Age of Egalitarianism simply does not seem fitting in a history of Jackson's own city *(Concept of Jacksonian America,* 336).
2. Elkins and McKitrick, "A Meaning for Turner's Frontier, Part 1" 321–53.
3. Zane Miller and James B. Crooks commented upon an early paper that I delivered in 1969 to a session of the Southern Historical Association.
4. Thernstrom, "New Urban History," 43.
5. See Thernstrom, *Poverty and Progress,* and Thernstrom and Sennett (eds.), *Nineteenth-Century Cities.*
6. See Doyle, *Social Order of a Frontier Community;* Frisch, *Town into City;* and Warner, *Private City.*
7. I have consulted with profit, in addition to the works cited above, the following books: Amos, *Cotton City;* Blumin, *Urban Threshold;* Gold-

field, *Urban Growth in the Age of Sectionalism;* and Conzen, *Immigrant Milwaukee.*

8. See, for example, Dawley, *Class and Community;* Laurie, *Working People of Philadelphia;* Ryan, *Cradle of the Middle Class;* and Wilentz, *Chants Democratic.* See also Blumin, "The Hypothesis of Middle-Class Formation in Nineteenth-Century America," and Sutcliffe, "Urban History in the Eighties."

9. See Goldfield, "The New Regionalism" and "The Urban South," and Mahoney, "Urban History in a Regional Context."

10. Leuchtenburg, "The Pertinence of Political History."

11. Wilentz, "Class and Politics in Jacksonian America," 58.

12. Turner, *The Frontier in American History.*

13. My reading of Nashville's frontier eras owes a great deal to Thomas P. Abernethy's pioneering work and especially to his *From Frontier to Plantation in Tennessee.*

14. Hofstadter, *The American Political Tradition,* especially chap. 3, and Hammond, *Banks and Politics in America.*

15. Elkins and McKitrick, "A Meaning for Turner's Frontier, Part 1."

16. See Elkins and McKitrick's reservations about the southern frontier in "A Meaning for Turner's Frontier, Part 2."

17. Wade, *Urban Frontier,* chap. 4.

18. Bogue, "Social Theory and the Pioneer." See also Doyle's cogent critique of the Elkins and McKitrick thesis in *Social Order of a Frontier Community,* 1–10.

19. Doyle, *Social Order of a Frontier Community,* 41–61, 91; Warner, *Private City,* x, 62, 100; and C. S. Rosenberg, *Religion and the American City,* 7–8, 38–39.

20. Pessen, *Jacksonian America,* 251–66.

21. Gilkeson, *Middle-Class Providence,* chap. 2; Ryan, *Cradle of the Middle Class,* chap. 3; Doyle, "Social Functions of Voluntary Associations"; and Banner, "Religous Benevolence as Social Control."

22. A fine exception to this statement is Bridges, *A City in the Republic.*

23. McCormick, *The Second American Party System;* Watson, *Jacksonian Politics and Community Conflict;* and Howe, *Political Culture of the American Whigs.* J. Mills Thornton, in *Politics and Power in a Slave Society,* is especially enlightening on Democratic political culture in the South.

24. Nashville's popular political rhetoric was very close indeed to central themes of the Republican party's ideology as documented in Foner, *Free Soil, Free Labor, Free Men.*

25. David R. Goldfield makes the case for the southernness of antebellum southern cities depending upon slavery, staple agriculture, and northern money markets in *Cotton Fields and Skyscrapers,* chap. 2.

26. Curry, "Urbanization and Urbanism in the Old South."

27. See Kruman, *Parties and Politics in North Carolina,* 133, 181, 196–212.

Chapter 1: Leadership in a Frontier County

1. The nineteenth-century narratives remain the best sources for "telling the story": J. Haywood, *Civil and Political History of Tennessee;* Putnam, *History of Middle Tennessee;* Ramsey, *The Annals of Tennessee.*
2. Abernethy, *From Frontier to Plantation in Tennessee,* 24ff.
3. "Articles of Agreement, or Compact of Government, entered into by settlers on the Cumberland River, 1st May 1780," in Putnam, *History of Middle Tennessee,* 94–102.
4. Information about the members of the court of notables has been assembled from public records in TSLA: Davidson County, Minute Books of the County Court, Deed and Will Books, 1798 Tax List; Sumner County, Will Books and Tax Lists of 1793, 1795, 1796; Montgomery County, Will Books; Index to North Carolina Land Grants; Index to Tennessee Land Grants. In addition to Haywood, Putnam, and Ramsey, cited above, see also Williams, *Dawn of Tennessee Valley and Tennessee History;* Cisco, *Historic Sumner County, Tennessee;* Durham, *The Great Leap Westward;* and J. E. Pike (ed.), "A Letter Home."
5. Robertson deserves a better biography than Thomas E. Matthews's rambling account, *General James Robertson.* In addition to the public records and narratives cited above, see "Correspondence of General James Robertson" and Whitaker (ed.), "Letters of James Robertson and Daniel Smith," 409–12.
6. The best account of this episode remains Abernethy, *From Frontier to Plantation in Tennessee,* 52–58, 348, 352.
7. J. Haywood, *Civil and Political History of Tennessee,* 218–20, lists preemptioners.
8. William Blount to John Gray Blount, Nov. 7, 1797, *John Gray Blount Papers,* 3:178; Masterson, *William Blount,* especially 88, 164-65, 298.
9. Chapell, "Land Speculation and Taxation" 35, 51; Masterson, *William Blount,* 235; William Blount to James Robertson, Oct. 1, 1794, and Oct. 3, 1795, "Correspondence of General James Robertson," 3:359, 4:74.
10. The eight representatives were James Robertson, Elijah Robertson, Anthony Bledsoe, David Hay, Robert Hays, Thomas Hardeman, William Polk, and Joel Rice.
11. For information about these justices, see, in addition to the sources listed in note 4, "Papers of General Daniel Smith," 213–35; Durham, *Daniel Smith;* Des Champs, "Early Days in the Cumberland Country," 6:195–229; Goodpasture, "Beginnings of Montgomery County," 8:193–215. Manuscript sketches in TSLA's Miscellaneous Collections include Glenn I. Johnson, "Epoch from His Pills: The Legacy of Dr. John Sappington," and Charles A. Marlin, "Sketch of Ephraim McLain."

12. Arnow, "Education and the Professions in the Cumberland Region," 123; Index to North Carolina Land Grants (TSLA); DC Will Book 9, 54 (1826); DC Tax List 1798 (TSLA).

13. Sumner County Will Books, 1, 153.

14. DC Will Book B, 63 (1797); Index to North Carolina Land Grants (TSLA); DC Tax List, 1798 (TSLA).

15. In 1795 Blount was able to buy Robertson's share of some of their jointly owned lands at twenty-five cents per acre, and in the same year Elijah Robertson exchanged thirty-three thousand acres of land for Andrew Jackson's store, a transaction that probably netted Elijah less than twenty-five cents an acre (William Blount to John Gray Blount, Sept. 22, 1795, *John Gray Blount Papers* 1:595). See also Remini, *Andrew Jackson and the American Empire,* 89.

16. William Blount to John Gray Blount, Nov. 7, 1790, *John Gray Blount Papers,* 1:131; William Blount to Governor Sevier, July 6, 1798, THS: Miscellaneous Collections, TSLA.

17. Information about these justices was gathered from the sources listed in note 4 and from the following sources, all located in TSLA: Claybrooke and Overton Papers, Nichol-Britt Collection, Samuel A. Weakley Papers, THS: Murdock Collection, Overton Papers, THS: Miscellaneous Collections. See also Spence and Spence, *History of Hickman County;* Leach, "John Gordon" 322–44; James Byrn's obituary, *Whig,* Jan. 31, 1825.

18. Jackson's most recent biographer, Robert V. Remini, emphasizes the importance of Blount to Jackson's early career (*Andrew Jackson and the American Empire,* 53).

19. In addition to sources cited above in note 5, see Robertson's correspondence in the John Coffee Papers, TSLA, and in *American State Papers,* 1:253, 453, 467. For a description of Robertson's farm in 1787, see Arnow, *Flowering of the Cumberland,* 233–34; for a description of his ironworks, see Corlew, "Aspects of Slavery in Dickson County," 226, 228. The quotation from the Indian chief appears in Lewis, "James Robertson, Nashville's Founder," 286.

20. In addition to sources cited above in notes 4, 11, and 15, see the James McGavock Dickinson Papers, the Robert Whyte Papers, TSLA; William G. Nicholson, "Sketches of Nashville People," in THS: Miscellaneous Collections, TSLA; Clayton, *History of Davidson County;* Gower and Allen (eds.), *Pen and Sword;* Speer (ed.), *Sketches of Prominent Tennesseans;* Williams, *History of the Lost State of Franklin;* Glass, "Sketch of Henry Rutherford," 225–29; Kinard, "Frontier Development of Williamson County," 3–33, 127–53; and N. L. Parks, "The Career of John Bell," 229–42.

21. Tax List, 13th Assessment District, Oct. 1, 1798, TSLA; 618 names are listed. Two pages of the list are missing; the figure of 700 is, therefore, an approximation.

22. In 1800 approximately 1,746 white males over the age of sixteen re-

sided in the county (*Return of the Whole Number of Persons within. . . . the U.S. . . . 1800*, 88).

23. Nine landholders are listed; the holdings of W. T. Lewis, John McNairy, and James Robertson, all large landowners, are illegible or on the missing pages (Tax List, 13th Assessment District, Oct. 1, 1798, TSLA).

24. John Overton to Tench Coxe, Dec. 2, 1795, Overton Letter Book, 34, TSLA.

25. Abernethy, *From Frontier to Plantation in Tennessee*, 359.

26. P. M. Hamer, *Tennessee*, 1:202. See also Durham, *Daniel Smith*, 143–44.

27. P. M. Hamer, *Tennessee*, 1:217–18.

28. Remini, *Andrew Jackson and the American Empire*, 119.

29. J. H. Parks, *Felix Grundy*, 34–37.

30. Sellers, *James K. Polk, Jacksonian*, 68.

31. The work of the court is described in the Minute Books of the Davidson County Court, 1784–1803. A similar pattern is described in Browning, "Washington County Court," 328–43.

32. DC Will Book, 1, 41, 43.

33. DC Minute Book A, 220 (1788).

34. DC Minute Book A, 55 (1785); C, 177 (1799).

35. DC Minute Book A, 240, 243 (1788); DC Minute Book B, 358, 372 (1796); DC Minute Book C, 168 (1799), 289 (1800); DC Minute Book D, 30 (1802), 101 (1803). For quotation see Minute Book B, 264 (1795).

36. See, for example, DC Minute Book A, 55 (1785).

37. DC Minute Book A, 240 (1788), B, 372 (1796), and C, 168 (1799).

38. DC Minute Book B, 345 (1796).

39. DC Minute Book A, 153 (1787), 27 (1784); DC Will Book, 245–47 (1802), 319–21 (1803).

40. DC Minute Book A, 29, 31, 36 (1784).

41. Putnam, *History of Middle Tennessee*, 639.

42. For information on Craighead, see Clayton, *History of Davidson County*, 215, 312, and Doak, "Development of Education in Tennessee," 71.

43. John Gray Blount to Willie Blount, May 11, 1800, *John Gray Blount Papers*, 3:376–77.

44. Sumner County Will Book, 1, 153 (1812).

45. The crucifix is reported some years later: see Flanigen (ed.), *Catholicity in Tennessee*, 9.

46. "Report of the Journey of the Brethren Abraham Steiner and Frederick C. De Schweinitz to the Cherokees and the Cumberland Settlements" (1799), in Williams (ed.), *Early Travels in the Tennessee Country*, 512.

47. *Journal and Letters of Francis Asbury*, 3:125.

48. Elijah Robertson's assessment for the support of the Reverend Mr. Craighead, 1793, THS, TSLA, Miscellaneous Collections.

49. McFerrin, *History of Methodism in Tennessee*, 1:397; on church mem-

bership, see also 134, 157, 217, 224, 336. For Bishop Asbury's comment, see *Journal and Letters of Francis Asbury*, 3:256.

50. "Report. . . . of the Brethren Abraham Steiner and Frederick C. De Schweinitz . . ." (1799), in Williams (ed.), *Early Travels in the Tennessee Country*, 513.

51. "The Conference Business of the Baptist Church under the Care of James Whitsitt, on Mill Creek, Davidson County," Record Book, 1797–1814, TSLA.

52. Reps, *The Making of Urban America*, 210, 217.

53. Chacere to Bouligny, Dec. 10, 1785, "Papers from the Spanish Archives," 140. See also Louis Brantz, "Memoranda of Journey, 1785," in Williams (ed.), *Early Travels in the Tennessee Country*, 285.

54. DC Deed Books, passim, 1784–90.

55. DC Minute Book B, 58.

Chapter 2: Leadership on the Urban Frontier

1. James C. Bonner, *Milledgeville: Georgia's Antebellum Capital*, a study of a frontier village that became a state capital but remained a political and legal center only, underscores the significance of a merchant community in promoting urban development. Milledgeville never really claimed city status.

2. The phrase, of course, is that of Richard Hofstadter (*The American Political Tradition*, 57).

3. Cf. Wade, *Urban Frontier*, 77.

4. *Return of the Whole Number of Persons within the U.S. 1800*, 88.

5. In 1816, 953 landholders were taxed; two-thirds of them held no more than 300 acres. While in 1798 twelve men claimed more than 5,000 acres, in 1816 only one, William Tait, did so (D. C. Tax List, 1816, TSLA).

6. Nashville Population Schedule, 1820, transcribed from the manuscript U.S. census by Martha Lou Houston, TSLA. References to the 1820 census are to this mimeographed typescript.

7. See Appendix, table 1.

8. Ibid. When "frontier" is defined to refer to only rural areas, the male-female ratio resembles that of long-settled areas (J. E. Davis, *Frontier America*, 22, 67).

9. This may overstate the transiency of the population. In 1820, 1830, and 1840, only the heads of households were identified by name. Some men on the 1811 militia roll may have been included in other people's households in 1820. The problem is the same for the later years. As historian Mary E. Young once put it, working with antebellum statistical data can be like "sculpting in butter."

10. See Appendix, table 3. Of the 386 household heads on the 1820 census, 115 are found again on the 1830 census. The persistence rate of

Nashville's population was calculated by tracing the heads of households from one census to the next from 1820 to 1860.

11. Thernstrom, *Poverty and Progress*, 158–59; Knights, *Plain People of Boston*, 121.

12. Knights, *Plain People of Boston*, 103. Some of the difference in these cases may be accounted for by the difference in the size of the populations measured.

13. Goldfield, *Urban Growth in the Age of Sectionalism*, 64; Conzen, *Immigrant Milwaukee*, 42. The 1850–60 transiency rates for Richmond and for Milwaukee were approximately 66 percent and 61 percent, respectively.

14. Doyle, *Social Order of a Frontier Community*, 95.

15. *Whig*, June 11, 1825; for information on White, see F. Robertson, "Address," 446–54; for information on Yandell, see Clayton, *History of Davidson County*, 285.

16. *Gazette*, Mar. 31, Apr. 7, 1802.

17. Frontier conditions undoubtedly aggravated but did not wholly account for the low status of doctors, which prevailed even in major cities. See C. Rosenberg, *The Cholera Years*, 70, 222.

18. The *Whig* pled, "A rule is desirable for *county* days that not more than *six* persons speak at once" (Jan. 17, 1825). The letters of the "modern attorney" were published in the *Whig* from July 1823 to Jan. 1824; see especially Oct. 20, Nov. 17, 1823, Jan. 19, 1824. On Sam Houston's career, see Caldwell, *Sketches of the Bench and Bar*, 97. In 1815 George Campbell offered to take law students at $150 for a full course or $75 for a year (George W. Campbell to James Winchester, May 29, 1815, THS: James Winchester Papers, TSLA).

19. The standard biography of Grundy is J. H. Parks, *Felix Grundy*. On Overton, see Clifton, "The Life and Activities of John Overton"; Caldwell, *Sketches of the Bench and Bar*, 77–79; and a sketch by John Lea in THS: John Overton Collection, TSLA. On Whiteside, see Caldwell, 52–53, and *Constitutional Advocate*, Oct. 22, 1822.

20. Whiteside and Alfred Balch bought from Judge McNairy a tract adjoining Nashville that was divided into ninety-three lots in 1824 and incorporated into the town in 1837.

21. Wooldridge (ed.), *History of Nashville*, 516–18.

22. *Whig*, July 11, 1815. Dickinson earned a baccalaureate at Dartmouth when he was sixteen and then came to Tennessee with his tutor-turned-land-locater, Moses Fisk. Dickinson taught school, boarded and read law with Judge McNairy, and was licensed to practice in Davidson County when he was nineteen.

23. Lists of directors were published in the newspapers: *Clarion*, Dec. 6, 1808, Jan. 18, 1811, Jan. 5, 1813, Jan. 11, 1814, Jan. 8, 1817, Jan. 6, 1818, Jan. 5, 1819, Jan. 4, 1820; *Whig*, Jan. 4, 1815, Jan. 3, 1821. See also Wooldridge (ed.), *History of Nashville*, 265, 272–73.

24. Francis Baily, in Williams (ed.), *Early Travels in the Tennessee Country,* 412; David McGavock, May 3, 1801, in Gower and Allen (eds.), *Pen and Sword,* 19.

25. Anthony Foster to John Overton, Sept. 24, Nov. 4, 1798, Claybrooke and Overton Papers, TSLA; Foster to Governor Blount, July 1792, in *American State Papers,* 1:283–84; Inventory of the Estate of Francis Sappington, DC Will Book 2, 189, 224; *Impartial Review,* Nov. 15, 1806; *Whig,* Dec. 1, 1819; Index to North Carolina Land Grants, TSLA.

26. *Tennessee Gazette,* Sept. 22, 1802, Mar. 27, 1805.

27. John Overton to David Henley, Dec. 10, 1795, David Henley Papers, TSLA; DC Minute Book C, 84; William Blount to James Robertson, Apr. 29, 1792, in Carter (ed.), *Territorial Papers,* 4:146; Blount to Robertson, Jan. 19, Mar. 7, 1794, "Correspondence of General James Robertson," 3:282–83, 287.

28. List of certificates delivered to William Tait. . . . July 26, 1793, July 26, 1794, THS: Miscellaneous, TSLA.

29. Deposition of Sampson Williams, July 7, 1795, David Henley Papers; David Henley to James Robertson, July 9, 1794, "Correspondence of General James Robertson," 3:376–77.

30. Deaderick advanced funds to federal officials for the boats that would follow Aaron Burr's suspect adventurers down the Mississippi (Andrew Jackson to William B. Lewis, Aug. 19, 1828, *Correspondence of Andrew Jackson,* 3:427).

31. Moon, *Sketches,* 121.

32. *Whig,* Feb. 9, 1820; DC Will Book 10, 57; DC Will Book 4, 311–13; Jesse Wharton to John Overton, Aug. 19, 1832, Claybrooke and Overton Papers, TSLA.

33. Clayton, *History of Davidson County,* 212; *Clarion,* Feb. 22, 1811.

34. Whitaker, *The Mississippi Question,* 131.

35. *Tennessee Gazette,* Feb. 18, July 29, 1801.

36. Ibid., Feb. 16, 1803. For earlier agitation concerning this issue in Nashville, see "Proceedings of a Meeting Held by Representatives of Militia Companies of Davidson and Sumner Counties," June 2, 1786, Microfilm, 5XX18 Draper Collection of Manuscripts, State Historical Society of Wisconsin, Madison (photostats in TSLA); Lardin [sic] Clark to Colonel Hawkins, Sept. 8, 1789, *The Diaries of George Washington,* 4:88–89.

37. Andrew Ewing, "Memorandum Book, 1780–1851," microfilm, Vanderbilt University.

38. *Clarion,* Oct. 26, 1810.

39. See, e.g., advertisements in the *Clarion,* May 21, 1811, June 7, 1814, June 10, 1817.

40. Atherton, *Frontier Merchant* 18, 115; *Clarion,* Feb. 22, 1811.

41. David Allison to John G. Blount, Jan. 21, 1796, *John Gray Blount Papers,* 3:11.

42. See, e.g., DC Minute Book D, 211, 212, 243.

43. John C. McLemore to John Coffee, Oct. 13, 1822, Mar. 4, 1824, and Thomas Crutcher to John Coffee, 1823, John Coffee Papers, TSLA; DC Will Book 3/4, 426; DC Will Book 5, 366–371.

44. "S" to a friend "back home," *Whig*, Oct. 20, 1817.

45. Speer (ed.), *Sketches of Prominent Tennesseans*, 277.

46. R. C. Foster to E. H. Foster, Oct. 31, 1817, Foster Family Papers, TSLA.

47. J. R. Bedford to William Bedford, Mar. 3, 1815, THS: Miscellaneous Collections, TSLA. The emphasis is mine.

48. J. P. Erwin to James Erwin, Apr. 24, 1825, THS: Miscellaneous Collections, TSLA.

49. The twenty-eight men named in both the militia roll and the census were Robert Armstrong, John Baird, Stephen Cantrell, William Carroll, Thomas Deaderick, Anthony Foster, Elihu Hall, Thomas Hill, Andrew Hynes, Alpha Kingsley, Thomas Kirkman, William Lytle, John Nichol, Josiah Nichol, Joseph Park, Alexander Porter, John Price, Ephraim Pritchett, Thomas Read, Alexander Richardson, Duncan Robertson, Robert Searcy, Samuel Seay, Robert Stothart, Wilkins Tannehill, Joseph Woods, Thomas Yeatman, and John Young. Nineteen of these men were listed "in commerce" on the 1820 census; the nine others had been merchants at some time since 1800 and are included to give perspective on merchants' careers during the period. The sources of greatest utility for the description that follows are the Nashville newspapers (*Impartial Review and Cumberland Repository*, 1805–8; *Clarion*, 1800–1822; *Nashville Whig* 1812–25); DC Deed and Will Books; manuscript and typescript tax lists of Davidson County for 1787, 1798, 1816, and 1829, TSLA. Clayton's *History of Davidson County* includes a number of sketches of nineteenth-century businessmen.

50. See, for example, Goldfield, *Urban Growth in the Age of Sectionalism*, 40.

51. DC Will Book 3/4, 451–55.

52. Remini, *Andrew Jackson and the American Empire*, 132–34; see also Hardeman, *Wilderness Calling*, 40–45.

53. Andrew Jackson to Josiah Nichol, June 9, 1814, *Correspondence of Andrew Jackson*, 2:5–6.

54. Farrell and Farrell, *Burlington*, TSLA; DC Will Book 9, 128; DC Will Book 7, 176–98.

55. DC Will Book 10, 186, 239.

56. A. C. Hall, "Economic and Social Beginnings of Tennessee," 33; *Whig*, Nov. 2, 1814, June 20, 1815, Nov. 8, 1820; McDonald, "Milling in Middle Tennessee," 164, 167–68, 170; U.S. Census of Manufactures, Nashville, Feb. 1, 1820, TSLA.

57. *Correspondence of Andrew Jackson*, 1:261.

58. Newcomer, "Two New England Teachers," 77; *Clarion,* June 14, 1814; *Whig,* Aug. 8, 1818; Clayton, *History of Davidson County,* 213.

59. Applewhite, "Early Trade and Navigation," 80.

60. DC Will Book 10, 506–11; "Recollections of Colonel Willoughby Williams," in Clayton, *History of Davidson County,* 203; for a description of the Cumberland Iron Works see *National Banner and Daily Advertiser,* Nov. 27, 1833.

61. DC Will Book 10, 175, 186.

62. *Whig,* Nov. 10, 1823, Jan. 15, 1817; Wooldridge (ed.), *History of Nashville,* 265; John Overton to James Winchester, Aug. 5, 1814, THS: James Winchester Papers, TSLA.

63. Jesse Wharton to John Overton, Feb. 8, 1815, THS: John Overton Collection, TSLA.

64. H. L. White to John Overton, Sept. 11, Nov. 3, 1820, Claybrooke and Overton Papers, TSLA. White's anxiety to consolidate his bank with the Nashville Bank is clear (Gresham, "The Public Career of Hugh Lawson White," 79–80).

65. Andrew Jackson to Thomas H. Benton, June 1832, *Correspondence of Andrew Jackson,* 4:445; *Clarion,* Feb. 3, 1818.

66. "Debts Due Farmers and Mechanics Bank," June 29, 1820, PMLT, DC 1820, TSLA; *Whig,* Jan. 3, 1818, July 3, 1819. Seven of the twenty-three men who served as officers of the bank were investors in steamboats.

67. F. Roulhac to John Overton, Nov. 24, 1820, Claybrooke and Overton Papers, TSLA.

68. Thomas Emmerson to John Overton, Mar. 23, 1815, John Overton Papers, microfilm, Vanderbilt University Library.

69. *Whig,* Mar. 1, 1815.

70. *Niles Register* 31 (1826): 161.

71. In 1816 only 132 people were assessed on town property, and in 1829, only 171 (DC tax lists 1816, 1829, TSLA).

72. Seventeen of the merchants held five or more slaves; Lytle held twenty, and Porter, twenty-three.

73. *Clarion,* Jan. 11, 1820. By the spring of 1821 the notes of the Farmers and Mechanics Bank were being sold at a 45 percent to 75 percent discount (Wooldridge [ed.], *History of Nashville,* 263).

74. Golden, "Carroll and His Administration," 29.

75. Sellers, *James K. Polk, Jacksonian,* 67.

76. PMLT, DC 1820, TSLA; *Whig,* June 26, 1819, Aug. 2, 1820, Apr. 18, 1821; *Clarion,* Apr. 18, 25, May 2, 23, Aug. 8, Oct. 3, 10, 17, 24, 1820, Mar. 14, 1821.

77. Charles G. Sellers links the infighting between the old and new banks and political factionalism. See his "Banking and Politics in Jackson's Tennessee," 64–68, 83–84.

78. Abernethy, *From Frontier to Plantation in Tennessee,* 265; *Constitutional Advocate,* Sept. 17, Oct. 15, 1822; *Whig,* June 30, 1823.

79. *Whig,* Apr. 30, June 4, 1823; *Constitutional Advocate,* June 24, July 15, 1823; Andrew Jackson to John Coffee, Apr. 15, May 24, 1823, *Correspondence of Andrew Jackson,* 3:194, 195, 198.

80. *Whig,* June 23, 1823, July 26, Aug. 24, 1824.

81. J. H. Eaton to John Overton, Nov. 10, 1823, Claybrooke and Overton Papers, TSLA.

82. Abernethy, "Commerce and Banking in Tennessee," 319–20; Golden, "Carroll and His Administration," 17–21; Phelan, *History of Tennessee,* 253; Sellers, *James K. Polk, Jacksonian,* 85.

83. Wooldridge (ed.), *History of Nashville,* 272. Charles G. Sellers points out that after 1825 all political factions in Nashville supported the move for a branch of the BUS ("Banking and Politics in Jackson's Tennessee," 82).

84. *Clarion,* July 4, 1821.

85. Applewhite, "Early Trade and Navigation," 106.

86. Wooldridge (ed.), *History of Nashville,* 280, 284.

Chapter 3: Building Institutions on the Urban Frontier

1. John Dickinson to Moses Fisk, Apr. 17, 1800, Aug. 12, 1805, Moses Fisk Papers, TSLA.

2. James Robertson to Andrew Jackson, Feb. 1, 1806, in Matthews, *General James Robertson,* 540; Jacob McGavock to Hugh McGavock, June 11, 1813, photostat, James McGavock Dickinson Papers, TSLA; Clayton, *History of Davidson County,* 200.

3. Jacob McGavock to Randal McGavock, May 31, 1850, photostat, James McGavock Dickinson Papers, TSLA.

4. Willie Blount to Moses Fisk, Mar. 14, 1799, John Overton Papers, microfilm, Vanderbilt University Library.

5. See, for example, P. D. Hall, "Family Structure and Economic Organization," 40 41, and Eblen, "Nineteenth-Century Frontier Populations," 413.

6. Jennie Thompson Howell, "Family Talk," typescript, loaned to the writer by Isabel Howell.

7. L. Davis, "Banker in Knee Pants."

8. DC Will Book 2, 299.

9. Cate, "Timothy Demonbreun," 221.

10. M. A. Jones, *American Immigration,* 93; Hansen, *Atlantic Migration,* 77.

11. Hansen, *Atlantic Migration,* especially 107–19.

12. *Clarion,* Apr. 25, May 2, 1820.

13. Andrew Jackson to William Eustis, May 10, 1810, *Correspondence of Andrew Jackson,* 1:205.

14. "Recollections of Colonel Willoughby Williams," in Clayton, *History of Davidson County*, 199–203, 72–76.

15. Thomas, *Old Days in Nashville*.

16. *Orthopolitan*, Oct. 16, 1845.

17. Andrew Jackson to William Eustis, May 10, 1810, *Correspondence of Andrew Jackson*, 1:205; *Journal of the Senate*, 15, 40, 54; *Impartial Review and Cumberland Repository*, Oct. 3, 1807; DC Minute Book B, 387.

18. *Whig*, Jan. 4, Nov. 22, 1814, Mar. 3, 1817; Christie, *Cantrill-Cantrell Genealogy*.

19. See below, chap. 4.

20. For examples of town meetings, see *Clarion*, Apr. 6, 1810; *Whig*, Nov. 23, 1818, Mar. 27, 1819; *Banner and Whig*, Aug. 6, 22, 1826.

21. Anson Nelson, "Historical Memoranda, Cumberland Lodge Number Eight," THS: Miscellaneous Collections, TSLA, includes a membership list for 1818; forty-eight of the fifty-eight men listed are characterized by occupation. See also M. Haywood, *Freemasonry in North Carolina*, 24, 27.

22. *Nashville Gazette*, Feb. 11, July 8, 1801, June 13, July 20, 1803.

23. See Green, *Democracy in the Old South*, 123–24.

24. Beaumont, *Marie*, 32.

25. Crabb, "Wilkins Tannehill," 314–21; notes relating to Tannehill are in the Catherine B. Avery Papers, TSLA.

26. *Impartial Review*, Oct. 15, 1807; *Clarion*, Jan. 18, 1814, Feb. 3, 1818; M. D. Moore, "Library History in Tennessee," 3.

27. *Clarion*, Aug. 19, 1817, Sept. 29, 1818, May 16, 1821; G. S. Miles, "Literary Beginnings in Nashville," 194.

28. *Impartial Review*, Feb. 1, 1806; *Whig*, Apr. 23, 1813.

29. *Clarion*, Feb. 28, 1821.

30. G. S. Miles, "The Tennessee Antiquarian Society," 96–97, and "Literary Beginnings in Nashville," 62ff. Judge John Haywood's *Duty and Authority of Justices of the Peace in Tennessee* was the first book published in Tennessee. The work of the aborted antiquarian society undoubtedly provided material for the judge's *Civil and Political History of the State of Tennessee*, first published in 1823.

31. Thweatt, "James Priestley," 423–39; Grant, "Career of Cave Johnson," 196; Sally Priestley to Patsy, June 21, 1795, Small Collections (Priestley), TSLA; Daniel S. Donelson to Andrew J. Donelson, Mar. 12, 1819, THS: Dyas Collection, John Coffee Papers, TSLA.

32. Priestley taught between one hundred and two hundred students who did not sit for degrees (University of Nashville Records, 1, microfilm, Vanderbilt University Library).

33. For enrollment figures, see Wooldridge (ed.), *History of Nashville*, 392; see University of Nashville Records, 1, passim for lists of graduates, 4 for lists of trustees.

34. F. Garvin Davenport emphasizes the uphill struggle to create and

maintain cultural institutions ("Culture versus Frontier,"18–33). For descriptions of private libraries, see Arnow, *Flowering of the Cumberland*, 158–62, and DC Will Book 7, 391–96.

35. *Impartial Review*, Feb. 1, 1806.

36. *Return of the Whole Number of Persons within . . . the United States . . . 1800. . . . 1820.*

37. Harriette S. Arnow points out that "around two-thirds of the wives of the original settlers were widowed before the ending of the Indian Wars." (*Flowering of the Cumberland*, 31.) She provides a sympathetic and carefully wrought profile of the women of the first frontier (30–57); for her rendering of the language of the pioneers see 121–55, especially 125–27, 143.

38. M. B. Norton, *Liberty's Daughters*, 216–17.

39. See William Martin's letter, May 13, 1843, in Draper Collection of Manuscripts, State Historical Society of Wisconsin, Madison, photostat in TSLA, for the quotation and a description of Mrs. John Buchanan; on Charlotte Robertson see Kelley, *Children of Nashville*, 129.

40. For the Hays, see DC Will Book B, 205, 215, 322, DC Will Book 4, 291, 303, 336, 345, and Ann Hay to David P. Hay, Oct. 30, 1808, John Coffee Papers, TSLA. Margaret Tait's will was signed with a mark (Will Book 3/4, 462).

41. See Mathews, *Religion in the Old South*, 109.

42. Flanigen (ed.), *Catholicity in Tennessee*, 10–13; *Clarion*, June 22, 1810.

43. Posey, "Bishop Asbury Visits Tennessee," 267.

44. Doak, "Development of Education in Tennessee," 71; Bass, "Rev. Thomas Craighead," 88–96; Clayton, *History of Davidson County*, 215, 255, 312; *Clarion*, July 20, 1813.

45. *Clarion*, Aug. 13, 1811.

46. D. Berry to Bentley, Aug. 5, 1818, in Newcomer, "Two New England Teachers," 78; Bunting, *Manual of the First Presbyterian Church*, 4; Royall, *Letters from Alabama*, 129; Clayton, *History of Davidson County*, 312.

47. Bunting, *Manual of the First Presbyterian Church*, 13. See Sessions Book, First Presbyterian Church Records, microfilm, TSLA, for the numbers of merchants who joined the church.

48. Bunting, *Manual of the First Presbyterian Church*, 31.

49. Thomas, *Old Days in Nashville*, 33; *Whig*, May 5, 1817, Apr. 11, 1818. Carol Smith Rosenberg dates the founding of the Female Society for the Poor of New York in 1816 (*Religion and the American City*, 54). Mary P. Ryan makes the point that women who participated in these organizations "enhanced the elite status of their mates" (*Cradle of the Middle Class*, 84). For comparable activities of women in a southern city, see Amos, *Cotton City*, 171–75. See also Scott, "On Seeing and Not Seeing," 9–11.

50. Ament, "First Sunday School Organized in Nashville," typescript, TSLA. This was, again, an early development in Nashville relative to the rest of the country: cf. Boyer, *Urban Masses and Moral Order*, 34–35.

51. *Whig*, Apr. 17, May 11, 1819; Russel Campbell, "History of the Sunday School of the First Presbyterian Church," typescript, 1939, TSLA.

52. McFerrin, *History of Methodism in Tennessee*, 3:156.

53. Fowler et al., *History of McKendree Methodist Church*, 9.

54. Thomas, *Old Days in Nashville*, 60, characterizing Mrs. Moore.

55. McFerrin, *History of Methodism in Tennessee*, 3:78–79.

56. Phelps (ed.), "Diary of a Chaplain," 268; see also 269–72, 278, 281.

57. Cf. Mathews, *Religion in the Old South*, 66–67, 196–97, 203ff.

58. "Memorial of the First Baptist Church," manuscript, microfilm, TSLA; Wooldridge (ed.), *History of Nashville*, 476–77.

59. Wooldridge (ed.), *History of Nashville*, 472–73; Crabb, *Nashville*, 139–40.

60. Beard, "The Church of Ante Bellum Times," 78n, and Woods, "The First Christ Church," 70.

61. Flanigen (ed.), *Catholicity in Tennessee*, 15–18, 20.

62. *Whig*, Feb. 28, 1821; *Constitutional Advocate*, June 17, 1823.

63. *Whig*, Feb. 13, 1819.

64. Minutes of the Auxiliary Bible Society of Davidson County, 1823–58, Oct. 20, 1828, TSLA.

65. Minutes of the Board of Trustees of the University of Nashville, Mar. 19, 1825, Nov. 28, 1827, Apr. 1828, microfilm, Vanderbilt University Library.

66. Thomas, *Old Days in Nashville*, 87.

67. A list of subscribers appears in Windrow, "Elliott and the Nashville Female Academy," 80. See also THS: C. D. Elliott Papers, TSLA, for a list of stockholders as of 1822.

68. *Whig*, July 18, 1818, Jan. 9, 1819, Feb. 23, 1824, Jan. 3, 1825; *Banner and Whig*, June 21, 1826; "Female Academy Minutes," in THS: C. D. Elliott Papers, TSLA, Dec. 23, 1824.

69. M. B. Norton, *Liberty's Daughters*, 256–57.

70. C. D. Elliott, "Piety in the Nashville Female Academy," in Female Academy Minutes, THS: C. D. Elliott Papers, TSLA, July 14, 1818. See also entry for September 27, 1827, in which the girls gain permission to go to a ball given by the University of Nashville on condition they do not ask leave to go to any other party or the theater during the session, and entry for September 12, 1826, regarding students who went to dancing school against the rules.

71. Cf. Boyer, *Urban Masses and Moral Order*, 11, 60–61.

72. Minutes of the Board of Commissioners, 1802–3, TSLA.

73. PMLT, DC 1803, TSLA.

74. *The Laws of the Corporation of Nashville*, 1828, 15–17. For the amendment of 1811 see 18–19.

75. Ibid., 9. However, the board of commissioners of 1802 was not to

be elected regularly. Provision was made only for replacing individual commissioners who resigned or were incapacitated.

76. Teaford, *Municipal Revolution*, 75.

77. DC tax lists, 1798, 1816, 1829, TSLA.

78. For information on the aldermen, the most useful sources are the Nashville newspapers: *Impartial Review and Cumberland Repository*, 1805–8; *Clarion*, 1800–1822; *Nashville Whig*, 1812–25. See also tax lists of Davidson County for 1816 and 1829, TSLA.

79. Farrell and Farrell, *Burlington*, TSLA; Kelley, *Children of Nashville*, 133–34; DC Will Book 17, 367–69.

80. Stuart M. Blumin makes a similar point with reference to Kingston, New York (*Urban Threshold*, 24).

81. *Whig*, Sept. 15, 1817; *Clarion*, Sept. 9, 30, 1817.

82. Eugene J. Watts uses the term *social filter* to explain a similar phenomenon in postbellum Atlanta politics (*Social Bases of City Politics*, 48, 154).

83. *Clarion*, Mar. 1, 1808; Wooldridge (ed.), *History of Nashville*, 114–15. Nashville was not unusual in its lack of attention to public services. David R. Goldfield points out that as late as the fifties, cities in Virginia lacked police and fire forces, and that the services provided were dictated by the needs of the business districts (*Urban Growth in the Age of Sectionalism*, 143ff.).

84. Nathaniel Cross, "Nashville Water Works," manuscript, THS: Miscellaneous Collections, TSLA.

85. *Whig*, Dec. 26, 1818, Sept. 20, 1824, Mar. 12, 1825; *Clarion*, Feb. 3, 1821.

86. *Whig*, Jan. 2, 1819; *Clarion*, Feb. 28, 1821; Nagy, "Wanted: A Teacher," 171, 176, 178; G. S. Miles, "Literary Beginnings in Nashville," 59.

87. Malvina Grundy to Maria Reed, Mar. 5, 1826, photostat, James McGavock Dickinson Papers, TSLA.

88. *Gazette*, May 16, 1807; *Clarion*, Mar. 15, 1814; *Whig*, Mar. 24, 1814, Oct. 31, 1821, Apr. 9, May 7, 1823.

89. *Banner and Whig*, Feb. 10, 1829.

90. *Whig*, Sept. 1, 1823.

91. *Banner and Whig*, Aug. 25, Sept. 1, 1829.

Chapter 4: Black History on the Nashville Frontiers

1. See chapter 1 of Chase C. Mooney, *Slavery in Tennessee*, for a discussion of the retention of North Carolina law. I wish to acknowledge a special debt to the pioneer studies of black history in Tennessee by Mooney and by James M. England. Mooney's work also includes "Slavery in Davidson County, Tennessee," and "Slavery in Tennessee"; England's work includes, among other studies, "The Free Negro in Davidson County, Tennessee, 1780–1860," and "The Free Negro in Ante Bellum Tennessee."

2. Gutman, *The Black Family*.

3. Cf. Goldfield, *Urban Growth in the Age of Sectionalism*, xxvii, 38. This is, of course, the thesis of Morgan in *American Slavery, American Freedom;* see also D. B. Davis, *The Problem of Slavery* 2:262, and Cooper, *The South and the Politics of Slavery*, xiii, 69.

4. J. Haywood, *Civil and Political History of Tennessee*, 128, 341, 379, 380; "Letters of Benjamin Hawkins," 174–75.

5. John Sevier to Little Turkey, Aug. 25, 1796, "Journal of Governor John Sevier," 119.

6. Cisco, *Historic Sumner County*, 219; "Letters of Benjamin Hawkins," 174; J. Haywood, *Civil and Political History of Tennessee*, 95, 130, 101–4; Matthews, *General James Robertson*, 206–7, 210–12; Kelley, *Children of Nashville*, 77.

7. DC Minute Book A, 49; Putnam, *History of Middle Tennessee*, 119, 227; J. Haywood, *Civil and Political History of Tennessee*, 128. The list of preemptioners appears in Haywood, 218–20.

8. One reason given for the Donelsons' temporary retreat from Nashville in 1780 was the number of their slaves, who would have to be fed out of the pioneers' meager stores (Putnam, *History of Middle Tennessee*, 621). The inventory of John Donelson's personal estate in 1791 listed thirty Negroes "valued at $4,344 . . . hard dollars" (DC Will Book 1, 196–98).

9. DC Deed Book B, 111–13; DC Will Book 1, 164.

10. DC Will Books, 1784–1803. Some of the slaves counted here were sold more than once in this period. On the other hand, records of slaves sold as part of the inventory of deceased masters have not been included.

11. Seventy-eight slaves were involved in the transactions recorded between 1784 and 1789. Between 1790 and 1803 the greatest number in any given year was eighty-four (1797) and the smallest number was twenty-five (1792).

12. Only in some cases were children clearly identified as those of the female slave sold with them, but where a woman was sold with young children I have counted the group as a "matriarchal family." I have designated groups of slaves as families or couples where the sexes and ages of the individuals make this likely. For use of the words *family* and *wife* in bills of sale, see DC Will Book 2, 234, 378.

13. DC Will Book 1, 240, 71.

14. DC Will Book 2, 158; DC Will Book 1, 179, 189, 220.

15. DC Will Book 1, 172.

16. See, for example, DC Will Book 1, 237, 248, 263, 270, 279, 280; DC Will Book 2, 35, 98, 104, 118, 146; DC Will Book 3, 276.

17. DC Will Book 1, 277–79; DC Will Book 2, 94, 343–44; for provisos that a slave sold might be redeemed by substitution of another slave, see DC Will Book 1, 96, 173, 244, and Will Book 2, 9.

18. Gutman, *Black Family*, especially chap. 4.

19. DC Will Book 1, 86, 90, 97, 146; *State v. Thompson*, in Catterall, *Cases concerning American Slavery*, 2:483.

20. David B. Davis, in a review of Herbert G. Gutman's *Black Family in Slavery and Freedom*, argues that the hiring of slaves worked against the family stability Gutman emphasizes (745).

21. DC Will Book 2, 245–47; Estate Papers: Thomas Molloy, in Claybrooke and Overton Papers, TSLA; DC Minute Book C, 390; PMLT, DC, 1821, TSLA; England, "The Free Negro in Davidson County," 6, 41.

22. Jenkin Whiteside to John Overton, Dec. 4, 10, 1809, Jan. 4, 19, Mar. 12, 1810, THS: Murdock Collection–Overton Papers, TSLA; Will Book 5, 88; DC Court Minutes, 1810, 77.

23. John Coffee to John McLemore, Jan. 2, 1819, John Coffee Papers, TSLA.

24. DC Will Book 1–2, 32; DC Minute Book A, 299; DC Will Book 5, 458–62; England, "The Free Negro in Davidson County," 44, 45.

25. C. H. Brown, *Agents of Manifest Destiny*, 175.

26. DC Will Book 3/4, 239.

27. *Tennessee Gazette*, Oct. 19, 1803.

28. Mooney, "Slavery in Davidson County," 60, 62, 63. Mooney estimates that only fifty slaves were emancipated in the seventy-year period after 1790. England reports emancipations indicated in wills (although emancipation was not legal until the county agreed to it) and, therefore, suggests a slightly higher figure; see "Free Negro in Ante Bellum Tennessee," 42–48, 85.

29. DC Minute Book A, 91.

30. Tax List, 13th Assessment District, 1798, TSLA.

31. England, "The Free Negro in Davidson County," 10–19; DC Will Book 3, 110, 184, 208, 233, 234, 236–42; DC Will Book 4, 79, 112, 113, 122, 149, 167, 184, 186, 187, 195, 197, 201–3, 235, 236, 284, 346, 347, 375, 399.

32. *Return of the Whole Number of Persons within . . . the United States . . . 1791 . . . 1800 . . . 1810;* for the 1795 census schedule, see Carter (ed.), *Territorial Papers*, 4:404.

33. England, "The Free Negro in Davidson County," 14, 15, 17, 18, 265, 266; PMLT, DC, 1821, TSLA.

34. James E. Davis documents the scarcity of free blacks on the southern frontier in *Frontier America*, 132.

35. DC Minute Book A, 78; DC Will Book 2, 134; DC Minute Book C, 294ff. Scott's lawyers promised to appeal (England, "The Free Negro in Davidson County," 131).

36. *Tennessee Gazette*, Sept. 26, 1804.

37. DC Minute Book B, 150; PMLT, DC, 1801, TSLA; *Journal of the Sen-*

ate. . . . *of the State of Tennessee, 1801*, 43, 48; *Tennessee Gazette*, June 23, 1802; *Clarion*, Oct. 18, 1808, Aug. 11, 1812; *Whig*, Jan. 6, 1813; Reverse Index to Davidson County Deeds.

38. DC Will Book 4, 202; Will Book 3/4, 234; Minute Book C, 418.

39. England, "The Free Negro in Davidson County," 41, 46, 83.

40. For examples see DC Will Book 1, 276; DC Will Book 2, 69, 167, 340.

41. Wade, *Slavery in the Cities*, 38–54, especially 40. David R. Goldfield points out that despite persistent complaints slave hiring was too profitable to be discontinued in urban Virginia (*Urban Growth in the Age of Sectionalism*, 136–37). Savannah also instituted badges and a pass system for hired slaves in the 1850s, but enforcement was lax (Haunton, "Law and Order in Savannah," 77).

42. *Clarion*, Oct. 5, 1810, Dec. 13, 1814.

43. Will White to Eliza C. White, Dec. 12, 1820, Whiteford R. Cole Collection, TSLA.

44. Ibid., Dec. 19, 1820.

45. *The Laws of the Corporation of Nashville* (1828), 50; England, "The Free Negro in Davidson County," 140; Mooney, "Slavery in Tennessee," 63.

46. *Correspondence of Andrew Jackson*, 3:87.

47. England, "The Free Negro in Davidson County," 154 (see also 33–34, 139); England, "The Free Negro in Tennessee," 46.

48. PMLT, DC, 1799, 1813. At this point there was no evidence of the self-conscious planning to prevent the alleys of a later period that Richard C. Wade describes in *Slavery in the Cities*, 61.

49. Minutes of the Board of Commissioners, TSLA; *Tennessee Gazette*, Sept. 22, 1802, Aug. 3, 31, 1803.

50. *Whig*, Oct. 13, 18, 1823.

51. DC Minute Book A, 411; DC Minute Book B, 119, 406.

52. James Robertson to Secretary Smith, Aug. 17, 1793, *American State Papers*, 1:466–67; *Whig*, Jan. 11, 1815.

53. Martin, "Anti-Slavery Activities," 108; Patterson, *The Negro in Tennessee*, 108–17.

54. McFerrin, *History of Methodism in Tennessee*, 3:64, 68, 81.

55. "The Conference Business of the Baptist Church under the Care of James Whitsitt, on Mill Creek, Davidson County," Record Book, 1797–1814, TSLA. Mechal Sobel points out that black members did not vote and apparently never "criticized" white members (" 'They Can Never Both Prosper Together'," 298).

56. Woodson, *History of the Negro Church*, 56–57.

57. Genovese, *Roll, Jordan, Roll*, especially 232–54.

58. DC Minute Book C, 291–92 (1800); *Union*, Aug. 19, 22, 1837; Na-

tional Banner and Nashville Whig, Aug. 21, 1837; Circuit Court Minutes, Sept. Sessions, 1837, 234, 265, 266, 268.

59. The discussion that follows is based on figures from the 1820 manuscript federal census as transcribed by M. L. Houston, TSLA. See Appendix, tables 1 and 2.

60. DC Will Book 3/4, 420, 436–37; DC Will Book 2, 77.

61. DC Minute Book 1817, 370; DC Minute Book 1820, 435.

62. DC Will Book 3/4, 237; DC Minute Books, 1820, 435, 1824, 925, 1826, 420, 514, 566, 1827, 693; *Banner and Whig*, Sept. 27, 1830.

63. DC Minute Book, 1820, 436; Reverse Index to Davidson County Deeds.

64. DC Minute Book, 1817, 298, 1825, 330.

65. Ibid., 1817, 123, 142.

66. Thomas, *Old Days in Nashville*, 22.

67. DC Minute Book, 1817, 120.

68. See Schweninger, *James T. Rapier and Reconstruction*, 1–8, for the story of Sally Thomas. Barber Frank Parrish is another example.

69. Wade, *Slavery in the Cities*, passim.

Chapter 5: Municipal Politics in the Age of Jackson

1. Cf. the descriptions of Alabama politics in the 1820s in Thornton, *Politics and Power in a Slave Society*, especially chap. 1, and of North Carolina politics in one county in Watson, *Jacksonian Politics and Community Conflict*, 15–25.

2. Remini, *Andrew Jackson and American Freedom*, 12–31, 116–17; Meyers, *The Jacksonian Persuasion*, 11–23.

3. See Appendix, table 1.

4. Bergeron, *Antebellum Politics in Tennessee*, 7–8.

5. Capers, *Biography of a River Town*, 44–45.

6. PMLT, DC, 1813, TSLA; Howell, "Early Corporate Limits of Nashville," 113.

7. See ward map of Nashville, 95.

8. George Williams decided to remain in Dover, where he could rent a four-room house for $36 a year, rather than move to Nashville, where the only house he could find rented for $175 and where it was "impossible to get a front or back shop" (Williams to Samuel Williams, in Mooney [ed.], "Some Letters from Dover," 160).

9. These 412 individuals were included within 127 households. This reference is once more to the 1820 census as transcribed by M. L. Houston. The figure for households in manufactures corresponds remarkably well with the 125 craftsmen's and mechanics' establishments listed by the town constable in 1823 (newspaper clipping, THS, Box N1, TSLA).

10. *Whig*, Feb. 14, 1815; *Impartial Review and Cumberland Repository*, May 17, 1806; *Banner*, May 15, 1833.

11. In 1820, 50 of 382 households (13 percent) included three or more white males aged 16 to 26 years old; in 1830, 88 of 742 households (12 percent); and in 1840, 72 of 911 households (8 percent) claimed three or more white males 15 to 30 years old (compiled from the 1820 census and the 1830 and 1840 microfilm censuses).

12. See appendix, table 2.

13. *Whig*, Dec. 26, 1818, May 1, June 19, Aug. 7, Sept. 25, 1819.

14. Wooldridge (ed.), *History of Nashville*, 119–20.

15. In each of these years a director of the new and more popular state "loan bank" was also elected.

16. William G. Nicholson, "Sketch of James Condon," THS: Miscellaneous Collections, TSLA; *Republican Banner*, Sept. 5, 1837; *Whig*, Aug. 22, 1812, Feb. 14, 1825; DC Will Book, 1835, 241–42.

17. *Clarion*, Sept. 26, 1820.

18. *Whig*, Oct. 13, 1823.

19. Wooldridge (ed.), *History of Nashville*, 31, 113; *Clarion*, Feb. 20, 1821; *Whig*, Oct. 13, 20, Nov. 3, 1823, Sept. 20, 1824. The tax on auctioneers was deemed unconstitutional by the state supreme court (*Whig*, Feb. 7, 14, 1825).

20. J. P. Erwin to James Erwin, Apr. 24, 1825, THS: Miscellaneous Collections, TSLA; J. P. Erwin to Samuel Stock, Aug. 5, 1828, Correspondence by Author File, TSLA; James Jacks to John Coffee, Jan. 28, 1824, John Coffee Papers, TSLA; J. Newnan to Peter Force, July 12, 1826, Emil E. Hurja Collection, TSLA; *Whig*, Apr. 15, Sept. 6, 1826.

21. *Whig*, Nov. 24, 1823.

22. John Coffee to John Donelson, July 1, 1824, John Coffee Papers, TSLA. Erwin, too, thought he had "all the Yankees" on his side, but he was quickly put on the defensive by Jackson's popularity (J. P. Erwin to James Erwin, Apr. 24, 1825, THS: Miscellaneous Collections, TSLA).

23. *Whig*, Apr. 23, 1825.

24. Bergeron, *Antebellum Politics in Tennessee*, 3; Sellers, *James K. Polk, Jacksonian*, 88–89. See also Sellers's "Jackson Men with Feet of Clay," 537–51.

25. Thomas Yeatman to Henry Clay, Dec. 29, 1826, and Boyd McNairy to Henry Clay, Nov. 13, 1826, *Papers of Henry Clay*, 5:922, 1051, 1052.

26. *Banner and Whig*, Sept. 6, 13, 16, 1826.

27. *Clarion*, July 4, 1821; Sellers, "Banking and Politics in Jackson's Tennessee," 71.

28. *Clarion*, July 25, 1820.

29. *Banner and Whig*, Oct. 4, 1826. According to the federal census, in 1830 there were 1,078 white males older than twenty years.

30. Cooper, *The South and Slavery*, 26.

31. *Banner and Whig*, July 12, 1826.

32. *A Compilation of the General Laws of the City of Nashville*, 21, 22; *Banner and Whig*, Aug. 16, 22, 1826; PMLT, DC 33–1826, TSLA.

33. *Nashville Republican*, Sept. 30, 1828.

34. This may be an overstatement. The Davidson Academy's lands in the sixth ward carried with them a tax exemption that was upheld by the state supreme court in 1839. Tax lists did not always include owners in this "free territory." Jacob Brasher, for example, did own real estate in Nashville, though he was not on the 1839 tax roll (Reverse Index to DC Deeds).

35. Only 32 percent, or 41 of 127, of household heads "in manufactures" in 1820 were taxed on property in 1816 and/or 1829. This compares with 49 percent, or 35 of 71, of households identified as "in commerce" (DC tax lists, 1816, 1829). Only 51 percent of all households included slaves in 1830, but by 1840 this figure had risen again to 59 percent (U.S. Census, 1820, 1830, 1840).

36. Included in the spate of legislation of the first municipal government after reorganization was a minutely detailed bylaw for the regulation of the new market, one meant to deal with some of the lawyers' complaints (*The Laws of the Corporation of Nashville* [1828], 34–38).

37. *Banner and Whig*, Aug. 28, Sept. 9, Oct. 21, 31, 1828, June 19, July 24, Oct. 6, 1829.

38. Ibid., Aug. 14, 1829.

39. Ibid., Aug. 11, Sept. 1, 1829.

40. For a bibliography, a masterly summary of the Jacksonian controversy, and interpretations of the meaning of the American political and social experience during the Jacksonian period, see Pessen, *Jacksonian America*, 384–93.

41. *Nashville Republican*, Sept. 15, 1831; *Banner and Whig*, Aug. 11, 1829, Aug. 3, 1831. Claiborne had been both anti-Grundy and pro-Jackson (Sellers, "Jackson Men with Feet of Clay," 548).

42. *Banner and Whig*, Sept. 9, 1828, Aug. 4, 18, 1829.

43. Ibid., Aug. 25, Sept. 1, 4, 8, 1829.

44. *A Compilation of the General Laws of the City of Nashville*, 24–25.

45. Ibid., 26–27; Wooldridge (ed.), *History of Nashville*, 131; *Banner and Whig*, June 9, Aug. 11, 1829, Aug. 5, 1830. Banning hogs from the streets eliminated the best garbage disposal the town could command.

46. PMLT, DC, 208–1831, TSLA.

47. *Banner and Whig*, Dec. 1, 1829.

48. Ibid., Aug. 26, 5, Sept. 20, 1830.

49. Ibid., Aug. 19, 1830.

50. *Nashville Republican*, Sept. 29, 1830.

51. In 1833, the first year for which comparable data are available, 119 men voted from the sixth ward (*Banner and Whig*, Sept. 30, 1833). Brasher's failure may be explained in part by his not supporting Jackson in 1828, one

of the many ironies discouraging the use of the term *Jacksonian democracy* (ibid., Sept. 2, 1828).

52. Thomas, *Old Days in Nashville*, 22; *Union*, Aug. 9, 1850.

53. Vaulx was one of the commission merchants who did support the Broad Street Bridge effort.

54. PMLT, DC, 1831, TSLA.

55. Thirteen professionals served as aldermen. The occupations of seven aldermen are unknown.

56. Distribution of Property Holders and Aldermen as Property Holders, 1839:

Assessed on real estate	Property holders on tax roll (%)	Aldermen/ property holders (%)	Number of alderman
$1,000 or less	26	14	7
$1,001–$10,000	60	63	31
$10,001+	14	22	11

In addition, 43 percent of all those on the 1839 tax list were taxed only as white polls. Three aldermen fell into this category. Of the eleven aldermen who were assessed on more than $10,000 in real estate, two were mechanics, seven were merchants, one was a lawyer, and one was a banker (Tax List, DC, District No. 1, 1839, TSLA).

57. *Credit of the West*. See also Sellers, *James K. Polk, Jacksonian*, 196, and, for a summary of the personal quarrels with Jackson that led a number of prominent Tennesseeans to break with him, see Murphy, "Jackson and the Tennessee Opposition," 54ff.

58. Sellers, *James K. Polk, Jacksonian*, 270, 302, 303; Abernethy, "Origin of the Whig Party," 506–8; P. Moore, "Revolt against Jackson," 337–39.

59. Bergeron, "Polk and the Jacksonian Press," 266.

60. Bergeron, *Antebellum Politics*, chaps. 4 and 5.

61. Real Estate Holdings of Aldermen by Wards, 1839:

Ward 1	$ 82,500	Ward 4	$ 39,300
Ward 2	40,550	Ward 5	144,440
Ward 3	118,890	Ward 6	11,750

This is, of course, only an inexact measure of any given alderman's wealth. It does, however, give an indication of where wealth was concentrated (the third and fifth wards) and where the poor might be found in largest numbers (the sixth ward) (Tax List, DC, District No. 1, 1839, TSLA).

62. E. A. Miles, "Slave Insurrection Scare," 49 and passim.

63. *Union*, July 20, Aug. 5, 1835.

64. *Banner and Whig,* Aug. 8, 20, 1835; *The Narrative of Amos Dresser,* passim. The committee did persuade the mob to agree that there would be no further punishment after the flogging in the public square, thereby forestalling even greater violence.

65. *Union,* July 29, Aug. 5, 21, 1835; for membership in the colonization society, see *Banner and Whig,* Nov. 11, 1831, *National Banner,* Oct. 18, 1832.

66. For the vigilance committee, see *The Narrative of Amos Dresser,* 3–4.

67. See appendix, table 4.

68. *Banner and Whig,* Sept. 23, 1836.

69. Ibid., Nov. 9, 1836; Bergeron, *Antebellum Politics,* 10.

70. Bergeron, *Antebellum Politics,* 48; P. M. Hamer, *Tennessee* 1:293.

71. *Union,* Jan. 9, 1839; on Hollingsworth, see Clayton, *History of Davidson County,* 119, 120; Nicholson, "Sketches," THS: Miscellaneous Collections, TSLA.

72. *Union,* Oct. 5, 1838.

73. PMLT, DC, 160–1837, TSLA.

74. *Republican Banner,* Dec. 22, 1837.

75. PMLT, DC, 161–63, 1837, TSLA. Whigs, too, crossed lines. A number, including Anderson and Hunt, had signed the petition for repeal of suffrage restrictions.

76. *Republican Banner,* Sept. 30, 1839.

77. Minutes of the Board of Aldermen, Jan. 28, 1840, Office of the Metropolitan Clerk, Metro Courthouse; *Journal of the House of Representatives,* 565.

78. *Republican Banner,* Sept. 28, 1840.

79. *Union,* Sept. 28, 1840.

Chapter 6: Growing Apart

1. Blumin, *Urban Threshold,* App. A.

2. Capers, *Biography of a River Town,* 44–45, 59; James, *Antebellum Natchez,* 161.

3. Goldfield, *Cotton Fields and Skyscrapers,* 70; see also 28–35, 58–79.

4. In 1835, 231 arrivals and departures were counted, and 580 were counted in 1860 (Hunter, *Steamboats on the Western Rivers,* 646). See *Whig,* Mar. 23, 1848; *Union,* Feb. 8, 1841.

5. Douglas, *Steamboatin' on the Cumberland.*

6. The Union Bank building was described as "an ornament of our town" (*Banner and Whig,* Oct. 26, 1835).

7. C. A. Campbell, "Development of Banking," 63–67; Wooldridge (ed.), *History of Nashville,* 280, 284.

8. During the years when the branch bank was winding down its business (1832 to 1835), at least eleven of its Nashville directors served on the boards

of the Union and Planters' banks. John Sommerville, who was cashier of the branch bank, served as president of the Planters' Bank in 1836.

9. Sharp, *The Jacksonians versus the Banks,* 196.

10. Wooldridge (ed.), *History of Nashville,* 286, 287; Charles G. Sellers points out that in 1840 all the state bank officers were Whigs who had been retained by a Democratic administration (*James K. Polk, Jacksonian,* 393).

11. *Republican Banner,* Jan. 11, 1838.

12. C. A. Campbell, "Development of Banking," 79; J. M. Bass to M. D. Cooper, Feb. 1, 1837, Cooper Family Papers, TSLA.

13. *Whig,* Mar. 8, 1842.

14. *Banner and Whig,* June 8, 1831; *Union,* May 22, 1835.

15. Folmsbee, *Sectionalism and Internal Improvements,* 17, 126, 184, 247. For a formal accounting of the finances of the Nashville, Murfreesboro and Shelbyville turnpike, see *Republican Banner,* Apr. 25, 1838.

16. See, e.g., *Union,* Aug. 26, 1854. Samuel Seay was president of the Protection Insurance Company of Nashville, which offered the "Negro policies." Eight of the twelve members of the board of the Tennessee Marine and Fire Insurance Company, four of the eleven members of the board of the Nashville Insurance and Trust Company, and four of twelve members of the board of the Merchants' Insurance and Trust Company also served on the boards of the Planters' Bank and/or the Union Bank in the 1830s.

17. N. S. Mahoney, "Strickland's Introduction to Nashville"; Hoobler, "Karnak on the Cumberland," 258–59.

18. *Orthopolitan,* Oct. 16, 1845.

19. *Gazette,* Jan. 25, 1851.

20. See Appendix, table 6. Less than 25 percent of the household heads of Richmond, Virginia, sampled by David Goldfield were property holders in 1850, which compares well with the Nashville figures. Goldfield feels that these figures suggest a larger property-holding group than was available in northern cities (*Urban Growth in the Age of Sectionalism,* 62).

21. The census takers of 1860 evidently provided estimates closer to market value than did the census takers of 1850 (Lowrey, "Tennessee Voters," 142). Lee Soltow reports that, on the basis of federal census returns in the United States in 1860, 62 percent of adult free males claimed some property. Soltow's figures include both rural and city people, and property holding was twice as likely for farmers as for nonfarmers, so Nashville's figures do seem attractive, though 37 percent of her property holders claimed less than $1,000 in assets (*Men of Wealth,* 174–75).

22. Cf. Conzen, *Immigrant Milwaukee,* 75; Doyle, *Social Order of a Frontier Community,* 104, 263; Blumin, "Mobility and Change," 204. See also Soltow, *Men of Wealth,* 178–79.

23. Compiled from DC Tax List, 1839, TSLA, and Corporation of Nashville Tax List, 1847, Nashville Public Library.

24. Compiled from the manuscript U.S. population census for 1850 as

transcribed by Deane Porche, 1850, TSLA, and the microfilm manuscript population census for 1860.

25. William F. Cooper Letter Book, Aug. 6, 1845, Cooper Family Papers, TSLA. On the board of directors of the Adelphi Theatrical Society, which built a new theater in 1850, were, among others, John Bass and Hugh Kirkman; Francis Fogg was among the patrons of theater companies. The "young gentlemen" of the city often filled out the professional cast. See *Republican Banner*, Feb. 3, 1850; *Union*, Aug. 8, 1850; Davenport, *Cultural Life in Nashville*, 118 ff.

26. *Republican Banner*, Apr. 14, 1845.

27. Thirty-seven of the 64 household heads who owned property worth $100,000 or more and 26 of the 68 who owned property worth between $50,000 and $100,000 lived in the fifth ward in 1860. For quotation, see Gower and Allen (eds.), *Pen and Sword*, 465. Jennie Thompson Howell, "Family Talk," typescript, loaned to the author by Isabel Howell, and Mary Woods, "Memories," typescript, Archives, Jessie Ball duPont Library, The University of the South, contain descriptions of childhood in Nashville. See also Walter, "Growth and Residential Succession," 10.

28. *Whig*, Jan. 23, 1847; *Republican Banner*, Feb. 21, 1849, Aug. 25, 1855.

29. *Gazette*, June 2, July 26, 1853.

30. Nine lawyers, five doctors, three planters, two gentlemen, a hotelier, a carpenter, a plasterer, and nine women completed the richest group of Nashvillians, according to the federal census returns of 1860.

31. Of the fourteen individuals or estates reporting $30,000 or more on the 1839 tax list, at least eleven had been in Nashville or came from families who had been since before the War of 1812, and six of these or their families had been in the city since the eighteenth century. Eight would reappear among the richest sixteen Nashvillians on the tax list of 1847, and only two of these sixteen were relative newcomers to Nashville. Three years later, when the federal census recorded real-estate holdings, twenty-five individuals reported property worth $30,000 or more; no more than nine had come to Nashville after 1812.

32. Adam G. Adams Notebook and Account Book, TSLA; Flanagan, "Irish Element in Nashville," 41, 42, 49, 88.

33. The millionaire was W. W. Woodfolk, who listed his occupation as "gentleman." He was a director of the Bank of Nashville and owned a farm in Davidson County and a plantation in Arkansas. He had moved from land speculation to breeding fine horses and cattle (McBride and Robison, *Biographical Directory*, 819).

34. Two-thirds of the mutual acquaintances of the sons of a lawyer and of a Baptist minister began their careers as clerks, most often in dry-goods stores in Nashville, Philadelphia, and St. Louis. Only two of thirty-two men specifically identified by their occupation attended college; one was a law clerk, one practiced medicine, and three were mechanics, two of them in

shops owned by their fathers (John Meigs to Morton B. Howell, May 13, June 3, 1853, Morton B. Howell Family Papers, TSLA).

35. James P. Thomas, "Autobiography," 19, Rapier Family Papers, Moorland-Spingarn Research Center, Howard University.

36. Clayton, *History of Davidson County*, 427, 428; Thomas, *Old Days in Nashville*, 3; Bransford Family Papers, TSLA. The daughter of James Condon, the tailor who was elected mayor in 1820, married a tinner, and at least one of Condon's sons was trained to be a tailor. Shoemaker Lientz's daughter attended the female academy and married the Honorable George Tompkins, judge of the supreme court in Boone County.

37. Of course, this accounting does not reckon with those who moved from Nashville within the decade.

38. Wooldridge (ed.), *History of Nashville*, 590–92; Flanagan, "Irish Element in Nashville," 40, 45, 48.

39. Speer (ed.), *Sketches of Prominent Tennesseans*, 237–39.

40. U.S. Census. . . . Manufactures of the U.S. in 1860, 562. Wooldridge, *History of Nashville*, 220–21, is helpful in identifying the firms listed in the 1860 census.

41. *Republican Banner*, Sept. 8, 1851.

42. *Union*, Nov. 7, 1854.

43. International Typographical Union of North America, *Golden Anniversary, 1855–1905, Nashville Typographical Union, No. 20*, 25; Robert, *Nashville and Her Trade*, 408; *Banner and Whig*, Oct. 15, 1833, July 29, 1834, Jan. 12, 1835, Apr. 15, 1836; *Union*, Apr. 12, 1838, July 11, 1849, Nov. 17, 1854.

44. *Republican Banner*, Feb. 10, 1840; see also *Republican Banner*, Apr. 30, 1833, *Banner and Whig*, Sept. 9, 1836.

45. *Gazette*, Aug. 27, Sept. 2, 1853; *Nashville City and Business Directory*.

46. Cf. Dawley, *Class and Community*, 145, 224, 225.

47. PMLT, DC, 160–1837, TSLA; 1848 quotation in Weathersby, "J. H. Ingraham and Tennessee," 267; W. F. Cooper to W. B. Webb, Feb. 11, 1850, Cooper Letter Book 2, Cooper Family Papers, TSLA.

48. See Appendix, table 3.

49. Nashville was declared a port of entry in 1831, and appropriations totaling $135,000 were made by the federal government between 1832 and 1837 to improve the Cumberland River (Folmsbee, *Sectionalism and Internal Improvements*, 68).

50. The *Orthopolitan*, Dec. 20, 1845, reported the results of a census taken by Alpha Kingsley.

51. *Union*, Jan. 21, 28, 1837; *Banner and Whig*, Jan. 23, 1837.

52. *Republican Banner*, Jan. 21, 1841; *Whig*, Nov. 14, 1844; *Orthopolitan*, Oct. 9, 26, Nov. 9, 1845.

53. *Whig*, Dec. 31, 1842; Gohmann, *Political Nativism in Tennessee*, 56.

54. Gohmann, *Political Nativism in Tennessee*, 126, 122.

55. E. J. Smith, "Free, Foreign-Born Population," 71, 95.

56. Ibid., 79, 89, 113; the persistence rate was calculated from data on p. 118.

57. The foreign-born population was 42 percent female in 1860 as compared with 34 percent in 1850 (ibid., 73, 100).

58. Frank, *Beginnings on Market Street*, 150. See also Frank's *Five Families*.

59. Data garnered from the census of 1860; for quotation see *Republican Banner*, Nov. 8, 1858.

60. Frank, *Beginnings on Market Street*, 152, 153, and *Five Families*, 115.

61. *Republican Banner*, Jan. 13, 1855, Dec. 18, 1856.

62. Macpherson, "Nashville's German Element," 28, table 2; Walter, "Growth and Residential Succession," 14.

63. Connelly, "Old North Nashville and Germantown," especially 119–27 and the excellent photographs of buildings in North Nashville.

64. A petition and a motion for incorporation were presented to the board of aldermen in 1856. Almost a year later a citywide vote on incorporation was lost by a vote of 545 to 635 (*Republican Banner*, Oct. 25, 1856, Sept. 27, 1857).

65. Berlin and Gutman, "Natives and Immigrants," tables 7A and 7B, 1183, 1197; E. J. Smith, "Free, Foreign-Born Population," 108–13.

66. E. J. Smith, "Free, Foreign-Born Population," 107, 112. Flanagan counted only 409 Irish laborers ("Irish Element in Nashville," 26).

67. E. J. Smith, "Free, Foreign-Born Population," 113–14.

68. Flanagan, "Irish Element in Nashville," 30, 31.

69. Flanigen (ed.), *Catholicity in Tennessee*, 28, 29; Wooldridge (ed.), *History of Nashville*, 499, 500; *Union*, Oct. 11, 1849, Dec. 23, 1854; *Whig*, Oct. 8, 1848; *Gazette*, Jan. 26, 1851.

70. Berlin and Gutman provide data that emphasize the significance of immigrants as components of the working classes of southern cities ("Natives and Immigrants," 1179–83).

Chapter 7: Growing Apart: Black Nashville

1. Curry, *The Free Black*, 195.

2. Cf. ibid., 205–12.

3. See Appendix, table 1. The decline in the percentage of slaves in urban populations has been interpreted as a result in part of the influx of immigrant labor rather than as evidence of the incompatibility of slavery and urban life (Goldin, *Urban Slavery*, xiii–xiv, 22, 25; Wade, *Slavery in the Cities*, 243 ff.) For the percentage of blacks in Memphis, see Capers, *Biography of a River Town*, 110.

4. In 1850 and 1860 the census provided a separate slave schedule rather than listing slaves in the households of free inhabitants. The figure of 37 percent for slaveholding households in 1860 was obtained by dividing the total number of households into the number of slave owners or employers.

Since some owners/employers would not have been household heads, 37 percent is an overstatement (U.S. Census ... Slave Schedules, 1850, 1860; the descriptions of the slave population below are based on these schedules).

5. James P. Thomas, "Autobiography," 25 Rapier Family Papers, Moorland-Spingarn Research Center, Howard University. There are two sets of page numbers in the manuscript; I refer to the numbers on the righthand corner of each page. See also Simmons, *Men of Mark*, 573, for the reminiscences of Randall B. Vandervall.

6. A rewarding attempt to deal with black family stability is Herbert G. Gutman, *The Black Family in Slavery and Freedom*.

7. Thomas, "Autobiography," 60.

8. See Appendix, table 2. The imbalance between male and female slave populations was significantly less in Nashville than in Baltimore, Louisville, St. Louis, or Washington (Goldin, *Urban Slavery*, 65).

9. Thomas, "Autobiography," 2, 13, 218–19.

10. From 1842 to 1849 the county court was allowed to permit a freed slave to remain in Tennessee, but in 1849 the 1831 restrictions were reimposed, and in 1854 manumission was made dependent on emigration to Liberia (Howington, "'Not in the Condition of a Horse or an Ox'," 260; England, "The Free Negro in Ante Bellum Tennessee," 135, 196, 198; MBA, Dec. 8, 1838).

11. See, e.g., *Banner*, June 28, 1834, Nov. 13, 1835, July 25, 1836; *Whig*, Jan. 3, Feb. 7, 1825. See also Mooney, "Slavery in Davidson County," 113.

12. *The Narrative of Amos Dresser*, 7.

13. *Banner and Whig*, Aug. 21, 1837; *Union*, Aug. 19, 22, 1837; DC Circuit Court Minutes, Sept. 1837, 234, 265–68.

14. *Banner and Whig*, Jan. 8, 1830, Aug. 10, 17, Nov. 4, 11, 1831. By 1849 all of the officers of the Nashville Colonization Society were ministers, professionals, or professors at the University of Nashville (*Republican Banner*, Mar. 19, 1849). George Weller, rector of Christ Church, was one of the more committed early members of the society, reporting to James Birney on the condition of freedmen in Nashville awaiting passage to Liberia (*Letters of James Gillespie Birney*, 58, 59, 87, 88). See also Curry, *The Free Black*, 233.

15. Berlin, *Slaves without Masters*, 257.

16. Thomas, "Autobiography," 33, 72.

17. "U.S. Census ... Schedule of Free Inhabitants," 1860.

18. Elizabeth Moore advertised for her runaway slave, Mary: "It is expected that she will be concealed by some free negroes or whites of no better standing in or about the suburbs of Nashville" (*Banner and Whig*, Nov. 14, 1831). See also *Republican Banner*, Apr. 30, 1857.

19. Ten of 85 blacks in the sixth ward claimed $40,600. The total Irish population of the ward was 411, and property claimed by Irish inhabitants totaled $18,900. Property owned by some of the 80 Germans in the ward

amounted to $29,200 (*U.S. Census . . . Schedule of Free Inhabitants, 1860*). There is some evidence that blacks who owned property sometimes held that property in the name of a white patron "because of the peculiarly uncertain standing of the free Negro in the courts and before the laws" (Imes, "Negroes in Tennessee," 49; Imes's study is especially interesting, for he gathered data from old people of the black community early in this century). See also *Republican Banner,* Jan. 30, 1858, quoted in Berlin, *Slaves without Masters,* 262.

20. Of the 112 black household heads in Nashville in 1840, 26 appear again in 1850, a persistence rate of 23 percent; of 135 black household heads in 1850, 34 reappear in 1860, a persistence rate of 25 percent. Black persistence rates may have been even higher because individuals who remained in the city and who were not heads of households in the second listing were not counted. However, because the persistence of white household heads was calculated in this way, it seems best to maintain consistency in the way in which the samples were counted. Cf. Appendix, table 3.

21. Cf. Provine, "Economic Position of Free Blacks," 66–67; Berlin, *Slaves without Masters,* 236–38.

22. It may be that the decline from 1850 to 1860 in the number of households that included nuclear families and the larger number in 1860 of individuals living in white households resulted from the increase in blacks who had moved to the city during that decade.

23. Schweninger, *Rapier and Reconstruction,* 1–10. I am especially grateful for Schweninger's "A Slave Family in the Antebellum South" and his "The Free Slave Phenomenon: James P. Thomas and the Black Community in Ante-Bellum Nashville," which alerted me to the existence of Thomas's "Autobiography."

24. H. A. Norton, *Tennessee Christians,* 131–34; Simmons, *Men of Mark,* 144–45; PMLT, DC, 1837, 1839; MBA, May 28, 1857; Reverse Index to DC Deeds.

25. James C. Napier Papers, Fisk University Library; Napier, "Negro Members," 117; clippings, Oberlin College Archives.

26. McFerrin, *History of Methodism in Tennessee,* 3:68, 81, 87, 103, 124, 147.

27. *Banner and Whig,* Aug. 11, 14, Sept. 5, 1829.

28. Ibid., Aug. 18, 1829. The editor of the *Banner and Whig* objected that "slaves ought not to be permitted to hold separate meetings—religious or secular—at any time" (Dec. 17, 1834). Cf. Raboteau, *Slave Religion,* 180.

29. McFerrin, *History of Methodism in Tennessee,* 3:111, 117.

30. Gwinn, quoted in Harrison, *The Gospel among the Slaves,* 167–68. Gwinn had come to the Tennessee frontier as a youngster of nineteen in 1788. A founder of the Methodist Society, he had served as chaplain to Jackson's New Orleans expedition (Fowler et al., *History of McKendree Methodist Church,* 10).

31. A report of Bishop Andrew's sermon on mission work includes a de-

scription of the slave convert: "'There he was mingling his morning song with the matin chorus of the birds, sending up his orisons to God under the light of the evening star, contented with his lot, cheerful in his labors, submissive for conscience sake to plantation discipline, happy in life, hopeful in death, and from his lowly cabin carried at last to Abraham's bosom'" (in Harrison, *The Gospel among the Slaves, 176–77*). Donald G. Mathews analyzes the changes in the Methodists' stance on slavery in *Slavery and Methodism*.

32. Thomas, "Autobiography," 63, 78.

33. Ibid., 34–36.

34. *Whig*, Aug. 22, 1848.

35. See, e.g., MBA, Apr. 25, 1838, Apr. 13, 1844, Aug. 28, 1846, Sept. 28, 1850, Feb. 14, 1851.

36. See Spain, "R. B. C. Howell: Progressive Baptist Minister in the Old Southwest," 99–119, and "R. B. C. Howell: Virginia Baptist Tradition Comes to the Old Southwest," 195–226, especially 220–25.

37. Compiled from R. B. C. Howell's Pastor's Book, Morton B. Howell Family Papers, TSLA. Only 28 black people were listed without a master's name from 1831 to 1848; almost half of these people joined the church between 1831 and 1833. There were 101 women and 63 men; the sex of 11 persons cannot be determined from the name given. Of these 175, 32 were expelled, 31 were dismissed by letter, 32 died, 14 were dropped, presumably for nonattendance, and 66 were transferred to the colored mission in 1848.

38. Sobel, "'They Can Never Both Prosper Together,'" 300n.16.

39. R. B. C. Howell, "Memorial of the First Baptist Church, Nashville, Tennessee, 1820–1863," microfilm, TSLA.

40. Sobel, "'They Can Never Both Prosper Together,'" 303.

41. Fuller, *History of the Negro Baptists*, 41, 72, 78.

42. H. A. Norton, *Tennessee Christians*, 23.

43. Scobey (ed.), *Franklin College*, 48. In the 1850s, when one faction of the church rejected its minister, J. B. Ferguson, one reason given was Ferguson's strong leadership, which left to the congregation a more passive role than it had enjoyed (Claiborne et al., *History and True Position*, 13).

44. Thomas, "Autobiography," 95.

45. H. A. Norton, *Tennessee Christians*, 25, 128, 129.

46. Ibid., 129; J. P. Campbell, *Directory;* MBA, May 27, 1857.

47. Hunt, "Leaves from an Old Diary," 93, 109; P. M. Radford, "History of Christ Church, Nashville," Archives, duPont Library, The University of the South.

48. Lines, "Slaves and Churchmen," 241.

49. Report of J. Thomas Wheat, rector of Christ Church, in *Journal of the Protestant Episcopal Church*, 17. Italics are mine.

50. See the penetrating analysis of Lines, "Slaves and Churchmen," 72ff.

Note also Raboteau's arguments for the popularity of the Baptist church among black people in *Slave Religion*, 135–36.

51. Thomas, "Autobiography," 78. Only seven black people are listed as members of the First Presbyterian Church through 1853 (Sessions Book, First Presbyterian Church Records, microfilm, TSLA).

52. This is an approximate figure based on a black population over the age of ten of roughly three thousand. It assumes that church membership was not extended to children ten or younger.

53. Wadkins's narrative appears in G. W. Hubbard, *A History of the Colored Schools of Nashville, Tennessee.*

54. MBA, Dec. 27, 1837, Jan. 10, 1828.

55. Hubbard, *History of Colored Schools*, 4.

56. Thomas, "Autobiography," 5.

57. Hubbard, *History of Colored Schools*, 5–6; J. C. Napier, "Negro Members," 116.

58. England, "The Free Negro in Ante Bellum Tennessee," 292.

59. *Union*, Sept. 20, 1850.

60. Hubbard, *History of Colored Schools*, 5–6; Napier, "Negro Members," 116; *Republican Banner*, Dec. 5, 1856.

61. Wilburn, *Hazard of the Die*, 38, 208; Simmons, *Men of Mark*, 144; Napier, "Negro Members," 116. The atmosphere of the Fannings' school must have been extraordinarily supportive of blacks in that time and place; see Wilburn, 25, 86.

62. G. D. Pike, *Jubilee Singers*, 62; Simmons, *Men of Mark*, 425; Napier refers to Sally Porter as Sallie Player in "Negro Members," 116.

63. Schweninger, "The Free-Slave Phenomenon," 297.

64. Thomas, "Autobiography," 13.

65. Ibid., 10, 38, 66.

66. *Banner and Whig*, Dec. 9, 1836.

67. Imes, "Negroes in Tennessee," 56; Thomas, "Autobiography," 110; Schweninger, *Rapier and Reconstruction*, 193.

68. William F. Cooper to M. D. Cooper, Dec. 29, 1856, Cooper Family Papers, TSLA. See also entries in McGavock's diary for Dec. 1856, in Gower and Allen (eds.), *Pen and Sword*, 385; *Republican Banner*, Nov. 1, 27, Dec. 5, 9, 25, 30, 1856; MBA, Dec. 23, 1856, Jan. 8, 1857. For present-day assessments of the insurrection scare, see Dew, "Black Iron Workers," 321–38, and cf. Strickland, "Insurrectionary Fears," 82.

69. Imes, "Negroes in Tennessee," 57; *Republican Banner*, Dec. 21, 22, 1856. There was some opposition to appropriating funds for the Shelby Guards for services rendered during "the Negro Excitement in December," but ultimately $200 went to the company (MBA, Jan. 9, 22, Feb. 26, Mar. 12, 1857).

70. *Republican Banner*, Jan. 15, 1857. Not until the following November were blacks legally allowed to move about the city from sundown to 9:00

P.M. on Sundays (*A Compilation of the General Laws of the City of Nashville*, 228–29).

71. PMLT, DC, 1837, TSLA.

72. All quotations in this paragraph are drawn from Thomas, "Autobiography," 14, 15, 19, 61, 67, 85.

73. Cf. Berlin, *Slaves without Masters*, 350–51, and Goldin, *Urban Slavery*, 29–30. The *Republican Banner*, Nov. 14, 1856, reports a clash between a white drayman and a colored hack driver. The black was subject to a "cleaning out"; the white was discharged by the court. Much earlier, the *Banner and Whig* had printed a letter from "A Subscriber" furious because the *Gazette* had implied that a corporation slave had been murdered by the corporation overseer. The letter writer was exercised as well by a lavish funeral for a slave that was attended by blacks in "their splendid carriages"; he concluded, pointedly, that "in comparison to a *moneyed oligarchy*, my patronage is but a grain of sand" (Aug. 26, 1830).

74. *Union*, Sept. 4, 1850. Imes reports that "the testimony of those who lived through this time" placed the responsibility for the terrorizing of blacks in 1856 on "the poor and middle classes of the whites rather than their masters" ("Negroes in Tennessee," 56–57). Masters occasionally preferred charges against police for the illegal arrest and punishment of their slaves; see, e.g., MBA, Aug. 15, 1839.

75. Men like William Cooper and Randal McGavock were aware that there was no Negro insurrection: see, e.g., Wyatt-Brown, *Southern Honor*, 62–87.

76. George F. Clark to Mary E. Clark, May 9, 1847, Correspondence File, TSLA.

77. MBA, July 13, 1840, May 11, 1841, Feb. 8, 1855.

78. Berlin, *Slaves without Masters*, 370–71.

Chapter 8: Whig City

1. See Appendix, table 5.

2. Bergeron, *Antebellum Politics*, especially 13, 16, 22, 59, 73, 78–79, 99–100.

3. Abernethy, "Origin of the Whig Party," 509–10, 517; Thornton, *Politics and Power*, 41–42; Watson, *Jacksonian Politics and Community Conflict*, 146, 184, 207, 234–35, 280, 313.

4. Watson, *Jacksonian Politics and Community Conflict*, 322–24; Kruman, *Parties and Politics in North Carolina*, 55, 63, 68, 77.

5. McCormick, *The Second American Party System*, 230–35; Bergeron, "The Jacksonian Party on Trial," 17, 128, 146, 147, 205. See also Bergeron's *Antebellum Politics*, 52.

6. *Republican Banner*, Aug. 9, 1839; *Whig*, Nov. 1, 1842.

7. *Republican Banner*, Aug. 3, 1839, Aug. 21, 1843, Aug. 20, Sept. 6, 1844;

Sellers, *James K. Polk, Jacksonian,* 474–75. Crowds of 30,000 to 100,000 were drawn to the city to hear Clay and Crittenden (Bergeron, "Jacksonian Party on Trial," 125).

8. *Republican Banner,* Aug. 2, Sept. 8, Nov. 22, Dec. 6, 1843, Sept. 13, 1844.

9. Ibid., Aug. 9, 1844; Bergeron, "Jacksonian Party on Trial," 175. In 1814, Robert Foster, eldest son of E. H. Foster, shot the editor of the *Union;* in 1842 there was a "shoot-out" between the editors of the Democratic and Whig papers; in 1852 there was a "duel" between the editors of the *Union* and *Republican Banner;* in 1859 the editor of the *Union* was killed by the editor of the *News* (*Union,* Jan. 14, 1841; *Republican Banner,* Aug. 24, 1852; Bergeron, *Antebellum Politics,* 143; John B. Lindsley Diary, Nov. 18, 1859, Lindsley Family Papers, TSLA).

10. R. H. McEwen to Kitty McEwen, Sept. 7, 1859, THS: Robert H. McEwen Papers, TSLA; *Republican Banner,* Aug. 23, 1844; Kincheloe, "Transcending Role Restrictions," 163–68. All of Kincheloe's descriptions of women at political rallies refer to Whig rallies.

11. *Union,* Sept. 14, 1840; *Republican Banner,* Aug. 16, 1844.

12. Lowrey, "Tennessee Voters," 26, 38.

13. Pessen, *Jacksonian America,* 264.

14. Barton W. Folsom III finds that antebellum elites in Davidson County were fairly evenly divided between Democrats and Whigs ("The Politics of Elites," 362, 368, 369). He is, however, concerned with Davidson County as a whole rather than with Nashville alone, and his occupational categories are very general. Lawyers and farmers/planters are much more heavily represented than "businessmen." Davidson County, like Nashville, tended to vote Whig; the city's Whig preponderance undoubtedly helped account for this. For Davidson County's voting record, see Bergeron, *Antebellum Politics,* 16, 21, 27.

15. Tax List for DC, District No. 1, 1839, TSLA; List of the Taxable Property in the City of Nashville, 1847, Nashville Public Library.

16. Lowrey, in his statistical study of voting patterns in Tennessee, points out the tendency of merchants to affiliate with the Whigs or anti-Democrats ("Tennessee Voters," 61, 78, 99). Seven Whigs and one Democrat sat on Union Bank's board and six Whigs and one Democrat on Planters' Bank's in 1835; in 1841 five Whigs and three Democrats were Union directors, and seven Whigs and no identifiable Democrats were Planters' directors. Party identity was discovered most often by newspaper reports of participation in party meetings.

17. The business directory was published in the *Republican Banner,* Jan. 15, 1849.

18. William F. Cooper to D. R. Arnell, Jan. 25, 1847, Letter Book, Cooper Family Papers, TSLA.

19. Cf. Pessen, " 'Era of the Common Man,' " 602. Lowrey notes that "ar-

tisans and clerks in Middle Tennessee appear to have been inclined substantially toward the Whig Party" ("Tennessee Voters," 60–61, 84–87).

20. Of the seventy-five aldermen serving from 1840 to 1853, thirty-four were mechanics; twelve were professionals; there were eight merchants, including a druggist, one grocer (as opposed to wholesale grocery dealer), and four clerks, including a bank teller and a secretary of an insurance company; there were three stable keepers, one drayman, and a confectioner; a night watchman, predictably from the sixth ward, and a registrar could be considered government employees; two men of some property might be labeled either "gentlemen" or retirees. The occupations of seven aldermen are unknown.

21. For information on the property of aldermen in office between 1841 and 1845, I referred to the 1839 and 1847 tax lists; for similar information on those in office between 1846 and 1852, I referred to the 1847 tax list and the census reports of 1850 and 1860.

22. See below, chap. 9.

23. John M. Lea reported real estate valued at $800,000 in 1860.

24. Howe, *Political Culture of American Whigs*.

25. *Union*, July 6, 1838; *Banner and Whig*, Jan. 12, 18, 1850. James R. Sharp notes that the stubborn, antibank ideology was not as common in states involved in the banking system (*The Jacksonians versus the Banks*, 195, 322). The *Union* did publish an attack on Yeatman-Woods and its attempt to gain incorporation and, of course, always attacked the Bank of the United States (Dec. 7, May 11, 1837).

26. Folmsbee, *Sectionalism and Internal Improvements*, 54, 55, 101, 184, 194, 195, 206, 247.

27. *Orthopolitan*, Oct. 6, Dec. 11, 1845.

28. *Whig*, July 14, 1842. S. H. Laughlin, in his contemporary diary entry, reported two Whig ward leaders commenting on what a Democratic merchant "had smuggled under the bankrupt law" ("Diaries of S. H. Laughlin," 68).

29. *Whig*, Nov. 3, 1842; *Union*, Jan. 30, 1850.

30. Phelan, *History of Tennessee*, 388; John Bell quotation is from Sellers, *James K. Polk, Jacksonian*, 373.

31. Ronald P. Formisano establishes for Michigan the connections among Presbyterians, benevolence and reform societies, and Whiggery. The division he makes between evangelical-activist and nonevangelical, laissez-faire advocates was not apparent in Nashville, especially on the leadership level. Presbyterians and Episcopalians overlapped in benevolent societies and reform causes, although Presbyterians had the strength of numbers (*Birth of Mass Political Parties*, 104, 138, 141). See also Howe, *Political Culture of American Whigs*, 9, 21, 32–33, 35.

32. First Presbyterian Church Records, microfilm, TSLA.

33. *Orthopolitan*, Dec. 4, 1845, Nov. 20, 1846; *Nashville Herald*, Mar. 24, 1831.
34. Gusfield, *Symbolic Crusade*, 39–57.
35. PMLT, DC 1837, TSLA; *Republican Banner*, Dec. 11, 1839.
36. *Whig*, Aug. 2, 1841; *Union*, Feb. 10, 1838.
37. *Whig*, July 2, 7, 12, 1842.
38. *Republican Banner*, Mar. 27, 1841.
39. Cf. P. E. Johnson, *Shopkeeper's Millennium*.
40. *Whig*, July 12, 1842.
41. Ibid., Jan. 27, 1846; *Republican Banner*, Jan. 18, 1857. In 1842 the Saint Charles Hotel advertised a reduction in the price of a drink of John W. Walker's liquor, from ten to five cents, because of "hard times and scarce money" (*Republican Banner*, Nov. 29, 1842).
42. *Whig*, Sept. 2, 1847, Dec. 29, 1846.
43. The pervasiveness of this appeal to social mobility as the solution to class division is well documented (see, e.g., Welter, *The Mind of America*, 143–44). It became as much a Democratic as a Whig appeal. As John W. Ward suggests, even the tension between the self-sufficient man of Jeffersonian rhetoric and the self-made man of the Jacksonian period may not have been peculiar to Democratic spokesmen ("Jacksonian Democratic Thought," especially 77-79). See also the range of Whig biographies covered in Howe, *Political Culture of American Whigs*.
44. PMLT, DC 1827, TSLA.
45. *Banner and Whig*, Oct. 9, 1833, reprinted from the *New England Artisan*.
46. Cf. Stuart M. Blumin's provocative article, "The Hypothesis of Middle-Class Formation in Nineteenth-Century America," especially 337, and note his quotation (316–17) from James W. Alexander's *American Mechanic and Working Man*.
47. *Nashville Republican*, Jan. 18, 1828.
48. Robinson to R. H. McEwen, Aug. 23, 1842, THS: Robert H. McEwen Papers, TSLA.
49. William R. Taylor brilliantly analyzed the antebellum writers who began to produce and probe sectional stereotypes. The northern stereotype was the striving, ever-ambitious Yankee (*Cavalier and Yankee*, especially 95–141). Eric Foner described the free-labor ethic and the concern for social mobility as the basis of northern Republican ideology (*Free Soil, Free Labor, Free Men*, 11–18). Obviously, the Whigs and usually the Democrats of Nashville were insisting on similar values—for white people. The cavalier stereotype was not rewarding politically.
50. *The Agriculturist*, 4:61; *Republican Banner*, Apr. 21, 28, May 1, 1843.
51. *Banner and Whig*, May 16, 18, June 8, 13, 15, July 6, 1831, Apr. 4, 1836; Wooldridge (ed.), *History of Nashville*, 216–19.

52. Coppersmith Joseph Knowles, coachmaker Monohan, brickmason Samuel Watkins, merchant tailor J. V. D. Stout, and architect and builder Adolphus Heiman were appointed to committees along with other master craftsmen. Only editor Hunt seemed a bit out of place in this company (*Republican Banner*, Dec. 25, 1837, Jan. 23, Feb. 21, 1838).

53. *Union*, Oct. 4, 1853, Nov. 25, 1839; *Republican Banner*, Nov. 27, 1839, Jan. 1, 1840; Crowe, "Tennessee's Prison Problem," 115.

54. "Benefit members" would be accepted on payment of five dollars in money or books. Active members paid a one-dollar fee (*Whig*, Aug. 23, 1841).

55. *Whig*, Oct. 4, Nov. 17, Dec. 8, 17, 1842, Oct. 5, 1848; Davenport, *Cultural Life in Nashville*, 170.

56. *Union*, Sept. 14, 1853. On Ament, see Clayton, *History of Davidson County*, facing p. 332.

57. McEwen, *Reform of Social Ranks*, 14, 16. See also Turner S. Foster's *Address* for a similar warning against "demagogues" and the insistence that mechanics "have the elements of social and scientific advancement in themselves and in the nature and spirit of their pursuits."

58. *Union*, Nov. 14, 1854; see also Sept. 27, Oct. 4, 14, 1854. The poll tax Ferguson referred to must have been the tax imposed for the new public schools.

59. Cf. Howe, *Political Culture of American Whigs*, 9, 101, and Dawley, *Class and Community*, 102. Dawley makes the point that democratic politics worked against the development of class consciousness (70).

60. *Republican Banner*, Aug. 26, 30, 1851.

61. In 1836 the newspapers urged the city to rent a boat and bring coal from the Cumberland mines lest the city be deserted "as in 1834" (*Banner and Whig*, echoing the *Republican*, Dec. 9, 1836).

62. *Orthopolitan*, Sept. 4, 1846.

63. S. V. D. Stout to S. H. Stout, Apr. 24, 1844 (?), THS: Samuel H. Stout Papers, TSLA; *Union*, Oct. 2, 1835; *Banner and Whig*, Oct. 26, 1835.

64. Cooper Letter Book 2, June 18, 1849, Oct. 2, 1850, Cooper Family Papers, TSLA; Lindsley Diary, June 29, 1849, Lindsley Family Papers, TSLA.

65. Charles Rosenberg points out how widespread these attitudes were (*The Cholera Years*, especially 138–39, 218, 229–30. He cites the *Nashville Republican* of October 29, 1832, as "relating cholera to intemperance and sexual excess" (41n.2). Carol Smith Rosenberg provides a comparable antebellum definition of "respectability" (*Religion and the American City*, 7–8n.2; see also 38, 39).

66. *Banner and Whig*, Mar. 17, 1837; *Orthopolitan*, Dec. 14, 1845. The house of industry came to concentrate on providing cultural and educational advantages to disadvantaged girls "so that they would someday make suitable wives." Musicals, outings, French lessons, and fine sewing seemed

to be what concerned the patrons of the school (Wheeler and Neblett, *Chosen Exile*, 108–10). Cf. C. S. Rosenberg, *Religion and the American City*, 118.

67. *Republican Banner*, Feb. 9, 1849, Feb. 9, 1850, Nov. 9, 1854; Wheeler and Neblett, *Chosen Exile*, 117; *Union*, Dec. 3, 1854.

68. *Republican Banner*, Dec. 17, 1845, Jan. 26, 1849; *Union*, Dec. 9, 1848; *Banner and Whig*, Jan. 5, 1850.

69. *Constitution of the Robertson Association*. The AOMC fancied the white robes and black cowls of monks for its members (*Republican Banner*, Oct. 4, 1859).

70. Gower and Allen (eds.), *Pen and Sword*, 486.

71. P. M. Radford, "Christ Church," "Church of the Holy Trinity," "Church of the Advent," manuscripts, Archives, Jessie Ball duPont Library, The University of the South; Coke, "Christ Church," 141– 50.

72. The bibliography on this topic is immense, but see, e.g., Formisano, *Birth of Mass Political Parties*, 5, 45, 102, 110; Welter, *The Mind of America*, 77–84; C. S. Rosenberg, *Religion and the American City*, 51.

73. *Union*, Jan. 9, 1839; MBA, Dec. 27, 1837, Jan. 10, 1838.

74. *Union*, Sept. 14, 1850. In 1860, faced with drought and a huge increase in freight, the Louisville and Nashville Railroad could not get labor to load its cars on Sundays because of the sabbatarian ordinances (Clark, *Beginnings of the L & N*, 50). Ronald Formisano sees Sabbath observance as a Whig issue (*Birth of Mass Political Parties*, 122).

75. *Republican Banner*, Sept. 16, 1851.

76. "Diaries of S. H. Laughlin," 61.

77. See Appendix, tables 4 and 5; *Orthopolitan*, Dec. 20, 1845.

78. Robert I. Moore owned slaves, a farm in Williamson County, land in Arkansas, and considerable city real estate; he was a director of the Franklin Turnpike Company (DC Will Book, Dec. 14, 1849, 447–52, Dec. 18, 1848, 198, 199, Dec. 31, 1851, 236–38).

79. With few exceptions they were men of small means. Three claimed no real estate in 1850; five claimed between $2,000 and $12,000.

80. John Coltart to William Coltart, Aug. 8, 26, 1838, June 15, 1839, THS: Miscellaneous Collections, TSLA; Acklen, *Tennessee Records*, 9. Coltart was also president of the Mechanics' Library Debating Society in 1846 (*Orthopolitan*, Sept. 29, Nov. 26, 1846).

81. Thomas J. Haile listed no occupation in the 1850 census and "shoemaker" in 1860, when he also acted as a census taker, and claimed no property in either year. In the late fifties he served the city as tax assessor.

82. William P. Downs served four terms as alderman in the fifties. In 1850 he claimed $26,000 in real estate and in 1860 $65,000 in real and personal estate. Either a bachelor or a widower, he was a boarder in both years.

Chapter 9: Urban Success and National Disaster

1. See especially Thornton, *Politics and Power,* xviii–xxi and passim.

2. Robert L. Partin, "The Secession Movement in Tennessee," provides close reporting of Tennessee newspapers' reactions to the sectional crisis from 1850 to 1860 (21, 29, 30, 36, 38, 39, 41, 56).

3. Cf. Kruman, *Parties and Politics in North Carolina,* 133, 181, 196–212.

4. Blumin, *Urban Threshold,* app. A, 223–26. Blumin's city, Kingston, ranked 56th, Lynn 47th, Springfield 60th, Petersburg 50th, and Norfolk 63d. Studies of each of these confirm urban patterns (Dawley, *Class and Community;* Frisch, *Town into City;* Goldfield, *Urban Growth in the Age of Sectionalism).* See also the map of "Leading Southern Cities, 1860," in Goldfield's *Cotton Fields and Skyscrapers,* 31.

5. *Banner and Whig,* Aug. 14, Sept. 18, 21, 1835.

6. Wooldridge (ed.), *History of Nashville,* 632.

7. *Banner and Whig,* Jan. 27, 1829, Oct. 7, 1830, Aug. 3, 1831; White, *Educational Organization,* 77.

8. Nagy, "Wanted: A Teacher," 182–86; *Union,* Jan. 11, 1839; MBA, Nov. 12, 26, 1839; *Whig,* Jan. 17, 1840. R. H. McEwen, superintendent of public instruction, defaulted on $121,000 of school funds that had been loaned "on good security" (*Republican Banner,* Dec. 14, 1839, and Jan. 1840 passim; White, *Educational Organization,* 48). Defaulting evidently did not compromise McEwen's position with his fellow Whigs or his son's later political career.

9. Morton B. Howell, "Memoir," typescript loaned to the author by Isabel Howell, 66–67. Numbers of students and teachers are reported by the *Whig,* Aug. 23, 1842, and in the manuscript federal census of 1840.

10. Ingraham was especially concerned to provide schooling for the children of the "destitute." He estimated that 610 of 1,500 school-age children in Nashville were in that category (Ingraham, *Report,* 21). See also Weathersby, "Ingraham and Tennessee," 264–72.

11. *Whig,* July, Aug. 1842, especially July 14, 21, 26, Aug. 9, 1842, Sept. 11, Oct. 4, 1845. On the high-school issue cf. Tyack, *The One Best System,* 57–58, and Katz, *Early School Reform,* part 1.

12. *Whig,* Dec. 10, 1842.

13. Ibid., Sept. 19, Oct. 5, 1848.

14. The members of the board were Francis Fogg, John McEwen, Return J. Meigs, W. F. Bang, publisher of the *Republican Banner,* successor to the *Whig,* Allen Hall, editor of the *Banner,* and Charles Tomes, rector of Christ Church. Isaac Paul and John B. Lindsley were added to the board in October 1855.

15. MBA, Nov. 3, Dec. 29, 1851, Sept. 7, 1853, Apr. 14, Aug. 10, Sept. 4, 14, 18, 29, 1854; *Republican Banner,* Sept. 20, 21, 30, Oct. 12, 14, 1854.

16. MBA, Sept. 29, 1860, Mar. 9, 1854, Nov. 22, 1855.

17. *Republican Banner*, Feb. 18, 1857.

18. McGavock, *Communication*, 14, 15; Davenport, *Cultural Life in Nashville*, 54; MBA, Sept. 30, 1858; *Republican Banner*, Feb. 18, 1857.

19. Gower and Allen (eds.), *Pen and Sword*, 510.

20. MBA, Nov. 11, Dec. 10, 1839, Aug. 24, 1854, Jan. 10, 1856.

21. An eggnog party at the University of Nashville wound up with a fight with the night watch on the public square; the mayor and a mounted company were called on when the fight spread to the wharf, where the students took on the boatmen (Coffee, "A Student," 156). For another example, see *Whig*, June 23, 1846.

22. Kaser, "Nashville's Women of Pleasure," 379–82. Robert W. Fogel and Stanley Engerman build, in part on these census figures, a complex if shaky argument for the relative lack of sexual exploitation of black women by white men (*Time on the Cross*, 135). In the winter of 1854 the eviction of prostitutes from Smokey Row by the police became something of a party issue, with the *Banner* defending the corporation and the *Union* urging some concern for the "shelter and subsistence" of the women (*Republican Banner*, Nov. 9, 1854; *Union*, Aug. 24, Sept. 26, 1837, Nov. 28, 1854; see also MBA, Nov. 9, Dec. 14, 1854, Jan. 11, 1855, Apr. 10, 1856; *Banner and Whig*, Nov. 1, 1830; and *Banner*, Apr. 23, 1833).

23. "Officer Reddick arrested a negro boy, property of Mr. Peabody, for flying a kite within the city limits"; the boy was flogged (*Union*, Sept. 21, 1850).

24. *Laws of the Corporation of Nashville* (1837), 24; *Revised Laws of the City of Nashville*, 41; MBA, Dec. 27, 1837, Sept. 11, Nov. 12, 19, Dec. 10, 1839; PMLT, DC 1837; *Republican Banner*, Dec. 30, 1837, Sept. 30, 1839.

25. McGavock, *Communication*, 12.

26. MBA, July 10, 1851.

27. Report of Dr. Thomas R. Jennings to the county court on the state of the jail, *Union*, Dec. 16, 1837; see also Aug. 31, 1850.

28. McGavock, *Communication*, 5, 10, 12; MBA, Sept. 20, 1857.

29. One company wore cream-colored hats and pink shirts with blue trim ("The Diary of Mary Hunt," *Kirkwood Historical Review* 6:6, TSLA; Susan Elliott to Elizabeth, Feb. 23, 1839, THS: C. D. Elliott Papers, TSLA; *Union*, Oct. 17, 1838).

30. *Whig*, Jan. 22, 1845, Aug. 31, Sept. 16, 1847; *Republican Banner*, Jan. 24, Feb. 5, Dec. 30, 1845.

31. J. B. Jones, "Mose the Bowery B'hoy," 175–81. See Appendix, table 7.

32. Wooldridge (ed.), *History of Nashville*, 131–33; Blake, *Water for the Cities*, 77, 120, 266.

33. MBA, Sept. 20, 1857, Sept. 20, 1858, Sept. 30, 1859, Sept. 29, 1860; *Republican Banner*, Aug. 16, 1852, Aug. 31, 1853, Nov. 21, 1856.

34. *Gazette*, Jan. 21, 1851, Feb. 14, 1851; McGavock, *Communication*, 195; Wooldridge (ed.), *History of Nashville*, 231.

35. Cf. Rothman, *Discovery of the Asylum*.

36. MBA, Feb. 13, Mar. 27, May 8, 1846; *Union*, Apr. 17, 1835.

37. Two hundred persons were reported dead within ten days in June 1849 and five hundred from June 9 to August 1, 1850 (William Cooper to D. Arnell, June 18, 1849, Letter Book 2, Cooper Family Papers, TSLA; Frank, *Five Families*, 128).

38. MBA, Oct. 25, 1852, Feb. 23, 1854; *Republican Banner*, Oct. 4, 1851. Cf. Vogel, "Patrons, Practitioners, and Patients," 128 and passim.

39. When Lindsley visited in the North, he attended the "Woman's Right" convention in New York and visited one of the city's schools and the annual exhibition of deaf-mutes as well as the Academy of Fine Arts and the navy yard. He made a special effort to attend Henry Ward Beecher's Congregational Plymouth Church. Lindsley's diary reports a circle of friends active in the politics or the new institutions of the community: Alexander Hume, John McEwen, William Cooper, the bookseller William Eichbaum, Return J. Meigs, and Francis Fogg's son, Henry. Lindsley went regularly to the "at homes" of Mrs. Bass, of Bishop Otey's daughter, Mrs. Hitchcock, of Mrs. Senator Weakley, and of Mrs. Rutledge, Henry Fogg's grandmother and a principal sponsor of the house of industry.

40. MBA, Feb. 21, 23, Mar. 9, 1854, Apr. 24, 1856; *Union*, Jan. 3, 1855.

41. *Republican Banner*, Nov. 10, 1855.

42. See Appendix, table 7; MBA, Apr. 11, 1856; *Republican Banner*, Dec. 7, 1856.

43. See Appendix, table 7.

44. MBA, Sept. 29, 1860.

45. For a list of the original commissioners of the railroad, see De Bow, *Legal History*, 4. For Stevenson, see Wooldridge (ed.), *History of Nashville*, 328–30. In 1854 Stevenson, a widower, married John Bass's daughter.

46. MBA, Oct. 10, 1850, Apr. 22, 1852, Apr. 28, 1853, Oct. 12, 26, Dec. 28, 1854; Wooldridge (ed.), *History of Nashville*, 330; *Republican Banner*, July 27, 1854, Aug. 10, 1855, Sept. 23, Oct. 3, 1859.

47. Quoted in McDonald, "Milling in Middle Tennessee," 184–85.

48. *Union*, Sept. 27, 1849, Aug. 7, 9, Sept. 2, 10, 28, 1850.

49. See, e.g., ibid., Sept. 14, 1850, Aug. 31, 1853; *Republican Banner*, Aug. 16, 1852, July 28, 1854, Nov. 21, 1856.

50. MBA, July 23, 1857. The city debt of $120,000 in 1842 had prompted Mayor Coleman to urge "retrenchment"—by hiring rather than purchasing corporation slave hands (*Whig*, Oct. 14, 1842).

51. *Republican Banner*, Sept. 30, 1854, Dec. 18, 1856; McGavock, *Communication*, 19.

52. *A Compilation of the General Laws of the City of Nashville*, 50–53. Aldermen still were required to be freeholders, and the mayor was required to be the owner of a freehold worth at least $500.

53. McGavock, *Communication*, 19; MBA, Oct. 1, 1858.

54. Teaford, *Municipal Revolution*, 99.

55. McGavock, *Communication*, 15, 17.

56. Cooper, *The South and Slavery*, 226, 278; Bergeron, *Antebellum Politics*, 79, 85–86.

57. Bergeron, *Antebellum Politics*, 99–100.

58. Ibid., 104–6; M. E. R. Campbell, *Attitude of Tennesseans*, 58–59.

59. William F. Cooper to J. B. Varnum, Dec. 7, 1850, Letter Book 2, Cooper Family Papers, TSLA.

60. Cooper, *The South and Slavery*, 340, 355–60.

61. *Republican Banner*, Aug. 30, Sept. 1, 1854; *Union*, Aug. 31, 1854; Gohmann, *Political Nativism in Tennessee*, 88. Michael F. Holt notes that this was a frequent stratagem of the Know-Nothings (*Political Crisis of the 1850s*, 157).

62. On the Know-Nothings and moralism, see Silbey, *Transformation of American Politics*, 12.

63. *Union*, Oct. 1, 3, 4, 1854, and Oct.–Nov. 1854, passim.

64. Lowrey, "Tennessee Voters," 11, 26, 38; Gohmann, *Political Nativism in Tennessee*, 83. Even M. Sulzbacher, a foreign-born Jew and a Whig, was elected as one of the twelve vice-presidents of the Fillmore and Donelson club (Frank, *Five Families*, 92). Cooper notes that Whigs' conversion to the American party was general throughout the South (*The South and Slavery*, 365).

65. William F. Cooper to M. D. Cooper, Apr. 10, 1855, Oct. 12, 1856, Cooper Family Papers, TSLA; Overdyke, *Know-Nothing Party*, 299; Gohmann, *Political Nativism in Tennessee*, 114.

66. *Republican Banner*, Oct. 9, 1854; MBA, Oct. 26, 1854.

67. *Republican Banner*, Sept. 25, 26, 30, 1855.

68. Cooper, *The South and Slavery*, 368–69.

69. *Republican Banner*, Sept. 28, Oct. 3, 1856.

70. A. Johnson, *Speech*.

71. A. V. Brown, *Address*.

72. *Republican Banner*, Apr. 29, Sept. 21, 23–25, 27, 1857; see *Nashville Gazette*, Nov. 15, 1865, for the obituary of Robert McEwen, father of the mayor.

73. *Republican Banner*, Sept. 18, 25, 26, 1858. It is interesting to note that a few months later a committee of the aldermen voted against Democrat V. K. Stevenson for president of the Nashville and Chattanooga Railroad, which he had nurtured. Stevenson won without the city's vote (Gower and Allen [eds.], *Pen and Sword*, 500).

74. Gower and Allen (eds.), *Pen and Sword*, 488, 489, 427; for McGavock's hesitations about democracy, see 313, 314.

75. *Republican Banner*, Sept. 26, 1858; see Appendix, tables 4 and 5.

76. *Republican Banner*, Sept. 13, 19, 20, 26, 30, 1859, Sept. 30, 1860. Smith indeed may have been flirting with the Democrats. During Recon-

struction he was in favor with Andrew Johnson's administration. Though "hated by the Nashvillians," he was mayor again from 1862 through 1864, judge of the circuit court from 1867 to 1870, and councilman from 1868 to 1869 (Rose, "Nashville and Its Leadership Elite," 66–67).

77. R. H. McEwen to Kitty, Sept. 7, 1859, THS: Robert H. McEwen Papers, TSLA.

78. Cooper, *The South and Slavery*, 74, 75, passim.

79. Chitty, *Reconstruction at Sewanee*, 60, 80n.119.

80. Goldfield, *Cotton Fields and Skyscrapers*, 76–77, and his "Cities and Southern Independence."

81. Holt, *Political Crisis of the 1850s*, 230ff.; cf. Kruman, *Parties and Politics in North Carolina*, 181, 191, 195–97, 219, 220.

82. *Republican Banner*, Sept. 6, 1859.

83. Ibid.

84. J. H. Parks, *John Bell of Tennessee*, 356, chaps. 18 and 19, passim.

85. Ibid., 362.

86. M. B. Hamer, "Presidential Campaign of 1860," 20–21.

87. Ibid., 16.

88. Partin, "The Secession Movement in Tennessee," 66.

89. Wooldridge (ed.), *History of Nashville*, 185; Cooper, *The South and Slavery*, 370.

90. Partin, "The Secession Movement in Tennessee," 80. Most of Douglas's Tennessee support came from the Memphis area.

91. Cf. Thornton, *Politics and Power*, 57–58.

92. John Lindsley Diary, Apr. 20, 29, 1861, THS, TSLA.

93. Partin, "The Secession Movement in Tennessee," 83, 167.

94. Wooster, *Secession Conventions*, 181, 173, 180, 185; Partin, "The Secession Movement in Tennessee," 181–82.

95. For the use of "conditional" to describe Tennessee Unionists' position, see Maslowski, *Treason Must Be Made Odious*, 13. Ralph A. Wooster uses "conditional unionists" in a similar way in *Secession Conventions*, 11n.1.

96. Gower and Allen (eds.), *Pen and Sword*, 582.

97. Not all opted for the Confederate uniform; Return J. Meigs's sons raised and officered a unit of black Tennesseans for the Union forces (Faulkner, "Return J. Meigs," 161).

98. Maslowski, *Treason Must Be Made Odious*, 149; Durham, *Nashville* and *Nashville and the Union*.

99. David R. Goldfield made a similar observation of Virginia's antebellum cities (*Urban Growth in the Age of Sectionalism*, 224).

100. Doyle, *Nashville in the New South*, 42, 65–68.

BIBLIOGRAPHY

Manuscripts Cited

Tennessee State Library and Archives
  Adam G. Adams Notebook and Account Book
  Samuel B. Ament. "First Sunday School Organized in Nashville." Transcript
  Auxiliary Bible Society of Davidson County. Minutes, 1823–58.
  Catherine B. Avery Papers
  Bransford Family Papers
  Russel Campbell. "History of the Sunday School of the First Presbyterian Church." Typescript.
  Claybrooke and Overton Papers
  John Coffee Papers
  Whiteford R. Cole Papers
  Cooper Family Papers
  Correspondence by Author File
  James McGavock Dickinson Papers
  First Presbyterian Church. Records. Microfilm.
  Moses Fisk Papers
  Foster Family Papers
  David Henley Papers
  Morton B. Howell Family Papers
  R. B. C. Howell. "Memorial of the First Baptist Church, Nashville, Tennessee, 1820–1863." Microfilm.
  Emil E. Hurja Collection
  Lindsley Family Papers
  Manuscript Sketches in Miscellaneous Collections
  Militia Companies of Davidson and Sumner Counties. Proceedings of a Meeting.... June 2, 1786. Microfilm 5XX18, Draper Collection of

Manuscripts, State Historical Society of Wisconsin, Madison. Photostats in TSLA.
Mill Creek Baptist Church. "The Conference Business of the Baptist Church under the Care of James Whitsitt." Record Book, 1797–1814.
Nichol-Britt Collection
John Overton Papers
Overton Letter Book
Small Collections (Priestley)
Samuel A. Weakley Papers
Robert Whyte Papers
Tennessee Historical Society: Dyas Collection, John Coffee Papers
THS: C. D. Elliott Papers
THS: Robert H. McEwen Papers
THS: Miscellaneous Collections
THS: Murdock Collection—Overton Papers
THS: Samuel H. Stout Papers
THS: James Winchester Papers
Fisk University Library
  James C. Napier Papers
Howard University Library
  James P. Thomas. "Autobiography." Rapier Family Papers. Moorland-Spingarn Research Center.
Jessie Ball duPont Library, The University of the South
  P. M. Radford. "Christ Church," "Church of the Advent," "Church of the Holy Trinity."
  Mary Woods. "Memories." Typescript.
Vanderbilt University Library
  Andrew Ewing. Memorandum Book, 1780–1851. Microfilm.
  John Overton Papers. Microfilm.
  University of Nashville Records. Microfilm.
Typescripts loaned to the author by Isabel Howell
  Jennie Thompson Howell. "Family Talk."
  Morton B. Howell. "Memoir."

Unpublished Public Records

Davidson County. TSLA.
  Deed and Will Books, 1784–1832.
  Minute Books of the County Court, 1780–1825.
  Tax Lists: 1787, 1798, 1816, 1829, 1839.
Montgomery County Will Books, 1789–1821. TSLA.

Sumner County. TSLA.
  Will Books, 1789–1842.
  Tax Lists: 1793, 1795, 1796.
Nashville
  Minutes of the Board of Commissioners, 1802–3. TSLA.
  Corporation of Nashville Tax List, 1847. Nashville Public Library.
  Minutes of the Board of Aldermen, 1837–60. Office of the Metropolitan Clerk, Metro Courthouse.
Index to Land Grants: North Carolina. TSLA.
Index to Land Grants: Tennessee. TSLA.
Petitions and Memorials to the Legislature of Tennessee. TSLA.
U.S. Census Records
  First through Eighth Censuses: Population Schedules.
  Nashville Population Schedule, 1820, as transcribed from the manuscript U.S. Census by Martha Lou Houston. TSLA.
  Nashville Population Schedule, 1850, as transcribed by Deane Porche. TSLA.
  U.S. Census. . . . Manufactures. . . . 1820.
  U.S. Census. . . . Schedule of Free Inhabitants, 1850, 1860.
  U.S. Census. . . . Slave Schedules, 1850, 1860.

Newspapers

The Agriculturist, 1843.
Clarion, 1800–1822.
Constitutional Advocate, 1822–23.
Impartial Review and Cumberland Repository, 1805–8.
Nashville Daily Gazette, 1851–53.
Nashville Herald, 1831–32.
Nashville Republican, 1825–31.
Nashville Union, 1835–60.
Nashville Whig, 1812–26, 1840–49.
National Banner, 1825–26.
National Banner and Nashville Whig, 1826–37.
Niles Register, 1826.
Orthopolitan, 1845–46.
Republican Banner, 1826, 1837–49.
Republican Banner and Nashville Whig, 1849–60.
Tennessee Gazette, 1800–1807.

Published Works Cited

Abernethy, Thomas P. "The Early Development of Commerce and Banking in Tennessee." *Mississippi Valley Historical Review* 14 (1927–28): 311–25.

———. *From Frontier to Plantation in Tennessee.* Chapel Hill: University of North Carolina Press, 1932.

———. "The Origin of the Whig Party in Tennessee." *Mississippi Valley Historical Review* 12 (1925–26): 504–22.

Acklen, Jeanette T. *Tennessee Records.* Nashville: Cullom and Ghertner Co., 1933.

American State Papers: Indian Affairs, vol. 1. Washington, DC: Gales and Seaton, 1832.

Amos, Harriet E. *Cotton City: Urban Development in Antebellum Mobile.* Tuscaloosa: University of Alabama Press, 1985.

Applewhite, Joseph D. "Early Trade and Navigation on the Cumberland River." Master's thesis, Vanderbilt University, 1940.

Arnow, Harriette S. "Education and the Professions in the Cumberland Region." *Tennessee Historical Quarterly* 20 (1961): 120–58.

———. *The Flowering of the Cumberland.* New York: Macmillan, 1963.

Asbury, Francis. *The Journal and Letters of Francis Asbury.* 3 vols. Ed. Elmer T. Clark, Manning Potts, and Jacob S. Payton. Nashville: Abingdon Press, 1958.

Atherton, Lewis E. *The Frontier Merchant in Mid-America.* Columbia: University of Missouri Press, [1939] 1971.

Banner, Lois W. "Religious Benevolence as Social Control: A Critique of an Interpretation." *Journal of American History* 60 (1973): 23–41.

Bass, J. M. "Rev. Thomas Craighead." *American Historical Magazine* 7 (1902): 88–96.

Beard, William E. "The Church of Ante Bellum Times." In *Christ Church, Nashville.* Nashville: Marshall and Bruce Co., 1929.

Beaumont, Gustave de. *Marie, or Slavery in the United States.* Stanford: Stanford University Press, [1835] 1958.

Benson, Lee. *The Concept of Jacksonian America: New York as a Test Case.* Princeton: Princeton University Press, 1961.

Bergeron, Paul H. *Antebellum Politics in Tennessee.* Lexington: University Press of Kentucky, 1982.

———. "The Jacksonian Party on Trial: Presidential Politics in Tennessee, 1836–1856." Ph.D. diss., Vanderbilt University, 1965.

———. "James K. Polk and the Jacksonian Press in Tennessee." *Tennessee Historical Quarterly* 41 (1982): 257–77.

Berlin, Ira. *Slaves without Masters: The Free Negro in the Antebellum South.* New York: Pantheon Books, 1974.

———, and Herbert G. Gutman. "Natives and Immigrants, Free Men and Slaves: Urban Workingmen in the Antebellum South." *American Historical Review* 88 (1983): 1175–1200.

Birney, James Gillespie. *Letters of James Gillespie Birney.* Ed. Dwight D. Dumond. New York: D. Appleton-Century, 1938.

Blake, Nelson. *Water for the Cities.* Syracuse, NY: Syracuse University Press, 1956.
Blount, John Gray. *The John Gray Blount Papers,* vol. 1. Ed. Alice B. Keith. Raleigh: North Carolina Department of Archives and History, 1952.
———. *The John Gray Blount Papers,* vol. 3. Ed. William H. Masterson. Raleigh: North Carolina Department of Archives and History, 1965.
Blumin, Stuart M. "The Hypothesis of Middle-Class Formation in Nineteenth-Century America: A Critique and Some Proposals." *American Historical Review* 90 (1985): 299–338.
———. "Mobility and Change in Ante Bellum Philadelphia." In *Nineteenth-Century Cities: Essays in the New Urban History,* ed. Stephen Thernstrom and Richard Sennett. New Haven: Yale University Press, 1969.
———. *The Urban Threshold: Growth and Change in a Nineteenth-Century American Community.* Chicago: University of Chicago Press, 1976.
Bogue, Allan. "Social Theory and the Pioneer." *Agricultural History* 34 (1960): 21–34.
Bonner, James C. *Milledgeville: Georgia's Antebellum Capital.* Athens: University of Georgia Press, 1978.
Boyer, Paul. *Urban Masses and Moral Order in America, 1820–1920.* Cambridge: Harvard University Press, 1978.
Bridges, Amy. *A City in the Republic: Antebellum New York and the Origins of Machine Politics.* Ithaca, NY: Cornell University Press, [1984] 1987.
Brown, Aaron V. *Address on the Parties and Issues of the Presidential Election Delivered at Philadelphia, August 15, 1856.* Nashville: G. C. Torbett and Co., 1856.
Brown, Charles H. *Agents of Manifest Destiny.* Chapel Hill: University of North Carolina Press, 1980.
Browning, H. M. "The Washington County Court, 1778–1789: A Study in Frontier Administration." *Tennessee Historical Quarterly* 1 (1915): 328–43.
Bunting, Robert F. *Manual of the First Presbyterian Church.* Nashville: Southern Methodist Publishing House, 1868.
Caldwell, Joshua W. *Sketches of the Bench and Bar of Tennessee.* Knoxville: Ogden Bros., 1898.
Campbell, Claude A. "The Development of Banking in Tennessee." Ph.D. diss., Vanderbilt University, 1932.
Campbell, J. P. *The Nashville, State of Tennessee, and General Commercial Directory.* Nashville: L. P. Williams and Co., 1853.
Campbell, Mary E. R. *The Attitude of Tennesseans toward the Union, 1847–1861.* New York: Vantage Press, 1961.
Capers, Gerald M. *The Biography of a River Town.* Chapel Hill: University of North Carolina Press, 1938.
Carter, Clarence E. (ed.). *The Territorial Papers of the United States,* vol. 4. Washington, DC: Government Printing Office, 1936.

Cate, Wirt A. "Timothy Demonbreun." *Tennessee Historical Quarterly* 16 (1957): 214–27.
Catterall, Helen T. *Judicial Cases concerning American Slavery and the Negro*, vol. 2. Washington, DC: Carnegie Institution of Washington, 1929.
Chapell, Gordon T. "Land Speculation and Taxation in Tennessee, 1790–1834." Master's thesis, Vanderbilt University, 1936.
Chitty, Arthur B. *Reconstruction at Sewanee*. Sewanee, TN: University Press, 1954.
Christie, Susan C. *The Cantril-Cantrell Genealogy*. New York: Grafton Press, 1908.
Cisco, Jay G. *Historic Sumner County, Tennessee*. Nashville: Charles Elder, [1909] 1971.
Claiborne, Thomas, et al. *History and True Position of the Church of Christ in Nashville*. Nashville: Cameron and Fall, 1854.
Clark, Thomas D. *The Beginnings of the L & N*. Louisville, KY: Standard Printing Co., 1933.
Clay, Henry. *The Papers of Henry Clay*, vol. 5. Ed. James F. Hopkins and Mary W.M. Hargreaves. Lexington: University of Kentucky Press, 1973.
Clayton, W. W. *History of Davidson County*. Philadelphia: J. W. Lewis, 1880.
Clifton, Frances. "The Life and Activities of John Overton." Master's thesis, Vanderbilt University, 1948.
Coffee, John D. "A Student at the University of Nashville: Correspondence of John Donelson Coffee, 1830–1833." Ed. Aaron M. Boom. *Tennessee Historical Quarterly* 16 (1957): 141–59.
Coke, Fletch. "Christ Church, Episcopal, Nashville." *Tennessee Historical Quarterly* 38 (1979): 141–57.
A Compilation of the General Laws of the City of Nashville. Nashville: James E. Rains, 1860.
Connelly, John L. "Old North Nashville and Germantown." *Tennessee Historical Quarterly* 39 (1980): 115–48.
Constitution of the Robertson Association of the City of Nashville. Nashville: W. F. Bang, 1856.
Conzen, Kathleen N. *Immigrant Milwaukee, 1836–1860*. Cambridge: Harvard University Press, 1976.
Cooper, William J., Jr. *The South and the Politics of Slavery, 1828–1856*. Baton Rouge: Louisiana State University Press, 1978.
Corlew, Robert E. "Some Aspects of Slavery in Dickson County." *Tennessee Historical Quarterly* 10 (1951): 224–48, 344–65.
Crabb, Alfred L. *Nashville: Personality of a City*. Indianapolis: Bobbs-Merrill, 1960.
———. "Wilkins Tannehill, Business and Cultural Leader." *Tennessee Historical Quarterly* 7 (1948): 314–21.
Credit of the West: Reports of a Committee Appointed at a Meeting of Merchants

    and Other Citizens of Nashville, Tennessee, April 2, 1833. Nashville: Office of the *Nashville Banner*, 1833.
Crowe, Jessie C. "The Origin and Development of Tennessee's Prison Problem, 1837–1871." *Tennessee Historical Quarterly* 15 (1956): 111–35.
Curry, Leonard P. *The Free Black in Urban America, 1800–1850*. Chicago: University of Chicago Press, 1981.
———. "Urbanization and Urbanism in the Old South: A Comparative View." *Journal of Southern History* 40 (1974): 43–60.
Davenport, F. Garvin. *Cultural Life in Nashville on the Eve of the Civil War*. Chapel Hill: University of North Carolina Press, 1941.
———. "Culture versus Frontier in Tennessee, 1825–1850." *Journal of Southern History* 5 (1939): 18–33.
Davis, David B. *The Problem of Slavery in the Age of Revolution, 1770–1823*, vol. 2. Ithaca, NY: Cornell University Press, 1957.
———. Review of *The Black Family in Slavery and Freedom* by Herbert G. Gutman. *American Historical Review* 82 (1977): 745.
Davis, James E. *Frontier America, 1800–1840*. Glendale, CA: A. H. Clark Co., 1977.
Davis, Louise. "Banker in Knee Pants Owned a Skyscraper Site." *The Tennesseean Magazine*, July 29, 1973.
Dawley, Alan. *Class and Community: The Industrial Revolution in Lynn*. Cambridge: Harvard University Press, 1976.
De Bow, J. D. B. *Legal History of the Entire System of the Nashville, Chattanooga and St. Louis Railway*. Nashville: Marshall and Bruce, [1900?].
Des Champs, Margaret B. "Early Days in the Cumberland Country." *Tennessee Historical Quarterly* 6 (1947): 195–229.
Dew, Charles B. "Black Iron Workers and the Slave Insurrection Panic of 1856." *Journal of Southern History* 41 (1975): 321–38.
Doak, H. M. "The Development of Education in Tennessee." *American Historical Magazine* 8 (1903): 64–90.
Douglas, Byrd. *Steamboatin' on the Cumberland*. Nashville: Book Co., 1961.
Doyle, Don H. *Nashville in the New South, 1880–1930*. Knoxville: University of Tennessee Press, 1985.
———. "The Social Functions of Voluntary Associations in a Nineteenth-Century Town." *Social Science History* 1 (1977): 333–56.
———. *The Social Order of a Frontier Community: Jacksonville, Illinois, 1825–1870*. Urbana: University of Illinois Press, 1978.
Dresser, Amos. *The Narrative of Amos Dresser*. New York: American Anti-Slavery Society, 1836.
Durham, Walter T. *Daniel Smith*. Nashville: Sumner County Library Board, 1976.
———. *The Great Leap Westward*. Gallatin, TN: Sumner County Public Library Board, 1969.

———. *Nashville and the Union.* Nashville: Tennessee Historical Society, 1987.

———. *Nashville: The Occupied City.* Nashville: Tennessee Historical Society, 1985.

Eblen, Jack E. "An Analysis of Nineteenth-Century Frontier Populations." *Demography* 2 (1965): 399–413.

Elkins, Stanley, and Eric McKitrick. "A Meaning for Turner's Frontier, Part 1: Democracy in the Old Northwest." *Political Science Quarterly* 69 (1954): 321–53.

———. "A Meaning for Turner's Frontier, Part 2: The Southwest Frontier and New England." *Political Science Quarterly* 69 (1954): 565–602.

England, James M. "The Free Negro in Ante Bellum Tennessee." Ph.D. diss., Vanderbilt University, 1941.

———. "The Free Negro in Davidson County, Tennessee, 1780–1860." Master's thesis, Vanderbilt University, 1937.

———. "The Free Negro in Tennessee." *Journal of Southern History* 9 (1943): 37–58.

Farrell, Josephine E., and Mallie W. Farrell. *Burlington, A Memory.* Privately printed, n.d.

Faulkner, Ronnie W. "Return J. Meigs: Tennessee's First State Librarian." *Tennessee Historical Quarterly* 42 (1983): 151–64.

Flanagan, James J. "Irish Element in Nashville, 1810–1880." Master's thesis, Vanderbilt University, 1951.

Flanigen, George J. (ed.). *Catholicity in Tennessee.* Nashville: Ambrose Printing Co., 1937.

Fogel, Robert W., and Stanley Engerman. *Time on the Cross: The Economics of American Negro Slavery.* Boston: Little, Brown, and Co., 1974.

Folmsbee, Stanley J. *Sectionalism and Internal Improvements in Tennessee, 1796–1845.* Knoxville: University of Tennessee Press, 1939.

Folsom, Barton W., III. "The Politics of Elites: Prominence and Party in Davidson County, Tennessee, 1835–1861." *Journal of Southern History* 39 (1973): 359–78.

Foner, Eric. *Free Soil, Free Labor, Free Men: The Ideology of the Republican Party before the Civil War.* New York: Oxford University Press, 1970.

Formisano, Ronald P. *The Birth of Mass Political Parties: Michigan, 1827–1861.* Princeton: Princeton University Press, 1971.

Foster, Turner S. *An Address Delivered at the Close of the First Annual Exhibition of the Mechanics Institute of Tennessee.* Nashville: J. F. Morgan, 1855.

Fowler, H. Thornton, et al. *The History of McKendree Methodist Church.* Nashville: Parthenon Press, 1962.

Frank, Fedora S. *Beginnings on Market Street.* Nashville: Fedora Small Frank, 1976.

———. *Five Families and Eight Young Men.* Nashville: Tennessee Book Co., 1962.

Frisch, Michael H. *Town into City: Springfield, Massachusetts, and the Meaning of Community, 1840–1880.* Cambridge: Harvard University Press, 1972.

Fuller, Thomas O. *History of the Negro Baptists of Tennessee.* Memphis: Haskins Print–Roger Williams College, 1936.

Genovese, Eugene D. *Roll, Jordan, Roll.* New York: Random House, 1972.

Gilkeson, John S. *Middle-Class Providence, 1820–1840.* Princeton: Princeton University Press, 1986.

Glass, P. T. "Sketch of Henry Rutherford." *American Historical Magazine* 5 (1900): 225–29.

Gohmann, Sister Mary de Lourdes. *Political Nativism in Tennessee to 1860.* Washington, DC: Catholic University of America, 1938.

Golden, Gabriel H. "William Carroll and His Administration." *Tennessee Historical Magazine* 9 (1925–26): 9–30.

Goldfield, David R. "Cities and Southern Independence." Paper delivered in Nashville, September 24, 1984.

———. *Cotton Fields and Skyscrapers: Southern City and Region, 1607–1980.* Baton Rouge: Louisiana State University Press, 1982.

———. "The New Regionalism." *Journal of Urban History* 10 (1984): 171–86.

———. *Urban Growth in the Age of Sectionalism: Virginia, 1847–1861.* Baton Rouge: Louisiana State University Press, 1977.

———. "The Urban South: A Regional Framework." *American Historical Review* 85 (1981): 1009–34.

Goldin, Claudia. *Urban Slavery in the American South, 1820–1860.* Chicago: University of Chicago Press, 1976.

Goodpasture, Albert V. "Beginnings of Montgomery County." *American Historical Magazine* 8 (1903): 193–215.

Gower, Herschel, and Jack Allen (eds.). *Pen and Sword: The Life and Journal of Randal McGavock.* Nashville: Tennessee Historical Commission, 1959.

Grant, C. L. "The Public Career of Cave Johnson." *Tennessee Historical Quarterly* 10 (1951): 195–223.

Green, Fletcher M. *Democracy in the Old South and Other Essays.* Nashville: Vanderbilt University Press, 1969.

Gresham, Lunia P. "The Public Career of Hugh Lawson White." Ph.D. diss., Vanderbilt University, 1943.

Gusfield, Joseph R. *Symbolic Crusade: Status Politics and the American Temperance Movement.* Urbana: University of Illinois Press, 1963.

Gutman, Herbert G. *The Black Family in Slavery and Freedom, 1790–1925.* New York: Pantheon Books, 1976.

Hall, Albert C. "The Economic and Social Beginnings of Tennessee." *Tennessee Historical Magazine* 8 (1924–25): 24–86.

Hall, Peter D. "Family Structure and Economic Organization: Massachusetts Machinists, 1700–1850." In *Family and Kin in Urban Communities, 1700–1930,* ed. Tamara K. Hareven. New York: New Viewpoints, 1977.

Hamer, Marguerite B. "The Presidential Campaign of 1860 in Tennessee." *East Tennessee Historical Society Publications* 3 (1931): 3–22.

Hamer, Philip M. *Tennessee: A History.* 4 vols. New York: American Historical Society, 1933.

Hammond, Bray. *Banks and Politics in America from the Revolution to the Civil War.* Princeton: Princeton University Press, 1957.

Hansen, Marcus L. *The Atlantic Migration, 1607–1860.* New York: Harper and Brothers, [1940] 1960.

Hardeman, Nicholas P. *Wilderness Calling: The Hardeman Family in the American Westward Movement, 1750–1900.* Knoxville: University of Tennessee Press, 1977.

Harrison, W. P. *The Gospel among the Slaves.* Nashville: Publishing House of the Methodist Episcopal Church, South, 1893.

Haunton, R. H. "Law and Order in Savannah, 1850–1860." In *The Southern Common People,* ed. Edward Magdol and John L. Wakelyn. Westport, CT: Greenwood Press, 1980.

Hawkins, Benjamin. "The Letters of Benjamin Hawkins, 1796–1806." *Collections of the Georgia Historical Society* 9 (1916).

Haywood, John. *The Civil and Political History of the State of Tennessee.* Knoxville: Tenase Co., [1823] 1969.

———. *The Duty and Authority of Justices of the Peace in Tennessee.* Nashville: Thomas G. Bradford, 1810.

Haywood, Marshall. *The Beginnings of Freemasonry in North Carolina.* Raleigh, NC: Weaver and Lynch, 1906.

Hofstadter, Richard. *The American Political Tradition.* New York: Knopf, 1948.

Holt, Michael F. *The Political Crisis of the 1850s.* New York: Norton, [1978] 1983.

Hoobler, James A. "Karnak on the Cumberland." *Tennessee Historical Quarterly* 35 (1976): 251–62.

Howe, Daniel W. *The Political Culture of the American Whigs.* Chicago: University of Chicago Press, 1979.

Howell, R. B. C. "Early Corporate Limits of Nashville." *Tennessee Historical Magazine* 2 (1916): 110–18.

Howington, Arthur F. "'Not in the Condition of a Horse or an Ox': *Ford v. Ford,* the Law of Testamentary Manumission, and the Tennessee Courts' Recognition of Slave Humanity." *Tennessee Historical Quarterly* 34 (1975): 249–63.

Hubbard, G. W. *A History of the Colored Schools of Nashville, Tennessee.* Nashville: Wheeler, Marshall, and Bruce, 1874.

Hunt, Mary E. "Leaves from an Old Diary." In *Christ Church, Nashville.* Nashville: Marshall and Bruce Co., 1929.

Hunter, Louis C. *Steamboats on the Western Rivers.* Cambridge: Harvard University Press, 1949.

Imes, William L. "Negroes in Tennessee before the Civil War: A Sociological Study." Master's thesis, Fisk University, 1912.

Ingraham, J. H. *Report upon a Proposed System of Public Education, for the City of Nashville, Respectfully Addressed to Its Citizens.* Nashville: W. F. Bang, 1848.

International Typographical Union of North America. *Golden Anniversary, 1855–1905, Nashville Typographical Union, No. 20.* Nashville: n.p., 1905.

Jackson, Andrew. *Correspondence of Andrew Jackson.* 7 vols. Ed. James S. Basset. Washington, DC: Carnegie Institution of Washington, 1926–28.

James, D. Clayton. *Antebellum Natchez.* Baton Rouge: Louisiana State University Press, 1968.

Johnson, Andrew. *Speech Delivered in Nashville, July 15, 1856.* Nashville: G. C. Torbett and Co., 1856.

Johnson, Paul E. *A Shopkeeper's Millennium: Society and Revivals in Rochester, New York, 1815–1837.* New York: Hill and Wang, 1978.

Jones, James Boyd, Jr. "Mose the Bowery B'hoy and the Nashville Fire Department, 1849–1860." *Tennessee Historical Quarterly* 40 (1981): 170-81.

Jones, Maldwyn A. *American Immigration.* Chicago: University of Chicago Press, 1960.

Journal of the House of Representatives, Tennessee, 1839–1840. Knoxville: Lauson Gifford, 1839.

Journal of the Senate. . . . of the State of Tennessee, 1801. Knoxville: George Roulstone, 1933.

Kaser, David. "Nashville's Women of Pleasure in 1860." *Tennessee Historical Quarterly* 23 (1964): 379–82.

Katz, Michael B. *The Irony of Early School Reform: Educational Innovation in Mid-Nineteenth-Century Massachusetts.* Cambridge: Harvard University Press, 1968.

Kelley, Sarah F. *Children of Nashville.* Nashville: Blue and Gray Press, 1973.

Kinard, Margaret. "Frontier Development of Williamson County." *Tennessee Historical Quarterly* 8 (1949): 3–33, 127–53.

Kincheloe, Joe L., Jr. "Transcending Role Restrictions: Women at Camp Meetings and Political Rallies." *Tennessee Historical Quarterly* 40 (1981): 158–69.

Knights, Peter R. *The Plain People of Boston, 1830–1860.* New York: Oxford University Press, 1971.

Kruman, Marc W. *Parties and Politics in North Carolina, 1836– 1865.* Baton Rouge: Louisiana State University Press, 1983.

Laughlin, S. H. "Diaries of S. H. Laughlin of Tennessee, 1840 and 1843." Ed. St. George L. Sioussat. *Tennessee Historical Magazine* 2 (1916): 43–85.

Laurie, Bruce. *Working People of Philadelphia, 1800–1850.* Philadelphia: Temple University Press, 1980.

Laws of the Corporation of Nashville. Nashville: John S. Simpson, 1828.

Laws of the Corporation of Nashville. Nashville: William E. Matthews, 1837.

Leach, Douglas E. "John Gordon of Gordon's Ferry." *Tennessee Historical Quarterly* 18 (1959): 322–44.

Leuchtenburg, William E. "The Pertinence of Political History: Reflections on the Significance of the State in America." *Journal of American History* 73 (1986): 585–600.

Lewis, E. C. "James Robertson, Nashville's Founder." *American Historical Magazine* 8 (1903): 285–94.

Lines, Stiles B. "Slaves and Churchmen: The Work of the Episcopal Church among Southern Negroes, 1800–1860." Ph.D. diss., Columbia University, 1960.

Lowrey, Frank M., III. "Tennessee Voters during the Second Two-Party System, 1836–1860: A Study of Voter Constancy and Socio-Economic and Demographic Distinctions." Ph.D. diss., University of Alabama, 1973.

McBride, Robert M., and Dan M. Robison. *Biographical Directory of the Tennessee General Assembly*. Nashville: Tennessee State Library and Archives, 1975.

McCormick, Richard P. *The Second American Party System: Party Formation in the Jacksonian Era*. Chapel Hill: University of North Carolina Press, 1966.

McDonald, Kenneth M. "Milling in Middle Tennessee." Ph.D. diss., Vanderbilt University, 1938.

McEwen, John A. *Reform of Social Ranks*. Nashville: Smith, Camp, and Co., 1858.

McFerrin, John B. *History of Methodism in Tennessee*. 3 vols. Nashville: Publishing House of the Methodist Episcopal Church, 1886–95.

McGavock, Randal W. *Communication from His Honor the Mayor. . . . September 30, 1859*. Nashville: A. S. Camp, 1859.

Macpherson, Joseph T. "Nashville's German Element, 1850–1870." Master's thesis, Vanderbilt University, 1957.

Mahoney, Nell S. "William Strickland's Introduction to Nashville, 1845." *Tennessee Historical Quarterly* 9 (1950): 46–63.

Mahoney, Timothy R. "Urban History in a Regional Context: River Towns on the Upper Mississippi, 1840–1860." *Journal of American History* 72 (1985): 318–39.

Martin, Asa E. "Anti-Slavery Activities of the Methodist Episcopal Church in Tennessee." *Tennessee Historical Magazine* 2 (1916): 98–109.

Maslowski, Peter. *Treason Must Be Made Odious: Military Occupation and Wartime Reconstruction in Nashville, Tennessee, 1862–1865*. Millwood, NY: KTO Press, 1978.

Masterson, William H. *William Blount*. Baton Rouge: Louisiana State University Press, 1954.

Mathews, Donald G. *Religion in the Old South*. Chicago: University of Chicago Press, 1977.
———. *Slavery and Methodism: A Chapter in American Morality, 1780–1845*. Princeton: Princeton University Press, 1965.
Matthews, Thomas E. *General James Robertson*. Nashville: Parthenon Press, 1934.
Meyers, Marvin. *The Jacksonian Persuasion*. Stanford: Stanford University Press, 1957.
Miles, Edwin A. "The Mississippi Slave Insurrection Scare of 1835." *Journal of Negro History* 42 (1957): 48–60.
Miles, Guy S. "Literary Beginnings in Nashville." Ph.D. diss., Vanderbilt University, 1941.
———. "The Tennessee Antiquarian Society and the West." *East Tennessee Historical Society Publications* 18 (1946): 87–106.
Moon, Anna M. *Sketches of the Shelby, McDowell, Deaderick, Anderson Families*. Chattanooga: n.p., 1933.
Mooney, Chase C. "Slavery in Davidson County, Tennessee." Master's thesis, Vanderbilt University, 1936.
———. "Slavery in Tennessee." Ph.D. diss., Vanderbilt University, 1939.
———. *Slavery in Tennessee*. Westport, CT: Negro Universities Press, 1957.
———, ed. "Some Letters from Dover, Tennessee, 1814–1855." *Tennessee Historical Quarterly* 8 (1949): 154–84, 252–83, 345–65.
Moore, Mary D. "The First Century of Library History in Tennessee." *East Tennessee Historical Society Publications* 16 (1941–45): 3–21.
Moore, Powell. "The Revolt against Jackson in Tennessee, 1835–1836." *Journal of Southern History* 2 (1936): 335–59.
Morgan, Edmund S. *American Slavery, American Freedom*. New York: Norton, 1975.
Murphy, James E. "Jackson and the Tennessee Opposition." *Tennessee Historical Quarterly* 30 (1971): 50–69.
Nagy, J. Emerick. "Wanted: A Teacher for the Nashville English School." *Tennessee Historical Quarterly* 21 (1972): 171–86.
Napier, James C. "Some Negro Members of the Tennessee Legislature." *Journal of Negro History* 5 (1920): 113–17.
Nashville City and Business Directory. Nashville: L. P. Williams and Co., 1859.
Newcomer, Lee N. "Two New England Teachers in Nashville, 1818." *Tennessee Historical Quarterly* 19 (1960): 74–79.
Norton, Herman A. *Tennessee Christians*. Nashville: Reed, 1971.
Norton, Mary Beth. *Liberty's Daughters*. Boston: Little, Brown, 1980.
Overdyke, W. Darrell. *The Know-Nothing Party in the South*. Baton Rouge: Louisiana State University Press, 1950.
"Papers from the Spanish Archives Relating to Tennessee . . . 1783–1800." *East Tennessee Historical Society Publications* 9 (1937): 111–42.

Parks, Joseph H. *Felix Grundy*. Baton Rouge: Louisiana State University Press, 1940.

———. *John Bell of Tennessee*. Baton Rouge: Louisiana State University Press, 1950.

Parks, Norman L. "The Career of John Bell as Congressman from Tennessee, 1827–1841." *Tennessee Historical Quarterly* 1 (1915): 229–49.

Partin, Robert L. "The Secession Movement in Tennessee." Ph.D. diss., George Peabody College for Teachers, 1935.

Patterson, Caleb P. *The Negro in Tennessee, 1790–1865*. University of Texas Bulletin No. 2205. Austin: University of Texas, 1922.

Pessen, Edward. *Jacksonian America: Society, Personality, and Politics*. Homewood, IL: Dorsey Press, 1969.

———. "Who Governed the Nation's Cities in the 'Era of the Common Man.'" *Political Science Quarterly* 87 (1972): 591–614.

Phelan, James. *History of Tennessee: The Making of a State*. Boston: Houghton-Mifflin, 1889.

Phelps, Dawson A. (ed.). "The Diary of a Chaplain in Andrew Jackson's Army." *Tennessee Historical Quarterly* 12 (1953): 264–81.

Pike, G. D. *The Jubilee Singers*. Boston: Lee and Shepard, 1873.

Pike, James E. (ed.). "A Letter Home." *Tennessee Historical Quarterly* 12 (1953): 239–63.

Posey, Walter D. "Bishop Asbury Visits Tennessee, 1788–1815." *Tennessee Historical Quarterly* 15 (1956): 253–68.

Provine, Dorothy. "The Economic Position of Free Blacks in the District of Columbia, 1800–1860." *Journal of Negro History* 58 (1973): 61–72.

Putnam, A. W. *History of Middle Tennessee*. Nashville: printed for the author, 1859.

Raboteau, Albert J. *Slave Religion*. New York: Oxford University Press, 1978.

Ramsey, J. G. M. *The Annals of Tennessee*. Knoxville: East Tennessee Historical Society, [1853] 1967.

Remini, Robert V. *Andrew Jackson and the Course of American Empire, 1767–1821*. New York: Harper and Row, 1977.

———. *Andrew Jackson and the Course of American Freedom*. New York: Harper and Row, 1981.

Reps, John W. *The Making of Urban America*. Princeton: Princeton University Press, 1965.

Revised Laws of the City of Nashville. Nashville: H. M. Watterson, 1850.

Robert, Charles E. *Nashville and Her Trade for 1870*. Nashville: Roberts and Purvis, 1870.

Robertson, Felix. "Address.... to the members of the Medical Society of Tennessee." *Nashville Journal of Medicine and Surgery* 8 (1856): 446–54.

Robertson, James. "Correspondence of General James Robertson." *American Historical Magazine* 1, 3–5 (1896, 1898–1900): 71–91, 189–94, 280–91,

390-96 (vol. 1); 74–83, 267–98, 348–94 (vol. 3); 66–96, 163–92, 247–86, 336–81 (vol. 4); 67–96, 162–90, 252–86 (vol. 5).

Rose, Stanley F. "Nashville and Its Leadership Elite, 1861–1869." Master's thesis, University of Virginia, 1965.

Rosenberg, Carol Smith. *Religion and the Rise of the American City: The New York Mission Movement, 1812–1870.* Ithaca, NY: Cornell University Press, 1971.

Rosenberg, Charles. *The Cholera Years: The United States in 1832, 1849, and 1866.* Chicago: University of Chicago Press, 1962.

Rothman, David J. *The Discovery of the Asylum: Social Order and Disorder in the New Republic.* Boston: Little, Brown, 1971.

Royall, Anna N. *Letters from Alabama.* Tuscaloosa: University of Alabama Press, [1830] 1969.

Ryan, Mary P. *Cradle of the Middle Class: The Family in Oneida County, New York, 1790–1865.* New York: Cambridge University Press, 1981.

Schweninger, Loren. "The Free-Slave Phenomenon: James P. Thomas and the Black Community in Ante-Bellum Nashville." *Civil War History* 22 (1976): 293–307.

——. *James T. Rapier and Reconstruction.* Chicago: University of Chicago Press, 1978.

——. "A Slave Family in the Antebellum South." *Journal of Negro History* 60 (1975): 29–44.

Scobey, James E. (ed.). *Franklin College and Its Influence.* Nashville: McQuiddy, 1906.

Scott, Anne F. "On Seeing and Not Seeing: A Case of Historical Invisibility." *Journal of American History* 71 (1984): 7–21.

Sellers, Charles G. "Banking and Politics in Jackson's Tennessee, 1817–1827." *Mississippi Valley Historical Review* 41 (1954–55): 61–84.

——. "Jackson Men with Feet of Clay." *American Historical Review* 62 (1957): 537–51.

——. *James K. Polk, Jacksonian.* Princeton: Princeton University Press, 1957.

Sevier, John. "The Executive Journal of Governor John Sevier." *East Tennessee Historical Society Publications* 1 (1929): 95–153.

Sharp, James R. *The Jacksonians versus the Banks.* New York: Columbia University Press, 1970.

Silbey, Joel H. *The Transformation of American Politics, 1840–1860.* Englewood Cliffs, NJ: Prentice-Hall, 1967.

Simmons, William J. *Men of Mark: Eminent, Progressive, and Rising.* Chicago: Johnson Publishing Co., [1887] 1970.

Smith, Daniel. "The Papers of General Daniel Smith." *American Historical Magazine* 6 (1901): 213–35.

Smith, Earl J. "The Free, Foreign-Born Population of Nashville in the 1850s." Master's thesis, Vanderbilt University, 1968.

Sobel, Mechal. " 'They Can Never Both Prosper Together': Black and White Baptists in Antebellum Nashville, Tennessee." *Tennessee Historical Quarterly* 38 (1979): 296–307.

Soltow, Lee. *Men of Wealth in the United States, 1850–1860.* New Haven: Yale University Press, 1975.

Spain, Rufus B. "R. B. C. Howell: Progressive Baptist Minister in the Old Southwest." *Tennessee Historical Quarterly* 14 (1955): 99–119.

———. "R. B. C. Howell: Virginia Baptist Tradition Comes to the Old Southwest." *Tennessee Historical Quarterly* 14 (1955): 195–226.

Speer, William S. (ed.). *Sketches of Prominent Tennesseans.* Nashville: A. B. Tavel, 1888.

Spence, W. J. D., and D. L. Spence. *A History of Hickman County, Tennessee.* Nashville: Norval Gilbert, [1900] 1969.

Strickland, John S. "Insurrectionary Fears in North Carolina: An Examination of Antebellum Southern Society and Slave Revolt Panics." In *Class, Conflict, and Consensus: Antebellum Southern Community Studies,* ed. Orville V. Barton and Robert C. McMath, Jr. Westport, CT: Greenwood Press, 1982.

Sutcliffe, Anthony R. "Urban History in the Eighties: Reflections on the H. J. Dyos Memorial Conference." *Journal of Urban History* 10 (1984): 123–44.

Taylor, William R. *Cavalier and Yankee.* New York: G. Braziller, 1961.

Teaford, Jon C. *The Municipal Revolution in America: Origins of Modern Urban Government.* Chicago: University of Chicago Press, 1975.

Thernstrom, Stephen. "The New Urban History." In *The Future of History,* ed. Charles F. Delzell. Nashville: Vanderbilt University Press, 1977.

———. *Poverty and Progress: Social Mobility in a Nineteenth-Century City.* Cambridge: Harvard University Press, 1964.

——— and Richard Sennett (eds.). *Nineteenth-Century Cities.* New Haven: Yale University Press, 1969.

Thomas, Jane. *Old Days in Nashville.* Nashville: Charles Elder, [1897] n.d.

Thornton, J. Mills. *Politics and Power in a Slave Society: Alabama, 1800–1860.* Baton Rouge: Louisiana State University Press, 1978.

Thweatt, John H. "James Priestley: Classical Scholar of the Old South." *Tennessee Historical Quarterly* 39 (1980): 423–39.

Turner, Frederick Jackson. *The Frontier in American History.* New York: H. Holt and Co., 1921.

Tyack, David. *The One Best System.* Cambridge: Harvard University Press, 1974.

Vogel, Morris J. "Patrons, Practitioners, and Patients: The Voluntary Hospital in Mid-Victorian Boston." In *Victorian America,* ed. Daniel W. Howe. Philadelphia: University of Pennsylvania Press, 1976.

Wade, Richard C. *Slavery in the Cities.* New York: Oxford University Press, 1964.

———. *The Urban Frontier*. Chicago: University of Chicago Press, 1959.
Walter, Benjamin. "Growth and Residential Succession: Nashville 1850 to 1920." In *Growing Metropolis*, ed. James F. Blumstein and Benjamin Walter. Nashville: Vanderbilt University Press, 1975.
Ward, John W. "Jacksonian Democratic Thought: 'A National Charter of Privilege.'" In *Development of an American Culture*, ed. S. Cothen and L. Ratner. Englewood Cliffs, NJ: Prentice-Hall, 1970.
Warner, Sam Bass. *The Private City: Philadelphia in Three Periods of Its Growth*. Philadelphia: University of Pennsylvania Press, 1968.
Washington, George. *The Diaries of George Washington, 1748–1799*. Ed. John C. Fitzpatrick. Cambridge, MA: Houghton-Mifflin, 1925.
Watson, Harry L. *Jacksonian Politics and Community Conflict: The Emergence of the Second American Party System in Cumberland County, North Carolina*. Baton Rouge: Louisiana State University Press, 1981.
Watts, Eugene J. *The Social Bases of City Politics: Atlanta, 1865–1903*. Westport, CT: Greenwood Press, 1978.
Weathersby, Robert W. "J. H. Ingraham and Tennessee." *Tennessee Historical Quarterly* 34 (1975): 264–72.
Welter, Rush. *The Mind of America, 1820–1860*. New York: Columbia University Press, 1975.
Wheat, J. Thomas. "Report." In *Journal of the Proceedings of the Protestant Episcopal Church in the Diocese of Tennessee*. Nashville: S. Nye and Co., 1840.
Wheeler, Mary B., and Genon H. Neblett. *Chosen Exile: The Life and Times of Septima Sexta Middleton Rutledge, American Cultural Pioneer*. Gadsden, AL: Rutledge Co., 1980.
Whitaker, Arthur P. *The Mississippi Question, 1795–1803*. New York: D. Appleton–Century, 1934.
———. (ed.). "Letters of James Robertson and Daniel Smith." *Mississippi Valley Historical Review* 12 (1925–26): 409–12.
White, Robert H. *Development of the Tennessee State Educational Organization 1796–1929*. Kingsport, TN: Southern Publishers, 1929.
Wilburn, James R. *Hazard of the Die*. Austin, TX: Sweet Pub. Co., 1969.
Wilentz, Sean. *Chants Democratic: New York City and the Rise of the American Working Class*. New York: Oxford University Press, 1984.
———. "On Class and Politics in Jacksonian America." *Reviews in American History* 10 (1982): 45–63.
Williams, Samuel C. *Dawn of Tennessee Valley and Tennessee History*. Johnson City, TN: Watauga Press, 1937.
———. *History of the Lost State of Franklin*. New York: Press of the Pioneers, 1933.
——— (ed.). *Early Travels in the Tennessee Country*. Johnson City, TN: Watauga Press, 1958.
Windrow, John E. "Collins D. Elliott and the Nashville Female Academy." *Tennessee Historical Magazine*, 2d series, 3 (1932–37): 74–106.

Woods, Mary. "The Building of the First Christ Church." In *Christ Church, Nashville*. Nashville: Marshall and Bruce Co., 1929.

Woodson, Carter G. *The History of the Negro Church*. Washington, DC: Associated Publishers, [1921] 1945.

Wooldridge, J. (ed.). *History of Nashville, Tennessee*. Nashville: H. W. Crew, 1890.

Wooster, Ralph A. *The Secession Conventions of the South*. Princeton: Princeton University Press, 1962.

Wyatt-Brown, Bertram. *Southern Honor*. New York: Oxford University Press, 1982.

INDEX

Adams, Adam G., 123
Adelphi Theatrical Society, 235n25
African Church, 146
African Complaint, 78
Aldermen, 66–67, 69, 97, 102, 109, 161–62, 208, 232n56, 232n61, 243–44n20, 247n79
Allison, Alexander (mayor, 1847–48), 127, 162, 164
Ament, Henry, 125, 159, 170
American Party, 180, 195, 196, 197
Ancient Order of Mystic Chevaliers, 175, 24n69
Anderson, Andrew (mayor, 1856), 162, 195
Anderson, David, 148
Armstrong, Martin, 16
Armstrong, Robert, 33, 89, 105, 113, 114, 219n49
Armstrong, William (mayor, 1829–32), 105, 107, 111
Asbury, Bishop Francis, 15, 16, 57, 85
Austin, John, 110, 125
Auxiliary Bible Society of Davidson County, 62

Baird, John, 219n49
Bang, W. F., 125, 248n14
Bank directors, 97, 109, 233n8, 243n16
Banking, 36–40, 42–43, 118, 119, 163
Bank of the State of Tennessee, 118, 125
Bank of Tennessee, 25, 36
Bank of the United States, 36, 37, 42, 118
Baptist Church, 61; and black people, 85, 86, 147–48, 240n37; illustration, 46
Baptist Colored Mission, 148

Barnett, Peter, 80
Barton, Samuel, 3, 10
Bass, John M. (mayor, 1833), 111, 118, 169, 197, 235n25, 250n45
Bell, John, xv, 109, 164, 181; and Constitutional Union Party, 180, 198, 199, 200
Benton, Thomas Hart, 45
Black Bobb. *See* Rentfro, Robert
Blackburn, Rev. Gideon, 58, 59, 86
Blackman, Rev. Learner, 60
Bledsoe, Anthony, 6
Bledsoe, Isaac, 6
"Bloody Tenth," 200
Blount, William, 5, 7–8, 11, 12, 15, 26, 27
Board of Commissioners, 64, 224–25n75
Bogue, Allan, xi
Boosterism, 164
Bosley, James, 84
Bradford, Simon, 47
Brasher, Jacob, 102, 105, 106, 107, 231n34, 231n51
Breckinridge, John, 200
Brentz, George, 148
Brian, Sherwood. *See* Bryant, Sherrod
Broad Street and Market Street, split between, 103–4, 106
Brown, Aaron V., 195
Brown, Berryman H., 177
Bryant, Sherrod, 80
Buchanan, James, 196
Buchanan, Captain John, 7
Buddekke, J. H., 133
Burns, Michael, 125

Campbell, George, 217n18
Campbellites, 61
Cannon, Newton, 113

271

Cantrell, Stephen (mayor, 1817), 28, 33, 40, 41, 50, 219n49
Capitol Hill, 120, 181
Carroll, William, 35, 41–42, 45, 47, 48, 50, 100, 114, 144, 167, 219n49
Cartmell, Henry, 108, 125
Castleman, Robert (mayor, 1855), 162, 195
Catholic Church, 56–57, 61, 198; Catholic Ladies' Benevolent Association, 135; illustration, 49. *See also* Miles, Richard; Saint Mary's Cathedral; Sisters of Charity
Catron, John, 143, 155
Charity: organization of, 175–76; women and, 59
Chavois, Nancy, 89
Cheatham, B. F., 196
Cheatham, Richard (mayor, 1860), 162
Christ Church, 176
Christian Church, 61; black members of, 148, 149, 150
Church of the Advent, 176
Church of the Assumption, 133
Civil, Jack, 72–73
Claiborne, Thomas, 104–5, 181
Clark, Lardner, 16
Clay, Henry, 98, 99, 159, 160
Coffee, John, 33, 77, 89
Coleman, Thomas B. (mayor, 1842), 191
Coltart, John, 177, 194, 247n80
Condon, James (mayor, 1820), 97–98, 236n36
Conrad, Rufus, 152
Constitutional Union Party, 180, 198–99
Cooper, William F., 161, 174, 193, 194, 250n39
Court of Triers, 2, 3
Craighead, Rev. Thomas, 14, 15, 56, 57–58
Credit of the West, 109
Creek Wars, 12, 50
Cross, Nathaniel, 170
Cross, Richard, 89
Crutcher, Thomas (mayor, 1819), 31, 63, 66
Cumberland College, 51, 53, 54, 62, 181
Cumberland Compact, 2, 3
Cumberland Presbyterian Church, 61
Curry, Leonard, xiii, 137
Curry, Robert B. (mayor, 1822–23), 66

Darby, Patrick Henry, 40–41, 43
Dashiell, John, 187
Davidson Academy, 14, 54, 62
Davidson County Court: jurisdiction of, 12–14, 68; members of, 5–7, 8–11, 18; and town government, 17
Deaderick, George M., 27–29, 31, 46, 47, 58, 75, 218n30
Deaderick, Thomas, 219n49
De Bow's Review, 191
Democratic Party: aldermen, 110, 177, 195, 208; and Know-Nothing Party, 195; leaders of, 161; and mayor's office, 113, 193, 195, 196–97; and the poor, 176; programs of, xiii, 109, 157, 158–59, 163–64, 176, 179, 190
Demonbreun, Timothy, 15, 47
Dickinson, John, 25, 31, 44–45, 217n22
Disciples of Christ, 144
Donelson, Andrew Jackson, 195
Donelson, John, 2, 46, 73, 226n8
Douglas, Stephen, 200
Downs, William P., 177, 247n82
Dresser, Amos, 112, 140
Driver, William, 159
Dueling, 44–45, 243n9
Dunson, Ned, 141

Eakin Wholesale Dry-Goods Company, 123
Eastin, William, 31
Edmiston, Robert, 7
Education: in the early city, 52–55, 62–63; on the frontier, 14–15; in public schools, 181–85; and schools for black people, 150–52; in South Nashville schools, 173
Eichbaum, William, 250n39
Elkins, Stanley, ix, xi
Ellis, Noble, 126
Elliston, Joseph (mayor, 1814–16), 66
England, James M., 225n1
Epidemics: cholera, 174, 188; smallpox, 69, 174, 188
Episcopal Church, 61, 149–50
Erwin, John P. (mayor, 1821, 1834), 98, 99, 100, 105, 109, 111, 113, 169, 230n22
Estill, Sarah, 49, 146
Everett, Edward, 199
Ewing, Andrew, 3
Ewing, Robert, 7

Fall, Rev. Philip, 61
Family ties on the frontier, 46–47
Fanning, Tolbert, 144, 152, 168, 241n61
Farmers and Mechanics Bank, 25, 37, 40
Fauntleroy, Henry, 172
Female Bible and Charitable Society, 59
Female Orphan School of Nashville, 175
Fenn, Letha, 141
Fenn, Richard, 141
Fenn, Robert, 141
Ferguson, Rev. Jesse B., 172, 173, 240n43
Fillmore, Millard, 194, 195, 198
Fire, 69, 84, 187
Fire protection, 67, 97, 98, 125, 181, 186–87
Fletcher, Thomas, 24, 35, 47
Fogg, Francis, 197, 235n25, 248n14, 250n39
Fogg, Godfrey, 154
Foster, Anthony, 26, 74, 75, 85, 219n49
Foster, Eleanor, 61
Foster, Ephraim H., 31, 143, 153, 154
Foster, Robert Coleman, 32, 37, 58, 62, 64, 85
Foster, Turner S., 246n57
Franklin College, 144
Free people of color: churches of, 144–50; families of, 90–91, 143–44; free status of, 79; and housing, 141; legislation concerning, 140; and militia, 86; and murder of Guinea John, 140–41; numbers of, 80, 89, 137; patrons of, 91, 155, 238n19; persistence rates of, 239n20; schools of, 150–52; and social class, 155–56; and suffrage, 86
Free School, 181–82
Fremont, John C., 198
Frontier history, x–xi

Gains, Anthony, 79
Gaslights, 188
Geiger, Jacob, 133
German Methodist Episcopal Church, 133; illustration, 57
German settlers in Nashville, 15, 47, 133–34
Gilliam, William, 125
Glenn, W. A., 191
Gloucester, Rev. John, 86

Goodlett, John A. (mayor, 1846), 162, 163
Good Village, xiii, 173, 174, 176, 178, 181, 198, 203
Gordon, Captain John, 27
Graham, Reuben, 91
Grainger, Delphi, 141
Grundy, Ann, 59, 170
Grundy, Felix, 12, 24, 25, 36, 39, 58, 91, 163
Gutman, Herbert, 72
Gwinn, James, 145–46, 239n30

Haile, Thomas J., 177, 194, 196, 247n81
Hall, Allen, 248n14
Hall, Elihu, 47, 219n49
Hammond, Bray, xi
Hart, Samuel, 90
Hay, Ann, 56
Hay, David, 74
Hayes, Mary, 59
Hays, Robert, 8, 75
Haywood, John, 53–54, 73, 222n30
Heiman, Adolphus, 175, 246n52
Henderson, Richard, 2
Hibernian Society, 129
Hill, H. R. W., 151
Hill, John M., 108, 113
Hill, Thomas, 219n49
Hofstadter, Richard, xi
Hollingsworth, Henry (mayor, 1837–38), 113, 114, 176
Hollingsworth, S. N. (mayor, 1859), 162, 191
Horn, W. H. (mayor, 1853), 162
Hospitals, 188–90
House of Industry, 175, 246n66
Houston, Sam, 24, 100
Howell, Rev. R. B. C., 147–48
Hume, Alexander, 170
Hume, Alfred, 183, 250n39
Hume, Rev. William, 23, 56, 58, 63, 170
Hunt, William G., 113, 246n52
Hurt, William, 125
Hynes, Andrew, 34, 35, 50, 58, 84, 99, 219n49

Indian raids, 3
Immigrants, 129–35
Ingraham, J. H., 182
Insurance companies, 120, 234n16;

Insurance companies *(continued)*
  advertisement for Negro insurance by, 87
International Order of Odd Fellows, Lodge No. 1, 177
Irish businessmen in Nashville, 105, 125
Irish immigrants to Nashville, 125, 134, 162
Iser, Alexander, 131

Jackson, Andrew: and political alignments, 93–94, 98, 99, 103, 109, 177, 202; mentioned, 8, 12, 14, 24, 31, 33, 35, 37, 45, 74, 83, 89, 91
Jackson, James, 34
Jacksonian rhetoric, 40, 100, 104, 113, 167
Jeffersonian republicans, 11–12
Jennings, Rev. Obadiah, 58
Jewish population of Nashville, 131–33
Johnson, Andrew, 180, 195
Johnson, Anthony, 104, 124
Johnson, Rev. John, 60
Johnson, Oliver, 124
Johnson, Vice President Richard M., 154

Kingsley, Alpha, 219n49
Kirkman, Hugh, 235n25
Kirkman, Thomas, 219n49
Know-Nothings, 125, 130, 194, 195, 197
Knowles, Joseph, 110, 246n52

Ladies Catholic Orphan Society, 175
Lasky, Mayer, 131
Laughlin, Samuel, 112
Lavendar, Anderson, 86
Lea, John M. (mayor, 1849), 162
Lectures on social class and mobility, 171–73
Lefever, Catherine, 13–14
Legal profession, 24–25
Lewis, Joel, 81
Lewis, W. T., 80, 86
Lindsey, Isaac, 3, 7, 15
Lindsley, John Berrien, 170, 174, 189, 200, 248n14, 250n39
Lindsley, Rev. Philip, 54
Little Turkey, 72
Lockelier, Jeffrey, 50, 89
Louisville and Nashville Railroad, 198, 204
Lowery, Peter, 143, 144, 149, 150, 155
Lowery, Samuel, 144, 152
Lundy, Benjamin, 112
Lutheran Church, 133
Lytle, William, 33, 219n49, 220n72

McBean, Daniel, 88
McCombs, James, 111
McEwen, John (mayor, 1857), 162, 171, 196, 248n14, 250n39
McEwen, Hattie, 160
McEwen, Robert H., 113, 194, 248n8, 251n72
McGavock, Jacob, 45, 46
McGavock, Randal (mayor, 1824–25), 58
McGavock, Randal (mayor, 1858), 162, 175, 186, 192, 196–97, 200
McKitrick, Eric, ix, xi
McNairy, Boyd, 91, 99
McNairy, John, 8, 95
Mann, Horace, 182
Market House, 67, 97, 101, 103, 192, 231n36
Masonic Order, 50–51, 125
Maxey, Powhatan (mayor, 1843–44), 111, 162
Maxwell House, 125
Mayors of Nashville, 111, 162, 196–97, 207
Mechanics: households of, 96–97; lifestyle of, 124; in office, 108; property holdings of, 103, 125–26; and Whig Party, 159, 161, 162
Mechanics' Institute, 170–71
Mechanics' Library Association, 169–70, 247n80
Medical profession, 23–24
Meigs, Return J., 170, 248n14, 250n39, 252n97
Merchants: and credit, 30–31; on frontier, 25–38; persistence rates of, 32–33; as subscribers to Female Academy, 63; and town government, 64, 67
Merry, Nelson, 147, 148
Methodism, 15, 58, 60, 63; and black congregations, 144–46; and slavery, 84–85
Meyers, Trim, 91
Miles, Bishop Richard Pius, 130, 134
Militia, 2, 11, 50
Mill Creek Baptist Church, 16, 85
Molloy, Sophia, 76

INDEX 275

Molloy, Thomas, 3, 10, 14, 16, 76, 77
Monohan, M. M., 126, 246n52
Mooney, Chase C., 225n1
Moore, Robert I., 247n78
Morgan, Samuel, 164, 191; illustration of Morgan and Co., 171
Morrow, John, 126
Mulherin, James, 6–7
Municipal government: disbursements by, 190, 209; elections of, 66–67, 97, 98, 100, 102, 105, 107, 113, 157–58, 194, 195, 196, 197; and electorate, 100, 106, 108, 114; incorporation act of 1806, 65; railroad subscriptions of, 190–91; reorganization of, 100–102, 192–93; services of, 97, 98, 106, 181–92; and suffrage, 65, 114, 106–7, 113–14; and ward politics, 110–11. *See also* Aldermen; Board of Commissioners; Mayors of Nashville
Murrell, John, 111

Napier, William C., 143, 144, 152
Nash, William, 84
Nashville: description of, in 1820s, 70; housing in, 122; map of, 95; plat of, 16; population of, 20–22, 94, 117, 180; property holdings in, 121–24, 191, 205, 232n56; reminiscences about, 48–49, 121; town lots in, 17, 217n20; transiency figures in, 22–23, 128–29; wards in, 95–96. *See also* Municipal government; Wealth in Nashville
Nashville and Chattanooga Railroad, 122, 190, 251n73
Nashville and Northwestern Railroad, 125, 190
Nashville and Southern Railroad, 190
Nashville Bank, 25, 27, 28, 34, 36, 37, 40
Nashville Bridge Company, 25, 28
Nashville Car Manufactory, 126
Nashville Colonization Society, 141, 232n65, 238n14
Nashville Convention (1850), 193
Nashville Female Academy, 53, 63, 224n70
Nashville Gaslight Company, 188
Nashville Mechanical Society, 51
Nashville Protestant School of Industry, 175
Nashville Steamboat Company, 35

Nashville Sunday School Union, 59
Nathan, Sinai, 131
Nativism, 105, 129–30, 134, 195, 198
Nichol, John, 219n49
Nichol, Josiah, 33–34, 36, 105, 219n49
Nichol, William (mayor, 1835–36), 3, 111, 174, 181
Nickajack massacre, 10, 26
Norris, Rachel Myers, 80
North Carolina legislature, 4, 5, 8
Norton, Mary Beth, 63
Norvell, Aduella, 159
Norvell, Joseph, 39
Norvell, Moses, 37, 47

Opposition Party, 180, 197, 198
Overton, James ("Old Chattanooga"), 190
Overton, John, 8, 10, 12, 24, 26, 36, 39, 41, 76, 99, 162

Panic of 1819, 20, 38, 42; newspaper reaction to, 39–41
Panic of 1837, 118
Park, Joseph, 219n49
Parrish, Frank, 143
Paul, Isaac, 125, 160, 173, 248n14
Peak, Abner, 84
Pearl, J. F., 184
Penitentiary, 169
Pennington, Jacob, 7
Pessen, Edward, xii
Planters' Bank, 118
Police, 67, 84, 185–86, 249n23; and student riot, 248–49n21
Polk, James K., 109, 110, 159
Polk, William, 6
Poor, the, xiv, 173–76; and disease, 188–90; and indigent strangers, 192–93
Porter, Alexander, 34, 36, 47, 219n49, 220n72
Porter, Sally, 152
Porter, Solomon, 141
Porterfield, Susan, 123
Powers brothers, 131
Poyzer, George, 34
Preemption claims, 4
Presbyterian Church, 57–58, 61, 62, 63, 175; illustration of, 53; Second Presbyterian Church, 123; and slaves, 86; Strickland building, 120
Price, John, 219n49

Priestley, Rev. James, 54, 58, 61
Pritchett, Ephraim, 219n49
Prostitution, 141, 185, 249n22
Protestant Orphan Asylum, 175
Pryor, Nicholas, 89, 91
Public meetings, 37, 50
Public schools, 181–85
Putnam, W. A., 73

Railroads, 120, 181, 190–91
Read, Thomas, 219n49
Religion: and black churches, 144–50, 240n37; in the early city, 56–62; on the frontier, 15–16
Rentfro, Robert, 76, 81, 86, 95
Richardson, Alexander, 219n49
Rice, Joel, 75
Rice, John, 75
Robertson, Charlotte, 56
Robertson, Duncan, 47, 82, 219n49
Robertson, Elijah, 6, 14, 73, 214n15
Robertson, Felix (mayor, 1818, 1827–28), 23, 102, 114
Robertson, James: career of, 3–4, 9; as land agent, 5; mentioned, 1, 6, 7, 8, 10, 12, 17, 27, 45, 56, 73, 167, 214n15
Robertson, Mark, 14
Robertson Association, 175
Rutherford, Griffith, 8

Sabbatarian legislation, 176, 247n74
Saint Andrews Society, 129
Saint Charles Hotel, 245n41
Saint Mary's Cathedral, 134–35
Sappington, Dr. John, 7, 213n11
Schacht, Rev. Ivo, 133
Schoolhouse, 67, 98
School of Industry. *See* Nashville Protestant School of Industry
Schoolhouse, 67, 98
Scott, Jeffrey, 80, 86
Seabury, John M., 127
Searcy, Robert, 76, 219n49
Seay, Samuel, 144, 195, 219n49, 234n16
Secession, 193–94, 200
Second American Party System, xiii, 109
Second Presbyterian Church, 123
Sevier, John, 12, 72
Shapard, W. B. (mayor, 1854), 194, 195
Shaw, Josiah, 102
Shelby, Evan, 14
Simpson, William, 7
Singleton, Moses ("Old Tip"), 194

Sisters of Charity, 130, 135, 175, 188
Slave insurrection rumors, 111, 154–55
Slaves: distribution of, in households, 87–88, 138; emancipation of, 77–78, 86; family structure of, 88–89, 139; hiring of, 81–83, 137–38; municipal use of, 67; numbers of, 75, 89, 137; pioneers among, 72, 75; and religion, 84–86, 144–50; sales of, 73–75; slave dealers' advertisements, 38
Smiley, Robert, 54, 125
Smith, Daniel, 6
Smith, Joel, 194
Smith, John Hugh (mayor, 1845, 1850–52), 162, 163, 190, 197, 251n76
Smokey Row, 141
Social mobility, xiii, xiv, 245n43; arguments about, 167–68; lectures on, 171–73
Society for the Relief of the Poor, 175
Sommerville, John, 233n8
Sons of Temperance, 166
Southern nationalism, 197–98
South Nashville, 127, 173
South Nashville Furniture Manufacturing Company, 128
Spain, Joshua, 125
Speculation in land, 2, 5, 6, 7, 8, 10, 11, 214n15
Steamboats, 35, 42, 117
Stevenson, Vernon K., 122, 161, 190, 200, 250n45, 251n73
Stewart, William, 159
Stockell, William, 125, 175, 187
Stothart, Robert, 219n49
Stothart, William, 27
Stout, Catherine, 124
Stout, J. V. D., 246n52
Stout, Samuel V. D. (mayor, 1841), 54, 98, 107–8, 110, 113, 124, 125, 162, 174
Street lighting, 67, 97, 188
Strickland, William, 120
Summer, Alonso, 143, 151
Sunday patrol, 67, 84
Sunday schools, 59, 62, 152
Sycamore Shoals, Treaty of, 2

Tailors, 128, 169
Tait, Margaret, 56, 223n40
Tait, William (mayor, 1811–13), 27–29, 69, 75, 78, 79, 90

Talbot, Thomas, 47, 90
Talbot's hotel, 121; advertisement for, 28
Tannehill, Wilkins (mayor, 1825–26): as author, 55; career of, 51–52; as judge advocate, 50; reminiscence of Nashville by, 121; and Whig causes, 164, 165; mentioned, 48, 49, 58, 102, 105, 113, 169, 170, 219n49
Tate, Mrs. A. L., 152
Tate, Armistead, 91
Tate, Billy, 91
Tate, Easter, 90
Tate, Franky, 91
Tate, Harry, 90
Tate, Mary, 90
Temperance, 160, 165–67
Tennessee Antiquarian Society, 51, 53–54
Tennessee Colonization Society, 113
Tennessee Hospital for the Insane, 125
Thernstrom, Stephen, x
Thomas, Aggy, 90
Thomas, James P., 124, 139, 143, 153, 154, 155
Thomas, Jane, 48, 49, 120
Thomas, Philip, 90
Thomas, Sally, 143
Tomes, Charles, 176, 248n14
Transportation routes on the frontier, 29–30
Transylvania Company, 2
Trimble, Judge, 24, 91
Turbeville, W. J., 126
Turner, Frederick Jackson, xi
Turner, Lemuel, 31
Turnpikes, 42, 120, 181
Turnverein, 133
Typographical Union No. 20, 127, 169

Union, 110
Union Bank, 118, 125; building, 233n6
United Sisters of Temperance, 166–67
University of Nashville, 51, 54, 62, 125, 170, 185; and hospital, 188; and public high school, 184
University of the South, 198
Urban historiography, ix–x

Van Buren, Martin, 109, 110, 113, 154, 178, 197
Vannoy, Mason, 126
Vardiman, Rev. Jeremiah, 61

Vaulx, Joseph, 108, 231n53
Vigilance Committee, 112–13, 125
Voluntary societies, xii, 52, 59, 62, 64, 70, 164–67, 169–70, 187

Wade, Richard C., ix, xi, 92
Wadkins, Daniel, 150, 151, 152
Walker, John W., 122
War of 1812, 12, 50
Washington, Thomas, 89
Waters, Dr. John, 110
Waterworks, 181, 187–88, 194
Watkins, Sam, 155, 246n52
Weakley, Robert, 8
Wealth in Nashville, 121–24, 205, 232n56, 232n58, 235n30, 235n31
Welch, Thomas, 98
Weller, B. S., 126
Wells, Heydon, 3
Wessel, G. H., 133
West, John B., 47
Wharton, Jesse, 36
Whig Party: ascendancy of, 114, 157–58; and churches, 165; dissolution of, 180; and mechanics, 161, 162; origins of, in Tennessee, 109–10; organizational efforts of, 159–60; programs of, xiii, xiv, xv, 158, 163; and rich men, 160–61; and ward battles, 110–11; and workers, 164
White, Hugh Lawson, 36, 109, 113
White, Dr. James, 23
Whiteman, W. S., 122
Whiteside, Jenkin, 12, 24, 76–77, 78
Wilentz, Sean, x
Williams, Col. Willoughby, 48, 49
Winchester and Alabama Railroad, 190
Winston, C. K., 195
Women in Nashville, 48, 49, 223n37, 250n39; foreign-born, 134; free black, 142; frontier, 55–56; and religion, 58–60; schoolteachers, 184–85; and Whig conventions, 160
Woodfolk, W. W., 235n33
Woods, James, 162
Woods, Joseph, 35, 47, 219n49
Woods, Robert, 35, 47, 58
Workhouse, 186
Workingmen, 126–29; free black, 142; and temperance societies, 167; and trade unions, 127–28
Wright, Fanny, 181

Yaegers, 133
Yancy, William, 199
Yandell, Dr. William, 23
Yandle, John, 151
Yeatman, Thomas, 35, 36, 99, 109, 219n49
Yeatman and Woods, 32, 36, 42, 47, 118, 244n25
Young, Mary E., 216n9
Young, Thomas, 219n49
Young Men's Benevolent Society (Jewish), 132